UNMAKING THE PRESIDENCY

UNMAKING THE PRESIDENCY

DONALD TRUMP'S WAR ON THE
WORLD'S MOST POWERFUL OFFICE

SUSAN HENNESSEY AND BENJAMIN WITTES

FARRAR, STRAUS AND GIROUX | NEW YORK

Farrar, Straus and Giroux
120 Broadway, New York 10271

Portions of this book previously appeared, in different form,
in *Lawfare*, *The Atlantic*, and *Foreign Policy*.

Library of Congress Cataloging-in-Publication Data
Names: Hennessey, Susan, 1985– author. | Wittes, Benjamin, author.
Title: Unmaking the presidency : Donald Trump's war on the world's most powerful office / Susan
Hennessey and Benjamin Wittes.
Description: First edition. | New York : Farrar, Straus and Giroux, 2020. | Includes bibliographical
references and index. | Summary: "How Donald Trump has reshaped the norms of the American
presidency"—Provided by publisher.
Identifiers: LCCN 2019028858 | ISBN 9780374175368 (hardback)
Subjects: LCSH: Trump, Donald, 1946– | Presidents—United States—Case studies. | Political
leadership—United States—Case studies. | Executive power—United States—Case studies. |
United States—Politics and government—2017–
Classification: LCC E912 .H46 2020 | DDC 973.933092—dc23
LC record available at https://lccn.loc.gov/2019028858

Designed by Richard Oriolo

Our books may be purchased in bulk for promotional, educational, or business use.
Please contact your local bookseller or the Macmillan Corporate and Premium Sales Department
at 1-800-221-7945, extension 5442, or by e-mail at MacmillanSpecialMarkets@macmillan.com.

www.fsgbooks.com
www.twitter.com/fsgbooks • www.facebook.com/fsgbooks

1   3   5   7   9   10   8   6   4   2

For Brendan and Tamara

CONTENTS

UNMAKING THE PRESIDENCY

"It's MODERN DAY PRESIDENTIAL"

THE STEEL-GRAY SKIES ON THE MORNING OF JANUARY 20, 2017, opened now and then for the occasional drizzle of rain. It was not the worst weather that had afflicted a presidential inauguration. At William Howard Taft's inauguration, a snowstorm forced the entire ceremony indoors. By contrast, the temperature the day that Donald J. Trump became the forty-fifth President of the United States reached a comparatively balmy 49 degrees. Yet the inaugural parade route, typically filled to capacity with well-wishers, had only sparse crowds, and empty bleachers lined Pennsylvania Avenue. Cameras broadcast the scene around the world as commentators narrated the day's events in hushed and somber tones more befitting a state funeral than the dawn of a new presidential administration.

The scene on the Capitol dais was undeniably strange—"some weird shit," as former president George W. Bush reportedly called it as he left the stage when it was all over. It was strange even before the newly inaugurated president began speaking of "American carnage" in his first address in that capacity. As is the custom, the living former U.S. presidents attended the event. Jimmy Carter was there. George H. W. Bush was too ill to attend at the time, but the younger Bush and his wife, Laura, represented the family. Trump had vanquished Bush's other son, Jeb, eleven months prior in the early Republican primaries. And he had savaged George W. Bush rhetorically at various points. It was no secret that neither the elder nor the younger Bush had voted for Trump in the end, even though Trump was the standard-bearer for their party. Most eyes, however, rested on a different family of Trump foes: former secretary of state Hillary Clinton, attending with her husband, Bill, in her capacity as the former First Lady.

Ten weeks earlier, Trump had defeated Hillary Clinton in a stunning upset that reverberated around the globe. The 2016 campaign was without question the nastiest in modern American history. Trump had hurled nightly invective against his opponent, whom he called "Crooked Hillary." Stadium crowds at his rallies—and at the Republican National Convention—had chanted "Lock her up!" In one especially low moment before a debate—after Trump held a press conference with women who earlier had accused Bill Clinton of sexual misconduct—the two candidates could not even bring themselves to shake hands onstage. In the run-up to the inauguration, some observers had speculated that the Clintons might not attend at all, but would break with tradition out of a sense of injury or hostility or mortification—or perhaps some combination of the three.

But Bill Clinton came. And Hillary Clinton came. She wore her trademark pantsuit in suffragette white. She said on Twitter that she attended in order to "honor our democracy and its enduring values." But her presence loomed over the day, a physical reminder that Trump the candidate and Trump the president were, at the end of the day, the same man.

The inauguration prayers seemed to be as much a rebuke of Trump as a benediction. The Reverend Samuel Rodriguez, an Evangelical minister, selected the Sermon on the Mount, reading the Beatitudes one by one.

"God blesses those who are poor," he prayed before a self-professed billionaire.

"God blesses those who are humble," before the notorious braggart.

As Rodriguez ticked through the list of favored attributes—those who are merciful, clean of heart, peacemakers—each stood in sharper contrast to Trump than the one before.

The clock counted down to the key moment, shortly before noon, when Donald Trump stood before Chief Justice John Roberts. Trump's wife, Melania, held two Bibles, on which he placed his left hand; one was from Trump's childhood; the other was the Bible that Abraham Lincoln used to take his oath of office in 1861. And then Trump raised his right hand and, repeating after Roberts, swore the presidential oath of office.

A momentary silence hung in the air. No lightning bolt struck. The ground did not open. The passage of power in the United States of America had taken place as quietly as ever. Yet in that moment an earthquake of sorts did occur. Because although the United States may have had more tragically misguided executives at its helm, never before had it had as president a man more obviously misplaced in the office. The mismatch reverberated across the country with the very words of the oath itself. While for millions of Trump's supporters the moment was one of triumph, for a great many others a sense of dread pervaded the air that morning. This dread had little to do with politics or policy programs; it was not the normal apprehension one might have at the swearing-in of a politician one opposes. Even many people who had cast their ballots for Trump shared in a collective recognition that the man swearing this oath was simply not the sort of man who was *supposed* to be President of the United States. That mismatch and the challenge it poses to the office Trump assumed that day are the subjects of this book.

This mismatch is fundamentally a question of character. At its core, to a far greater degree than Americans commonly imagine, the office of the presidency depends on a measure of civic virtue. We don't mean civic virtue in the lofty or nostalgic sense of expecting our elected leaders to be scholar-statesmen who can theorize a system of government as easily as they can lead one, nor do we mean virtue in the sense of personal righteousness and purity. Americans have long since given up the expectation that the country's leaders will be on a par with its founders, even as the founders' own luster has tarnished over time. The presidency has had its share of rogues and villains and incompetents.

That said, a certain common understanding of the presidency has prevailed over more than two centuries, and this understanding—call it the traditional presidency—carries with it certain expectations. It does not expect presidents to be paragons of virtue, but it does expect them to espouse shared values and to at least pose as role models. It expects presidents to speak of service and putting others before self. It expects presidents to, at a minimum, pay lip service to following the law and embracing an ethos of civic duty. And it pervasively depends on presidents thinking that they enforce and comply with rules in good faith.

By contrast, it was resoundingly clear on January 20, 2017, that Donald Trump's life and candidacy were an ongoing rejection of civic virtue, even if we define the term loosely. From the earliest days of his campaign, he declared war on the traditional presidency's expectations of behavior. He was flagrant in his personal immorality, boasting of marital infidelity and belittling political opponents with lewd insults. He had constructed his entire professional identity around gold-plated excess and luxury and the branding of self. As a candidate, he remained unabashed in his greed and personal ambition; even his namesake charitable foundation was revealed to be merely a shell for self-dealing. He bragged that finding ways to avoid paying taxes made him "smart." The overriding message of Trump's life and of his campaign was that kindness is weakness, manners are for wimps, and the public interest is for suckers. He never spoke of the presidential office other than as an extension of himself.

In America in 2016, that turned out to be a winning message. The reasons why have been treated in depth elsewhere. It was a function of political polarization domestically, of myriad forces driving the appeal of authoritarian populists globally, of the dramatic loss of confidence in political elites, and of a media ecosystem in which voters can increasingly choose their own realities. It was a function, no doubt, of the resurgence of race as a salient political identity for many white voters. And, critically for present purposes, it was a function of political parties' loss of control over their own nominating processes. We will leave to others the question of how to assess Trump's appeal and the social conditions that allow him to flourish. The relevant fact for now is that the appeal was broad enough for Trump to win 306 electoral votes and thus acquire the privilege of taking the oath of office that day.

And so a man who quite proudly rejected personal and public virtue now occupied an office designed by people who valued nothing higher. George Washington had said that "virtue or morality is a necessary spring of popular government." John Adams had insisted that public virtue, "the only foundation of republics," could not "exist in a nation without private" virtue. Alexander Hamilton had written that "virtue and honor" were the "foundation of confidence" that underpinned "the institution of delegated power." The contemporary Anglo-Irish philosopher Edmund Burke had famously declared that "society cannot exist unless a controlling power upon will and appetite be placed somewhere, and the less of it there is within, the more there must be without. It is ordained in the eternal constitution of things, that men of intemperate minds cannot be free." Trump had said to hell with all that. And he had gotten elected anyway. It's true that many presidents seem petty when measured against the founders.

But Trump was different even from prior unsavory men who had attained the presidency. They had at least feigned that they cared about these values and expectations. Trump had campaigned against them and won on that basis.

Therein lay the mismatch between Trump and the office he now occupied: he did not even pretend to share a common understanding with his predecessors of its nature and purpose. Trump had his own vision—and it was radically different from what the traditional presidency assumes and demands. At the moment he swore his oath, the mismatch screamed across the city, across the airwaves, and across the centuries. From the very moment of his inauguration he was violating the deepest normative expectations of the traditional presidency.

And the violations continued. The first years of the Trump administration saw such frequent and profound disruptions to widespread expectations of the presidency that the word "norm" became something of a cliché. It became commonplace to observe that many deeply ingrained assumptions about what presidents will and will not do were matters not of law, but of custom. Within a few days of Trump's inauguration, *The Washington Post* had launched a podcast entitled *Can He Do That?*, which announced in its introductory trailer that "Trump is approaching the presidency in ways that nobody has done before, so one of the questions that keeps coming up is: What exactly can the president do?"

But viewing Trump's presidency merely as a series of breaches doesn't quite capture its significance or radicalism, and asking "Can he do that?" isn't exactly the right question either. The answer is almost invariably yes, he can do some or all of "that"—or at least he can try. As we will see, the presidency itself, stripped down to its legal essence, is actually a pretty spare institution. The Constitution doesn't describe much about what a modern-day president should actually do. It doesn't address whether he or she should run an interagency policy process through the National Security Council or just shoot from the hip. It doesn't say whether it's proper for a president to demand loyalty from her FBI director or to menace her attorney general for recusing himself from an investigation that directly concerns the president. It doesn't say that he shouldn't use the presidency to enrich himself or his family. It doesn't even say that she should tell the truth or, more generally, be a decent or honorable person—except that she should swear an oath of office in which she promises fidelity and care in the execution of the laws. These and countless other expectations of the modern presidency are extra-constitutional grafts onto the Constitution's bare-bones model—some of them early, some of them surprisingly recent, some of them containing statutory elements, but many of them simply a reflection of developed public expectation over time.

In some ways, therefore, the Trump presidency is a warped throwback to the presidency before countless expectations and bureaucratic structures developed around it. It's a reminder that honoring those expectations and engaging those bureaucratic structures is ultimately optional—something presidents do because that's what presidents do, because it worked for their predecessors, and because they, like so many other Americans, have been conditioned never to consider the possibility of anything else. Think of Abraham Lincoln personally firing off telegrams to his generals with an aide or two by his side—where the aides are Steve Bannon and Stephen Miller and the president is not the man who spoke of a "new birth of freedom," but the one who spoke of "shithole countries." Trump reminds us that all the accumulated grafts onto the presidency are not essential features of the office. Under certain circumstances, they can be sloughed off at will.

Throughout the presidential transition and in the wake of Trump's inauguration, many of his supporters—and many nonsupporters as well—imagined that the office would tame him. Trump's opponents would never embrace his policies, of course, but their fears would prove overblown, the argument went, as this radically unconventional candidate would nevertheless be disciplined by the nature of the office and its strictures. Had this prediction proved correct, we would not have written this book. Presidents can build trust that they may lack upon first entering office.

With a different man, it is possible to imagine that the uneasiness felt by those who watched him on the dais that day would have gone away over time.

But the office did not change Trump. Special Counsel Robert Mueller's final report offers the most authoritative account of his presidency's disruptions, but those disruptions go well beyond the ones explored by the special counsel. Within a day of his swearing the oath, Trump had lied about basic factual information—such as the size of his inauguration crowd—launching a war against the press. Within a week, he had attacked traditional notions of executive branch process, unleashing a major national security policy initiative without any meaningful consultation with the government agencies that are most qualified to know what the consequences might be. He began an unsettling series of interactions with his law enforcement hierarchy almost immediately, demanding loyalty from the FBI director and then asking him to drop an investigation of his national security adviser. His presidency raised a series of ethical questions about his and his family's business dealings, about which he has been simultaneously unapologetic and secretive. He adopted a management style as chaotic as it was theatrical, one that quickly had pundits across the political spectrum comparing the White House to a reality television show. He pioneered a new form of presidential communication with the public—the unfiltered Twitter tantrum—in which he lashed out in highly personal terms and often with malicious lies at political foes and at anyone who angered him. And he entered office dogged by the question, unique in American history, of his relationship with the intelligence apparatus of an adversarial foreign power—and then made overt efforts to stymie the investigation of that question.

Any hope that the presidency would discipline Trump, let alone tame him, vaporized quickly. Talk continued of the so-called pivot, but as the weeks and months wore on, it became more ironic than hopeful. There would be no pivot. There was just the man and the role to which he was so obviously unsuited. If the Mueller report does nothing else, it portrays a person wholly lacking in the moral and temperamental and characterological attributes the traditional presidency demands.

Indeed, what became clear was that Trump was attacking the core expectations of the traditional presidency, forged by more than two centuries of history and behavior, yet apparently held in contempt by tens of millions of Americans. These expectations have been historically enforced by a political party structure that has impeded the public's access at the general election ballot box to figures who don't minimally conform to its norms. Radical departures from the traditional presidency have not happened in the past because the parties have filtered them out. But the traditional presidency is not just the province of party apparatchiks, media elites, and commentators. It is a creature of mass expectations as well. Large numbers of voters believe in and reinforce its expectations; remember that Clinton received more votes than did Trump.

So as the Trump presidency progressed and his attacks on the norms of the traditional presidency continued, the question shifted from whether the presidency would change Trump to whether and how Trump would change the presidency.

Our object in this book is to take this question seriously. The presidency is not a static institution. As we shall see, it evolved dramatically over the course of the nineteenth and twentieth centuries—evolved in how it is organized, evolved in how it interacts with the public and Congress, evolved even in how it sounds. The presidency is changeable, and in systematically violating the norms of the traditional presidency, Trump is proposing to change it. He is proposing not just that a president can do certain things, but that a president *should* do these things—that his use of the office is legitimate and proper. He is proposing a reimagination of the office. He campaigned on that proposal, which had resonance for millions of Americans who turned out to hold the strictures of the traditional presidency in low regard. He won the presidency in part by inflaming and exploiting the contempt his supporters felt for the strictures of the office. And he has governed in a fashion consistent with that part of his campaign. Trump's idea of the presidency has shown sufficient proof of concept that it warrants a systemic examination.

As a starting point, we take as a given the legal scholar Jack Goldsmith's blunt assessment of the man:

> We have never had a president so ill-informed about the nature of his office, so openly mendacious, so self-destructive, or so brazen in his abusive attacks on the courts, the press, Congress (including members of his own party), and even senior officials within his own administration. Trump is a Frankenstein's monster of past presidents' worst attributes: Andrew Jackson's rage; Millard Fillmore's bigotry; James Buchanan's incompetence and spite; Theodore Roosevelt's self-aggrandizement; Richard Nixon's paranoia, insecurity, and indifference to law; and Bill Clinton's lack of self-control and reflexive dishonesty.

But what follows is not in any sense a biography of Trump or a narrative history of his presidency. We do not purport to evaluate his policy proposals or the reasons for his election. Rather, we offer a study of what happens to an institution like the American presidency when a person like this takes the oath of office and comes to embody it. It is an examination—to put it a different way—of what happens to the structure when King Kong climbs the Empire State Building.

Saying that Trump is proposing a revision to the American presidency may sound like it gives him too much credit. This is not, after all, a reflective man; he is not a theoretician. But if he's no Woodrow Wilson—a man who assumed the presidency having developed a systematic intellectual critique of the U.S. political system and its institutions—Trump is clearly acting intentionally, even if he is not operating according to any plan. He quite consciously poses the question of how he fits into the historical presidency when he mocks what it means to be "presidential." He full well understands that he is plotting his own course. He takes pride in it. He declared, on Twitter of course, "My use of social media is not Presidential—it's MODERN DAY PRESIDENTIAL." At a rally for a Republican congressional candidate named Rick Saccone in Pennsylvania a year into his term in office, Trump told the crowd, "You know . . . how easy it is to be 'presidential'? But you all would be out of here right now. You'd be so *bored*. Because I could stand up"—and he assumed an overly stiff demeanor and a deep, sonorous voice, saying—"I'm very presidential. 'Ladies and gentlemen, thank you for being here tonight. Rick Saccone will be a great, great congressman. He will help me very much. He's a fine man . . . And to all of the military out there, we respect you very much. Thank you. Thank you.' And then you go, 'God bless you, and God bless the United States of America. Thank you very much.'" And he tottered away from the microphone—only to swing back a second later. "See that? Easy. That's much easier than doing what I have to do . . . If I came [here] like a stiff, you guys wouldn't be here tonight." Trump knows he is proposing an alternative. Our aim in this book is to examine the proposal.

Most of all, Trump proposes a presidency that elevates the expressive and personal dimensions of the office over everything else. It is one in which the institutional office and the personality of its occupant are almost entirely merged—merged in their interests, in their impulses, in their finances, and in their public character. In elevating the expressive, vanity-plate dimensions of the office and making it a personal vehicle for the public self-expression of the officeholder, he proposes sublimating nearly all other traditional features of the presidency: its management functions; its expectation of good-faith execution of law; its expectation of ethical conduct, truthfulness, and service. This vision of the presidency thus unsurprisingly produces a genuinely novel set of deployments of the executive's traditional powers, ones that are profoundly different from those of prior presidents.

Trump's proposed revision is notably holistic in its nature. Previous presidents have most often sought to transform their office by expanding the edges of their authority; sometimes they succeeded, and sometimes they were pushed back. Consider Abraham Lincoln unilaterally suspending habeas corpus during the Civil War and ultimately deciding to go to Congress for ratification of his decision. Or Harry Truman trying to seize the steel mills and having the Supreme Court block him. Or presidents over time going to war on their own authority and Congress letting it happen. Or Franklin Roosevelt threatening to pack the Supreme Court after it serially ruled against his New Deal program, and the court backing down just in time to head off the plan. Consider the electoral rebuke Republicans suffered after Richard Nixon's abuses.

Given such history, it is no surprise that when Trump—a man who wore his propensity to abuse power on his sleeve—was elected president, many commentators and critics feared similar efforts. They instinctively knew to treat his enthusiastic remarks in favor of torture and certain war crimes as potentially more than mere words. They knew, without being told, to be concerned about the possibility of intelligence abuses. They worried about what he might do with drones. They worried about which "bad dudes" he might bring to Guantánamo Bay.

But while commentators reflexively looked to the edge cases of presidential power in anticipating Trump's abuses, the authorities he has actually abused have not lain at the edges. Over the first two years of his presidency, the fights over the major issues of presidential power that have divided Americans since September 11, 2001, largely disappeared from view. For all the fretting during the campaign about Trump's comments on torture, interrogation policy didn't change. Neither did detention policy. The authorities of the intelligence agencies to collect and process information did not materially increase under the new administration. And, ironically, the person most vocal in complaining about alleged intelligence abuses was Trump himself, who serially claimed illegality on the part of the intelligence community—from his predecessor's having allegedly had Trump's "wires tapped" to his gripes about the "unmasking" of anonymized names in intelligence reports, to his sudden opposition to a key intelligence authority sought by his own administration the very morning Congress finally managed to pass it.

Trump's abuses, as we shall describe, have almost uniformly occurred in areas where the president's power is not contested, areas at the very heart of what the Constitution calls "the executive Power."

Few serious constitutional scholars, after all, doubt the president's power to "appoint . . . Officers of the United States"—and thus to remove them. Nor is there any serious debate over the president's power to direct his administration to take actions that are based on bad information and no coherent process. No language in the Constitution requires Trump to follow a process of any kind before setting the executive branch on some course of action or another. The president also has the authority to pardon people: guilty people, people who support him politically, people convicted in an investigation in which he has personal interests. He has the power to strip former officials of security clearances. Even the president's power to spill highly classified information to foreign adversaries is pretty clearly established. If he wants to receive ambassadors in the Oval Office and divulge secrets to them there, well, they are his secrets to tell.

And, of course, the president's authority to speak his mind, including on Twitter, is likewise beyond any serious question. Many of the abuses of authority in which Trump has engaged have taken the form of tweets—from maligning people in a fashion that would certainly give rise to defamation suits were Trump not president to announcing new military policies on transgender service members without first establishing an official change in procedure. But the president has the right to say what he wants.

It turns out that one doesn't need to push the limits of executive power to become an abusive president. One need only personalize and abuse the powers the presidency indisputably holds. The Trump presidency is rethinking the institution not at its edges, but at its core, transforming it from the inside out, as it were.

Trump's broad attack on the traditional presidency raises an uncomfortable question: Is he right that the presidency needs transforming and is out-of-date? How much, if at all, should people really care about traditions that are not as old or as authoritative as we thought they were? And what happens if the American political system fails to enforce the norms of the traditional presidency over time? What if those norms are elitist claptrap rather than essential guardrails? Perhaps Trump's throwback presidency should be understood as a refreshing reversion to first principles, not as a dangerous assault on the protective structures we have built around the presidency's core. Put another way, is there any merit to Trump's proposed revisions to the office—and if so, what parts of the proposal have value?

These are not questions on which we will feign neutrality. The traditional presidency, in our view, requires a defense. For all its limitations and flaws, it is a successful institution that has, over a long period of time, well served Americans of many different political views.

As this book goes to press, Congress is considering President Trump's impeachment and possible removal from office, and less than a year from the time this book is published, Americans will vote on whether to re-elect Donald Trump as president. That decision, we hope to persuade the reader, includes the question of whether to ratify and accept the changes Trump proposes to the presidency itself or whether instead to repudiate and discard the vision he has put forward.

The examination of that vision necessarily begins with a close look at Trump's inauguration and the oath of office he swore that day.

ONE

"I do solemnly swear"

THE OATH

BARELY TWO MONTHS AFTER THE RAINY JANUARY MORNING when Donald Trump took the oath of office, the U.S. Justice Department was compelled to confront, formally in a court filing, the question of whether Trump's oath meant anything at all.

The occasion was the mounting litigation over the administration's travel ban. The department found itself in the unenviable position of having to convince a federal court that, although candidate Trump had campaigned on implementing a "Muslim ban" and made many disparaging statements about Islam, the executive order issued by President Trump

barring entry from a number of Muslim majority countries had nothing
to do with religious bigotry. There wasn't much the department's lawyers
could do to persuade the courts that Trump's multiple campaign statements didn't mean what they said. And so they adopted a strategy to avoid
dealing with those statements entirely: the department argued that anything Trump said about Muslims or proposed travel bans before he swore
the oath of office didn't count.

"Taking that oath marks a profound transition from private life to the
Nation's highest public office, and manifests the singular responsibility
and independent authority to protect the welfare of the Nation that the
Constitution necessarily reposes in the Office of the President," the department wrote. One cannot evaluate an "action by the President of the
United States because of his statements as a private citizen—before he
swore an oath to support and defend the Constitution, formed his Administration, assumed the responsibilities of governance, and consulted
with Executive officials responsible for legal, national security, foreign-
relations, and immigration matters."

The Justice Department's contention was that the oath of office is not
just a ceremonial formality—rather, it has an operative, almost mystical
effect. The oath, the department argued, transforms a person into a president. After taking the oath, when a president speaks and acts, he or she
must be presumed to do so with necessary deliberation and with the interests of the nation in mind. When a person swears the oath of office, the
logic goes, it doesn't just remake the person; it obliterates past acts that
might be unbefitting. The oath renders prior ignorance, racism, and outright lying irrelevant—at least for purposes of official consideration. The
oath does this even when the person swearing it is someone who seems
unlikely to make a clean break with his past.

As a legal matter, the department was on solid enough ground in invoking the distinction. How, after all, would the institutional presidency
function if it had to answer for everything its current occupant might ever
have said in the past? The department's invocation of Trump's oath was a

way of reminding courts that they should treat Trump, with all his oddities, like a normal president entitled to the same deference that any other
president would receive from the judiciary. But a normal president does
not need to remind the courts that he or she should be treated like a normal
president. That the department felt compelled to offer such a reminder was
a recognition of the stark reality that judges might not instinctively think
of Trump's oath in the same way they regarded the oaths of his predecessors. They might, like tens of millions of other Americans, have doubts.

When a ruling doge died in Renaissance Venice, a spokesman for the
Collegio, the collective assembly, would announce: "With much displea-
sure we have heard of the death of the Most Serene Prince, a man of such
goodness and piety; however, we shall make another." The governmental
elite had a script to begin the public transfer of power; through words, they
could make a prince, who would be transformed from whatever lesser
being he might have been before.

The U.S. Constitution was not about creating princes, but if words can
make a prince, then why not a president? The Constitution also contains a
script to mark the transfer of power between leaders; indeed, the relevant
passage is the only place in the entire document that uses quotation marks.
Article II, Section 1 directs that before a president takes office, he or she
pledges: "I do solemnly swear (or affirm) that I will faithfully execute the
Office of President of the United States, and will to the best of my Ability,
preserve, protect and defend the Constitution of the United States." The
founders of the American republic considered the presidential oath to be
so important that they, like the Venetian nobility, wrote the script into the
document itself.

Modern American political culture tends to give the oath short shrift.
The words spoken by George Washington and Donald Trump alike have
come to be viewed principally as a formality, part of the pageantry of inaugurations. The swearing of the oath is seen as a quaint nod to the conti-
nuity of our history, even as it serves as a time stamp marking the moment
of transition: the magic words that—Abracadabra!—transform someone

into a president, a president back into a normal citizen, and one presidential administration into another. To the extent that the oath is understood to have substantive content, it is in the promise to "faithfully execute" the office—a promise that is understood to pledge fidelity and is linked thematically to the Constitution's other general requirement of the president, that he or she "take Care that the Laws be faithfully executed."

Americans can perhaps be forgiven for undervaluing the oath. If it has pride of place in the Constitution, the presidential oath barely appears in Supreme Court case law. It has not historically been the subject of extensive scholarly literature. While there is exhaustive legal analysis of the meaning of the "take care" clause, the oath has largely remained unexamined, creating a false impression that it is inert and ceremonial.

Yet the people who wrote our founding document took oaths very seriously. The founders specifically considered the presidential oath—its inclusion, its words, its meaning—because they recognized that it has profound significance in the American system of government. Its execution, unlike virtually every other presidential duty, is purely mechanical; the president merely has to say the right words in the right order, and the Constitution's terms are satisfied. At the same time, it contains substantive promises to behave in a certain way, and it embeds a conception of civic virtue in our political order. The oath is the crux of the covenant between the president, the rest of government, and the people.

Textually, the oath has two dimensions. The first is a promise regarding execution of the law. The second is a more general promise of assistance to the constitutional order. The former promise is modified by the notion of fidelity ("faithfully execute"); the latter promise is modified by a promise of effort ("to the best of my Ability"). Crucially, both modifiers presume the existence of a presidential conscience—they are operative only if some minimal level of virtue is present.

The political scientist Edward Corwin, in his book *The President: Office and Powers, 1787–1984*, describes the coronation oath of the English kings "from which the President's oath is lineally descended," saying that "its purpose, definitely, was to put the King's conscience in bonds to the law." The early constitutional treatise writer Justice Joseph Story considered the purpose of the oath so obvious that he began his one-paragraph discussion of it by saying that there "is little need of commentary upon this clause" because "no man can well doubt the propriety of placing a president of the United States under the most solemn obligations to preserve, protect, and defend the constitution." Story described the oath as actively cultivating virtue in a president, "creat[ing] upon his conscience a deep sense of duty, by an appeal, at once in the presence of God and man, to the most sacred and solemn sanctions, which can operate upon the human mind."

In a recent law review article about the original meaning of the oath and the take care clause, the legal scholars Andrew Kent, Ethan Leib, and Jed Shugerman note that the promise of faithful execution in the clauses was commonly associated at the time of the founding with "true, honest, diligent, due, skillful, careful, good faith, and impartial execution of the law or office." The oath, they write, is thus a promise on the part of presidents "to exercise their power only when it is motivated in the public interest rather than in their private self-interest, consistent with fiduciary obligation in the private law."

This idea of a fiduciary obligation on the part of the president to act in the public interest gets to the heart of the matter. Without the oath's second clause—the promise to "preserve, protect and defend" the Constitution—it might be possible to read the oath as a narrow promise to comply with and enforce the law. This language, however, invokes something more elevated, a positive duty to serve the constitutional order. Interestingly, this is the clause that Story considered so obvious in its propriety that no explanation was necessary. So yes, the oath is a promise to execute the laws with care on behalf of others, not on behalf of oneself. But it is also a promise of something more, a promise of service. It is not an especially high bar. It's not a promise that one will be a philosopher-statesman or a moral paragon, or that one's nonofficial activity will be always above reproach. But it is a promise to use the powers of the office in pursuit of the public good. It's a promise of a certain minimal level of decency and trustworthiness—just enough to allow even the president's political foes to believe she is trying to do her best.

The Constitution's logic here is hard to argue with. The oath, one might say, fills what would otherwise be a disturbing void. There is, after all, no way for a two-century-old document to force a president to act in a public-spirited manner. There is no way for it to force a president to do his or her best for the country. The Constitution can give the president the power to veto legislation, but it can't directly compel a president to use that power to veto only legislation he honestly believes to be detrimental to the public interest. It can make the president commander in chief of the military, but it cannot directly compel her to issue only military orders in which she earnestly believes. It can make the president impeachable for bribery, but it cannot directly compel a president to be pure of heart when making important decisions. It cannot force the president to think of others, instead of himself, when making critical judgments. The most it can do, beyond the generic requirement of the take care clause and the document's various efforts to hem in the president with structural separation of powers constraints, is to make the president *promise* to behave with good faith and public-spiritedness with respect to the office—and to formalize that promise in a way calculated to influence actual behavior. That's the role of the oath, which is an attempt to harness honor and decency and civic virtue and the possibility of shame—indeed, to instill a measure of civic virtue by harnessing the threat of shame—and put them to work so that presidents make earnest efforts to use their office on behalf of the country.

If Americans were designing the presidency today, they probably wouldn't spend a lot of time debating the precise words the incoming president would say at his inauguration. But the founders debated the matter; they actually cared a great deal about the oath of office. While they recognized that oaths did not provide a sufficient condition for a stable republic, they certainly considered it a necessary one. If you're going to have a government in which people hold titles not by virtue of birth or status, but through election by their peers, what binds them to the conduct of their offices? The constitutional system the framers constructed required an oath imposing duty and obligation upon its executive.

The idea that an oath would actually serve this function may seem counterintuitive to people today. But the founders lived in an honor culture, and they put a lot of stock in oaths. Oath-taking had religious origins and retained religious overtones for many people—the natural self-enforcement mechanism being godly retribution for violation. Washington impulsively added "so help me God" to his first oath of office. And Lincoln, in his first inaugural address, pleaded with secessionists that they had "no oath registered in Heaven to destroy the government, while I shall have the most solemn one to 'preserve, protect, and defend' it."

What's more, the founders were steeped in the English liberal tradition that emphasized the utilitarian value of oaths. Thomas Hobbes had argued that to "put one another to swear by the God he feareth" provides a basis of the modern social contract. Jeremy Bentham, a contemporary of the founders and a skeptic of oaths, suggested that people really care about not lying under oath in order to avoid punishment by the state and moral sanction by the public—not from fear of divine retribution. Bentham's thesis is borne out in the degree to which we rely on oaths to this day in the entirely secular contexts of the courts: breaking one's promise "to tell the truth, the whole truth, and nothing but the truth" might not bring eternal damnation, but it could mean going to prison for perjury. In a society in which just government relies on the consent of the governed, the way we form a social contract with one another is by making promises and agreeing to be punished if we break them.

It was in recognition of all this, as the political scientist Matthew Pauley observes in his book on presidential oaths, that the founders made it "the President's first official duty" to swear "a solemn oath worthy of the majesty of the people who had elected him." As the legal scholar Sanford Levinson put it, "The constitutional oath may not be a 'religious test' . . .

but it is surely a test establishing one's devotion to the civil religion as a predicate condition for the ability to hold office."

If the oath's text and the fact of swearing it are law, the rest is all custom. Nothing dictates the place of the oath. It doesn't have to be sworn on a Bible, or on any book. The chief justice of the United States does not have to administer it. The highest-ranking judicial officer of New York, Robert Livingston, administered the first presidential oath to George Washington. At Washington's second inauguration, Supreme Court justice William Cushing administered the oath, and that has been the pervasive norm since. But exigent circumstances have occasionally called for different practice, as when the federal judge Sarah Hughes—the only woman ever to have administered the oath—swore in Lyndon Johnson aboard Air Force One following John F. Kennedy's assassination. Theodore Roosevelt had been out climbing Mount Marcy when he received news that President William McKinley had died, and following a perilous midnight stagecoach ride, Roosevelt met a federal district judge at a friend's house in Buffalo to take his oath. The only part that matters is the very thing that tens of millions of people found unsettlingly absent on January 20, 2017: the solemnization of the commitment to the office, the earnest promise by a figure chosen by the people to serve the constitutional order itself.

And indeed, if the goal of the founders was, as Story suggested, to "create upon [the] conscience [of the oath-taker] a deep sense of duty," it seems historically to have had exactly that effect on a number of presidents. When George Washington swore the first presidential oath on April 30, 1789, he was overwhelmed with the gravity and significance of the moment. Prior to his departure from his estate at Mount Vernon, Washington wrote to a friend that the sense of dread that marked his trip from private life in Virginia to the seat of government, then in New York, made him feel like "a culprit who is going to the place of his execution." The overwhelming sense of responsibility he felt to faithfully discharge the trust of his fellow citizens made him unable to enjoy the outpouring of support he received along his route of travel.

He swore the oath standing on a balcony at New York's Federal Hall, finishing with his ad-libbed "so help me God" and bowing to kiss the Bible. Fisher Ames of Massachusetts was in attendance, and he didn't say, "That was some weird shit." Rather, he wrote, "It was a very touching scene . . . It seemed to me an allegory in which virtue was personified, and addressing those whom she would make her votaries. Her power over the heart was never greater, and the illustration of her doctrine by her own example was never more perfect."

Washington, in short, deeply felt his oath of office. And everyone around him understood his sincerity. Washington's sensibility endured throughout his tenure; his second inaugural address was entirely occupied with the question of upholding his oath. In it, he said that if he should be found to have violated this oath, "besides incurring constitutional punishment," he wished that he may "be subject to the upbraidings of all who are now witnesses of the present solemn ceremony."

Of modern presidents, Lyndon Johnson most openly shared Washington's anguish at the gravity and responsibility of the presidential oath. Johnson spoke of taking his oath aboard Air Force One "in an hour of indescribable grief and sadness aboard a hushed and sweltering airplane" mere hours after the assassination of Kennedy. In that moment, Johnson said, he recognized the "magnitude of the job" and "the burden that no President can adequately explain or describe and no citizen can fully understand." After his presidency, Johnson wrote about the sense of relief he felt when he heard Nixon swear the presidential oath: "The most pleasant words . . . that ever came into my ears . . . because at that time I no longer had the fear that I was the man that could make the mistake of involving the nation in war. That I was no longer the man that would have to carry the terrifying responsibility of protecting the lives of this country, and maybe the entire world, unleashing the horrors of some of our great power, if I thought that was required."

The problem is that the oath works only when the president actually means it. It instills a sense of duty only when the oath's words and the solemn occasion of its delivery matters to the president and when others recognize that he means it. What if the person swearing is the sort of person who cannot credibly swear an oath?

Return for a moment to the strange scene on the dais at Trump's inauguration. Even in this unusually fractured period of American politics, the day offered a rare show of bipartisanship: Democrats and Republicans sat there united both in their shared commitment to the peaceful transition of power and—we suspect, but cannot prove—also in a profound unease about the man who raised his right hand before them. It's true that around the country, tens of millions of Trump voters delighted in his inauguration. But there was still an undeniable anxiety etched on the faces of many people on that dais about whether this was a man capable of solemnly swearing anything, let alone swearing to "faithfully execute" something like the office of the presidency. It wasn't just the Democrats. House Speaker Paul Ryan managed a weak smile but tightly gripped the arm of his wife, Janna. Past him, Senator John Cornyn and Representative Kevin McCarthy, both of whom should have been witnessing a moment of Republican triumph, gazed on somberly. Senate majority leader Mitch McConnell frowned, even more than usual, and appeared to wish he were anywhere else.

Pinning down the precise defect in Trump's oath is impossible. Indeed, the claim that there *is* a defect is inherently unprovable. One cannot know what was in Trump's heart as he said the words the Constitution prescribes. No public opinion experts polled anyone on public faith in President Trump's oath. Very few of the many Americans who fear or hate Trump frame their suspicions, either intellectually or emotionally, in terms of doubt as to the integrity of his oath.

Moreover, the history of hating a president, and of suspecting his illegitimacy in office, is old. A great many voters—including Trump himself—harbored deep enough questions about Obama's legitimacy to doubt his American birth. Many Democrats did not believe that George W. Bush was legitimate in office because he had prevailed in the 2000 election only after the intervention of the Supreme Court. And that contested election, in turn, reran aspects of the earlier contested election of 1876 between Rutherford B. Hayes and Samuel Tilden—one that left a mark of illegitimacy on Hayes's presidency. Most famously, it was an earlier presidential election and impending inauguration that triggered the South's secession from the Union in 1861.

The defect in Trump's oath was certainly not technical. Presidents have flubbed their oaths before. Herbert Hoover swore to "maintain" the Constitution rather than protect it; Nixon inserted an "and" that didn't belong. At Obama's first inauguration, Chief Justice Roberts fumbled his role, resulting in the new president swearing to "execute faithfully" rather than "faithfully execute" the office; the fastidious Roberts re-administered the oath the next day to be safe. For his part, Trump said all the right words—prompted by the chief justice, surrounded by his family, congressional leadership, and justices of the Supreme Court—and he did so without faltering or ad-libbing. He shook Obama's hand afterward, as one would expect. He observed all the niceties. Yet an unformed question tugged at the back of millions of minds even as he did so: Is this a man capable of being faithful to anything? Does he even know what it means to preserve, protect, and defend something other than himself?

Underlying these questions was Trump's public conduct over the preceding months and years. In addition to his statements about Muslims and travel bans, the oath would have to relieve him of a lot of other baggage if it was to serve its traditional function of assuring people that their president was a good-faith enforcer of law and committed to the defense of the Constitution. This was a man, after all, who only a few months earlier had been promising to commit war crimes, who had repeatedly described the election that brought him to power as "rigged," and who would not promise to respect the outcome if he lost. This was also a man who had lied serially about all manner of things, from the profound to the mundane. The oath here was being asked to do an uncommon amount of work.

This was particularly true because Trump had not changed in any way since the election. Even during a normal presidential campaign, candidates say all kinds of reckless things, and the transition period before the victor takes office serves to temper the rhetoric and ameliorate division. In Trump's case, however, there had been no healing words. The erratic statements never stopped. No evident process of pivoting to the task of governing had taken place. Nor did the transition see any elevation to leadership on the part of Trump personally. And so, when the new president took the oath, it did not seem like the culmination of a "profound transition from private life to the Nation's highest public office." It seemed like a man, his hand on the Bible, mouthing the correct words and minimally observing the proper forms. Everything was right, yet everything was also pervasively wrong.

This sense of something being wrong was, we submit, rooted in what James Comey would later call "the nature of the person." Comey would use this phrase before the Senate Intelligence Committee in an attempt to explain why he had felt compelled to memorialize his first interaction with Trump in writing. Senator Mark Warner asked Comey what it was about the interaction with the president-elect that made him so keen to write down the details right away, typing the memo out on a laptop in an FBI car as he was being driven away from Trump Tower. Comey's response is worth considering in relation to the oath Trump would swear two weeks after their meeting:

> I was alone with the president of the United States, or the president-elect, soon to be president . . . I was talking about matters that touch on the FBI's core responsibility, and that relate to the president, president-elect personally. And then *the nature of the person*. I was honestly concerned he might lie about the nature of our meeting, and so I thought it really important to document. [Emphasis added]

Consider Comey's invocation of "the nature of the person." He means, of course, that Trump is the sort of person one does not trust. And Comey was not alone. In the days following Comey's firing, his successor—Andrew McCabe—also memorialized his conversations with Trump, later writing that he "wrote memos about my interactions with President Trump for the same reason that Comey did: to have a contemporaneous record of conversations with a person who cannot be trusted." It matters if a person swearing the presidential oath is so lacking in civic virtue and trustworthiness that an officer of the government feels compelled to document conversations with him—and that the desirability of doing so is so self-explanatory that it can be justified by a mere reference to "the nature of the person" with whom he is dealing.

If the Trump presidency has shed many expectations that have attached themselves over time to the original presidency, Trump has most flamboyantly shed those expectations the oath of office purports to embody: the expectation of public-spiritedness in the man who wields the executive authority of the United States.

Put simply, it makes a difference that Trump's inauguration was, in the view of one—and probably all—of his living predecessors, "some weird shit." It matters if people on the stage had pits in their stomachs. And it matters if tens of millions of people around the country had an inchoate feeling of dread about the integrity of the oath. At every presidential inauguration there is a side that didn't win, of course. But it matters, even if it can't ever be proved, that the pits in the stomachs were deeper and more numerous this time around, the dread more widespread and profound. The American presidency simply doesn't work in the absence of the good faith we have come to expect in a president. What makes Trump's oath different is that he couldn't even fake it credibly.

The sincerity and integrity of the presidential oath does not present any sort of justiciable legal question. It is not a matter one could ever bring before a judge. Nonetheless, it is the glue that holds together many of our system's functional assumptions about the presidency. It is the fundamental underpinning of many of our cultural expectations regarding presidential behavior. And it is a key part of the reason the judiciary grants deference to the executive, extending what lawyers call a "presumption of regularity" to executive branch actions. The idea is that when someone has sworn an oath to do something, a coordinate branch of government owes it to that person to assume—at least in the absence of evidence to the contrary—that he or she is doing it properly. When large numbers of people doubt a president's oath, that assumption ceases to operate. It ceases without anyone's ever announcing, let alone ruling from the bench, that the president didn't satisfy the presidential oath clause and thus is not really president. It just stops working—or works a lot less well.

There's a big, if somewhat ineffable, difference between opposing a president and not believing in his oath of office, though the line can be fuzzy. All presidents face opposition, some of it passionate, extreme, and delegitimizing. All presidents face questions about their motives and integrity. And many presidents face at least some suggestion that their oaths do not count.

Yet there is something different about the questions that can be asked about Trump's oath. Such a person simply does not receive certain presumptions our system normally attaches to presidential conduct. The presidential oath, after all, does not discipline only the president; it also disciplines other actors in relation to the president. Deference to it tends to restrain people—including people who dislike, even hate, the president at any given time. Yet in his years in office, President Trump has seen remarkable resistance from judges, from the press, and from the members of the bureaucracy who serve him. The bureaucracy leaked information in a fashion the country has never seen before. Judges refused to credit executive branch statements about national security matters. And the press often treated presidential statements as presumptively untrue unless and until they could be corroborated independently. Part of this was self-defense against an individual who openly attacked them, but the predominant reason these actors declined to defer to Trump's oath was that they did not trust it.

Upon swearing his oath, Trump immediately made plain the extent to which he was not transformed by it and would not be changed by his office. To many people, Trump's refusal to maintain certain appearances is actually an important part of his appeal. His supporters had not sent him to Washington to be transformed. The oath—to the extent that it has come to embody certain expectations of the traditional presidency—was asking Trump to change, which is precisely what he promised not to do. So there was a strange integrity in his refusal to even pretend to take his oath seriously.

It's worth acknowledging as well that Trump's behavior also reveals an important truth about our collective civic life: if a president is a good and virtuous person, he doesn't need an oath to feel bound to faithfully execute his office—though it may amplify the feeling. Conversely, if he is a dishonorable rogue, then no oath will bind him anyway. In 1846, Enoch Lewis, a mathematician who dabbled in legal theory, observed that "no rational man would choose to put one into an office of honor or trust, if he believed his principles so loose as to require an oath to bind him to the performance of his official duties." Trump is revealing the oath's chains as a kind of myth; they only bind the president who chooses to feel bound by them.

And much of Trump's base cheers when he exposes civic mythology. Many of his supporters are tired of fiction and pretense, and he has delivered a kind of perverse authenticity. Whatever Trump is, after all, he is not a hypocrite in this regard. He doesn't pretend to civic virtue. Indeed, what made his oath so discordant was precisely its absence of hypocrisy. He did not remotely pretend to be experiencing the transformation that his Justice Department would later claim. For someone who lies so often, there is something refreshingly honest about Trump's oath. Yes, he said the words, and as surely as Washington and Johnson were moved by them, Trump made abundantly clear that the pledge meant nothing to him.

The ultimate evidence of this is that immediately upon taking the oath, he turned around and began lying about the very occasion of his having done so. Trump swore his oath and became president on a

Friday. On Saturday, he traveled to the CIA, where he stood in front of the agency's hallowed memorial wall for its fallen officers and boasted falsely about his inaugural crowd size. That day, his new press secretary, Sean Spicer, harangued the press about how many people had seen Trump's inauguration—claiming falsely, but no less energetically and angrily for the statement's falsity, that "this was the largest audience to ever witness an inauguration—period—both in person and around the globe." And that same weekend saw Trump's counselor Kellyanne Conway defending Spicer's lies about crowd size on *Meet the Press*, where she coined the memorably Newspeak term "alternative facts."

When the National Park Service's Twitter account shared a side-by-side photograph of the Trump and Obama inaugurations—leaving no question that Obama drew a larger group—the administration ordered the entire agency to stop using social media until further notice. The confused department hurried to implement contingency planning for emergencies, during which it usually relies on social media to communicate with the public. Did the president really intend to prioritize his personal feud over the ability to rapidly alert the public about mudslides or flood routes? It didn't matter. The president said no tweeting, and so the guidance went out.

The degree to which the overt lying over crowd size was driven personally by the man who had just sworn an oath to "faithfully execute" the presidential office emerged only later. After White House chief of staff Reince Priebus was fired, he described Trump's calling him just after 6:00 a.m. on that first Saturday in a rage over *The Washington Post*'s pictures of the comparative inaugural crowd sizes. "This story is bullshit," the new president shrieked. Priebus recounted, "He said, 'There's more people there. There are people who couldn't get in the gates . . . There's all kind of things that were going on that made it impossible for these people to get there.'" The president ordered Priebus to call the new interior secretary and the Park Service: "Tell him to get a picture and do some research right away." As Priebus tried to calm the implacable president, he realized he had a decision to make: "Am I going to go to war over this with the president of the United States?" The White House went to war with the press instead.

The traditional presidency—indeed, the structure of the Constitution—does not account for the president's caring about something profoundly dumb. It doesn't allow a federal agency to decide that a presidential directive wasn't issued in good faith or that it was a silly whim. It doesn't allow the executive branch to ignore a presidential order on grounds that the president is not really behaving in the public-spirited fashion the oath requires. So the new administration had no choice but to set itself to telling the public that plainly documented facts, clear to their own eyes in pictures, were untrue.

The episode provided an early glimpse of how Trump understands the presidency. Even on the day after his oath, the government's foremost task was to create a public reality that conformed to his desires.

The Department of Justice can argue that a president is necessarily transformed by the oath and by the duties of his office. But if a president assumes office and directs the powers and priorities of the executive branch to promote his personal self-expression, the oath does not restrain him.

The expressive presidency was an innovation Trump proposed from the very beginning. What this meant for his management of his office and policy-making decisions would become clear quickly.

"The President needs help"

WHITE HOUSE DECISIONS

GOD MAY HAVE RESTED ON THE SEVENTH DAY, BUT DONALD Trump did not. God took a week to form an ordered universe out of a void of emptiness. But on the seventh day of his presidency, Trump truly began his work of restoring the executive branch to the chaos from which two centuries of American history had crafted elaborate form.

Trump had devoted the first week of his presidency largely to self-expression; it was about crowd sizes, vote counts, and magazine covers. On Monday, Trump made his first policy moves, such as signaling withdrawal from the Trans-Pacific Partnership. He also faced his first lawsuit as president, an allegation that the operation of his hotels violated the emoluments clause of the Constitution. On Tuesday, he approved the Keystone XL pipeline, an oil pipeline from Canada to Nebraska, which had stalled under the Obama administration for environmental reasons. On Wednesday, Trump issued executive orders on his promised border wall and on sanctuary cities. On Thursday, Mexican president Enrique Peña Nieto responded by canceling a trip to the United States. But mostly, the week had been spent fighting with the press.

On the seventh day, a Friday, Trump issued an executive order entitled "Protecting the Nation from Foreign Terrorist Entry into the United States." The first major national security initiative of the new administration, the document boldly—if partially—attempted to fulfill one of the new president's most inflammatory campaign promises. "Donald J. Trump is calling for a total and complete shutdown of Muslims entering the United States until our country's representatives can figure out what the hell is going on," the candidate had said. And though the administration insisted that the new policy was not a Muslim ban, it was certainly a ban, and it just as certainly was a ban that affected mostly Muslims. The president himself, when he wasn't protesting that the action had nothing to do with banning Muslims, offered it as the fulfillment of his pledge, saying with a verbal wink at the signing ceremony, "This is the protection of the nation from foreign terrorist entry into the United States. We all know what that means."

Unlike Trump's earlier policy pronouncements, which had little immediate effect on anyone—the Trans-Pacific Partnership had never gone into effect, and no new brick had been laid on the border wall—the promulgation of the travel ban unleashed immediate chaos and hardship on the lives of many thousands of people. The order was signed without warning, without meaningful consultation with affected federal agencies, and without anything beyond cursory legal review. With the stroke of a pen, Trump showed not just what he could do with little more than the force of his words and will, but what he could do *to others*.

For supporters of a president who had campaigned for office on the idea that he would come in and do things—including securing the border—the moment was electrifying. Trump had swept in and, without wasting any time, done something. He had said he was going to ban Muslims, and he hadn't asked anyone's permission or gotten bogged down in deliberation. Nor had he compromised or backed away from his promise. Trump's vision of the presidency may not have been punctilious about the oath or good faith, but it was muscular and it acted decisively. It's not hard to understand the appeal: here was a presidency that was actually responsive to the will of the voters who elected the man. The lack of consultation was evidence of that responsiveness. Voters hadn't elected Trump to be talked off his path by a bunch of bureaucrats. They had sent him to Washington to tame the bureaucracy, not to be tamed by it. And he had done just that—or so it seemed at first.

The order suspended all entry to the United States and all issuance of visas for people from seven countries: Iran, Iraq, Libya, Somalia, Sudan, Syria, and Yemen. It also temporarily suspended all refugee admissions from anywhere and indefinitely suspended refugee admissions from Syria.

The impact was immediate: people were trapped in airports, pulled off airplanes, and turned back from ports of entry. Permanent residents of the United States suddenly were stuck abroad and couldn't get home. Students home on vacation couldn't return to school. Refugees who had been cleared for entry suddenly had no place to go. Protests began at airports; lawyers quickly filed lawsuits. Within a day, the ACLU had petitioned a federal court for a stay of deportations of immigrants and refugees trapped in airports by Trump's order. And a federal judge in Virginia issued a temporary restraining order preventing the removal of green card holders detained in airports and requiring that legal residents of the United States have access to counsel. By the end of the following week, there were similar orders temporarily restraining enforcement of the whole ban nationwide.

The chaos the travel ban unleashed outside the administration reflected a certain chaos within the administration that had produced it.

Normally, a major presidential action in the national security realm that affects the lives of millions of people and the security of the country at large involves a complex process within the government. An action like the travel ban affects many different agencies with different interests. The Department of Homeland Security mans the ports of entry. The State Department issues visas and has to respond to the diplomatic fallout from countries that don't want their citizens banned from entering the United States—not to mention the negative backlash from Muslim countries that perceive such an action as discriminatory with respect to Islam. One would expect consultation with the intelligence agencies as to whether a ban is even necessary—and, if so, how broadly it should sweep, against which countries it should be directed, and on what sort of people it should focus. If the goal is to protect national security, one would presumably want to hear from the folks who have insight into which kinds of people do and do not pose threats to national security. It turned out that the military had important dogs in this fight too: people who had helped U.S. forces in Iraq, to whom the military had promised shelter, were suddenly barred from entering the country. And, of course, the Justice Department has to consider the legality of any major federal action to make sure it can survive the legal challenges that have to be anticipated.

This sort of complex integration of different governmental entities is why the executive branch developed the so-called interagency process, a system of coordination and discussion between the federal agencies, at escalating levels of authority, designed to unify and deconflict policy and make sure all of the different agencies' concerns are accounted for and addressed. The goal is ultimately to tee up policy decisions for a president adequately informed of the costs and benefits of different courses—and, in order to preserve presidential time and focus, to resolve matters between the agencies that do not require presidential involvement at the lower levels.

Process is hard to love. It slows things down. It is frustrating to people who want action. No one votes for process. All presidents have chafed at and sidestepped it to some degree. But all presidents have been forced to rely on it too. This is because the executive branch is, in reality, a network of giant bureaucracies, not just a person who wants to express herself. Some kind of system has to make sure that these bureaucracies are not working at cross-purposes and that the president gets the information she needs in order to act wisely. In the preparation of the travel ban, there was as little process as the modern presidency has seen on a major decision. Consultation with the Justice Department was limited to a facial review of the order's text for obvious illegality. The Homeland Security Department was briefed only shortly before the ban was released. Neither the military nor the intelligence community was meaningfully consulted.

If the president had consulted with those agencies, the executive order would have looked quite different. It would have applied to fewer groups of people for shorter periods of time; its language would have been cleansed of the lingering hints of racial and religious animus; and it would have contained safety valves in the forms of carve-outs and discretionary exemptions. In other words, it would have been less like what Trump had said he wanted: "a total and complete shutdown of Muslims entering the United States." For many of the president's supporters, this would have been far less satisfying, and they surely would have viewed such an outcome as the kind of business-as-usual watering down of campaign promises delivered by regular politicians. They didn't want that. By contrast, a number of critics had counted on executive branch processes to temper Trump's worst impulses and ugliest campaign promises. Process would discipline Trump, they had said. He simply couldn't do the many things he had promised as a candidate; the vast bureaucracies of the executive branch would delay policies, imposing facts and levels of review and injecting carve-outs and exemptions. These commentators didn't imagine that Trump would simply sidestep the process entirely.

In signing the order without substantial consultation, the new president stunned Washington by treating a major policy change no differently from the other self-expressive acts of his first week in office. His supporters had sent him to the White House to shake up the way things are done in

Washington, and Trump had done just that. In doing so, he drew back a curtain and revealed the remarkable personal power of the office.

The result was a document with enormous negative impact on the United States and on countless innocent people. It was a document that emotionally satisfied Trump's hardest-line supporters better than anything a coordinated interagency process could have produced, precisely *because* it defied bureaucratic and policy niceties. But it was also a document that ultimately could not withstand legal scrutiny.

Within a few days, Acting Attorney General Sally Yates had instructed the Justice Department not to defend the order, declaring, "I am responsible for ensuring that the positions we take in court remain consistent with this institution's solemn obligation to always seek justice and stand for what is right. At present, I am not convinced that the defense of the Executive Order is consistent with these responsibilities nor am I convinced that the Executive Order is lawful." Trump immediately fired Yates, replacing her with an acting attorney general who would agree to defend the order. It did not make a difference. The order could not be successfully defended and ultimately was abandoned. After a federal appellate court enjoined its enforcement, the government withdrew the order, replacing it with one that had gone through at least minimal interagency review. This one lasted marginally longer before it too was struck down and replaced. On its third try, the administration came up with a version of the policy that was rolled back substantially from the original travel ban—and this one it could defend successfully in court. In June 2018, the Supreme Court finally okayed implementation of Travel Ban 3.0.

In other words, while Trump's highly personal, expressive, and processless brand of decision-making won that first week in dramatic fashion, the more modern presidency—the process presidency—ultimately did prevail, with a healthy assist from the courts. It turns out to be hard to do things—at least to do large, sustainable things that require the movement and coordination of thousands of participants—without process. And in an age in which presidential action is subject to judicial review, process turns out to be essential to surviving judicial scrutiny. So while Trump successfully unleashed temporary chaos that first week and made a strong statement to his political base, he didn't ban Muslims from entering the United States—temporarily or otherwise—even from the specific countries at issue. And when all the dust had settled, the final travel ban the Supreme Court upheld bore only some marks of Trump's original imagined policy.

If Trump is proposing a truly novel vision of a personally expressive presidency, his vision of a processless presidency is actually not new. Structurally and constitutionally speaking, the complex interlocking bureaucracies that make up the executive branch are mostly of recent origin. And they are the president's instruments to use as he or she sees fit. To the extent the presidency has rules, those rules are, to a great degree, themselves simply expressions of presidential will.

There are important exceptions to this last statement. Formal processes have over the years been written into law. Civil service rules, for example, govern aspects of the career federal bureaucracy; the Uniform Code of Military Justice governs aspects of military life; the Administrative Procedure Act sets up formal rules for promulgating regulations; and federal agencies have statutory responsibilities that assign roles and functions to officials below the president. But mostly, the rules of the executive branch exist because presidents want them to exist. Basically, the presidency worked better with rules than without them, and as the office grew, more rules were added and more stuck over time. Some of these rules got written into law, but many never did.

Trump is far from the first president to fail to run processes that allowed sufficiently diverse input into key decisions. Indeed, all presidents supervise process failures of some kind, though these failures are of very different types and very different magnitudes. The George W. Bush administration's post–September 11 decisions to authorize certain intelligence programs at CIA and NSA and its decision to invade Iraq were all rightly criticized for the narrowness of the advice the president received and the decision to marginalize internal dissent. Even the normally process-conscious Barack Obama made the politically costly decision to seek congressional approval for planned military action against Syria—approval that never came—after taking a walk around the White House grounds with a single aide. His advisers had no warning about plans to go to Congress before he informed them of that decision. Normally, when presidents have failed to run good processes, the political and legal price paid has been sufficiently high to induce relatively quick self-correction. And of course, people tend not to fixate on process fouls, or even define them as such, when the outcomes are good. For example, before Obama approved the raid that killed Osama bin Laden, a senior CIA official told him that the intelligence placing bin Laden at the targeted building in Abbottabad, Pakistan, was weaker than the intelligence that Iraq had weapons of mass destruction. The bin Laden raid is lauded as one of the high points of Obama's presidential decision-making, but we probably wouldn't have evaluated his process as admiringly had the intelligence turned out to be false.

The point is that presidential process is not a switch that is either on or off; it varies depending on the personality of the president in question and other factors. And a good process is no guarantee of a successful outcome. That said, in the end, interagency consultations take place in a structured fashion because presidents have *wanted* input from different sources of expertise before making fateful decisions. The interagency process reduces mistakes, and the traditional presidency cares about not making mistakes. And when it works well, the interagency process enables the complex mustering of diverse information sources and government entities to enable the very best decisions a president is capable of making. Obama authorized the bin Laden raid having heard a diversity of points of view about the intelligence, the diplomatic fallout, and the military options and risks. George H. W. Bush was able to draw on the entire military and diplomatic resources of the country to put together a coalition to confront Iraq after its invasion of Kuwait. The confrontation with the Soviet Union over decades required—both in acute episodes such as the Cuban missile crisis and in longer-term strategic approach—the coordination of massive but bureaucratically distinct sources of American power and capability.

But very little of this coordination is ultimately constitutionally required. If a president wishes to act like presidents in the earliest days of the republic, when the presidency really was processless, he is free to try.

George Washington's cabinet famously contained within it the seeds of the American party system, with Alexander Hamilton as Treasury secretary and Thomas Jefferson as secretary of state pursuing radically divergent agendas. There was no process to speak of. There were just individual actors who could be fired if they got too out of hand, and Washington eventually dismissed key cabinet members for straying too far. Hamilton advocated for what became the Federalist position, and Jefferson opposed him vociferously. They sometimes compromised, and when they could not, Washington tended to side with Hamilton. What the administration lacked in processes, it made up for in personalities. The presidency was truly personal.

One reason that the early republic was so processless was that the executive branch departments were quite small, and the early presidents had essentially no professional staff. At the outset of the republic, there were only three cabinet-level departments: Treasury, State, and War. And this remained the case until 1849. Only five more were added between then and 1953: the Departments of Interior, Agriculture, Justice, Commerce, and Labor. The First Congress created an attorney general, but the office did not head an executive department. Instead, U.S. attorneys—then called district attorneys—reported to the Treasury Department from 1797 until the Ulysses S. Grant administration, although in practice, the sluggish pace of communication meant that there was little supervision. The attorney general, meanwhile, was responsible for providing legal advice to the president and the various departments and was responsible for representing the government in court.

Unlike today, when much of the presidency is on autopilot by necessity of scale, the personal presidency meant that the president actually

did a lot of the work himself. In his biography of John Adams, David Mc-
Cullough describes the second president's work habits at home in Quincy,
Massachusetts, one summer when Abigail Adams was gravely ill:

> He worked no less diligently than usual, spending long hours
> at his desk. Official reports from Philadelphia, dispatches from
> department heads, documents requiring his signature, requests
> for pardons, applications for jobs, reports of all kinds, arrived in
> assorted bundles, daily by post rider. Decisions were called for
> on matters large and small. Benjamin Rush asked that his brother
> be considered for the Supreme Court. There was a request for
> the President's approval to build a lighthouse at Cape Hatteras,
> a request from Secretary Wolcott for authority to borrow up to
> $5,000,000 on behalf of the United States, reports from Wolcott on
> the yellow fever epidemic. Secretary McHenry sent an extended
> review, numbing in detail, of expenditures required for the
> Department of War . . . Nor was there any letup in the stream of
> patriotic addresses.

The early presidents personally handled tasks that would never get
anywhere near the president's desk today. Washington himself, for example, reviewed all letters written by cabinet officials. He also regularly
reviewed the line-item expenditures of the U.S. Post Office, even going
so far as to review contractual language for carriage of the mail. Jefferson also engaged with minutiae. At one point he instructed a subordinate on post-road river crossings, specifying down to the foot the width
of rivers and streams that should be bridged. In another instance he approved the pay increase of a single official. Treasury Secretary Albert
Gallatin once reported that he had issued an emergency authorization
for an expenditure to repair a leaky roof of a hospital in Norfolk, Virginia, that President Jefferson normally would have approved directly.

And President Grover Cleveland personally answered the White House telephone.

Perhaps no example illustrates the personal presidency better than Washington's actions during the Whiskey Rebellion. In 1794, Washington personally led a column of thirteen thousand troops through Pennsylvania in order to put down the incipient revolt.

One of the reasons the early presidency was so personal was that presidents did not have staffs as we understand them today. When Jefferson was president, he had only one messenger and one secretary. When Grant took the presidency sixty years later, the size of the staff had expanded to three. The political scientist John Burke writes that by 1900, the presidential staff consisted of a private secretary, as well as "two assistant secretaries, two executive clerks, a stenographer, three clerks, and four other office personnel," for a total staff of thirteen.

It was not until 1857 that Congress even appropriated money for presidential staff. Prior to that, presidents paid staff out of their own pockets—which probably helps explain why the staffs were so small. It may also help explain why so many presidents hired family members. Interestingly, one of Trump's many means of circumventing process is by entrusting important questions to his children. This too recalls earlier eras, before presidential process had developed.

Cabinet departments also had few actual employees. Jefferson, as secretary of state in the Washington administration, had an initial staff consisting only of a chief clerk, three other clerks, one translator, and a messenger. When the Treasury Department moved to Washington, D.C., in 1800, just sixty-nine employees worked in the building. By 1818 the staffing at the State Department had not grown much larger: eight clerks and a few other minor employees. In 1836 the department was split into six bureaus. Even so, six clerks managed all overseas correspondence. Even as of 1860, the Diplomatic Service had only forty-five employees staffing thirty-three overseas missions.

The notion that the executive branch should have processes—other than the process of the president thinking about things, getting advice, and making decisions—developed only as the executive branch grew and the need thus developed for more structured decision-making. As the world became more complicated, more information was necessary to make decisions responsibly, and the number and kinds of decisions that government had to make increased as it took on more functions. A small group with a single leader can decide things in a minimally process-driven fashion. The president can have hub-and-spokes relationships with a few key advisers of radically different views—indeed, with advisers who, like Hamilton and Jefferson, constitute the leaderships of rival parties in the incipient party system. We can romanticize an earlier, more freewheeling executive style, but the model doesn't scale. It works because the relationships are highly individualized. If each of those advisers now represents a gigantic bureaucracy with entrenched and long-standing interests, how do decisions get made? Under such circumstances, not only does the president no longer do nearly as much of the executive management personally, but the branch has a coordination question as to which department—indeed, which part of which department—is going to do it for him.

Under circumstances like these, important questions emerged: What parts of the job was the president still going to do herself? What happens when various parts of the different bureaucratic entities have functions that overlap? What happens when they disagree, when what used to be Jefferson is suddenly a giant building full of people and what used to be Hamilton is suddenly a different giant building full of people? What happens when the government is so big that the secretaries of state and Treasury don't even know that their departments are disagreeing many rungs below?

Franklin Roosevelt once mocked his role as presidential referee of minor executive branch decisions, firing off a sarcastic memo to his budget director to say that he agreed with the interior secretary that "fur-bearing animals" should remain within that department's jurisdiction. Roosevelt added: "You might find out if any Alaska bears are still supervised by (a) War Department, (b) Department of Agriculture, (c) Department of Commerce. They have all had jurisdiction over Alaska bears in the past and many embarrassing situations have been created by the mating of a bear belonging to one Department with a bear belonging to another Department . . . P.S. I don't think the Navy is involved, but it may be. Check the Coast Guard. You never can tell."

Modern executive branch process, as we currently conceive it, did not take shape until the 1930s. When it did begin to emerge, it was viewed as a way for the president to regain control over administrative agencies that had grown unaccountable and unmanageable in the preceding Progressive Era. Although FDR joked about it, the problem was not a joke.

The advent of such administrative agencies as the Federal Communications Commission and the Federal Trade Commission presented a new function for the executive branch. These agencies made rules, after all. They didn't simply perform tasks and carry out laws. Congress delegated to the executive branch important new rulemaking functions, and bureaucracies cropped up to implement the proliferating new regulatory powers. To the extent that the executive branch was suddenly making rules, it was arguably playing a role the Constitution had assigned to Congress. And to the extent that the president wasn't meaningfully supervising the executive branch in doing so, there was an additional problem of democratic control over rulemaking. Thus was born the "administrative state" that Trump aide Steve Bannon threatened to dismantle.

Burke writes that Roosevelt was painfully aware of this lack of control and was dedicated to "significant efforts to create a presidential staff that would perform a substantive role in policy decisions." This led him to form the Committee on Administrative Management, otherwise known as the Brownlow Committee.

In 1937 the Brownlow Committee made a simple, arresting claim: "The President needs help." Its recommendations were ambitious, and they included expanding the White House staff, revolutionizing the civil service merit system, grouping the one hundred independent agencies and commissions into twelve reorganized cabinet-level departments, and strengthening overall the managerial control of the government. The eventual bill Congress passed in 1939 rejected many of the Brownlow Committee's reforms, but it did approve an expansion of the presidential staff.

The reforms in this period created the Executive Office of the President and subsumed the Bureau of the Budget, known today as the Office of Management and Budget, under it. During the reorganization, the staff of the Bureau of the Budget grew from 35 to 600 people. Additional reforms followed over the successive decades. The result is an OMB that is significantly involved in legislative clearance and program coordination, giving it a leading role in determining policy and spending. It now has a management role in advising the president on the efficiency and effectiveness of various federal programs.

The national security sphere saw a particular need for interagency coordination. The explosive growth of the foreign policy bureaucracy during and after World War II meant that the country suddenly had—for the first time—a large standing army with permanent overseas deployments, an intelligence community, and a large diplomatic service, all notionally working as part of the same unitary executive branch.

In 1947 Congress created the National Security Council to coordinate foreign policy measures and to advise and assist the president in arriving at coherent and cohesive foreign policy judgments. Since then, the NSC has grown substantially, and it both advises the president and coordinates agency activities in the national security arena. Think of it as a two-way communications mechanism through which the White House hears from agencies, coordinates their action, and resolves disputes among them. It is the switchboard through which the president controls the national security bureaucracy.

By the early 1990s the White House staff had grown to include a raft of different staffs, in addition to the White House Office itself. These various offices of the White House staff are all there to "help" the president, who is theoretically sitting at the apex of the executive branch. They are there to coordinate policy implementation, manage information flow to the president, and help with crises and communications. The president has become a kind of CEO, supervising giant organizations that largely run themselves. Matters come to him or her only if the normal autopilot of day-to-day government is inadequate and specific presidential guidance and decision are thus necessary. This process creates remoteness for the presidency from the work of the executive branch; it also creates order and predictability.

Or that's the way it is supposed to work in the traditional presidency.

There is an embedded assumption here, though, and it goes back to the oath of office. That assumption is that the president is actually taking care to make sure the laws are faithfully executed—rather than, say, servicing his own vanity or manias—and that he actually wants help in order to do so effectively. The system is designed to be accountable to the president. There is no obvious mechanism to manage the flip side of that particular coin: that the president may be out of control and that the branch beneath might have to manage *him*. If the president doesn't care about getting the right answer, or has such a fixed sense of the right answer that he's not interested in conflicting inputs, remarkably few of these processes truly bind his hands. If he wants to listen only to the CIA, not the NSA, and if he wants to ignore the processes designed to get him the views of all other agencies, he can certainly do that. Beneath the process presidency, the personal presidency always lies latent. If the president does not want help, the executive branch cannot force it on him.

The pattern Trump set in that first week—of an executive disconnected from his branch—became a recurrent one. Trump's personal presidency was not a function of the size of the government or the lack of staff or agency support. Unlike Adams, President Trump wasn't doing the work of the executive branch himself. The personal nature of his presidency was a function of his imagining the presidency as a platform for his personal expression, not as an executive office whose job is actually to run things.

Perhaps the most vivid early example arose during the campaign, when Trump resisted allowing the organization of a presidential transition to prepare for the possibility that he might win the election. Former New Jersey governor Chris Christie had volunteered to run the Trump transition team, but as the journalist Michael Lewis recounts, Trump was allergic to the idea of paying for it. He didn't want to fund it personally, and he didn't want to use campaign funds either. Christie managed to get a transition operation organized anyway—until, that is, the media reported that he had raised money separately to support it. Trump actually ordered the transition shut down, and he relented only when Steve Bannon suggested to him that television pundits would say he was shutting down his transition team because he didn't think he could win.

The reprieve turned out to be brief. The transition team created various materials and proposed procedures, and it evaluated a slate of possible nominees for important offices. But shortly after the election, Trump had Christie fired, and Bannon even went to the transition office and demonstratively dumped its entire work product into a garbage can. Meanwhile, voluminous Obama administration transition briefing materials went unread. The Trump transition didn't even have teams ready to meet with the staffs of the agencies they were going to take over. Trump turned out to have meant it when he said to Christie, "You and I are so smart that we can leave the victory party two hours early and do the transition ourselves."

Trump's contempt for the processes and management of the branch he heads is so extreme that over three years into his administration, he still hasn't bothered to staff the executive branch. As of the end of his first year in office, he had made only 502 executive branch nominations, well behind the pace of either of his two predecessors. As of August 2019, he had filled only 488 of 730 key positions requiring Senate confirmation. While some of this reflected the slow pace of Senate confirmation of nominees, 138 positions still have no nominee at all. As of this writing, Trump has no permanent director of national intelligence, no permanent secretary of homeland security, no permanent secretary of the interior, and no permanent White House chief of staff. He has said he prefers it this way. "I like acting. It gives me more flexibility."

"The one that matters is me," Trump told Fox News on November 2, 2017, in addressing why he hadn't filled so many State Department vacancies. "I am the only one that matters, because when it comes to it, that's what the policy is going to be. You've seen that. You've seen it strongly." Referring to this comment, the journalist Major Garrett writes, "Trump truly believes this," observing that

> Trump has been known to derail policy discussions formed over weeks and moved through key agencies—humiliating senior White House staff or cabinet officials in the process. Sometimes he would decide an issue abruptly, skipping over that same policy process, because he grew bored or impatient. Both tendencies left senior White House advisors and cabinet officials wondering how to approach their core mission, uncertain how to present or move options through a rational process. Trump's approach was dismissive of almost everyone around him and the very jobs they did in service of his agenda and his government. Fundamentally, Trump believed most government jobs were useless and the process to create a solution too cumbersome and slow.

The irony is that Trump regularly pays a huge price for this vision of the presidency. Mostly it's a price in effectiveness. The travel ban debacle turned out to be a kind of template. Time after time, traditional processes have simply vanished, to the detriment of the administration's ability to carry out the president's own objectives in a timely, efficient, and coherent manner. Trump, for example, announced a ban on transgender service members in the military by tweet, without meaningful prior consultation with the military. Predictably, the policy saw swift judicial rebuke; as with the travel ban, the military had to start over and create a process that would support the outcome the president had announced. As of this writing, the litigation over the second version of the transgender service ban remains ongoing. In the foreign policy realm, Trump impulsively announced a meeting with the North Korean leader Kim Jong Un—whose country he had only weeks earlier been threatening with nuclear annihilation—after a single meeting with a South Korean representative who pitched the idea. His announcement of the withdrawal of U.S. forces from Syria followed a similar pattern. The absence of process behind any of these announcements, the attempt to conduct a presidency by whim and will, has not served Trump well. Indeed, it is not an accident that the phrase "malevolence tempered by incompetence," coined by one of the present authors to describe the travel ban order, has become a kind of buzzword for the Trump presidency more broadly.

If the goal is a presidency that can successfully do things, there is little logic to what Trump is doing here. But that's actually the point: in his vision, the presidency is emphatically not about the successful management of bureaucracies or the implementation of policy objectives. It is about the showmanship and flamboyance of the person and about entertaining and captivating audiences. So, whereas the traditional presidency developed process because administering government effectively required it to work optimally, Trump is proposing a kind of disconnect between the workaday functions of government and the show going on at the top. He doesn't care if it works optimally; optimal effectiveness is not the goal. He wants to mouth off and announce things and have the executive branch below him effectuate his will.

Here it is important to step back and acknowledge that Trump may be onto something important. Although the process presidency is essential to good decision-making, it is also legitimately frustrating in its remoteness and lack of immediacy and democratic responsiveness. Trump's critique of the traditional presidency—that Americans elect a person who makes promises, but they are stuck with a permanent government that is not elected and thwarts their democratic demands—is often descriptively accurate. And it is a frustration that has been shared even by those who strongly oppose Trump and condemn his disregard of process as reckless. For example, at least some members of that group probably celebrated when Obama signed, in his first week in office and without much advance process and deliberation, an executive order to close the military detention facility at Guantánamo Bay. And these people likely felt frustrated to discover—as Obama himself did—that it wasn't so easy. There's a reason that the facility remained open and operational on Obama's final day in office eight years later: there were lots of complex governmental and political interests at stake, which a better process might have identified even in that first week. Trump's appeal is evidence that people want a presidency that does not just act, but is seen to act. It is evidence that the underbrush that has grown up around presidential decision-making, however necessary it may be, is for many people an unwelcome accretion of debris.

For this reason, though it is difficult to imagine that future presidents will wish to run the executive branch in the self-defeating fashion Trump has adopted, it is worth asking whether there are aspects of the Trumpian personal presidency that may have more staying power. For example, although future presidents likely won't aspire to Trump's management ineptitude and replacement of process with personal whim, it's not hard to imagine the highly self-expressive elements of the Trump presidency having a certain appeal. Married in some future figure to a minimal level of managerial competence, it's possible to imagine them having a profound impact on presidential behavior and our expectations of it.

It is also possible to imagine the management of the executive branch adapting over time so that a president will have fewer meetings and consultations and briefing books to read and more time to vent in public or declare dramatic initiatives if he or she so desires. We haven't organized the executive branch this way to date, because that's not what presidents have wanted. But to the extent that future presidents adopt Trump's elevation of the expressive presidency over the process presidency, some mechanism to manage chaos would be necessary—some kind of chief operating officer for the executive branch. Perhaps the White House chief of staff would effectively run the federal government and render a great many decisions we have typically expected the president personally to make, leaving the president freer for immediately responsive self-expression. The chief of staff's relationship to the president would resemble that of a prime minister to a king in a constitutional monarchy where the king has not yet given up his power. Trump wants to be head of state. His interest in being head of government is sporadic.

Another feature of the personal presidency that may outlast Trump is the president's use of family members, instead of traditional governmental systems, for the most important presidential functions. As we noted earlier, it used to be common for presidents to employ their family members; this practice gradually became disreputable as the presidency became less personal. The inverse relationship is not an accident. Process in the executive branch is designed to create decision-making systems that presidents can trust. In less developed governmental systems, trust often relies on blood ties. And indeed, who needs a State Department to conduct foreign policy when you have a son-in-law? Who needs an expert delegation when you can send a daughter to an international security conference? An expert delegation might be more knowledgeable on substance and more adept at advocating American security policies, but Trump isn't looking for someone to represent U.S. security policy on the global stage when he is too busy. Instead, he wants someone to represent him personally, so he sends his children.

The journalist Bob Woodward recounts Reince Priebus's frustrations with Jared Kushner and Ivanka Trump: "They were in their own silo, in Priebus's view. He could not get them into some orderly program." In government, family is in many ways the opposite of process; it is fundamentally about privileged status rather than organized systems. "No one could fire the family. That was not going to happen," Woodward writes. At one point, Woodward recounts, Steve Bannon and Ivanka had a shouting match over her status: "'You're a goddamn staffer!' Bannon finally screamed at Ivanka. 'You're nothing but a fucking staffer!' She had to work through the chief of staff like everyone else, he said."

"I'm not a staffer!" she shouted in return. "I'll never be a staffer. I'm the first daughter!"

And there it is—the demands of process yielding to the privileges of family. Bannon, after all, no longer works at the White House. Ivanka, as of this writing, still does. It is reasonable to expect that the more personal and expressive the presidency becomes, the more legitimate this will appear.

In the end, the highly personal, expressive, processless presidency scares many people because it offers a daily reminder of the titanic power the presidency ultimately wields but normally hides beneath layers of interagency deliberation. The rejection of process is part of the personalization of power, especially when it operates in tandem with efforts to merge the individual with the office. The personalization of power has inherent links to personality cults and ultimately to tyranny.

And so it is a telling coincidence that the seventh day of his presidency was not only the day Trump did violence to traditional executive branch processes by issuing the travel ban. That evening, January 27, 2017, he also had dinner with his FBI director, James Comey, whom he had summoned to the White House for a tête-à-tête. At that dinner, he told Comey, "I need loyalty, I expect loyalty." Comey later testified that he understood that what the president was requesting was not allegiance to the country or the Constitution, but a declaration of personal loyalty to him.

In Trump's proposed presidency, process falls away for the same reason the oath of loyalty becomes a personal oath rather than an institutional one to the constitutional order: the presidency is merged with the personality of the president. No line separates them.

THREE

"This president runs this government"

THE NON-UNITARY EXECUTIVE

A FEW MONTHS INTO DONALD TRUMP'S FIRST YEAR IN OFFICE, on April 25, 2017, a political scientist named Daniel Drezner tweeted a screenshot of a *Washington Post* article, along with a cheeky comment: "I'll believe that Trump is growing into the presidency when his staff stops talking about him like a toddler." The screenshot showed the following text, which the newspaper had reported two days earlier: "Trump turns on the television almost as soon as he wakes, then checks in periodically throughout the day in the small dining room off the Oval Office, and continues late into the evening when he's back in his private residence. 'Once he goes upstairs, there's no managing him,' said one adviser." Drezner had highlighted the quotation from the adviser.

So began the "toddler-in-chief thread," surely the most quixotically lengthy Twitter thread in the history of the American presidency. Every time a White House adviser or a Republican member of Congress spoke about Trump in a news story as though he or she were talking about managing a small child, Drezner would tweet the relevant passage with the same sentence, adding it to the thread. The highlights from the first month of the thread alone were enough to make one wonder if Trump aides weren't intentionally vying for inclusion in Drezner's running joke. On May 5, 2017, *The New York Times* reported: "Over time, Mr. Trump bridled and demanded the unstructured time he had so valued as an executive at Trump Tower. Mr. Priebus, who initially outsourced the details of Oval Office scheduling and paper flow to a deputy, has now taken over those tasks himself. He has reduced the pace of public events and, like a Montessori teacher, modulates structured work time with the slack periods Mr. Trump craves." Two days later, *Axios* reported, "Aides often leak stories about the difficulty of managing Trump—as if they were his babysitters."

Drezner emphasizes that these are not examples of the president's political enemies looking to embarrass him. Quite the contrary. Asked to explain what he was trying to convey with the toddler-in-chief thread, Drezner wrote in an email that to qualify for the thread, "a respected media outlet had to source the toddler-like descriptions of the president from individuals who had a vested interest in Trump succeeding as president." Although Drezner noted that the bulk of the sourcing comes from Trump's White House staff, often anonymously, there are also contributions from Republican members of Congress and their staffs and allied governments. In hundreds "of instances, a source with a rooting interest in Donald Trump's political success could not help but describe him as acting like a toddler. That's how bad Trump's behavior truly is."

As of this writing, there are more than one thousand separate entries, each reflecting a news story in which someone—usually a member of the executive branch—talked about managing the president, not the other way around, and talked about doing so in an explicitly infantilizing fashion.

The thread is a source of humor, but Drezner was onto something profound. Whereas the president's job is to supervise the White House staff and the executive branch agencies that report to the White House, in the Trump presidency, the inverse is what's really happening most of the time, and people don't even bother to pretend otherwise. Yes, when Trump gives an actual order in a form directed to a subordinate person or agency, that order has to be carried out—or something has to happen that can be said to count as carrying it out—on pain of possible dismissal. But until the moment of an actual order—and even afterward for those willing to take risks with their jobs—Trump can be avoided, evaded, cajoled, patronized, manipulated, or misrepresented in public by underlings who purport to serve him. This can all happen even as he presents himself with bombastic machismo as tough or strong, even as he in a meaningful sense personalizes the presidential office. As Drezner's thread illustrates, Trump's staff, the congressional leadership, and traditional U.S. allies do this unapologetically.

Infantilizing the president is a natural adaptive response to circumstances—if an entirely extra-constitutional one. Staffers and officials have reason to question the integrity of the president's oath of office or his mental stability. Confronted with a president who rejects traditional executive branch processes and management in favor of unfiltered personal expression and a merging of the office with his own personality, they have to do something. The toddler-in-chief thread—as bizarre and funny as it may be—is the organic outcome of this. Toddlers are impulsive, they will not play by the rules, and there is no point in reasoning with them. That the toddler's worldview is narcissistic and self-expressive is simply a fact to be accepted and managed; as she learns to navigate the world, she must be encouraged, but she cannot be permitted to hurt herself or others along the way. So deception and distraction are necessary tools. Every parent knows that sometimes you have to pretend that a little kid is doing it all by himself, when he isn't. Every parent knows that sometimes you just have to turn on the television so the adults can work in peace. When the task of those with a vested interest in Trump's succeeding is, in so many ways, the same as managing an unruly small child, these reference points come naturally.

But of course, it wasn't supposed to be this way. The Constitution creates a unitary executive branch in which, in the pure version at least, the president supervises the staff and they actually do what he tells them to do—or are removed if they do not. Constitutionally speaking, notwithstanding the internal processes that have built up over time, the executive branch is run by the president, and the president at some level supervises the entire branch. The federal courts are divided regionally and stratified by the three layers of the judicial system—district courts, appeals courts, and the Supreme Court. Congress has two chambers, each with its own formal rules. But the American presidency is a single person. And the executive branch is little more than the people who work for her. There is a debate, of course, about how unitary the "unitary executive" really is, and that debate is wrapped up in a larger set of arguments about the scope and nature and limits of presidential power. But there is a core to the unitary executive theory that is not in dispute: there is only one president, and he appoints the leadership of the executive agencies, who serve at his pleasure and thus must follow his direction or risk being fired.

Historically, this core unity has always tolerated some degree of fractiousness within the executive branch. One extreme example from early in the republic's history is that of Thomas Jefferson, who funded and ran an opposition newspaper while serving in George Washington's cabinet. Lower executive branch officials often have statutory responsibilities of their own delegated to them by Congress, and civil servants are not appointed and removed at will by the president. The unity fiction became a bit more strained as the executive developed into an immense series of interlocking bureaucracies, including the supposedly independent federal regulatory agencies, over the course of the twentieth century. Presidential lack of control over the State Department has long been a source of some consternation. And of course, notwithstanding the president's status as commander in chief, the military is a world of its own. The question of unity has always been one of degree; it is not absolute. That said, the idea of unity remains true in important respects.

When Trump took the oath of office, he assumed certain powers, all of which Article II, Section 2 of the Constitution vested personally in him: he became commander in chief of the military; he became responsible for appointing and supervising all heads of agencies and cabinet departments—including having the power to remove them from office; he was empowered to pardon criminals and those being prosecuted, to reprieve sentences, and to remit fines; he was empowered to make treaties with foreign governments, and thus to withdraw from them; he was given the power to appoint ambassadors and judges with the Senate's advice and consent; he was given the power to veto legislation. All these powers came to Trump personally—not to his cabinet officials, not to his staff, not to Republican congressmen, but to him.

Notwithstanding Alexander Hamilton's sudden hip-hop fame, it is not especially cool these days to admire the first Treasury secretary's views of executive authority and unity. Yet *Federalist* 70 is still the essential starting point in a discussion of why we have the presidency that we do.

"Energy in the Executive," wrote Hamilton, "is a leading character in the definition of good government. It is essential to the protection of the community against foreign attacks." The reason? "A feeble Executive implies a feeble execution of the government. A feeble execution is but another phrase for a bad execution; and a government ill executed, whatever it may be in theory, must be, in practice, a bad government." Translation: If you want government to *do* things, you have to have an executive capable of it.

The key to "energy in the Executive," in Hamilton's view, is the branch's unity. It is from that unity that the executive's other capacities derive. "That unity is conducive to energy will not be disputed. Decision, activity, secrecy, and despatch will generally characterize the proceedings of one man in a much more eminent degree than the proceedings of any greater number; and in proportion as the number is increased, these qualities will be diminished." Translation: The fact that the president's power is all vested in a single person makes it possible for that person to act quickly and decisively.

"This unity," Hamilton goes on, "may be destroyed in two ways: either by vesting the power in two or more magistrates of equal dignity and authority; or by vesting it ostensibly in one man, subject, in whole or in part, to the control and co-operation of others, in the capacity of counsellors to him." Translation: If you put legal or institutional restraints on the presidency even in the name of preventing tyranny, you will deprive the office of the flexibility that makes it effective.

And critically, Hamilton argued, "plurality in the Executive . . . tends to conceal faults and destroy responsibility." In Hamilton's account, the argument for unity is rooted not merely in efficient and effective government but also in accountability for failures. When executive power is divided, Hamilton contended, "it often becomes impossible, amidst mutual accusations, to determine on whom the blame or the punishment of a pernicious measure, or series of pernicious measures, ought really to fall. It is shifted from one to another with so much dexterity, and under such plausible appearances, that the public opinion is left in suspense about the real author." Translation: If you want to know whom to blame, there has to be someone in charge. Harry Truman's famous line, "The buck stops here," reflects a structural truth about the design of the presidency.

The modern presidency has considerable institutional fetters that Hamilton surely never imagined—of which he frankly might not have approved. But it also has powers he did not imagine. In particular, the war powers have migrated—to what degree is a matter of debate but certainly to *some* degree—from the legislature to the presidency, bringing unity of action and decision-making to the powers of war and peace to a degree the founders certainly did not envision. Similarly, the rise of informal international agreements that are not subject to the demands of the treaty power have concentrated a great deal of foreign policy authority in the hands of the president. And the growth of the standing, institutional military transforms the commander in chief power in peacetime into something much bigger than it was in Hamilton's time. What's more, in many areas, Congress has delegated huge swaths of authority to the executive branch.

The basic structure, however, remains more or less as it was in Hamilton's day, albeit much larger and with important exceptions that limit presidential control over independent agencies and lower-level officials across the government. The executive branch remains, broadly speaking, a vertically integrated organization with a single person at its apex. Justice Antonin Scalia once famously wrote that the vesting of the executive power in the hands of the president "does not mean *some* of the executive power, but *all* of the executive power." Although the totalism of Scalia's description is not an accurate account of modern constitutional law, the line still describes a good rule of thumb for thinking about how the presidency works.

Designing the executive branch in this fashion was controversial even in Hamilton's day, with many of the opponents of the Constitution arguing that the president's broad powers too closely resembled the monarchical power the colonies had only recently shaken off. The Declaration of Independence may be best known for its lofty introduction on the inalienable rights of men, but its substance is actually a list of grievances against the king's use of his individual authorities. When the delegates met at the Constitutional Convention, the question of whether the executive would be unitary or plural—a single president or some kind of council of officials—was very much an open one. The Revolutionary Era fear of creating an elective monarchy had led state constitutions to favor weak executives. As the legal scholar Michael Klarman notes in his book *The Framers' Coup*, "In response to perceived abuses of executive power by the king and his royal governors, state constitutions of the Revolutionary era generally provided for eviscerated executive branches, which were made largely subordinate to state legislatures." Klarman argues that "the immediate backdrop against which the delegates in Philadelphia were designing the executive branch—state constitutions—was one of emasculated executives" and that most convention delegates "were determined to change this state of affairs" in reaction to overly empowered legislatures too ready to succumb to populist pressures. Still, such delegates as Edmund Randolph argued that the unitary executive was the "fetus of monarchy." Along with George Mason and others, Randolph advocated for a three-person executive, but the convention rejected the idea in favor of a unitary presidency.

Having decided that the executive would be a single person, the convention debate then turned to whether that person should be bound by the advice of some kind of executive council. Such a council would not merely advise the president, but would act as a constraint upon him. The council would, in the words of George Mason, ensure that the executive had "safe and proper information and advice." And it would do so whether the president liked it or not. Benjamin Franklin argued that such "a council would not only be a check on a bad president but a relief to a good one." And yet any division of unity threatens to destroy accountability. So the convention rejected an executive council in favor of merely allowing the president to get the opinion in writing of any principal officer; the president would be able to get advice if he wanted, but he wouldn't be obligated to follow it or to consult with anyone.

These choices were intentional, and they were made in full cognizance of the risks they carried that the president would have too much control.

The American presidency, in its unity, is profoundly dissimilar from nearly all other executives in democratic systems that have persisted over time. The founders of other democracies have, quite intentionally, decided differently from the founders of this one. For example, in Israel—another democratic country that faces ongoing security issues and fights wars semi-regularly—the power to take the country to war is generally vested not in the prime minister, but in the government, a collective body. What's more, although the government has legislative powers that in this country the president does not have, the government—and the prime minister himself, for that matter—serves at the discretion of the legislature. So not only is the Israeli executive power not unified, but the executive can be dismissed for policy reasons alone. While Israeli governments have unified control over legislative and executive power, if the Knesset decides that the prime minister is a nut or a crook or incompetent, it passes a vote of no confidence and the government falls. Most parliamentary democracies align far more closely to Israel on these points than to the American separation of powers, which vests the entire executive authority—including the power to order the military into battle—in a single person who cannot be removed with a vote of legislative no confidence. Within eighty days of taking office, Trump had unilaterally ordered a cruise missile strike on the Syrian government in response to Bashar al-Assad's use of chemical weapons. He did not have to consult with Congress to do this. He merely ordered it.

In normal times, the American system has a lot to recommend it. It generates not merely decisiveness of action but also political accountability for that action—what Hamilton called "a due dependence on the people" and "a due responsibility." Divide up the executive authority, and nobody really knows who gets credit for success and who gets blame for failure. Nobody is truly responsible for anything in Israel, for example. By contrast, this isn't a problem if you give all the responsibility to one president. Nobody doubts that Obama is ultimately responsible for Obamacare or that George W. Bush was responsible for the second Iraq War.

But the American system gets sticky when you contemplate vesting the executive power in one person who cannot be easily removed when that person is as mercurial and as peculiar as Trump—or as incapacitated as Woodrow Wilson after the stroke he suffered in 1919 or, for that matter, as impaired as Ronald Reagan may have been by the end of his presidency. In such situations, the structure can start to seem downright reckless. In concentrating power so that this person directs the federal government to *do* things—and in making this person exceptionally difficult to depose for a protracted period of time—one has to have a certain amount of confidence in that person's intentions and abilities.

In some ways, as we saw in the previous chapter, Trump's personal presidency is a throwback to the Hamiltonian executive. Trump certainly was making "decisions" in a frenzy of "activity" that was all taking place with a great deal of "despatch"—if never "secrecy." And he certainly talked in bombastic Hamiltonian terms about his powers. In the first month of the new administration, Trump's aide Stephen Miller went on CBS's *Face the Nation* to warn that "our opponents, the media, and the whole world will soon see, as we begin to take further actions, that the powers of the president to protect our country are very substantial and will not be questioned."

But a funny thing happened on the way to a restoration of the Hamiltonian presidency in Trump's image: the executive branch's unity dissolved visibly before the public's eye. And as the toddler-in-chief thread showed, in important respects, the president ceased to be at the helm of the executive branch and instead became its mascot. Trump was proposing such a massive and radical change that the rest of the executive branch could not simply continue with business as usual; it had to adapt—and resist. Its response was in equal parts understandable and destructive of important constitutional norms.

The disuniting of the executive under Trump began immediately on his assumption of the presidency. Recall again that incident in which he was so incensed by the National Park Service crowd size retweet that on his first full day in office, he personally called the acting National Park Service director to demand that the agency produce photos to support Trump's claim that his crowds were larger. Indeed, an "urgent directive" went to thousands of people at the U.S. Department of the Interior that "all bureaus and the department have been directed by incoming administration to shut down Twitter platforms immediately until further notice." Despite the potential impact on emergency communications, officials were permitted to reactivate department Twitter accounts only once messages of atonement—apologizing for the "accidental" retweet—had been posted.

Ironically, it was not the apology or the disciplining of the wayward agency that had a lasting impact. It was the defiance and contradiction of the president by subordinate officers who quickly stopped bothering to retract or to apologize when they strayed.

The fracturing of the unitary executive is a close cousin of the breakdown in process we described in the previous chapter, but it is also a distinct phenomenon. Process is, after all, only one of the mechanisms the executive branch has developed to maintain a unitary position on matters. Process is the set of systems designed to make sure the branch as a whole considers its multivariate interests before the president makes a decision. But there are other systems too, the most obvious of them being that executive branch officers are supposed to do what the president says. They are not supposed to have policies of their own that conflict with presidential policy. Nor are they supposed to contradict the president. All these expectations associated with the traditional presidency began breaking down quickly in the face of Trump's expressive presidency.

Consider only a few of the countless examples of the breakdown in the president's control over the executive branch. He said repeatedly that he wasn't convinced that Russia had attempted to interfere in the U.S. election in 2016. He said he believed Russian president Vladimir Putin's denial of any involvement, regularly calling the allegations a "hoax" and the resulting investigation a "witch hunt." All his top intelligence officials, however, contradicted him—at a single conference. Speaking at the 2017 Aspen Security Forum, Trump's then homeland security adviser, Tom Bossert, said that interference had occurred and that Russia had been responsible for it. So did Trump's then CIA director, Michael Pompeo; his then director of national intelligence, Dan Coats; his then director of the National Security Agency, Admiral Michael Rogers; and the chairman of the Joint Chiefs of Staff, General Joseph Dunford. Indeed, over the first two years of Trump's presidency, not a single one of his senior national security officials publicly backed his claims on the subject.

The FBI contradicted him on electronic surveillance. Asked about Trump's claims that President Obama had wiretapped Trump Tower, then FBI director James Comey testified, "With respect to the president's tweets about alleged wiretapping directed at him by the prior administration, I have no information that supports those tweets and we have looked carefully inside the FBI." He went on: "The Department of Justice has asked me to share with you that the answer is the same for the Department of Justice and all its components. The department has no information that supports those tweets." The Justice Department later declared in a court filing that both its National Security Division and the FBI "have no records related to wiretaps as described by [Trump's] tweets."

Meanwhile, the former United Nations ambassador Nikki Haley may have worked for Trump and been removable at the president's will, but that didn't stop her from running her own foreign policy throughout her service in the Trump administration—or at least trying to. In April 2018, one day after Haley announced that the United States would impose new sanctions on Russia for facilitating Syria's use of chemical weapons against civilians, Trump contradicted her policy announcement, saying the government had not arrived at a decision. When White House officials said that Haley's statement was the result of "momentary confusion," she retorted, "With all due respect, I don't get confused."

Nor was she alone in conducting foreign policy in defiance of the White House. When the White House lent its support to the Saudi-led blockade of Qatar, the State Department and the Pentagon openly contradicted it on the subject. Then defense secretary James Mattis quickly reassured the Qatari government that it had the United States' backing, knowing that U.S. military aviation in Afghanistan, Iraq, Syria, and Yemen relies on an airfield on the outskirts of Doha. Mattis signed a $12 billion arms deal with the Qataris days later. Meanwhile, Secretary of State Rex Tillerson cautioned the Saudis to make only "reasonable and actionable" demands of Doha.

When Turkish president Recep Tayyip Erdoğan won a referendum granting him new powers, Trump called to congratulate him. This happened even as the State Department noted "irregularities on voting day and an uneven playing field during the difficult campaign period" and used the occasion to call on Turkey "to protect the fundamental rights and freedoms of all its citizens." Trump also extended his congratulations to Philippine president Rodrigo Duterte on the success of his controversial antidrug campaign. The State Department nonetheless released its human rights report finding the campaign to be rife with human rights violations, including extrajudicial killings, law enforcement tampering with evidence and crime scenes, life-threatening prison conditions, and basic disregard for human rights.

When Russian president Vladimir Putin won another term, the inter-governmental Organization for Security and Co-operation in Europe released a report criticizing the election as irregular and unfair. Perhaps sensing a theme, White House staffers warned Trump against appearing to endorse the election, writing "DO NOT CONGRATULATE" on the notes for his call with Putin. Trump ignored them and congratulated Putin anyway. While reporters noted the discrepancy between Trump's apparent position and the OSCE report, the State Department spokeswoman at the time, Heather Nauert, said, "We have every reason to believe that the [report's] conclusions are correct."

Perhaps the most dramatic example came in the wake of the white supremacist attack in Charlottesville, Virginia, that killed a peaceful protester. Trump infamously said that "both sides" were at fault for the violence and refused to treat the entire march as a white supremacist endeavor. In a highly unusual move, the military chiefs took to Twitter to condemn the attacks and underlying racism, though they didn't refer to Trump directly. Meanwhile, Haley and Attorney General Jeff Sessions likewise condemned the attacks without rebuking the president. But Rex Tillerson, then secretary of state, was more direct on the matter. When pressed on whether Trump's "both sides" comments about Charlottesville reflected American values, Tillerson said, "The president speaks for himself."

Pause for a moment over those words. A subordinate officer of the U.S. government declared—in public and without consequence—that the President of the United States does not speak for the country, the government, or him. Trump later fired Tillerson, but not for this. And in any case, Tillerson wasn't the only one. "Citizens standing up for equality and freedom can never be equated with white supremacists, neo-Nazis and the KKK," said the president's top economic adviser, Gary Cohn, to the *Financial Times*. "This administration can and must do better." According to the journalist Bob Woodward, Cohn's rebuke of the president was actually done with Trump's permission; Cohn had come to him to resign over the Charlottesville fiasco, and Trump prevailed on him to stay to see through tax legislation. Cohn said he couldn't stay without saying something publicly. "Go out there and say whatever you want," Trump told him. "Say whatever you want to say."

Contrast that with President Obama's actions in dismissing General Stanley McChrystal for his comments in 2010 to *Rolling Stone* magazine. McChrystal's aides had remarked that McChrystal was disappointed in his first meeting with the new president, whom he found disengaged. He went on to insult Vice President Joe Biden and members of the Obama national security staff. Obama responded by accepting McChrystal's resignation "with considerable regret" two days before the article hit the newsstands. McChrystal released a statement thereafter, saying, "I strongly support the president's strategy in Afghanistan and am deeply committed to our coalition forces, our partner nations, and the Afghan people. It was out of respect for this commitment—and a desire to see the mission succeed—that I tendered my resignation."

A more famous and fateful collision between a president and his general was that between President Harry Truman and General Douglas MacArthur during the Korean War. MacArthur was a celebrity military figure, commanding all U.S. forces in Korea at the height of the conflict. He flexed the muscle of his independent stature to publicly disagree with the president on matters of military policy—and made little secret of his political ambitions to one day occupy the Oval Office himself. President Truman tolerated a barrage of public criticism from MacArthur for months, but upon discovering that the general had again aired policy disagreements, this time in a letter to the House minority leader, Truman had had enough. On April 6, 1951, the president scrawled in his diary, "This looks like the last straw. Rank insubordination. Last summer he sent a long statement to the Vets of Foreign Wars—not through the high command back home, but directly! He sent copies to newspapers and magazines particularly hostile to me." In firing MacArthur, he told the American people, "With deep regret I have concluded that General of the Army Douglas MacArthur is unable to give his wholehearted support to the policies of the United States Government and of the United Nations in matters pertaining to his official duties . . . Full and vigorous debate on matters of national policy is a vital element in the constitutional system of our free democracy. It is fundamental, however, that military commanders must be governed by the policies and directives issued to them in the manner provided by our laws and Constitution. In time of crisis, this consideration is particularly compelling."

That is what the unitary executive looks like in the traditional presidency. Allowing the secretary of state to declare the president a carnival barker whose words are not policy is a stunning deviation from American historical practice—even if Tillerson's offending words happened to contain a deep truth.

Nor did the freelancing stop with Tillerson's departure. His successor, Mike Pompeo, actually went so far as to tell Congress in an open hearing that presidential statements do not count as policy. A few months after his confirmation as secretary of state, Pompeo was testifying before the Senate Foreign Relations Committee. For almost three hours the prickly Pompeo had been sparring with senators of both parties over what to make of Donald Trump's statements about Russia and how to read his conduct at a Helsinki summit with Vladimir Putin and at a Singapore summit with Kim Jong Un of North Korea. Pompeo had belligerently insisted that senators should ignore presidential musings, statements, tweets, and dismissals of Russian electoral interference and focus only on administration actions. He had listed the many times President Trump acknowledged

Russian electoral interference and waved away as mere noise the many more times Trump had seemed to question it—or even deny it outright as a "hoax." And then Pompeo said it. Confronted by Democratic senator Chris Murphy with the notion that presidential statements are U.S. policy, he responded derisively, "Oh, that's not true."

He continued, "That's absolutely not true. People make lots—I make lots of statements. They're not U.S. policy."

As the hearing was winding down, the committee's ranking member, Bob Menendez of New Jersey, called Pompeo on this remarkable claim that one can separate repeated presidential public statements from official policy: "I want you to think about the suggestion that what the president says is not the policy of the United States."

"Can I clean that up, Senator?" Pompeo asked, his jaw clenched with anger. "You're right. I misspoke."

Pompeo clarified: "It is the case that the president calls the ball. His statements are, in fact, policy. But it's the case that when all of us speak in informal settings in response to questions, we're not covering the full gamut of things that impact the world. That's what I intended to say. I saw the glee on your side walking away, trying to make a political point from that. That's silliness. This president runs this government. His statements are, in fact, U.S. policy."

Menendez, in response, gloated over Pompeo's admission that he could not so blithely ignore Trump's words. He offered a peremptory lecture emphasizing that contradictory presidential statements create policy confusion. When he finished, the committee's then chairman—Tennessee senator Bob Corker—asked the secretary if he wanted to say anything in reply.

Responded a glowering Pompeo, "Not a word."

The damage was done. The humiliating spectacle of the secretary of state appearing before the Senate, pretending for hours that policy has nothing to do with the words spoken, and tweeted, by his boss, and then—with evident fury on his face and in his voice—having to retreat and genuflect before the formal structure of the executive branch revealed this strangest feature of the empty machismo of Trump's presidency. The mere fact that Pompeo felt compelled to say "This president runs this government" was proof enough that he doesn't.

In the American constitutional structure, this sort of executive defiance of the president is akin to a body's rejection of a transplanted organ. The body cannot recognize the alien thing as part of itself and seeks to fight off the foreign object without understanding that it is actually attacking something that is, in fact, itself. For those inclined to take satisfaction in Trump's ineffectiveness at running the federal government, let us emphasize that it is very much a mixed blessing. Yes, in a thousand ways large and small, it has ameliorated things. But it has also created habits of executive defiance, of presidential detachment from the management of policy-making and execution of the law. It risks cultivating habits in the bureaucracy of not doing as it's told, habits far beyond those that have long made the executive branch a slow ship to turn. The consequences may be a presidency that will be much harder to manage in the future. Trump complains of a "deep state" that operates independently of the president. The slander has a quality of self-fulfilling prophecy. One of the consequences, after all, of Trump's mismanagement is a presidency with less control over the government; the bureaucracy today is far from a "deep state," but its actions are less transparent than before. None of this is good.

It might be temporary. If the presidency returns to the mean, the executive branch may snap back toward unity too. There is some reason to expect this. After all, the formal authorities of the president have not changed. A future president could restore the executive to unity by being as intolerant of executive freelancing as Obama was toward McChrystal or Truman was toward MacArthur. The executive has fractured only because Trump has let it fracture, because he tolerates a chaotic disunity that other presidents have not and that future presidents can choose not to tolerate. It's hard to imagine, in fact, future presidents tolerating the kind of insubordination Trump tolerates daily, from which he seems to benefit so little and suffer so much.

But there is an alternative possibility, which is that the expressive presidency may have staying power and that lessened presidential control over the executive branch is, to one degree or another, an organic feature of the expressive presidency. As we saw in the last chapter, a presidency without process may also be a presidency that is in its nature more plural. Just as a chief of staff may become something like a prime minister, other officials may take on more autonomy.

Another way to understand Trump's combination of a highly personal, expressive presidency with a non-unitary executive is to imagine a person sitting at a complicated switchboard frantically pulling levers, turning knobs, and pushing buttons. The problem is that the switchboard is only loosely connected to the machinery, and the operator doesn't know which buttons and knobs actually connect to any activity in the complex processes the switchboard supposedly controls. The president can push all the buttons and pull all the levers he wants, but the relationship between that activity and any action of the machine is episodic and unpredictable. A striking feature of the Trump presidency is that he has dramatically loosened the connections between the switchboard and the activities it notionally controls. Trump himself doesn't seem to know, or even care, that the buttons no longer do anything. He cares mostly whether he is perceived to be operating the switchboard in a commanding fashion. A good working assumption is that future presidents will care; they will need firm and predictable connections between the buttons and the actions they are supposed to produce; and those connections will thus need to be reestablished. But if Trump proves successful, maybe the idea that the switchboard is a set piece, not a control system, will catch on.

There's a quieter side to the breakdown of the unitary executive— one that is less visible than the public defiance. That's the daily efforts to manipulate the president and maneuver around him by staff and cabinet alike. The comic side of this is the sort of infantilization that shows up in the toddler-in-chief thread. But there's a less comic side too. And again, it has good elements and bad. The most positive element is the diminished effectiveness of likely presidential criminality. The Mueller report describes repeated instances in which Trump ordered staffers to take actions to curtail the Russia investigation and those staffers refused. Trump ordered that Mueller be fired, and White House counsel Don McGahn declined to transmit the order. Trump asked the attorney general to "unrecuse" himself, assert control over the investigation, and investigate Hillary Clinton—and Sessions did not do it. Trump's control over the executive branch is so loose that at one point in his effort to bully Sessions, he went entirely outside the executive branch hierarchy and asked former campaign manager Corey Lewandowski—a private citizen—to convey his demands to Sessions. Mueller writes wryly that "the President's efforts to influence the investigation were mostly unsuccessful, but that is largely because the persons who surrounded the President declined to carry out orders or accede to his requests." This ineffectiveness does not mitigate, morally or legally, the president's conduct. But it does mitigate the results of his misconduct, and it offers a striking portrait of Trump's inability to direct his staff.

If that inability were limited to instructions to commit crimes, it would be an unqualified good, but it isn't so limited. It extends to policy matters too, and here the picture gets complicated. In the summer of 2018, *The New York Times* reported on the machinations of John Bolton—the president's then national security adviser—to get NATO countries to agree on their joint communiqué before the NATO summit in Brussels, which Trump was planning to attend. The reason? "To prevent President Trump from upending a formal policy agreement" by throwing the kind of tantrum at the summit that his own staff suspected he might. The feverish diplomacy to get an agreement before the summit event began, the paper reported, was "a sign of the lengths to which the president's top advisers will go to protect a key and longstanding international alliance from Mr. Trump's unpredictable antipathy." Bolton, a highly controversial figure, at the time faced little public criticism for shielding U.S. alliance policy from the personality of the president he served.

Other examples of this tendency are legion. Perhaps the most famous came in the anonymous September 2018 op-ed in *The New York Times*, "I Am Part of the Resistance Inside the Trump Administration." By a writer who claimed to be "a senior official in the Trump administration," the article asserts "that many of the senior officials in [Trump's] own administration are working diligently from within to frustrate parts of his agenda and his worst inclinations." The author describes how "many Trump appointees have vowed to do what we can to preserve our democratic institutions while thwarting Mr. Trump's more misguided impulses until he is out of office." Most, he or she says, "are working to insulate their operations from his whims." And while sometimes "cast as villains by the media . . . they have gone to great lengths to keep bad decisions contained to the West Wing, though they are clearly not always successful."

The journalist Bob Woodward's book *Fear* is replete with other examples. It opens with Cohn stealing off the *Resolute* desk (the main desk in the Oval Office) a one-page letter that would have terminated the U.S.-Korea Free Trade Agreement. Cohn was worried that if Trump saw the draft letter, which was dated September 1, 2017, he would sign it. So he removed it and placed it in a blue folder marked "KEEP."

"I stole it off his desk," Cohn later said. "I wouldn't let him see it. He's never going to see that document. Got to protect the country." Trump never noticed. And when then staff secretary Rob Porter discovered that there were other copies, he and Cohn made sure all of them were removed. "Cohn and Porter worked together to derail what they believed were Trump's most impulsive and dangerous orders," Woodward writes. "That document and others like it just disappeared."

There were other, similar incidents. When Trump's trade adviser, Peter Navarro, wrote a blistering memo in March 2017 complaining about the frustration of the president's trade agenda by free traders in the White House, Porter, with Priebus's agreement, buried the two-page memo. At one point, at Trump's insistence, Porter drafted a notification that the United States would withdraw from NAFTA. After doing so, Porter went to see Cohn, who declared that he would take the paper off the president's desk—and proceeded once again to do so. "If he's going to sign it, he's going to need another piece of paper," he said. Responded Porter, "We'll slow-walk that one too." When then EPA chief Scott Pruitt gave Trump a public statement announcing the withdrawal from the Paris climate deal, Porter was appalled by the total absence of process or legal review. So he removed the proposed statement from Trump's desk. The defiance wasn't limited to trade deals or White House staff. Early in his presidency, Trump—horrified by the gas attack by Syrian president Bashar al-Assad that killed large numbers of civilians—got on the phone with then defense secretary Mattis and declared, "Let's fucking kill him. Let's go in. Let's kill the fucking lot of them." Mattis agreed and said he would get right on it. When he hung up, however, he said to staff, "We're not going to do any of that." The real policy? "We're going to be much more measured."

This sort of subterfuge of presidential will is perhaps inevitable when, as Tillerson put it in one argument with then national security adviser H. R. McMaster, "the President can't make a decision. He doesn't know how to make a decision. He won't make a decision. He makes a decision and then changes his mind a couple of days later." Such subterfuge has undoubtedly saved the country from policy disasters. But it's also poisonous stuff. Nobody elected these men to run the government, after all. One big piece of the argument for the unitary executive is that it creates clear accountability for policy and policy outcomes. But if the president's staff and cabinet officers openly contradict him and gleefully undermine him internally or just ignore him entirely, who is accountable for what?

The stakes in this question are high. Years ago, while speaking on a panel, Brad Berenson—who served in the White House counsel's office under President George W. Bush—made an arresting statement about the American presidency. The presidency, Berenson argued, is an office of terrifying power. There is no question, at least as a matter of domestic constitutional law, that the president has the legal authority under some circumstances to order a preemptive nuclear strike on Tehran or Beijing—or any foreign capital of his choosing, for that matter. That decision, and the ensuing consequences for our very planet, rests with a single individual. Berenson observed that there is only one thing more frightening than an American president who has such power in his sole command. And that is an American president who does *not* have that power.

Imagine trying to reach a decision on a nuclear launch by committee in the moment of gravest emergency, the theory goes. The possibilities range from a reduction in flexibility and agility to outright paralysis.

The nuclear launch power is the ultimate expression of the personal presidency that lies beneath the modern process presidency. By virtue of sheer destructive force, nuclear weapons have a clarifying effect on conversations related to presidential power, unitary command, process, and the conduct of military and foreign affairs. To be sure, the president's launch authority did not develop to make the use of the American nuclear arsenal more personal, in the sense of idiosyncratic or impulsive. It developed— driven largely by Dwight Eisenhower in the 1950s—because of the desire not to have field commanders freelance with nuclear weapons. As with presidential control over regulatory agencies, the idea was Hamiltonian; it was to ensure accountability. Because these were not ordinary weapons, the decision to use them was no mere tactical choice to be left to fighting officers. An order that could mean the end of the world was an order that only a president should be able to give.

At noon on January 20, 2017, Trump very personally came into control of the nuclear arsenal. And suddenly a system designed to combine operational effectiveness with accountability—and designed to maximize security benefits—started to seem like not such a great idea after all. The former director of national intelligence James Clapper put it succinctly in a television interview: "In a fit of pique, [if] he decides to do something about Kim Jong Un, there's actually very little to stop him. The whole system is built to ensure rapid response if necessary. So there's very little in the way of controls over exercising a nuclear option, which is pretty damn scary."

Reasonable minds will differ on whether Berenson's argument is generally correct and personal presidential launch authority is the worst idea in the world except for all of the others. But Clapper's suggestion raises the question of which is scarier: the personal presidency with launch authority in the wrong hands or a non-Hamiltonian executive with its hands tied in a crisis. Clapper's sentiment was echoed by the commentators and members of Congress who, within weeks of Trump's taking office, began discussing curtailing the president's unilateral powers. Some commentators tried to mute the reality that Trump had personal launch authority, speculating that military officers would refuse an illegal or deeply imprudent order to launch a nuclear weapon. Hope springs eternal that process, any process, will save us, after all. But the reality is that the more fateful the decision, the *more* personal and less process-driven the presidency is, or at least can be.

Ironically, the Trumpian presidency may be the worst of all possible worlds on this score. Because Trump does not propose any alternative to vertically integrated executive unity, he maximizes all the dangers of which Berenson warned. He retains the raw power to do all kinds of things—up to and including ordering the destruction of the world. Yet he wields his powers so ineptly as to leave them functionally unattended to much of the time. Thus power is centralized and concentrated in the hands of someone who is profoundly incapable of exercising it wisely or even effectively. At the same time, as with a plural executive, the public gets no benefit from executive unity, because Trump's staff defies him publicly and manipulates him semipublicly; the breakdown in unity produces all the ills of which Hamilton warned. So the public ends up with the dangers of both the unitary and the plural executive, the dangers of rash action and the dangers of the inability to act decisively or swiftly. The truth is that in a crisis, nobody has any idea which executive will show up: Will the country be dealing with Trump's impulses or with the sensibilities of aides who will not do as they're told and may not agree with one another? This choice is not how the presidency is supposed to work.

At least it's not how the traditional presidency is supposed to work. But again, Trump is proposing something new here, even if it's wholly untheorized and not thought through. He's proposing a presidency that does not enforce unity, in which the president imposes no discipline on agencies, staff, or cabinet secretaries—even while demanding unswerving personal loyalty. The executive is characterized less by energy than by mania; meanwhile, the president tolerates the propagation of multiple policies and the undermining of his own authority, thus eroding the core value of accountability that executive control is supposed to bring. He does this as part of a presidency that is all about the expressive dimensions of the office. And yet unity requires management—perhaps the feature of the traditional presidency in which Trump has the least interest.

Exacerbating it all is the unending stream of presidential statements with which the president's staff, who imagine themselves his nannies, have to contend—statements that they have to decide whether to contradict, affirm, comply with, or simply pretend did not happen.

"When a President speaks . . . it is for keeps"

THE OFFICIAL VOICE

O N DECEMBER 12, 1792, GEORGE WASHINGTON ISSUED HIS "Proclamation Against Crimes Against the Cherokee Nations," declaring that he had "received authentic information that certain lawless and wicked persons of the western frontier in the State of Georgia did lately invade, burn, and destroy a town belonging to the Cherokee nation . . . and put to death several Indians of that nation." The proclamation went on to declare that "such outrageous conduct not only violates the rights of humanity, but also endangers the public peace, and it highly becomes the honor and good faith of the United States to pursue all legal means for the punishment of those atrocious offenders." When the father of the nation issued the document, he did not impulsively replace this considered passage with the ad-lib "You had some very bad people in that group. But you also had people that were very fine people—on both sides."

More than seventy years later, Abraham Lincoln spoke at the Gettysburg battlefield during the dedication of a cemetery for the Union dead. "We have come to dedicate a portion of that [battle]field, as a final resting place for those who here gave their lives that that nation might live. It is altogether fitting and proper that we should do this," he said. He resisted the urge to shift gears and note that "they're war heroes because they were killed. I like people that weren't killed."

In his first inaugural address in 1933, Franklin Delano Roosevelt opened by saying, "Let me assert my firm belief that the only thing we have to fear is fear itself—nameless, unreasoning, unjustified terror which paralyzes needed efforts to convert retreat into advance." He did not go on to promise that under his leadership, "We're going to win. We're going to win so much. We're going to win at trade, we're going to win at the border. We're going to win so much, you're going to be so sick and tired of winning. You're going to come to me and go 'Please, please, we can't win anymore' . . . You'll say 'Please, Mr. President, we beg you sir, we don't want to win anymore. It's too much. It's not fair to everybody else.'"

Announcing the dawn of the atomic age, at the time of the attack on Hiroshima, Harry Truman declared, "The force from which the sun draws its power has been loosed against those who brought war to the Far East." He did not say, "We bombed the shit out of them!"

Ronald Reagan said to the Soviet leader in Berlin, "Mr. Gorbachev, tear down this wall!" But he didn't taunt Gorbachev by saying, "Nobody builds walls better than me, believe me—and I'll build them very inexpensively. I will build a great, great wall, and I will make the Soviet Union pay for that wall. Mark my words."

It is safe to say that if Donald Trump's predecessors as president had spoken in any way as Trump speaks, the American presidency would never have developed as it did. It would have emerged as a profoundly different office from the one Trump inherited. Indeed, in no aspect of the presidential role does Trump's performance of his job deviate more flamboyantly from traditional expectations than in the way he sounds.

In no area is his rejection of the traditional presidency more explicit; in no area is he more obviously proposing an alternative vision of the office. When he was running for the office, he didn't sound like a candidate for president. As he took the oath of office speaking of "American carnage," he didn't sound like a new president giving his inaugural speech. He hasn't sounded like a sitting president on any day since. He certainly doesn't sound like a president when he tweets. Trump has largely treated the U.S. presidency as an ongoing campaign rally, a stream of consciousness constantly emanating from the Oval Office across the airwaves and internet—not always coherent, but always bombastic, always combative, often untethered from fact, and ever electrifying to his base.

Trump knows he doesn't sound the way he is supposed to. He is actually proud of it and boasts of it—as at that Pennsylvania rally, quoted in the introduction, when he mocked the cadences of being "presidential." Insofar as Trump is capable of strategy, his use of the power of presidential speech is strategic. It is not merely some accidental quirk of his personality, though it certainly has elements of that. He has been warned repeatedly of the need to stop tweeting, to speak more conventionally, to read from the teleprompter, and to restrain himself from off-the-cuff rants. Unlike, say, George W. Bush, who faced criticism for an unpresidential reference to wanting Osama bin Laden "dead or alive" after September 11 and dialed back his rhetoric in response, Trump consistently brushes the warnings aside. He does this because he wants to sound as he does. He is, in short, quite intentionally using the power of presidential speech in a fashion different from any of his predecessors. The difference represents one of Trump's most revolutionary challenges to the presidency itself.

And one should not underestimate its power. Trump is right that standard political rhetoric feels rote and boring; he is right that conventions of political correctness often inhibit politicians from saying what they truly believe. Bush's comment on bin Laden may have been flippant for a president sending American troops to war, but it also connected with the public's visceral desire for justice in the wake of the 9/11 attacks in a way that measured statements on military strategy simply could not do. For a great many citizens, Trump's rhetoric feels authentic. It shows that he is a fighter who is on their side. The formalities and the cautious doublespeak of professional political discourse alienate lots of Americans, who find Trump's utter indifference to observing even the basic forms more relatable. Trump's speech, in content and style, also communicates love for in-groups and hate for out-groups, which resonates with his audience.

Analysts often don't think of presidential speech as a distinct power of the office. There is, after all, no presidential speech clause in Article II of the Constitution, no clause that conveys to the executive the power to say things. All people have the right of speech under the First Amendment. And the president is no different from anyone else in that regard. And certain types of speech are inherent features of other presidential authorities. The commander in chief power, for example, embeds the authority to speak to the troops, and to speak on behalf of the military. The power to appoint officials comes with the power to announce their service, and their dismissal. Indeed, speech is a component sufficiently embedded in certain presidential authorities that the Constitution explicitly contemplates presidential communications in those contexts. For example, the obligation to "from time to time give to the Congress Information of the State of the Union" contemplates presidential communications to the legislature. The veto power comes with an attendant obligation to "return" a vetoed bill "with [the President's] Objections to that House in which it shall have originated." It is possible to imagine the power of presidential speech modestly, as closely tied constitutionally to such provisions—and for much of American history, as we shall see, Americans imagined it more modestly than as the bully pulpit the presidency became in the twentieth century.

But the power of presidential speech, at least as it has developed, is best understood as an executive power of its own. Lawyers don't tend to imagine it in these terms, as legally speaking, the notion that the president has the power of speech is either a truism (of course he can talk) or a falsehood (the president has no legally distinctive power of speech). Political scientists, however, have long treated the power to speak as an important feature of presidential power.

As the political scientist Jeffrey Tulis puts it at the end of his magisterial book *The Rhetorical Presidency*, "Rhetorical power is a very special case of executive power because simultaneously it is the means by which an executive can defend the use of force and other executive powers and it is a power itself."

The president's rhetorical power is the power to speak on behalf of the country internationally and domestically. It is the power to make commitments that may bind the government, at least in the political sense. Domestically, in the federal system, it is the power to do the same on behalf of the federal government in interactions with the states. Within the federal government, it is the power to do this on behalf of the executive branch in interactions with the legislature and, to a lesser extent, the judiciary.

In his famous 1960 book on presidential power, the political scientist Richard Neustadt described presidential power as "the power to persuade." The idea was that the formal powers of the presidency "are no guarantee of power" in fact. "Despite his 'powers' [the president] does not obtain results by giving orders—or not, at any rate, merely by giving orders. He also has extraordinary status, ex officio, according to the customs of our government and politics." Despite that status, Neustadt contended, "he does not get action without argument." Effective presidential administration requires leadership, which is persuasive in character. Neustadt wrote, "In form all Presidents are leaders nowadays. In fact this guarantees no more than that they will be clerks." One element of this leadership is private persuasion, or semipublic persuasion—the ability to cut deals and the like. But another element of it is public persuasion. A president with the public's backing is far less likely to be a clerk and far more likely to be persuasive both within the executive branch and in interactions with Congress and foreign governments.

At least in this sense, the power to speak is an essential element of the power to persuade. It is not an accident that such phrases as "bully pulpit"—itself coined by Theodore Roosevelt to describe the rhetorical powers of the office—attach themselves to the presidency. It's also not an accident that presidencies are sometimes defined in relation to their communications—that Ronald Reagan was nicknamed the Great Communicator or that Franklin Roosevelt's "fireside chats" were a defining feature of his early presidency or that Jimmy Carter's so-called malaise speech came to symbolize, perhaps unfairly, the condition of the country in the late 1970s. The power of speech is, among other things, the power to define one's presidency—and, in some cases, one's era.

Some of the ways Trump uses speech are clearly pathological. He says certain things because he is undisciplined and just cannot help himself. In other ways, as we shall explain, Trump's speech represents an extreme example of trends in presidential rhetoric that were long under way. But in still other respects, Trump's speech represents a genuinely unprecedented and quite intentional deployment of rhetorical power for a purpose to which other presidents have not put it in the past. Trump behaves differently from other presidents not just because they predated Twitter and he lacks their sense of decorum. He behaves differently because he has a different sense of the nature and purpose of the office than his predecessors did.

In the beginning, the presidency was not a rhetorical office, at least not in the sense of public rhetoric. As Tulis summarizes, before the twentieth century, public speeches by presidents were actually rare: "Presidents preferred written communications between the branches of government to oral addresses to 'the people.'" Popular addresses, when they did take place, were mostly "patriotic orations for ceremonial occasions, some raised constitutional issues, and several spoke to the conduct of war." But domestic policy speeches, commonplace today, and "attempts to move the nation by moral suasion in the absence of war were almost unknown."

In Tulis's account, the nineteenth-century presidency followed strict rules that flowed from a constitutional understanding of the presidential office. Presidential communications on policy questions were generally made directly to Congress. When presidents spoke in public, addressing policy was verboten because direct appeals to the public, rather than argumentation to the coequal branch, were considered a form of demagoguery. Tulis recounts a striking incident in which Abraham Lincoln, shortly before his inauguration, appeared before an assembly in Pittsburgh and refused to discuss a matter as fateful as the coming Civil War. Refusing to address the secession crisis, which was then ongoing, Lincoln told the crowd:

> And here, fellow citizens, I may remark that in every crowd through which I have passed of late, some allusion has been made to the present distracted condition of the country. It is naturally expected that I should say something upon this subject, but to touch upon it at all would involve an elaborate discussion of a great many questions and circumstances, would require more time than I can at present command, and would, perhaps, unnecessarily commit me upon matters which have not yet fully developed themselves.

The crowd, a contemporary newspaperman reported, responded with cheers and cries of "Good" and "That's right." Counterintuitive though it may seem, the "pre-twentieth-century polity," Tulis argues, "proscribed the rhetorical presidency as ardently as we prescribe it."

The founders greatly feared demagogues and designed the Constitution to resist them. The source of their fear was both historical and contemporary. At the historical level, Roman antiquity, with which the framers were deeply familiar, is replete with examples of popular figures who appealed to the base instincts of the people, swept them off their feet with irresponsible promises, and proceeded to hoard power for themselves. On a more contemporary level, the period immediately prior to the Constitutional Convention provided an apt example of the dangers of demagoguery: an armed uprising in Massachusetts led by a Revolutionary War veteran named Daniel Shays, which stemmed from protests against the crushing debt burdens that farmers were facing in the wake of the war. With these examples in mind, the framers eschewed anything that might allow or facilitate what they derisively termed "democracy"—by which they meant something almost akin to mob rule. Alexander Hamilton once went so far as to argue that monarchy could only ever be established in the United States through "the acts of popular demagogues." He seemed almost to be describing Trump when he wrote in 1792, "The truth unquestionably is, that the only path to a subversion of the republican system of the Country is, by flattering the prejudices of the people, and exciting their jealousies and apprehensions, to throw affairs into confusion, and bring on civil commotion." The person Hamilton believed most threatened Republican government was "a man unprincipled in private life desperate in his fortune, bold in his temper, possessed of considerable talents, having the advantage of military habits—despotic in his ordinary demeanour—known to have scoffed in private at the principles of liberty." He concluded eerily, "When such a man is seen to mount the hobby horse of popularity—to join in the cry of danger to liberty—to take every opportunity of embarrassing the General Government & bringing it under suspicion—to flatter and fall in with all the non sense of the zealots of the day—It may justly be suspected that his object is to throw things into confusion that he may 'ride the storm and direct the whirlwind.'"

This point was so important to Hamilton that it actually shows up in the very first Federalist paper, in which Hamilton notes that "a dangerous ambition more often lurks behind the specious mask of zeal for the rights of the people than under the forbidden appearance of zeal for the firmness and efficiency of government." Populists, he argued, offer "a much more certain road to the introduction of despotism than [advocates of efficient government], and . . . of those men who have overturned the liberties of republics, the greatest number have begun their career by paying an obsequious court to the people; commencing demagogues, and ending tyrants."

The nineteenth-century pattern of speaking publicly almost exclusively in ceremonial settings and addressing policy matters chiefly in written communications to Congress—a pattern that reflected then settled expectations of the office—was followed remarkably scrupulously, with one big exception: Andrew Johnson. Johnson's rhetoric had a remarkably Trumpian quality. Johnson was, of course, not elected, having come into the presidency on Lincoln's assassination in 1865. But he had a stump speech during his period of intense conflict with Congress that, as Tulis summarizes it, closely resembles what one would hear at a Trump rally:

> In the typical speech, Johnson would begin by disclaiming an
> intention to speak, proceed to invoke the spirits of Washington and
> Jackson, claim his own devotion to the principles of the Union,
> deny that he was a traitor as others alleged, attack some part of
> the audience (depending on the kinds of heckles he received),
> defend his use of the veto, attack Congress as a body and single out
> particular congressmen (occasionally denouncing them as traitors
> for not supporting his policies), compare himself to Christ and offer
> himself as a martyr, and finally conclude by declaring his closeness
> to the people and appealing for their support.

The response of the political system to this style of rhetoric—direct, demagogic appeals to the people—was remarkable: Johnson's advisers counseled him against it. Newspapers were appalled. And Johnson was actually impeached for it. That the articles of impeachment against Johnson included an article—the tenth article, to be precise—exclusively about his rhetoric is mostly forgotten these days; the Johnson impeachment is remembered now chiefly as about the struggle over Reconstruction and the

Tenure of Office Act. But at the time, Johnson's speech and rhetoric were considered by a majority of the House of Representatives to be grounds for his removal from office.

The House alleged that Johnson, "unmindful of the high duties of his office and the dignity and propriety thereof" did "make and declare with a loud voice certain intemperate, inflammatory, and scandalous harangues, and did therein utter loud threats and bitter menaces as well against Congress [and] the laws of the United States." Such speeches, the House concluded, are "highly censurable in any" and "are peculiarly indecent and unbecoming in the Chief Magistrate of the United States." By giving such speeches, the House alleged, "Andrew Johnson has brought the high office of the President of the United States into contempt, ridicule, and disgrace, to the great scandal of all good citizens."

Johnson was, to put it bluntly, impeached for acting like a more restrained version of Donald Trump.

Tulis's book is, among other things, an account of how normative rules against demagoguery in presidents—rules that approached constitutional status—eroded over the course of the twentieth century.

What we think of as the "rhetorical presidency," a presidency that speaks directly to the populace at large, is really a creature of the early twentieth century, when first Teddy Roosevelt and then Woodrow Wilson began going over the heads of Congress and addressing policy matters directly with voters in attempts to build popular support. Roosevelt did so cautiously, and Tulis treats him as a transitional figure between the nineteenth-century norms of presidential speech and the more modern expectations of a president in dialogue with the public. Wilson represented a dramatic and decisive departure from past practice, one who took a theoretically different approach and thus changed the norms of presidential behavior. Tulis writes that Wilson articulated "new standards and new forms of address" that reflected his broader vision of presidential leadership. Presidential rhetoric previously aimed at Congress and delivered in writing would "now be *spoken* and addressed principally to the *people* at large." It was from this change that we got the fireside chats, the major policy addresses, and, ultimately, the regular presidential press conference.

Wilson also brought back a tradition from the era of Washington and Adams, which had been jettisoned by Jefferson, of giving the State of the Union speech in person. Back when Washington and Adams gave their State of the Union addresses, the traditional speech had an accompanying coda. Congress formally responded to the address, with the congressional leadership coming to the president and offering their comments. Wilson revived the live presidential speech, but not the response from Congress. The State of the Union thus shifted decisively under Wilson from a communication of information between the president and Congress to a communication between the president and the body politic, using Congress as a venue.

One shouldn't, of course, overstate the degree to which these shifts reflect presidents having different conceptions of the office. There was an element of their simply favoring their specific personal talents. Yes, Jefferson warned about impassioned orators like Patrick Henry, who aimed to inflame public emotion rather than persuade through reason. But Jefferson was also lousy at giving speeches; he didn't have the voice for it and was far more compelling in written form. Wilson, by contrast, not only had a philosophical commitment to the idea of appealing directly to the people; he also recognized what he called his own "unmistakably oratorical temperament" and was enamored with its ability to persuade and "the control of other minds by a strange personal influence and power."

Tulis presents striking data on the changing rhetorical norms of the presidency between the nineteenth and twentieth centuries. For one thing, there is dramatically more presidential speech in the twentieth century than in the nineteenth. Tulis counts approximately one thousand presidential speeches to public audiences throughout the entire nineteenth century. This figure represents essentially the entirety of public presidential communications. Presidents, after all, did not hold press conferences. They did not issue press releases or statements. They did not tweet.

By contrast, a search of the database of the American Presidency Project at the University of California, Santa Barbara, illustrates how radically different the modern presidency is from the nineteenth-century norm. A search through the entire nineteenth century of twelve common types of presidential public communications produced a grand total of sixty-four documents. Each modern president alone produces thousands of such statements.

What's more, the audience for presidential communications changed decisively. In the nineteenth century, presidential communications were overwhelmingly directed at Congress; very few were directed at the public. In the twentieth century, the balance shifted dramatically. And this shift in audience led to a dramatic shift in style of argumentation. Twentieth-century presidential communications are dramatically likelier than their nineteenth-century antecedents to contain laundry lists of points; they are much less likely than their nineteenth-century counterparts to mention the Constitution.

Other scholars have traced the development of presidential rhetoric differently. The political scientist Elvin Lim, in *The Anti-Intellectual Presidency*, shows how the complexity level of presidential speech has declined markedly over both the nineteenth and the twentieth centuries. The twentieth century, in his view, continued a trend already under way in the nineteenth century toward "rhetorical simplification." The average presidential sentence grew shorter. Sound bites got sound-bitier. What's more, Lim argues, the addresses came to involve less argument; they have been substantively impoverished, increasingly "disregard[ing] the weighing and judging of reasons" and resorting instead "to rhetorical tactics that are antithetical to deliberation."

The broad point is that presidents in general are speaking far more often these days than they did in the past; they are speaking more directly with the public than they used to; and they are speaking in less sophisticated terms than did their predecessors. All of that was true long before Trump burst onto the scene.

If it all sounds a bit like a long road that leads directly to Trump, in some ways it is. In some sense, Trump represents a radical acceleration of trends already long under way in presidential rhetoric. He speaks not merely more frequently than past presidents did but almost constantly. He aims to flood the zone with his speech, and he largely succeeds at it. He would rather be condemned for what he is saying than have the news cycle focus on something, or someone, other than himself. So his public communication is not merely regular, not merely daily, but many times a day. It is also intermodal. On a given day, he will do interviews; he will call favored talk-show hosts; he will also tweet; and he might speak at a rally at which he extemporaneously holds forth. The broad strategy is not merely to go over the heads of Congress directly to the people—the premise of the rhetorical presidency—but to go over the heads of the press as well, and with it the fact-checking and context the press might provide, thus establishing a direct and incessant means of speaking directly to the people. Think of it as a fireside chat, or a fireside rant, but one that has no beginning and no end.

Trump's Twitter feed is a key element of this direct line of communication. He knows this and has made clear it is the reason he will never give up tweeting—despite the entreaties of many aides with his best interests at heart. His Twitter feed represents a rolling intelligence stream about his thoughts and resentments and angers, only occasionally mediated by what he—much less anyone else—thinks it appropriate for a president to say. Yet it is a tool for staying directly in the popular consciousness at all times, and in this respect it is immensely effective. And even refusing to follow the president on Twitter does not insulate a person from his outbursts there, because those outbursts produce paroxysms of rage among his opponents, news stories, and ritual discussion on cable news. Trump can change the public conversation on a dime at any time, and Twitter is a big part of that capacity. He can use it to rally the base. He can use it to fight public boredom and keep people engaged. He can use it to create the illusion—and to some degree the reality—of direct engagement between the president and the public.

In some respects, therefore, his presidency can indeed be seen as the completion of the long-term trends already under way, with Trump as a kind of acceleration to apotheosis of what had been a slow erosion of traditional expectations of presidential speech. These rules were once so robust that Andrew Johnson actually could be impeached for, among other things, behaving as Trump behaves every day. Today the notion that Congress might impeach Trump over his rhetoric is laughable. For many Republicans in Congress, even acknowledging the impropriety of his speech is too heavy a lift. Instead they offer euphemisms—that the president has his own way of communicating, they say—or they pretend not to have heard the comment in question or read the tweet. Or they offer only embarrassed silence.

Whereas the rhetorical presidency shifted the balance of presidential communication toward the public and away from Congress, Trump's speech completes that trend. Indeed, even when he appears to speak to Congress, he generally does so in a high-visibility format that is meant for public consumption. Tweets, for example, are sometimes optically directed at members of Congress, but they are really aimed at generating political pressure on the body or members to do as the president wishes—or sometimes to deflect blame onto them for failures Trump fears will be laid at his door. For example, when Trump's health-care bill failed to pass the Senate, he tweeted a string of messages notionally addressing Senate majority leader Mitch McConnell but actually *about* McConnell. "Mitch, get back to work and put Repeal & Replace, Tax Reform & Cuts and a great Infrastructure Bill on my desk for signing. You can do it!" read one. Read another the same day, "Can you believe that Mitch McConnell, who has screamed Repeal & Replace for 7 years, couldn't get it done. Must Repeal & Replace ObamaCare!" These tweets were certainly not efforts to persuade McConnell to work harder to pass the Obamacare repeal. They were, rather, attempts to publicly humiliate McConnell in order to deflect blame from the president for the failure. This behavior is not novel; it is, however, dramatically exaggerated in Trump.

Trump's speech also represents a kind of apotheosis of Elvin Lim's thesis about the degradation of presidential rhetoric, both in substantive terms and in linguistic complexity. This is because Trump isn't even trying to map his rhetorical conduct onto prior traditions of presidential behavior. That is the significance of his belittling the idea of being "presidential." He actually has contempt for the way the presidency has traditionally sounded. Nobody has done the same linguistic analysis on Trump's speech that Lim did concerning prior presidents. But nobody needs to. Trump's speech represents a comically extreme endpoint of all the trends detailed in Lim's book. It boasts a proud illiteracy. Trump does not bother to spell words correctly or to write, let alone speak, sentences that scan properly. His speech, nearly always extemporaneous, never aspires to logical organization but emerges as a stream-of-consciousness rant. This feature of his communication is partly organic to his less-than-organized mind, but it's also deliberate—part of his strategic alteration of what it means to sound presidential. It is a feature of his populism, an attempt to lessen the gulf between the sound of a president and the sound of a guy in a bar.

During George W. Bush's two presidential runs, against Al Gore and John Kerry, commentators frequently invoked some iteration or other of the "regular guy" test, which amounted to the observation that it was a particular strength of Bush's—and a weakness of his opponents— that people would rather have a beer with him than with Gore or Kerry. Trump's studied illiteracy is, at least in part, an extreme play at a similar appeal. It communicates to a certain significant segment of the population that the president is not so high and mighty and that he speaks in a way that is different from the political speech they are used to hearing. It also communicates a canny understanding of how empty and platitudinous most political rhetoric sounds to the people who gravitate toward him. Trump's inability to speak in a more polished fashion is one of his limitations; the finest politicians can switch among idioms. But Trump's decision not to correct that limitation—to let "wires tapped" and "covfefe" go out uncorrected and to let the White House release a statement on the murder of the Saudi dissident and journalist Jamal Khashoggi that reads as if it were dictated verbatim in a fit of pique—is a strategy.

It's a strategy that no previous president has deployed. And if Trump in some respects represents merely the logical endpoint of prior presidents' rhetorical styles, in other ways he represents a complete break with anything the country has seen before. And it ultimately does him a disservice simply to dismiss his use of the presidency's rhetorical power as a degradation of preexisting forms. The innovations of Trump's speech and rhetoric are worth highlighting because they, in turn, highlight the degree to which he is using the presidency's rhetorical power for a purpose different from that of prior presidents—that is, he is once again proposing here an innovation to the presidency, one that makes it more expressive and knits the office and the man more closely together.

Indeed, Trump's use of this most inherent power of the presidency inverts every public expectation that has developed around it since George Washington gave his first inaugural address. If the traditional presidency expects presidential rhetoric to unify the country, or at least to seek to do so, Trump's rhetoric consistently and quite consciously seeks to divide it—identifying and vilifying enemies on a routine basis. If the traditional presidency expects presidents to model democratic leadership—something of grandeur from the office that brought us the "day which will live in infamy" and the call to "ask not what your country can do for you"—Trump's speech lives in the tawdry and small.

There are a few clear, salient features of his use of the presidency's rhetorical powers. First, his speech is not intended to "persuade," in the traditional sense of winning over sufficiently broad coalitions to inspire political action. Notably, he almost never makes an argument in his speeches, much less in his tweets. He promises things. He demands things. He announces what should happen and declares outcomes. He never makes an argument that a reasonable citizen, or legislator, would engage as such. But this is not surprising; his speech is not intended to change minds. It is, rather, designed to mobilize an existing constituency, to keep it involved and in line.

A second and related feature—one of the most jarring of Trump's rhetorical innovations—is his use of personal attacks and insults and the general combativeness of his speech. He is not the first president to use insults. Lyndon Johnson once responded to a reporter's question by accusing him of asking "the leader of the Western world . . . a chickenshit question." He publicly addressed his own press secretary, George Reedy, as "you stupid sonofabitch." Woodrow Wilson was more philosophical on the need to resort to personal attack in a "blunt business [that] . . . lacks a certain kind of refinement," cautioning a friend "not [to] read the speeches in which I use the bludgeon. I do not like to offend your taste; but I cannot fight rottenness with rosewater."

Even the restrained Barack Obama wasn't above an occasional dig at his foes, once joking in his White House Correspondents' Dinner speech, which was admittedly a roast, that "some folks still don't think I spend enough time with Congress. 'Why don't you get a drink with Mitch McConnell?' they ask. Really? Why don't *you* get a drink with Mitch McConnell?" But even to quote such lines today is to render them quaint. The ad hominem, grade-school insult that is Trump's daily fare makes such jibes read like the soul of wit. Whether it's calling Senator Elizabeth Warren "Pocahontas," calling the soon-to-be chairman of the House Intelligence Committee "little Adam Schitt," declaring any number of people to be "a national disgrace" or "low IQ" (if they happen to be African American), deriding journalists as the "enemy of the people," or attacking in highly personal terms mid-level career FBI and Justice Department officials, Trump has made the personal attack an integral, organic feature of presidential speech for the first time.

An additional feature is that Trump's speech is proudly offensive. Most presidents seek to avoid giving offense to significant segments of the population, even segments not rich with political supporters. Political foes might someday be won over, after all; and even voters who will never become supporters may become comparatively lackluster foes. Why energize them with needless offense? Moreover, presidents tend to see themselves as representatives even of those who are not their supporters; that is, the nature of their oath of office obliges them to respect and represent their opponents.

Trump is different. He actively prefers to give offense. He goes out of his way to do it. He does it with the insults. He does it with broad characterizations of ethnic and religious minorities. He does it with policy declarations that aim to infuriate those who don't support him. Offense is preferable for Trump to anodyne, unifying presidential rhetoric both because it gets people talking—Trump always prefers to be the story than to be in the background—and also because giving offense to his foes energizes his supporters. He appears to see no prospect of expanding his base, nor has he ever visibly endeavored to do so; the result is that his presidency relies pervasively on energy and enthusiasm among his core supporters, many of whom admire him for being blunt-spoken and not politically correct. His rhetoric thus consistently reflects the active desire to keep the base entertained, mobilized, and validated at the expense of those who might be affirmatively offended or merely put off or disgusted by a given comment. No previous president has ever made this rhetorical choice on a consistent basis.

Importantly, Trump's speech is also profoundly personal. He rarely speaks in a voice on behalf of the U.S. government or its people. He speaks generally in his own voice—as himself. There is no difference between his voice as President Trump and his voice as Donald Trump. This point may sound either obvious in some literal sense or like a refreshing departure from political rhetoric. But it actually represents one of Trump's most consequential distortions of the common understanding of presidential speech, which is that it is something different from regular speech.

At a legal level, the inability to distinguish the man from the office creates impunity. To cite only one relatively trivial, if vivid, example, a president cannot be sued for presidential speech—even if it is defamatory in a fashion that would give rise to liability for others. So long as the speech is within the outer limits of the president's official acts, the Supreme Court has held that he or she is "entitled to absolute immunity from damages liability . . . We consider this immunity a functionally mandated incident of the President's unique office, rooted in the constitutional tradition of the separation of powers and supported by our history." Making the line between official and unofficial speech indistinguishable serves to turn the presidency into a platform for defamation—for which any private citizen would incur liability. For example, the president can falsely suggest that individual American citizens are guilty of crimes—be it career FBI officials or family members of his former associates or political foes—and fear no consequences.

At a political level, the problem is even worse. For reasons we explored in depth in chapter 3, the inability to identify what should be considered an official presidential statement and what is just some old guy spouting off creates serious questions about executive accountability for policy. The public, the press, Congress, and foreign governments all assume that when the president is commenting on a matter regarding executive branch policy, which she supposedly sets, or classified national security information—which she alone ultimately controls access to—her words are something more than idle gossip or speculation. Presidents might not always be honest in their statements, but certainly their words are intentional. Even the famously mendacious Nixon said, "I know from experience that when a President speaks . . . it is for keeps. He doesn't get a second chance. He can't call a bullet back after he shoots from the hip. It goes to the target. In these critical times we cannot afford to have as President of the United States a man who does not think first before he speaks or acts."

Trump's highly personal speech creates endless legal headaches, with lawyers for the federal government having to explain in federal court that when the president speaks, he has no idea what he is talking about and should be ignored. When Trump tweeted that the Obama administration had tried to cover up wiretapping his campaign, government lawyers argued that the tweet was merely "generalized, vague allegations of misconduct based on no personal knowledge." Federal judges have ruled that Trump's comments amount to speculation and are not "assertions of pure fact." And when the president approvingly tweeted a quotation of someone accusing the government of misconduct, that, argued the Department of Justice attorneys, "cannot be assumed to be his confirmation of the media reporting based on government information, and it is not evidence of government misconduct." The department's position seems to be that the president is allowed to troll his enemies and that presidential trolling should not be confused with words that have actual legal meaning or consequence.

Additionally, Trump inverts the normal process by which form follows function in presidential speech. In the traditional presidency, first the president wants something or believes something, and *then* he or she says it. By contrast, Trump just says stuff and then lets other people figure out what it actually means. For his bewildered White House staff, this necessitates using the federal bureaucracy to construct some semblance of reality out of the president's words. If he has made an obviously false or unfounded statement of fact, then statistics or citations are trotted out, however unrelated or transparently wrong, in order to support the claim. Erica Newland, formerly an attorney at the Office of Legal Counsel during the Trump administration, authored an op-ed on the phenomenon following her resignation. She writes that when faced with a false claim from the president, she "would ask the White House to supply a fig leaf of supporting evidence. Or if the White House's justification for taking an action reeked of unconstitutional animus, [she] would suggest a less pungent framing or better tailoring of the actions described in the order." Eventually Newland concluded that these efforts violated her own oath of office. "After all," she writes, "the president had already submitted, through his early drafts or via Twitter, his reasons for issuing a particular order." She feared "using the law to legitimize lies."

Newland "felt more than a twinge of recognition" at a *New Yorker* story that described how editors of Trump's reality television show *The Apprentice* would shoot an episode with a planned conclusion and then, when Trump impulsively went off script and fired someone else, they would have to "reverse engineer" the footage to create some sense of order to justify Trump's whim. Like those editors—described by *The New Yorker* as "scouring hundreds of hours of footage . . . in an attempt to assemble an artificial version of history in which Trump's shoot-from-the-hip decision made sense"—Newland says she "caught [herself] fashioning a pretext, building an alibi."

A related, novel feature of Trump's use of the presidency's rhetorical power is the rapid integration of his speech into a conservative media ecosystem that has developed around it. This is partly a function of his unprecedented use of Twitter, which allows literally tens of millions of people instantly to retweet and amplify his words. It is also partly a function of news outlets, Fox News most notably, that have reoriented themselves as promotional vehicles for presidential messaging. A partisan press is certainly nothing new in American presidential history. The tradition of relatively apolitical news is actually comparatively recent. But a president engaged in near-constant public communication that is immediately amplified by aligned media (and attacked by hostile media) in what amounts to a public-private partnership in state propaganda is wholly new. Thomas Jefferson was the early master of the partisan press, but he could not have imagined Sean Hannity in his wildest dreams.

A final exceptional feature of Trump's rhetoric that operates in tandem with this media ecosystem is his mantra-like repetition of specific phrases—"Witch Hunt," "Make America Great Again," "Build the Wall," "No Collusion," "No Obstruction," "I have nothing to do with Russia," "It's a disgrace"—both in tweets and in speeches, and specifically the repetition of these memes in lieu of argumentation. Trump never made or developed an argument against Robert Mueller's investigation nor made a reasoned case against the suggestion that there was something untoward in his campaign's relationship with Russian operatives, for example. He simply repeated key phrases and let others fill in the gaps. These phrases come to represent the terms of the argument that others—Hannity, Lou Dobbs, Mark Meadows, and Jim Jordan, for example—will make in his place. Trump himself, instead of making the argument, simply announces the articles of faith around which others have to navigate in building it. His political allies could then criticize Mueller however they wanted and develop the argument against the prosecutor in any number of fashions, as long as they hit—or at least didn't contradict—these key points: Trump didn't do anything wrong with respect to Russia, however things might appear; he didn't corruptly seek to impede the investigation of his conduct; and the investigation against him was an unfair effort to damage him and his presidency.

A similar effect shows up in some of his more policy-oriented leitmotifs: Trump, for example, demanded Obamacare's repeal and replacement on countless occasions. He never articulated a health-care policy. He just repeated certain very specific catchphrases. For example, the word "imploding" appeared frequently alongside "Obamacare" in a great many tweets during the health-care fights in 2017—as did "repeal and replace." The idea being that the health-care law was imploding, so Congress needed to repeal and replace it. Endless repetition of such guidepost terms and phrases is a key feature of Trump's rhetoric.

Note that many of these guidepost terms do not seem to be scripted on his behalf. Trump appears to develop them himself and test them over time, much the way he develops the derisive, insulting nicknames he uses for people who upset him—"Rocket Man," "Little Marco," "Crooked Hillary," "Lyin' Ted," or "Slippery James Comey." Once he settles on one of these guidepost terms or epithets, he repeats it *constantly*; in fact, he says little else in reference to the subject in question. He tends to develop a cluster of such terms around a given subject, and his speech is composed almost entirely of the iteration and reiteration of terms and phrases within the cluster. What can you remember Trump saying about Hillary Clinton since his inauguration other than that she is crooked, that she has committed many crimes, and that the Justice Department should be investigating these crimes?

In his book *The Presidential Character*, the political scientist James

Barber describes the three political roles of the president as rhetoric, personal relations, and homework. Presidential style is determined by "how the President goes about doing what the office requires him to do—to speak, directly or through media, to large audiences; to deal face to face with other politicians, individually and in small, relatively private groups; and to read, write, and calculate by himself in order to manage the endless flow of details that stream onto his desk." Every president balances these roles somewhat differently—Wilson preferred rhetoric, Hoover homework, and Lyndon Johnson personal relations—but "no President can escape doing at least some of each." Trump is not just primarily a rhetorical president; he is an almost exclusively rhetorical president. His personal political relationships are overwhelmed by and subjugated to his rhetoric. The diligent task of homework—researching, reading, striving to understand—he simply does not do.

At the most fundamental level, all these novelties of Trump's verbal and written public communications flow from the same cause: Trump's speech has a different strategic purpose from that of prior presidents. Historically, presidents—even after the advent of the rhetorical presidency—have used speech to persuade the marginal voter and build and maintain the largest possible political coalition. Trump has not devoted one moment of his presidency to expanding the narrow political coalition that elected him. The purpose of his speech, rather, is to hold that narrow coalition together and to enforce a certain uniformity of thought among its ranks. He is the first president who does not speak as if he even imagines himself as representing the country at large. He represents, rather, a minority segment of the country, and he represents that segment chiefly in its resentments against the rest of the population. Other presidents, particularly Abraham Lincoln, have been forced into the role of representing one part of the population against the other by divisions in the country; and other presidents have certainly exploited national divisions, whether along racial, geographic, class, or policy lines. No prior president, however, has embraced or reveled in division to the point of not bothering to aspire to national leadership—indeed, not even pretending to aspire to it. This is a deployment of presidential authority unique to Trump.

Will he prove to be a pivot point—as Wilson did—in the deployment of the presidency's rhetorical power? Or will he prove to be, like Andrew Johnson, a deviation from the norms of acceptable presidential speech that will, in the disgusted reaction that the deviation triggers, reinforce prior norms? It is impossible to know. If Trump fails to win reelection, his rhetorical style will surely shoulder the lion's share of the blame. Analysts and historians will remember it as a major component of his failure as president. Conversely, imagine for a moment that Trump holds his coalition together successfully and wins a second term. Just as certainly, his relentless rhetoric will be credited for that success. And other politicians will notice. Speech is the area where Trump's expressive presidency is most deliberate and most self-conscious in proposing something different and new. It is safe to say that nowhere are traditional public expectations of the presidency more challenged than in this area; nowhere are fewer remedies legally available; and nowhere will the future presidency be more responsive to Trump's success or failure.

There is no law, after all, about how the presidency should sound. There is only what the populace over time tolerates and rewards.

FIVE

"An inexhaustible fund of political lies"

THE WAR ON TRUTH

T WAS ONLY THE FIRST WEEK OF AUGUST 2017, STILL IN THE first year of his presidency, that Donald Trump made what *The Washington Post* deemed his one thousandth false or misleading claim as president. The moment passed without fanfare; the *Post*'s Fact Checker column didn't manage to update its now-famous infographic that tracks the president's falsehoods until late in the month, when the respite of a presidential vacation allowed the columnists to catch up on the backlog. At the time, the writers Glenn Kessler, Michelle Ye Hee Lee, and Meg Kelly predicted that, at his current rate, the president was unlikely to "break 2,000 [false or misleading] claims in his first year in office. But with five months to go, all bets are off." It turned out that they were smart to hedge; ten days shy of the conclusion of Trump's first year, January 10, 2018, the number reached two thousand. And the pace continued to accelerate. By September 2018, the *Post* reported that Trump had made more than five thousand false or misleading claims in his first 601 days in office. A mere 226 days after that, the *Post* announced that Trump had exceeded ten thousand such claims.

The Fact Checker first started in 2007 and had been around long before Trump's presidency. Now helmed by Kessler, the column boasts the tagline "The truth behind the rhetoric." For the decade since its inception, the column had diligently plodded along on its mission of adjudicating whether statements from politicians or the government on important policy matters were true or false or debatable. The idea was to use fact-checking both to encourage accountability and to educate readers on substantive policy questions in the process. It aimed to run one or two fact checks each day.

Then came Trump.

Staffed by only three full-time employees, the Fact Checker was soon drowning in the deluge of falsehoods and misstatements uttered by the president. Unlike the occasional lie—be it a fib or a whopper—that has marked nearly every presidential administration, Trump lied about anything and everything, and he did it all the time. He repeated the same lies over and over again. He lied indiscriminately and about matters so mundane that factual correction served no particular educational function. He wasn't the slightest bit embarrassed when called out on his lies; indeed, getting caught did nothing to deter him from repeating the same lie.

His lies as president, as we have seen, started on day one. On his first full day as president, standing in front of the CIA's hallowed memorial wall, he claimed without evidence to have received "tremendous percentages" of military votes. He claimed that "probably almost everybody in this room voted" for him. He lied about his inauguration crowd size. He lied about the weather, claiming that the rain had stopped when he began speaking (which it had not) and that as he spoke, the sun emerged (it also had not). He lied about holding the record for the number of appearances on the cover of *Time* magazine, while questioning whether the magazine had corrected a recent reporting mistake, which it had. As Trump delivered these remarks, he stood across from a wall carved with the CIA's unofficial motto—a passage of scripture from the Gospel of John: "And ye shall know the truth and the truth shall make you free."

In the following days, weeks, and months, Trump piled on more lies. He lied about winning environmental awards. He lied about there having been millions of illegal votes for Hillary Clinton. He lied about two people being killed during a speech given by President Obama in Chicago. He lied about receiving a unanimous endorsement from Customs and Border Protection. He lied about immigration vetting procedures. He lied about his executive orders. He lied about saving money on some F-35 airplanes.

Within a couple of weeks, as Kessler later described it, the Fact Checker staff realized it couldn't keep up. Not only was Trump generating too many false statements to cover, but the manner in which he lied made it impossible to craft a traditional column around it. Much of what Trump said was so easily disproved that it would take only a sentence or two to debunk. What's more, the subjects of his dishonesty were, as Kessler put it, so "mindlessly dumb," so shallow and unserious that their explication did not illuminate policy. Kessler decided that the only way to cope was to start a list and keep a running tally. His team figured it would keep track for the first hundred days. It was a time-consuming "pain in the ass," but the team got through it. Over the first one hundred days it clocked 492 false or misleading claims uttered by the president. The group patted itself on the back, glad to be done. Then came a torrent of emails, all carrying the same message, Kessler says: You can't stop now, readers pleaded. And so the database continued—and it grew.

When we sat down with Kessler in mid-August 2018, the Fact Checker was still not using the word "lie." A column dedicated to policing exaggerations and false statements couldn't allow itself to get ahead of the facts,

Kessler explained. How could they sufficiently establish what was in some-one's mind, whether the false or misleading statement was intentional or not? Kessler mused that he wasn't especially preoccupied with the debate over whether journalists should use the word to describe Trump's state-ments: "'Lie' is a bit of a conversation stopper. And it turns people off when you start saying 'lie.'"

It took Trump less than a week more to push Kessler past these reser-vations. On August 22, 2018, the Fact Checker published its assessment of the president's numerous statements that he had no knowledge of hush money payoffs to multiple women who claimed to have had affairs with him: "Not just misleading. Not merely false. A lie," it wrote.

The database will continue, Kessler says, at least through the end of Trump's first term in office. The project has become so burdensome, how-ever, that were Trump to win reelection, Kessler isn't sure if it could continue.

Each item on the Fact Checker list carries an individual message: this specific statement is untrue. But the database itself—the aggregation of the lies—carries a much larger message: that this president is a liar, that the president's relationship with the truth is so lax that a major newspaper feels compelled to document his misstatements in a comprehensive cata-log as a service to its readers. Neither the *Post* nor any other major news-paper had ever undertaken such a project before.

"Every president lies," but according to Kessler, Trump is "different." And indeed, Trump's lies are not like those of the traditional presidency. The difference is not just a matter of volume, though the volume is radi-cally different. The lies are also of a different sort.

They are, for one thing, closely linked to Trump's radical use of pres-idential speech. As we argued in the prior chapter, Trump floods the field with a constant, overwhelming, and unfiltered flow of words. His lies op-erate in tandem with this effort; they transform what would otherwise be just an endless fireside chat into a persistent presidential disinformation campaign, amplified through Twitter and by the conservative media eco-system. The nature of the president's speech makes it impossible for the

press and the public to effectively filter for his dishonesty. And the chaotic and scattered messages from the disunified executive branch combine
with the president's tendency to frequently contradict himself, creating a
kind of house-of-mirrors effect; one can never be sure which direction to
look, or what is real and what is illusion.

In this area too, Trump is thus proposing a dramatic revision to the
traditional presidency. On its face, his proposal is simple: to do away with
the traditional presidency's expectation that the president will tell the
truth. But there is a more complex proposition embedded in the suggestion
that it doesn't matter if the President of the United States tells the truth,
which is that it doesn't matter if the President of the United States is believed.
The implications of this second point have taken time to emerge.

As if anticipating the Fact Checker's effort, while Trump was still
president-elect, our colleague Quinta Jurecic warned that the "sheer volume of Trump's bullshit ensures that any effort to archive or categorize
his false statements will inherently fall short." Jurecic argued that the
idea of "bullshit"— as distinguished from lying by the philosopher Harry
Frankfurt—better describes Trump's style of purveying untruths. Telling
a lie, after all, requires knowing—acknowledging—the truth; indeed, it
requires knowing and acknowledging that there is such a thing as truth.
Bullshit, by contrast, involves statements made without reference to truth,
and Trump "gives every appearance of proudly moving through the world
without ever bothering to consider how concepts of truth or falsehood
might potentially shape his behavior. Trump just says things, some of
which coincidentally happen to be true, many of which turn out not to be."

The notion of the politician as a bullshit artist is not in any sense new.
Three centuries ago, Jonathan Swift penned a famous essay entitled "The
Art of Political Lying." In it, Swift describes an English political figure of
a Trump-like disposition with respect to the truth, a man whose genius
lay in "an inexhaustible fund of political lies, which he plentifully distrib-
utes every minute he speaks, and by an unparalleled generosity forgets,
and consequently contradicts, the next half hour." A man who did not

concern himself with "whether any proposition were true or false," but only its convenience in a given moment and to the present audience. To presume that this man was always lying, and thus that the opposite of what he said was truth, was no help, for you "will find yourself equally deceived, whether you believe or not." Wrote Swift, "Although the devil be the father of lies, he seems, like other great inventors, to have lost much of his reputation, by the continual improvements that have been made upon him."

Trump's specific innovation—his personal improvement to the devil's invention, if you will—is brazen pervasiveness in the application of lies to the office of the American presidency. Trump does not just tell lies. He wields a water cannon of lies. He makes newspapers choose between cataloging his lies and giving up on accountability—newspapers he then accuses of making up sources and purveying "fake news." He lies about policy, about ethics matters, about his enemies and opponents, and about his personal behavior. He lies, routinely, about his prior lies. Trump's lies are so pervasive, so inherent to his presidency, that it is actually impossible to imagine his presidency without them. He is the first president in American history whose average public statement on any subject cannot be granted any kind of presumption of factual accuracy.

The Mueller report alone documented seventy-seven instances in which Trump and his associates lied or made false statements to the public, to Congress, or to federal investigators. An authoritative Justice Department report meticulously detailing these lies was so unsurprising that it provoked relatively little concern or outrage. While Congress and the public furiously debated whether the president had committed crimes, the idea that he was lying to the American people was shrugged off as a given. When Senator Dianne Feinstein asked Attorney General Bill Barr about Mueller's finding that the president had pressured his White House counsel to lie in order to deflect criticism of the president, Barr glibly replied, "Well, that's not a crime," rendering Feinstein momentarily speechless. Through audacity and exhaustion, Trump had gotten large segments of the public to accept the notion that if a presidential lie wasn't a crime, then it was no big deal.

The perils of dishonest officials did not go unnoticed at the founding. Honesty necessarily underlies the principles of civic virtue inherent in the oath of office. "Faithful" execution of the law, after all, necessarily involves *some* measure of honesty. And when the founders imagined civic virtue, integrity, and honesty in a president, they were describing not an abstract ideal, but an actual man: George Washington. The founders' well-placed faith in Washington's character invisibly embeds the assumption of basic integrity within the construction of the office itself. And Washington further molded the office by transforming strength of character into acts of precedent—the very first presidential norms. He was obsessed with his own personal probity, so much so that his first biographer, Mason Weems, invented the legend of the young Washington's confessing to cutting down a cherry tree. "I cannot tell a lie" may be a line too good to be true, yet it does capture Washington's sense that honesty is the core of civic virtue. In a letter to Hamilton in 1788, Washington wrote, "I hope I shall always possess firmness and virtue enough to maintain (what I consider the most enviable of all titles) the character of an honest man."

Washington's view of civic virtue as the irreducible core and highest aspiration of the political leader was shared by other transformative American presidents. The words of the man who would first make the Union are echoed in the youthful writings of Abraham Lincoln, who would re-make it less than a century later. In 1832, a twenty-three-year-old Lincoln concluded his first announcement of political candidacy by saying, "Every man is said to have his peculiar ambition. Whether it be true or not, I can say for one that I have no other so great as that of being truly esteemed of my fellow men, by rendering myself worthy of their esteem." Though Lincoln was himself a master of political feints and maneuvers, it is not an accident that he acquired the historical nickname Honest Abe.

Not all presidents, to be sure, lived up to the founding-era standard of civic virtue and honesty—and the country actually established early on that it could reconcile lies and deceit with the presidency. Thomas Jefferson is a complex historical figure, but honesty did not consistently rank among his virtues. While serving in Washington's cabinet, Jefferson once assured the president "in the presence of heaven" that he had played no role in influencing what appeared in the pages of Philip Freneau's opposition newspaper, which was published by a translator in his State Department. The presidential historian Alvin Felzenberg writes that Jefferson's claim "would have come as a surprise, not only to editor Freneau, but also to Representative James Madison, whom Jefferson beseeched on multiple occasion to 'pick up' his pen and 'cut [Hamilton] to pieces' on the pages of Freneau's publication." In other words, Jefferson was telling Washington a bald-faced lie.

Nor did Jefferson suddenly become a paragon of virtue when he became president. A remarkable man in many ways, he was, with respect to honesty, far more ordinary than either of his two predecessors—both of whom were genuinely extraordinary in their personal honor. In this way, Jefferson, more than Washington or Adams, offers the template for the way the presidency developed—mingling the capacity for deceit with some genuine civic virtue.

So the country learned early that the dream of impeccably honest leaders was an ideal to which to aspire, not a reality to demand in practice. That said, it also turned out that a core of presidential trustworthiness and honesty was both closely linked to and structurally embedded in the founding vision of the executive. When Hamilton advocated a unified and energetic executive, he did so, in part, to promote accountability; as he wrote, an official "ought to be personally responsible for his behavior in office." The most fundamental constraint on the executive, after all, is not the other branches, but political accountability to the people. If the president does something improper or imprudent, voters will respond by exerting forms of political pressure, which will force the president to correct his course or force Congress to take its own remedial action. Ultimately, a Congress that does not adequately respond has to face the voters, as does the president himself.

But this vision of accountability is predicated on the assumption that information would actually reach the public and that such information would be true and accurate. After all, the public cannot exert its political will without knowing what is going on.

The design doesn't work as intended when the president is a liar who will not own his errors—or, at least, such a liar adds a severe complication to the accountability endeavor. Accountability then requires not merely correcting the underlying error but also exposing it in the first instance. The expectation of integrity in leaders is thus in part an expectation aimed at facilitating democratic accountability. To some extent, of course, all presidents try to dodge political accountability for their errors; that's one of the big reasons why politicians lie. But Trump is surely the first to so pervade presidential communication with lies and bullshit as to make factual correction of any one misstatement an irrelevant raindrop in a typhoon.

Every person who has occupied the office has told falsehoods of varying degrees of intentionality at one point or another. There is the gray area of political spin into which all politicians frequently venture. There is some line between an exaggeration and a lie, a line on which many politicians live. And, of course, mistaken statements lack the intentional quality associated with lying—although some mistakes are highly consequential. Think, for example, of President George W. Bush's erroneous conviction that Saddam Hussein had weapons of mass destruction. This was false, but it was not a lie. The president honestly believed it and had reason to, given the reporting of the intelligence community. Still, nearly every president has gone firmly beyond the realm of spin and said something he knew at the time he said it to be untrue. Yet even in this category, not all presidential falsehoods are the same.

Normal presidents actually prefer not to lie, and the reason is not merely civic virtue. It's also effectiveness. To do the job, after all, the president has to get people to believe her. All presidents must eventually draw on a reserve of credibility in order to convince the public, as well as foreign governments, to take their representations seriously in circumstances in which the president is unable or unwilling to offer proof. U.S. allies must believe the nation's promises; the country's adversaries must believe its threats; the public must believe its sacrifices are for the greater good. When the president promises to support a senator's bill in exchange for the senator's support on some other policy priority, the senator needs to believe him. This is part of the reason presidential statements are normally vetted carefully by a staff whose job it is to make sure that the president's words are not just inspiring and politically clever, but also factually accurate. Spending down the president's reserve of trust unnecessarily is a terrible waste of political capital. Think of how much harder it was in early 2019 to negotiate over the government shutdown, first to avoid it and then to end it, as a result of the Democratic congressional leadership—and the Republican leadership, for that matter—not believing a word the president said.

In a true crisis, the problem of presidential credibility becomes critical. Imagine that the United States were hit with a massive cyberattack and the president had to justify publicly an armed response. Attributing the attack in a fashion the international community would accept would require credibility. Or imagine circumstances where the president might have good reason to order a preemptive strike of some kind against North Korea. Justifying such action would also require credibility. It is difficult to imagine that Trump currently has the requisite credibility should a genuine emergency materialize, particularly after his regular denials of intelligence findings about Russian hacking during the 2016 election.

In fairness, the problem of presidential credibility is bigger than Trump. Lots of people on the political right profoundly distrusted Obama and didn't believe a word he said, and lots of people on the political left didn't trust or believe George W. Bush, even though both operated well within the range of normal deviations from the truth for politicians. This lack of trust is exacerbated by such aspects of modern political culture as the decentralization of media and the rise of internet-driven conspiracy theories. But even before "Tricky Dick" Nixon and Lyndon Johnson's Vietnam-era "credibility gap," there are older examples of people not trusting presidents at critical moments. Whatever the general challenges, they are dramatically worsened when the president is openly known to be a liar. Elizabeth Drew, in her famous chronicle of Watergate, described in real time the profound skepticism with which Nixon's decision to put U.S. forces on alert during the 1973 Arab-Israeli war was greeted by people who had good reason by then not to trust the president. "The price, simply put," Drew wrote, "is that in what may be an international crisis there is widespread disbelief in our leaders. Either way, it is not good. If the crisis is, as some think, manufactured, that is not good. If it is real, and the public confidence in our leaders is at such a low ebb that they are widely disbelieved, that is not good, either. Democracy, if it is to work, requires more public trust than this."

Presidential political capital is not just the personal possession of the individual officeholder either. Each president has entered his office in the condition the prior occupant left it and has supplemented the existing balance of truth—positively or negatively—with his own reputation for probity. Some presidents build up the stores through candor, adherence to process, and transparency. If the last president has told the truth—and if presidents usually tell the truth—then the new president receives the benefit of the doubt that he or she too is honest. But when a president is believed to be dishonest, he or she depletes trust, and his or her successor is left the task of restoring it. It is possible that a genuinely honest man or woman will succeed Trump as president, perhaps even in reaction to him. In such a case, the new president may be able to rapidly renew the expectation of presidential truth telling and things will snap back to normal. But there is a risk that, even if later occupants of the office are not as extreme as Trump, they will be tempted to capitalize on the erosion of the traditional presidency's expectation of truth in circumstances when being less than fully candid proves expedient. There's also a risk that Trump's mendacity will translate over time into lessened public confidence in the words of any president.

The president's reserve of trust is a function of both his own statements and those made on his behalf, because the reserve of trust is both personal to the president and also held by the office he or she holds. This means that honesty matters when the president is speaking directly to the public and when he is speaking to the public through the press and through his own press office. The consequences of dishonesty are not merely to his personal effectiveness but also to the erosion of the effectiveness and prestige of the office itself. The president isn't obligated to have a press secretary, or even to communicate with the public in any specific manner. Early presidents communicated predominantly through the partisan press and via written letters. Teddy Roosevelt was the first to offer the press a space within the White House, pioneering a form of access journalism that served him well. The presidential press conference didn't exist until Woodrow Wilson held the first one in 1913. Warren Harding and Calvin Coolidge insisted that the press submit questions for review in advance. Truman convinced reporters to change his quotes if he'd said something he later decided was ill-advised. Kennedy distrusted the press, and Nixon loathed reporters.

This is all to say that the president can interact with the press in any way she might choose. And yet outright lies from the White House press podium are generally understood to be politically unacceptable. The White House press office is simply an extension of the president, so it traditionally seeks to preserve a reputation for basic honesty. Bill Clinton's press secretary Mike McCurry—who had to speak for Clinton during much of the Lewinsky scandal—has described the dance of answering press questions without lying as "telling the truth slowly."

Trump's White House press office, however, doesn't even attempt to mitigate the president's falsehoods—by spinning them into something marginally defensible, as we've seen in prior administrations. Rather, Trump has set his press operation to the task of amplifying and defending his lies and lying on his behalf. This was visible in Sean Spicer's first press conference on the "largest audience to ever witness an inauguration, period," and it remained visible in a great many of his successors' interactions with the press. Not only did Sarah Huckabee Sanders refuse to acknowledge Trump's lies as such, but she also routinely generated her own falsehoods—as when she claimed to have heard from "countless" numbers of FBI personnel expressing gratitude in the wake of FBI director James Comey's firing. This obviously was not true, as she subsequently acknowledged. She later told Mueller's office "that her reference to hearing from 'countless members of the FBI' was a 'slip of the tongue.'" The Mueller report states, "She also recalled that her statement in a separate press interview that rank-and-file FBI agents had lost confidence in Comey was a comment she made 'in the heat of the moment' that was not founded on anything."

Richard Nixon so thoroughly decimated faith in his office that two of his successors had to occupy themselves with restoring public confidence in it. This was only partly about lies. It was also about shocking criminality. But lies were integral to Nixon's degradation of the office, and honorable candor was crucial to restoring confidence in it. Gerald Ford, notwithstanding executive privilege, testified extensively and publicly before Congress about his knowledge during Watergate, his actions in the final weeks before Nixon resigned, and his decision to pardon Nixon. Jimmy Carter campaigned on the promise "I'll never lie to you." George W. Bush campaigned on a promise to restore personal integrity to the office, following Bill Clinton's sexual indiscretions and subsequent dishonesty about it under oath. And Barack Obama had to deal throughout his presidency with diminished trust in the government emanating from Bush's misrepresentations in the run-up to the Iraq War.

It is against this backdrop—a backdrop in which trust is a primary currency of the chief executive and has to be maintained—that a sympathetic journalist argued that Trump's supporters take his words "seriously, but not literally." The phrase "seriously, but not literally" became an effective tool for explaining away candidate Trump's most alarming rhetoric. Sure, he said things that the general public would usually deem presumptively disqualifying—that he would reinstate torture, that he might not concede the election if he lost—but only if you believed him. Instead, voters were urged to translate Trump's literal words into whatever version of related sentiment was marginally politically tolerable. When he said he'd bring back much "worse" than waterboarding, he just meant he'd be tough on terrorism. When he said "Second Amendment people" might do something about his campaign opponent, he didn't mean they would harm her with a gun, he meant at the polls. When he said he'd cover the legal fees of people who assaulted protesters at his rallies, he was only joking. When he urged Russia to find Hillary Clinton's missing emails, he wasn't endorsing a foreign intelligence operation directed against a political opponent. When he lied, he was not accountable for the lie, because he was telling some form of truth—just not a form expressed by the actual words he spoke.

Writing in *The New York Times*, the organizational behavior scholar Daniel Effron argues that Trump and his allies rely on "a subtle psychological strategy to defend his falsehoods: They encourage people to reflect on how the falsehoods *could have been* true." Effron argues that this allows Trump's supporters to excuse his lies and defend them as ethical, noting that when Trump shared "a video falsely purporting to show a Muslim migrant committing assault, [Sanders] defended him by saying, 'Whether it's a real video, the threat is real.'"

Yet however elastically they are understood by some supporters, a president's specific words matter; they can have precise legal consequences. When the president says that a foreign regime has used chemical weapons against civilians, the leaders of nations the United States asks to join in serious military or economic reprisals don't have the luxury of taking the statement seriously, but not literally. When a president tweets that he intends to take punitive action against a private company, investors likewise cannot afford to take the representation seriously, but not literally. These actors have to at least allow for the possibility that a president literally means what he says. Each presidential statement—whether politically persuasive or not—either adds or detracts from the reserve of trust in the office. Presidential lies necessarily and always undermine trust. Trump's lies, however, individually and cumulatively warp the office in ways the country has not seen before.

This is not because the president lies about subjects that haven't been lied about before. The public has confronted, for example, many instances in which politicians and presidents have hidden marital infidelity—the tradition dates back in American political history at least to Alexander Hamilton's decision to pay hush money to his mistress's husband. Critics of Bill Clinton, following the revelations of his affair with Monica Lewinsky, argued that even if his specific lies didn't go to questions of public policy, they nonetheless corroded trust in his ability to discharge his office faithfully. After all, they argued, if the president could lie to his wife, he could just as easily lie to the nation. And if he could lie under oath in a civil deposition and then to a grand jury, how could he be trusted with the duties of his office?

Trump's lies about his personal conduct not only amplify these anxieties; they are so pervasive as to put to shame all his predecessors. He lies about affairs. He lies about lying about the affairs. He lies about the hush money he paid to cover up the affairs. Trump supporters might be able to defend these lies as merely private matters—as many of Bill Clinton's supporters had—were it not for the fact that Trump is simultaneously lying about his personal conduct on a multitude of matters that bear deeply on the public interest. Even as he lies about his marital infidelity and its cover-up, the president also dictates a statement for his son to issue about the Trump Tower meeting with Russians during the campaign, a statement that intentionally omits the key facts. He then lies about having dictated the lie. He lies about his willingness to release his tax returns. He lied about his willingness to be interviewed by the Mueller investigation. He appears utterly unashamed when any of these lies are revealed. The result is that the lies on mundane matters that might be understandable—even forgivable—become impossible to disentangle from the lies on matters of great consequence.

The president's supporters thus cannot compartmentalize Trump's lies or dismiss them as unimportant or unrelated to the duties of his office. So they take a different tack when they address the matter at all: because the president lies about everything, there is no significance to any one lie. Former senator Rick Santorum, in attempting to explain why the president has lied so frequently about his contacts with Russia, offered a blunt formulation of this defense. "The president doesn't tell the truth about a lot of things fairly consistently," Santorum said, and so the "fact that he's not telling the truth about Russia fairly consistently, at least in the eyes of people around here, why is that any different?"

Santorum actually puts his finger on an important point, if not quite the one he intended to make: the public lacks the tools for filtering and processing this overwhelming number of presidential lies across nearly all areas. The mechanisms the nation's political culture has developed—normative and formal—to compensate for diminished trust in presidential honesty have evolved in response to discrete areas in which people do not trust presidents to tell the truth. These areas are discrete precisely because in the traditional presidency, presidents do not flood the zone with lies, let alone flood all zones with them. Trump has, perhaps needless to say, made a particular mockery of these specific expectations.

For example, the American political system has developed a certain set of norms concerning statements on presidential health—an area in which there is a well-documented strain of presidential deceit. The president's physical and mental stability is an issue that is both deeply personal and also of substantial public concern.

The history of lying about it is thus long. Grover Cleveland hid his jaw cancer while in office, had a secret surgery to remove the cancer, and few were the wiser until after his death. In perhaps the most egregious example, Woodrow Wilson suffered a debilitating stroke that left him unable to perform the basic functions of the office. His wife essentially ran the White House while she and aides hid the president's condition from the public. Franklin Roosevelt was so ill while seeking reelection to a fourth term that Democratic Party leaders prevailed on him to replace his sitting vice president with Harry Truman as a running mate, because they recognized that the vice president was likely to soon become the president. Kennedy outright denied that he had Addison's disease when asked by the press. Lyndon Johnson's aides hid his incapacitating depression. Nixon's staff hid his alcoholism, even as they made important national security decisions while the president was inebriated.

These lies were primarily lies of omission, but a powerful modern norm developed out of such deceptions that presidential candidates now offer independent certification of their health, and once a candidate is in office, the president's physician gives an annual assessment of his condition as a means of reassuring the American people. There is an accompanying norm that the information about the president's health that is made public ought to be accurate.

Following the norm in Trump's case would have served an important public purpose. He is not young. His diet is famously poor. He is overweight. There have been persistent questions about his mental acuity— and his mental health. If there was ever a major-party presidential nominee in the modern era about whom reasonable voters would have health questions, it was Trump.

Trump's response, however, was frankly fraudulent. During the campaign, his personal physician, Dr. Harold Bornstein, released a letter in which he called Trump's laboratory tests "astonishingly excellent" and said that Trump's "physical strength and stamina are extraordinary." He went on to say that if elected, Trump would be "the healthiest individual ever elected to the presidency," apparently believing that the then sixty-nine-year-old Trump, whose self-professed body mass index bordered on obesity, was in better condition than his immediate predecessor, who entered office at the age of forty-seven and played basketball regularly.

The letter was met with derision, and few observers were remotely surprised when, following the election, Bornstein acknowledged that Trump had personally dictated the entire letter to him. What would have been a major scandal for any other president—falsifying health records in order to deceive voters before the election—was simply shrugged off in the press as a comical farce.

The bizarre statements about Trump's health did not stop once he became president. The White House physician Ronny Jackson—a man who previously enjoyed a strong reputation—also raised eyebrows with his unusually rosy account of Trump's health while in office, proclaiming that the president had great genetics and that "if he had a healthier diet over the last 20 years, he might live to be 200 years old." The following year, questions arose about whether a new White House physician had actually authored a memo bearing his signature that offered a glowing assessment of Trump's health and predicted he would remain healthy "for the duration of his Presidency, and beyond."

Trump's lies about his health may seem inconsequential or even comical, but they offer a road map to understanding how his dishonesty interacts with traditional expectations of the office. Trump doesn't just lie about his physical fitness; he co-opts mechanisms designed to bolster public confidence to further his lie. The penchant for dishonesty he displayed as a candidate—back then aided by the buffoonish Dr. Bornstein—is as present in the Oval Office. Rather than Trump's questionable credibility being reinforced by the government processes intended to do just that, his dishonesty instead degrades public faith in the integrity of the government process used to validate him.

Ironically, the importance of these validating mechanisms becomes most apparent on the occasions in which they are necessary to perpetrate a justifiable lie.

And there are such things as justifiable presidential lies. Broadly speaking, those are lies or deceptions that serve some actual interest of the nation, where that interest warrants the erosion of trust engendered by the lie. Most people think it's okay for the president to deceive foreign governments in the conduct of diplomatic affairs, and most recognize that such lies might also require deceiving the American public. National security justifications are typically the most resonant in this area. Few people would consider a lawfully authorized covert action to be a lamentable lie, though it may involve deceit.

Even such justifiable lies can have substantial policy consequences if they are revealed. In 1960, the Eisenhower administration told the American public that the Soviet Union shot down a weather research plane. In reality, it was a spy plane on a reconnaissance mission. When the Soviets revealed that they had both the plane and its pilot, Eisenhower's lie became apparent. Eisenhower was so mortified at having been exposed as dishonest that he considered resigning from office. His instinct to resign was not a matter of some untoward motive, but rather it reflected his sense that the president must have a reputation for honesty in order to do his job. Even a justified lie, when exposed, compromised his reputation. Eisenhower later said that "the lie we told" about the U-2 was the greatest regret of his presidency.

After President Kennedy misled the public during the Cuban missile crisis, the Pentagon spokesperson Arthur Sylvester defended the decision, saying that the government has the "inherent" right to lie. He later testified, "Obviously, no government information program can be based on lies; it must always be based on truthful facts. But when any nation is faced with nuclear disaster, you do not tell all the facts to the enemy." In the same vein, Reagan's press secretary lied about the impending invasion of Grenada, as did Carter's press secretary regarding plans to rescue U.S. hostages in Iran. A common attribute of all these lies is that they were calculated from the outset to be temporary—a deceit to facilitate a short-term tactical gain, followed by an acknowledgment of the lie. This sequence bolsters the legitimacy of the lie.

But also bolstering the lie's legitimacy is the fact that its purveyor is not lying about everything else. Eisenhower had a reputation for honesty, so if he had to temporarily deceive the public about this one thing—and especially if he was mortified about doing so—his general reputation and his specific mortification fortified the justification. That defense does not work if the president is someone incapable of mortification, someone who lies so consistently that nobody trusts a word he or she says.

Presidential lies about important policy matters, when not justified by some immediately compelling rationale, are particularly democratically corrosive. The philosopher Sissela Bok writes that "deception of this kind strikes at the very essence of democratic government. It allows those in power to override or nullify the right vested in the people to cast an informed vote in critical elections."

Intentional deceptions about policy most frequently take place in the realm of national security, where presumptions of secrecy govern. And the line between justifiable and unjustifiable misrepresentations can be uncomfortably contingent on whether one agrees with the policy in question. In other words, one's assessment about whether Kennedy was justified in lying about the Cuban missile crisis, or secretly supporting the coup against Ngo Dinh Diem in South Vietnam, may depend more on one's views regarding U.S. policy at the time toward Cuba and South Vietnam than on general feelings about presidential dishonesty.

History, however, has judged particular presidential lies, even in the realm of national security, especially harshly. Lyndon Johnson's misrepresentations of U.S. policy and military success in the Vietnam War rank among the more consequential and historically condemned lies by a president. Throughout his tenure in office, Johnson systematically sought to disguise from the American public an unfolding U.S. policy of committing additional troops to Vietnam. Johnson's deception was epitomized in the Gulf of Tonkin incident, wherein the president used a purported North Vietnamese attack on a U.S. naval destroyer in order to obtain congressional authorization for the use of military force. The truth was, no such attack had occurred. While initial reports may have been confused, Johnson overplayed and misrepresented the incident to Congress long after he had intelligence suggesting that the attack had not happened. Johnson and his secretary of defense, Robert McNamara, went on to serially mislead the public about the success of covert and military operations in the region. An increasingly wary press began to use the term "credibility gap"—first coined around the time of the Cuban missile crisis—to describe the distance between the administration's account and reports from the ground.

When Richard Nixon took office following Johnson, his communications director, Herb Klein, pledged that "truth will become the hallmark of the Nixon administration . . . We will be able to eliminate any possibility of a credibility gap." To the contrary, Nixon would turn Johnson's credibility gap into a credibility gulf.

Johnson was not the first president to mislead the country into war. As a young congressman, Abraham Lincoln accused James K. Polk of taking the country into the Mexican War under false pretenses. Polk used a purported attack by Mexican troops in U.S. territory as justification to declare war. In reality, he had ordered troops into Mexican territory. The president's opponents famously labeled him Polk the Mendacious and, Felzenberg notes, they accused him of "relying on deceit and chicanery" and "fabricated intelligence" to embroil the country in an unjust war.

As a result of this long history, the U.S. government has adopted a general modern policy of avoiding lying about national security matters; rather than deny a covert action, for instance, it typically will simply refuse to comment on intelligence matters. As the Clinton spokesman Mike Mc-Curry put it, when faced with the dilemma of whether to make a misleading statement from the press podium for national security reasons, "you tap dance, but never lie."

At least so far, Trump has not engaged in this particular sort of lie about intelligence to justify major military actions. Nor has he, as other presidents have, used his access to secret intelligence information to justify his actions. Trump, rather, has shattered this mold in a peculiar fashion. Although he does lie about classified intelligence all the time, he does so less by mischaracterizing it for policy reasons than by denying its existence or refusing to believe it himself—or by making up intelligence facts of his own to support his preferred media narrative of the day. His serial denials of U.S. intelligence assessments regarding Russian interference in the 2016 election is the most prominent example of this. But it is not the only example. When Trump tweeted that President Obama had his "wires tapped" at Trump Tower, it set off a flurry of speculation as to whether Trump was confirming the existence of a warrant under criminal authorities or the Foreign Intelligence Surveillance Act. After all, he had access to all information from the Department of Justice and the intelligence agencies that he wished to see. As the Justice Department denied the existence of any such warrant in a court filing, it increasingly became clear that Trump's source of information was not sensitive government documents, but thinly sourced conspiracy theories reported by disreputable online publications. He was just bullshitting—announcing in a tweet what would be convenient if it were true as though it were, in fact, true.

Indeed, Trump's lies about intelligence are generally not of a strategic nature, designed to support some policy objective or conceal some short-term operation that publicity may put at risk. They are like his other lies—self-serving matters of momentary convenience that may deny intelligence, make it up, or mischaracterize it. And they are often less about the intelligence itself than about the agencies responsible for it. When he tweets something that is plausible on its face but lacks public evidence to support, it is impossible to know if he is disclosing sensitive government information or if he just watched a segment of *Fox & Friends*. Moreover, his policy lies are generally not attempts to persuade the country to follow him on a particular policy course; they are more often simply self-promoting bluster.

On occasion, he has also lied about factual matters by way of creating space for his policies. One of the present authors spent a year litigating a Freedom of Information Act request in an attempt to prove false a single line about immigrants and terrorism and Justice Department statistics in Trump's February 2017 speech to a joint session of Congress. The line was designed to gin up public fear of immigration and thus generate support for his travel ban executive order. But this sort of lie is actually the exception, not the rule. Far more often, Trump's lies serve no policy purpose. They are bloviating swagger and nothing else. In this sense, Trump not only depletes the reserve of trust and presumption of good faith in the presidency; he creates a presidency truly based on the Frankfurtian concept of bullshit. He is the politician of Swift's precise description—you "will find yourself equally deceived whether you believe or not."

This is inimical to the traditional presidency, which values credibility, effectiveness, policy-making efficiency, and prestige. But again, Trump is proposing a different vision. And if the point of a presidency is not to manage sprawling bureaucracies so as to develop and implement policy in a credible fashion domestically and in foreign relations, if the goal instead is personal exhibition and theater, then truth is actually not that important. Certainly truth that slows one down is an encumbrance, as is truth that contradicts policy outcomes or desires. Truth inhibits the expressive presidency—and thus is more foe than legitimizing friend.

There is, however, a pathological feature to Trump's dishonesty that is quite different from the liar of Swift's account. In numerous instances, the president seems incapable of telling the truth, even when the consequences of telling a lie far outweigh any harm that might be inflicted by revealing the truth. When Trump was filmed referring to Apple CEO Tim Cook as "Tim Apple" during a meeting, Trump insisted that he had actually said Cook's last name very quietly—an assertion that the tape demonstrates to be plainly false. He later tweeted that he had said Tim Apple in order to "save time &words." Rather than laugh it off, Trump insisted on lying about a harmless flub in a fashion that drove the news cycle for days.

This pathological feature is one reason why Trump's lawyers were quite open during the Mueller investigation in viewing their task as not merely to defend the president's prior conduct but also to prevent him from committing a new crime: lying to investigators or under oath, when the falsehood carries potential criminal penalties. That the special counsel investigation concluded without an interview with the president represented a substantial legal victory for Trump's team. As Bob Woodward writes at the conclusion of his book *Fear*, the attorney John Dowd had warned Trump that he'd end up in "an orange jumpsuit" if he gave Mueller an interview, because he would lie. "In the man and his presidency," Woodward writes at the book's end, "Dowd had seen the tragic flaw. In the political back-and-forth, the evasions, the denials, the tweeting, the obscuring, crying 'Fake News,' the indignation, Trump had one overriding problem that Dowd knew but could not bring himself to say to the president: 'You're a fucking liar.'"

This is Trump's radical proposed revision to the traditional presidency: not only that the president doesn't need to be honest, but that he can be known to everyone as a "fucking liar"—not an occasional liar, not a calculating liar, but a pervasive, constant liar and bullshitter on all subjects at all times. What would this revision mean in the long term for the presidency? In the broadest sense, nobody knows, because nobody knows how deeply such leadership will erode public confidence in the possibility of government—indeed, to what extent it will erode public belief in objective truth itself. Presidents are, among other things, modelers of public beliefs and aspirations politically. Does having a president who is a bullshitter change the public's sense of truth over time? The point of Trump's lies is not to convince the public that he can be believed, but rather to convince people that no one can be believed.

Certain effects, however, are clearly visible already and are unquestionably indelible features of the presidency—at least as long as Trump occupies it and possibly long after. The first is simply the decline in prestige and credibility of the office. A public presidential statement today comes with no presumption of factual accuracy. This means that allies cannot rely on America's word. The country's diplomatic interlocutors, friend and foe alike, do not know how to understand the country's intentions or representations. It also means that the office has no capacity to explain or persuade domestically. Trump cannot build coalitions. The author of *The Art of the Deal* cannot make deals, for who would rely on his word in a negotiation? His impairment is dramatic, all the more so because he does not appear to know it and has no capacity to correct it. His mendacity is a key feature of his incompetence.

Trump's mendacity is also a key feature of the erosion of his control over the executive branch, which we discussed in depth in chapter 3. When lower-level officials are constantly in the position of contradicting the president, it gravely disrupts executive unity. When the president misstates policy and some lesser official articulates the actual policy by way of clarification or correction, it widens the disconnect between the White House and the agency in question. When that happens every day and with every agency, it trains the public to accept that the executive branch is just this free-floating set of agencies and that the presidency is an unconnected, yammering head.

It may seem obvious that no future president would want to emulate Trump's behavior in this regard, as it seems so wholly self-defeating. The trouble is that it isn't clear how much of a price Trump really pays for his untruthfulness. To be sure, it impairs him in certain relationships, but those do not tend to be relationships he cares about in his expressive presidency. And even reasonably honest prior presidents were deeply mistrusted by partisans on the other side, so maybe the benefit of telling the truth was more limited than analysts assumed at the time. Trump's lies do not appear to have gravely harmed his standing with his base, and he remains as of this writing electorally viable. If a candidate can lie as much as Trump did and be elected, and a president can lie as much as Trump does and still be reelected, then future presidents may well feel freer to lie. They almost surely won't do it quite as flamboyantly as Trump does; the volume and the energy of his lying clearly have some element of pathology. But every prior president has faced inconvenient truths during his tenure—matters in which it would be far more expedient in the moment to simply lie. If someone like Trump can be reelected, it would be a demonstration that the importance of hoarding presidential credibility has been wildly overrated historically. It would mean that the traditional presidency utterly misjudged—at least recently—the political economy of truth, or that this political economy has shifted substantially of late. If that's the case, future politicians will notice.

There is, however, one price Trump has paid for his lies that future presidents will almost certainly want to avoid. And that price is leaks.

Leaks, of course, are a permanent feature of Washington. But once again, the Trump administration is different. The flow of leaks is near constant, and they pour from every direction. There are leaks about the president's calls with foreign leaders, leaks about his mood and private comments, leaks of sensitive national security information, leaks about policy strategy, about Trump's TV-watching habits, about disparaging comments and evaluations by his staff, and about his legal strategy. There are even leaks of memos addressing a plan to stop leaks. Staffers barely exit the Oval Office before texting their favorite member of the press to spill all.

The unprecedented number of leaks emanating from the White House, executive agencies, and Congress is an organic feature of the president's mendacity. This means that future presidents should view leaks as the inevitable consequence of following Trump's path away from presidential truth. The American democratic system requires accurate information in order to function. The president refuses to provide it, and the typical truth-seeking mechanisms—congressional oversight, most notably—have not effectively held him to task. The executive branch's internal immune response is to route around the damage and spill out secrets. Many of the leaks are specific responses to lies—as when the president insisted that he was not involved in his family members' security clearance process, only to have it leak that, over objections, he had personally ordered they be granted clearances.

The legal scholar David Pozen has argued that leaks bolster government credibility by reducing "the incidence of official lying." When the details of a classified program become public, even if the government refuses to formally confirm or deny its existence, there is little point in actually lying about it. According to Pozen, "Leakiness, in this context, not only pushes out specific revelations to the media but also creates an

environment in which official lying becomes an untenable and unnecessary strategy." Furthermore, the threat of future leaks may also reduce
governmental dishonesty generally. Officials are aware that despite formal
rules, they do not have complete control over the flow of information to
the public. In that sense, according to Pozen, "a pervasive culture of leaking may substitute, to some extent, for a pervasive culture of lying. The
executive benefits from this trade-off both because it likely better supports
public trust in government and because it prevents most officials from feeling pressure to violate an injunction ('thou shall not lie') that, unlike the
leak laws, continues to exert a strong moral pull on public servants."

Pozen wrote this paper in 2013, before the Trump administration, and
he surely would have written it differently had he imagined Trump. But
the Trump presidency has, in important respects, validated it. If Pozen's
theory was right, after all, one would expect to see a particularly mendacious president preside over a period of exceptional leaking. And that's
exactly what has happened.

But Pozen, in imagining that the leaks would limit lies, underesti-
mated Trump. Even the tidal wave of leaks from the Trump administration has been insufficient, after all, to displace the "pervasive culture of
lying." To the contrary, the culture of mendacity has simply driven more
leaks, which are in turn met with more lies. The lies and the leaks do not
counterbalance one another, but drive an ever-downward spiral. And, of
course, some of the leaks are more politically motivated than reflective
of civic commitment to truth, with individuals leaking damaging tidbits
about programs and policies and people they find objectionable or simply
in an effort to hurt an administration they dislike.

Most leaks have been merely embarrassing for the president, who
portrays himself in some heroic fashion only to have his staff or his agencies describe him completely differently. Some leaks, however, are more
serious, implicating especially grave national harms. In this sense, as Jack
Goldsmith has argued, the president's norm violations are inspiring reciprocal violations by his detractors that are themselves dangerous.

The most striking example of this is the leak of the contents of phone calls between the former national security adviser Michael Flynn and then Russian ambassador Sergey Kislyak, an episode described at length in the Mueller report. Less than a month before Trump's inauguration, on December 29, 2016—the day President Obama levied sanctions in response to the 2016 Russian election interference—Flynn phoned Kislyak "and requested that Russia respond to the sanctions only in a reciprocal manner, without escalating the situation." They spoke again two days later. The immediate public question at the time was whether the soon-to-be national security adviser was attempting to undermine the policies of the sitting president during the transition—and, if so, why he was doing that. It subsequently emerged that the calls had been scrutinized by counterintelligence investigators. As Mueller recounts, "When analyzing Russia's response, they became aware of Flynn's discussion of sanctions with Kislyak. Previously, the FBI had opened an investigation of Flynn based on his relationship with the Russian government. Flynn's contacts with Kislyak became a key component of that investigation." Flynn later admitted as part of his plea agreement that he did, in fact, discuss sanctions on the call.

However, in response to the revelations at the time, the Trump team again and again gave out false information. Then press secretary Sean Spicer claimed that there had been minimal contact to offer Christmas greetings and arrange for the scheduling of future calls between Trump and Putin. A flurry of leaks and counter-leaks ensued, many obviously sourced to the Trump team, until finally, Vice President–elect Mike Pence was sent out to CBS's *Face the Nation* to unequivocally—and, as it turned out, falsely—deny that Flynn had discussed sanctions with Kislyak.

Former acting attorney general Sally Yates later testified that she and others had personally warned the White House counsel that Flynn had apparently lied on the subject to the vice president. But Trump did not fire Flynn, despite Yates's warning, and the White House continued to distribute misinformation. In response to these lies, *The Washington Post* ran a story citing nine current and former national security officials who confirmed that—contrary to what Spicer, Flynn, Pence, and Trump himself had said—Flynn had in fact discussed sanctions on the call with Kislyak.

This revelation was an ugly moment. The content of the calls was almost certainly obtained through surveillance of Kislyak under the Foreign Intelligence Surveillance Act. The disclosure marked one of the first times the highly detailed contents of a FISA intercept had ever been leaked to the public. Such leaks represent a genuine security threat because they reveal the source and method of the collection, thereby foreclosing future use. It also presents a grave civil liberties violation to disclose information about an American citizen obtained through incidental intelligence collection—the precise harm that decades of guidelines and regulations had been designed to prevent. To see this information in newsprint threatened principles at the very core of the intelligence community's legitimacy.

And yet, seen in a different light, the leak was a reasonably predictable and adaptive response to a profound system failure. Flynn's presence in office presented a grave national security threat, and the president, having been informed of the risk, not only failed to act but allowed the White House to misrepresent the matter to the American public for weeks. The disclosure, in fact, worked as apparently intended. Flynn was forced to resign. By means of the leak, the nation was protected; by means of the leak, the nation was harmed.

The biblical passage from John inscribed on the walls at Langley—that the truth shall make you free—is fitting for the CIA, in part because it does not reveal all of itself to the public. It is a selective quotation from a larger text, the very one that Swift referred to in the early eighteenth century, when he said that "the devil be the father of lies" whose creation centuries of political liars have improved upon. A few lines down from the Gospel's proclamation that in truth lies freedom, reality sets in: "But now ye seek to kill me, a man that hath told you the truth." Through his lies and the position of his office, Trump can obfuscate, but he cannot prevent unwelcome truths from getting out.

And so he goes to war against those who would tell the truth about him—the press, which he calls "Fake News"; the intelligence community, which he calls the "Deep State"; and the FBI, which he says is on a "Witch Hunt."

SIX

"The love of power, and the love of money"

ETHICS IN THE WHITE HOUSE

THE CLOSER DONALD TRUMP CAME TO ACTUALLY BECOMING president, the less eagerness he showed to release his tax returns. Back in 2014, when the presidency was a mere gleam in his eye, doing so was a no-brainer; Trump told an Irish television show, "If I decide to run for office, I'll produce my tax returns, absolutely," adding, "And I would love to do that." By early the following year, he was a little bit less excited, telling the radio host Hugh Hewitt that he would "certainly" release the returns "if it was necessary." And by the fall of 2015, in an interview with George Stephanopoulos, he was "thinking about maybe" releasing them, but only "when we find out the true story on Hillary's emails." A few months later he said he would "get them out at some point, probably." But by February 2016, closing in on actually securing the nomination, he insisted on Twitter that "tax returns have 0 to do w/ someone's net worth" and opined that his financial disclosures with the Federal Election Commission were more than enough. By the end of the month, Trump introduced the rationale he would stick to for the rest of the campaign and into his presidency: he would really like to release his returns but was unable to do so while under audit. He never explained the failure to release tax returns for years that were no longer under audit.

As the election approached, the campaign reverted to pure legalism. During a vice presidential debate in October 2016, while maintaining that Trump would release the returns when the audit was complete, Mike Pence said, "Look, Donald Trump has filed over 100 pages of financial disclosure, which is what the law requires." The Indiana governor was moving the goalpost; he was also changing the subject. The controversy over Trump's tax returns had never been a controversy about legal compliance; rather, it was about Trump's rejection of a near-universal expectation of a serious presidential candidate—at least in modern times. In the four decades between 1976 and 2016, every major-party presidential candidate had released his or her tax returns, with the exception of Gerald Ford, who released only summary data and subsequently lost the election.

The norm began with Richard Nixon, who in 1973, amid the scandals that eventually consumed him, released his tax returns, famously telling the country, "I am not a crook." There was no law, then as now, that required him to do so. The practice caught on as a norm because candidates wanted to prove that they had paid their taxes—a baseline civic responsibility—and because releasing returns signaled a general embrace of financial transparency. After all, if a candidate *didn't* release tax returns, everyone would assume he or she had something to hide.

When Trump defied basic expectations of financial transparency, commentators speculated that doing so would hurt his electoral chances.

Mitt Romney, for example, called the failure to release returns "disqualifying." People like Romney presumed that financial transparency mattered to voters, and that a promise to comply with the norm at some future date would not suffice.

Trump was, in effect, daring the public to take traditional expectations of the presidency seriously—and the public elected him anyway, either because it blinked in the face of the dare or because it hadn't actually cared so much in the first place. At which point Trump went back on his commitment. Two days after the inauguration, White House counselor Kellyanne Conway announced that he would not be releasing his tax returns: "We litigated this all through the election. People didn't care." Conway later attempted to walk back the statement, reverting to the script about waiting out the audit. Two years later, the president's former lawyer, Michael Cohen, would testify before Congress that Trump had indicated that he was afraid that releasing the taxes would spur a future audit. Cohen said that he never saw evidence that the audit was real. Contrary to the representations of the president and his staff, Cohen testified that he presumed Trump "is not under audit."

Three months into office, Trump gave voice to his resentment that anyone took his promise to release his returns seriously. In April 2017 he tweeted, "I did what was an almost an impossible thing to do for a Republican—easily won the Electoral College! Now Tax Returns are brought up again?" Trump, always emotionally transparent even when resisting financial transparency, was openly complaining that anyone would suggest that, having successfully stalled long enough to get into office, he was still expected to keep his original promise. Having dared the public to do something about his refusal to release his returns in a timely fashion, he was now daring the public—and Congress—to do something about his refusal to honor the commitment he did make. Once again, the brazenness of the dare won the day. As of this writing, Trump has still released no returns; a congressional committee has formally sought them, and the Treasury Department refused the demand despite a clear statute authorizing the request, triggering litigation. In May 2019 he defiantly tweeted, "I won the 2016 Election partially based on no Tax Returns while I am under audit (which I still am), and the voters didn't care. Now the Radical Left Democrats want to again relitigate this matter. Make it a part of the 2020 Election!"

Refusing to disclose his tax returns may have been Trump's first breach of the traditional president's expectations of transparency and non-corruption, but it would hardly be his last. Indeed, the pattern he established with the tax return dare has played out over and over again across different ethical arenas—arenas in which Congress has generally refrained from directly seeking to regulate the presidency. In ways large and small, he has put the powers of the American presidency to work for his friends, his family, and himself. His cabinet has done likewise, resulting in serial resignations in disgrace of officials and a cloud of suspicion hanging over others still in office. Trump has scoffed at appearance problems and actual ethical misconduct alike. Each scoff calls a bluff.

Trump's challenge to the traditional presidency's approach to corruption, quite simply, is the "I dare you" principle. It is an approach that brazenly breaches ethical expectations and waits to see if the public and the other branches of government will force him to observe them. It is an approach that cheerfully advertises corruption, even while promising to "drain the swamp." It is an approach that, particularly from a liar, has an odd quality of honesty. Trump is not even pretending to civic virtue here. He is practically bragging about his conflicts. The message, across nearly all areas, is the same as his message about his tax returns: I will do as I please unless and until something forces me to do otherwise. Where Congress, the judiciary, or the electorate itself has bet that the president cannot get away with it, Trump flamboyantly bets that he can.

In making this bet, Trump isn't just banking on inertia in Congress or the lethargy or restraint of the judiciary. He is actively betting against the framers' vision of an at least minimally virtuous presidency and the Constitution they designed to achieve it. The framers cared a great deal about preventing corruption and very deliberately set out to safeguard the American government. Once again, Trump is proposing an alternative vision of the presidency, one that dispenses with the accumulated restraints of more than two centuries.

The drafters of the Constitution cared about preventing corruption because they recognized the stakes. They believed that the United States would survive only if elected officials worked for the public good. If, instead, corrupt officials used public office for private gain, the system would crumble. In non-republican systems, legitimacy flowed from birth and family. But if republicanism was to have legs, legitimacy would have to flow from public consent to the honest services of people who had no inherent right to rule. Corruption would make such consent impossible. In a letter read at the Constitutional Convention, Benjamin Franklin warned,

> There are two passions which have a powerful influence in the affairs of men. These are ambition and avarice; the love of power, and the love of money. Separately, each of these has great force in prompting men to action; but when united in view of the same object, they have in many minds the most violent effect. Place before the eyes of such men a post of honour that shall at the same time be a place of profit, and they will move heaven and earth to obtain it ... And of what kind are the men that will strive for this profitable pre-eminence, through all the bustle of cabal, the heat of contention, the infinite mutual abuse of parties, tearing to pieces the best of characters? It will not be the wise and moderate, the lovers of peace and good order, the men fittest for the trust. It will be the bold and the violent, the men of strong passions and indefatigable activity in their selfish pursuits.

George Mason put it in somewhat starker terms: "If we do not provide against corruption, our government will soon be at an end."

People don't tend to think about the various mundane technicalities of federal ethics regulations as central to furthering the framers' vision or as embodying an ideal that government officials should act for the common interest rather than their own. Usually, they think of ethics rules as dealing primarily with money and conflicts of interest and paperwork. Fundamentally, however, ethics rules are about loyalty and democratic legitimacy. They protect the basic premise that government officials should work exclusively for the benefit of the electorate. And in the founding era, they reflected another critical value: the nation's independence from foreign influence.

Indeed, fundamentally, ethics rules are about national security protections as well. Many national security and foreign policy decisions reflect a delicate balance of policies, values, and strategy. There are more close calls than obvious answers, and it can be impossible to identify the effects of improper bias in retrospect. Even those who differ on policy views share the common understanding that a president's decisions must be guided by the best interests of the United States as the commander in chief understands them. Ethical transparency is critical to national security because it ensures that personal financial interests are not placed before the interests of the country. The White House and the cabinet are charged with immensely consequential decisions; not infrequently, they determine matters of life and death. The legitimacy of the office of the presidency rests on public faith that the government is placing the interests of the country first. The demand for adequate ethics disclosure and vetting reflects the national security strategy of—as President Ronald Reagan put it—"Trust, but verify." The political system asks for verification that government officials are free from undue influence, for such influence goes to the core of basic democratic legitimacy. There should be no questions regarding the purity of the motives of individuals authorized to place American soldiers, foreign service officers, or intelligence agents in harm's way. Because of the necessary secrecy that surrounds a great many of these decisions, full vetting and transparency at the outset are critical to ensuring that the executive branch is, in fact, placing country first and also critical to maintaining basic integrity and legitimacy in the eyes of the people.

Corruption and foreign influence were actually major concerns of the constitutional framers. The law professor and political activist Zephyr Teachout argues that preventing corruption—or, conversely, fostering ethical behavior on the part of public officials—motivated many familiar constitutional features and also underpinned some of the Constitution's more obscure provisions. She calls this the "anti-corruption principle." Although people tend to think of the Constitution as dealing with governmental structures and powers and the protection of individual rights, preventing corruption is also a significant part of what the document is about.

The oath of office, as we have seen, embeds within the presidency an expectation of a certain minimal measure of civic virtue. In classical republicanism, in which the founders were steeped, civic virtue and corruption are opposing orientations. Officials with civic virtue act out of an interest in the public good rather than an interest in personal gain or enrichment. Teachout writes that corrupt officials, on the other hand, are "tempted by narcissism, ambition, or luxury, to place private gain before public good in their public actions." In *Federalist* 51, James Madison famously opined, "In framing a government which is to be administered by men over men, the great difficulty lies in this: you must first enable the government to control the governed; and in the next place oblige it to control itself."

The framers worried that a government of men carried with it the risks inherent in human nature: that officials would make decisions based on self-interest or monetary gain, that they would protect their positions of power by buying political loyalty, and that corruption would corrode faith in government and lead to the country's demise. Although the founders were more worried about corruption in the legislature, they recognized the possibility of corruption in the executive. The oath may embed an expectation of virtue, but the founders did not guard such an important principle with a promise alone. They designed a government that would, in a number of different ways, guard against corruption in elected officials. They did so through express constitutional provisions and through structural bulwarks.

There was, for starters, the basic structure of the Constitution. Federalism, the separation of powers, and the checks and balances generally promote good governance and ensure considered decision-making; divided power and multiple decision points also lessen the likelihood that corruption at any one point will infect government action and maximize the likelihood that it will be discovered and pushed back against by some empowered actor at some level of government.

There are also a number of structural constitutional features that ward off executive corruption specifically. For instance, the Constitution vests the taxing and appropriations powers—the ability to raise and spend money—in the legislature, in part to prevent the executive from buying political loyalty. The legislative role in foreign affairs itself was designed, in part, as a defense against foreign influence on and corruption of the presidency. And the Electoral College itself, as Hamilton noted, was designed to avoid making "the appointment of the President to depend on any preexisting bodies of men."

There are also specific constitutional constraints on the president's ability to accept gifts and money. Twin provisions of the Constitution, the so-called emoluments clauses, speak to the personal enrichment of officeholders. Article I's foreign emoluments clause, which constrains officeholders across the executive branch, declares, "No Title of Nobility shall be granted by the United States: And no Person holding any Office of Profit or Trust under them, shall, without the Consent of the Congress, accept of any present, Emolument, Office, or Title, of any kind whatever, from any King, Prince, or foreign State." Article II adds the so-called domestic emoluments clause, which imposes an express restraint on the president: "The President shall, at stated Times, receive for his Services, a Compensation, which shall neither be increased nor diminished during the Period for which he shall have been elected, and he shall not receive within that Period any other Emolument from the United States, or any of them."

Of course, the framers did not anticipate every bad thing that government officials might try to get away with. It was through the lived experience of democratic government over time that the country built onto the foundational constitutional principles specific ethics laws and executive regulations. In that process, the nation elaborated its ideas of what ethics and good government actually entail.

The rich history of ethics legislation and regulation developed largely as a reaction to specific events. The history of ethics laws is the history of political scandal—a history of the country figuring out what people could and could not get away with.

Ethics laws and regulations in the United States evolve reactively in conversation with political scandal. Usually those scandals don't involve the president himself. In the early republic, for example, government officials routinely moonlighted as representatives of private interests before government agencies. The practice was especially rampant in the years following the Mexican-American War, with veterans and citizens alike bringing claims against the government. Ohio senator Thomas Corwin won $500,000 for one such claimant for the alleged destruction of a silver mine. Corwin was later serving as secretary of the Treasury in the Millard Fillmore administration when, in 1852, it became known that this silver mine had never existed. The resulting scandal prompted the creation of the precursor to the U.S. Court of Federal Claims and the earliest legislative prohibition on federal employees representing private interests in matters before the government.

As government and its expenditures grew throughout the nineteenth century, so too did public concern over corruption. Civil War production and the exponential growth of government contracts, coupled with several high-profile scandals, spurred laws regulating government procurement practices and further restricting federal employees from representing private interests. The Whiskey Ring and other scandals exposed during Ulysses S. Grant's administration in the later 1870s drew significant public and congressional attention. In the 1920s, the Teapot Dome scandal, in which President Warren Harding's interior secretary was caught trading oil leases on federal land for bribes, enraged the public anew. Teapot Dome did lead to one of the first successful uses of the special prosecutor, a matter we will return to in later chapters. But that investigation drew to a close without prompting significant ethics reforms. Teapot Dome did, however, lead to the passage of the statutory provisions allowing Congress to inspect individual tax returns—the very law Congress is relying on in requesting Trump's returns now.

Later in the twentieth century, ethics scandals in the executive branch not only captured public attention but also spurred reforms to ethics laws. Amid scandal and pressure from political adversaries, President Harry Truman attempted to get ahead of ethics issues by proposing large-scale ethics reform, including, for the first time, that federal employees make broad financial disclosures. In a special message to Congress, he explained that, though he didn't like the idea of subjecting public officials to rules that didn't apply to the whole population,

> public office is a privilege, not a right. And people who accept the
> privilege of holding office in the Government, must of necessity
> expect that their entire conduct should be open to inspection by the
> people they are serving. With all the questions that are being raised
> today about the probity and honesty of public officials, I think all
> of us should be prepared to place the facts about our income on the
> public record . . . This is the best protection we can give ourselves
> and all of our co-workers against the charge of widespread graft and
> favoritism in the public service.

In the 1970s Watergate provided the impetus for the Ethics in Government Act of 1978, the most robust legislative reform to ethics laws. The act required extensive public financial disclosures by senior officials. The law also created the Office of Government Ethics, an independent overseer of ethics in the executive branch.

The Iran-Contra scandal likewise spurred ethics reform. The scandal culminated in the prosecution of Oliver North, a staffer on President Reagan's National Security Council, for, among other things, accepting a bribe. North's conviction was later overturned, but the scandal spurred action by the subsequent George H. W. Bush administration. Though Bush pardoned a number of those convicted as a result of the Iran-Contra investigation, in 1989 he ordered the creation of uniform ethics rules across the executive branch. These rules prevent federal employees from using public office for private gain, soliciting or accepting gifts from those with business before the government, and engaging in outside employment that might pose a conflict, among other basic principles. At the same time, Congress passed legislation prohibiting executive branch employees from receiving honoraria from nongovernmental sources—an attempt to prevent bribes—though the Supreme Court later overturned this law on First Amendment grounds.

The result of these developments was an edifice of modern regulation of conflicts of interest that has three broad components: disclosure, disqualification, and divestiture. First, government officials must make extensive financial disclosures, identifying conflicts being the first step in preventing harms. Second, executive employees are not only required to disclose nondivested assets; they are also criminally prohibited from substantially working on matters in which they have a financial interest. Because government ethics go to public legitimacy, even the appearance of a conflict is normally not allowed. For just about everyone, recusal is an elegant solution for sidestepping conflicts while preserving government legitimacy. But it does not work well for the president and the vice president, who have unavoidable constitutional duties. Legislation requiring the president to recuse himself in all instances of personal financial conflict might run up against the fact that the president cannot realistically recuse himself from ordering military action, for instance. Because Article II vests powers specifically in the person of the president, there are situations in which he simply cannot recuse himself. The president cannot really delegate the pardon power, for instance, or the power to veto legislation. In order to avoid confronting the complex constitutional questions regarding the extent to which Congress can constrain the president, laws about recusals expressly exclude the president and vice president.

Third and finally, executive branch officials can resolve conflicts altogether and not worry about recusal on a case-by-case basis by divesting themselves of assets likely to present problems. It is for this reason, recognizing that they cannot recuse themselves from certain matters, that modern presidents have tended to divest or otherwise shield themselves from knowledge about their financial assets—for example, by putting assets in a blind trust.

It has always been theoretically possible for presidents to flout the rules. As to executive regulations, the president can change those and is not bound by them anyway. The separation of powers dictates that Congress and the courts cannot constrain a president from performing her constitutional functions—even in the face of conflicts.

But normal presidents have had strong incentives for self-constraint, just as they have strong incentives to tell the truth when possible. The Office of Government Ethics has indicated to previous administrations that even though the president and vice president are exempt from such things as recusal laws "as a matter of policy, [they] should conduct themselves as if they were so bound." The policy goal furthered by the president's acting as if he is constrained by ethics rules is basic democratic legitimacy and public confidence in the conduct of government.

Presidents have behaved this way because the traditional presidency has assumed that the president needs to be viewed as ethical. By adhering to ethics practices, as with telling the truth, presidents develop reserves of credibility. The public has no trouble accepting that there are some areas in which a president has no way to avoid a conflict; for example, the president and his family and friends pay taxes, and the president's policies will certainly affect tax rates. But in order to achieve her policy goals, the president needs the public to believe that despite the unavoidable conflicts, she is advocating a particular tax policy because she believes it is in the interests of the country generally, even if it incidentally helps her or her family. She establishes the credibility needed in situations of unavoidable conflict by avoiding conflicts where she can. The result is a set of murky legal lines but fairly clear practice. Congress typically gives the executive branch constitutional breathing room by exempting the president in order to avoid constitutional issues. And the president voluntarily complies where possible, anyway. In other cases, where Congress does not impose an explicit carve-out, the president defers to the legislature by complying as a prudential and policy matter and not testing the issue in court. Neither side pushes to adjudicate matters, so questions remain unanswered in a formal sense while presidents benefit from meeting ethics expectations in functional terms. The assumption is that presidents will have strong incentives to behave ethically and to lead ethical administrations—and to be seen as doing both. That's what normal presidents do. But Trump has other ideas.

Shortly after the anniversary of his first year in office, he presided over a dinner of European business leaders during the World Economic Forum in Davos, Switzerland. Beginning a roundtable in which each attendee obsequiously praised him in turn, the president gestured to his left, urging "one of the very big, powerful businesspeople of the world" to go first. Joe Kaeser, the CEO of Siemens, introduced himself, saying, "Obviously, I work for Siemens," before going on to laud the president for the passage of his tax reform legislation. Trump interrupted Kaeser to jokingly chide the German on underselling his credentials, telling the group, "By the way, when he says he works for Siemens, he's the president of Siemens. But that's okay. It's a good way of saying it."

Without missing a beat, Kaeser responded, "But don't you work for your country?"

Nervous laughter filled the room as Trump quickly recovered, saying, "Yeah, we work for our country. That's right. I agree. Same thing," and he brusquely moved along.

The exchange lasted less than a minute but revealed more than Trump might have realized at the time. He needed to be reminded that a president—be it of a company or a country—works for someone else. Unlike the head of the Trump Organization, neither the president of Siemens nor the President of the United States is the owner. He is not a king. And he does not "work" for the country as some generous benefactor who makes the country great again. Rather, he works for the people in a more prosaic sense; he is their employee, and he is accountable as such. In the case of Siemens, the president is accountable to shareholders; in the case of the nation, he is accountable to voters.

One of the hallmarks of Donald Trump's personal narrative is that he has never worked for anyone but himself. Over the decades he has meticulously cultivated an image—built on fiction as often as fact—of a self-made man, the boss. Nothing about the way he described the presidency, before or after taking office, suggested a shift in this view of himself. He did not speak of public service and civic duty, but instead of running the country like his business and, as he put it years earlier, being "the first presidential candidate to run and make money on it." Trump's former lawyer, Cohen, testified that Trump often said the campaign "was going to be the 'greatest infomercial in political history.'"

That attitude has persisted into his presidency largely unabated. Trump has rejected routine disclosure of basic financial information—not just his tax returns, but all manner of information about the business activities, past and present, of the Trump Organization, which is a privately held entity owned by him. Trump has made a limited set of financial disclosures, but enormous questions remain about the most basic aspects of his financial life. Given the suspicions about his prior business with Russian entities, for one example, that's a huge omission.

The magnitude of that omission came to life especially vividly in October 2018, when *The New York Times* published a mammoth article about Trump's financial and tax history, based on tax returns and financial records the paper had obtained. According to the *Times*, "Trump participated in dubious tax schemes during the 1990s, including instances of outright fraud, that greatly increased the fortune he received from his parents." The paper also reported that Trump "received the equivalent today of at least $413 million from his father's real estate empire, starting when he was a toddler and continuing to this day" and that "this money came to Mr. Trump because he helped his parents dodge taxes" by setting up "a sham corporation to disguise millions of dollars in gifts," facilitating "improper tax deductions worth millions more," and undervaluing "real estate holdings by hundreds of millions of dollars on tax returns, sharply reducing the tax bill when those properties were transferred to him and his siblings."

Given the gravity of the suspicions, which range from tax fraud to anxieties about his business interactions with foreign actors, Trump's refusal to disclose represents a bit more than a slackening of the recent presidential commitment to financial transparency. It is the flat and very public refusal to play by the known rules. It is a statement that whatever concerns the public or the press may have about the president's finances—and the conduct that may lie beneath those finances—the president does not care and will do nothing that he is not forced to do to alleviate the concerns.

Even if Trump had disclosed sufficient financial information, disclosure is still a limited remedy. Fundamentally, disclosure itself does not resolve a conflict; it just makes the public aware of it. Because recusal is unavailable and disclosure is insufficient, most presidents have decided to divest in order to resolve financial conflicts. In the modern era, the key mechanism for handling personal financial conflicts of the president has been the creation of a blind trust. Establishing a blind trust is a halfway measure, short of full divestment but useful as it creates meaningful separation—including informational separation—between the officeholder and the management of the assets. To execute a blind trust, the official transfers control and responsibility of invested assets to a trustee, and though the official may at the outset put forth certain guidelines for how the trust is to be managed, communication between the official and the trustee is then sharply limited.

Trump is not the first president to struggle with how to handle his personal assets while in office—nor is he the first to keep a hand in his business affairs. Even George Washington turns out to have engaged in secret land purchases from the federal government while he was president. President Lyndon Johnson was the first to establish a supposedly blind trust, opting not to divest his ownership of the Austin, Texas, radio and television station KTBC, which was owned by his family. Robert Caro, Johnson's preeminent biographer, claims that this blind trust was a mockery and that the "establishment of the trust was virtually simultaneous with the installation in the Oval Office of private telephone lines to certain Texas attorneys associated with the administration of the trust—and over those lines, during the entire five years of his presidency, Johnson personally directed his business affairs, down to the most minute details." Caro goes so far as to argue that President Johnson "did not hesitate to use the power of the presidency itself, and to use it with utter ruthlessness" in the management of his private business affairs.

Although Johnson's blind trust may have been a ruse, presidents since Johnson have followed his example more honestly. Reagan executed a true blind trust, liquidating some of his assets and putting them into certifications to form the blind trust, which totaled $740,000. However, he kept the bulk of his assets outside of the trust, including his ranch near Santa Barbara and his private residence in Los Angeles. George H. W. Bush, even as vice president, used a diversified trust, which is more restrictive than a blind trust in that he could not even see dividends or summaries from the trustee. After scrutiny over health-care-related stocks, the Clintons put their assets into a blind trust in 1993. In 2007, during Hillary Clinton's first presidential run, additional concerns over the appearance of conflicts spurred the pair to fully liquidate the assets held in the blind trust.

If this all sounds like small potatoes, that's because Trump has taken the sorts of ethics concerns that have arisen in past administrations and—as he is wont to do—supersized them and slapped a gold-plated sign with his name on them. Right through the transition, the notion of a pres-

ident maintaining ownership and control of something like the Trump
Organization while in office was unthinkable—unthinkable, that is, except to Trump and tens of millions of his voters, whom he acculturated to
the idea that he could properly run a business empire and the country at
the same time. He did this even while blasting his opponent's sometimes
unflattering financial dealings as the height of corruption—presiding over
chants of "lock her up." In Trump's defense, he didn't try especially hard
to hide his plans to wear a business hat alongside his public service hat. He
never said he was going to actually give up his business, even as experts
warned that only full divestment would resolve the manifold conflicts.
He made it known that the transparently insufficient measure of handing
control of his business to his children was the most he was willing to do.
Trump was daring someone to make him comply. And again, no one did.

In November 2016, just after his election, Trump seemed for a moment to shift gears on this point. He tweeted that he would leave his "great
business in total." The Office of Government Ethics, which is responsible
for overseeing and enforcing ethics rules within the executive branch,
rushed to praise the move in hopes of further encouraging the president-
elect. Its official Twitter account responded, "@realDonaldTrump Bravo!
Only way to resolve these conflicts of interest is to divest. Good call!" The
office subsequently released an official statement, explaining the unchar-
acteristic tone: "Like everyone else, we were excited this morning to read
the President-elect's Twitter feed indicating that he wants to be free of
conflicts of interest. OGE applauds that goal, which is consistent with an
opinion OGE issued in 1983. Divestiture resolves conflicts of interest in a
way that transferring control does not."

The tweet turned out to be premature. Just nine days before his inauguration, Trump held a press conference to announce his plan for avoiding financial conflicts of interest. It was not divestment. It was not a blind
trust. It was, once again, the dare.

Trump's lawyer Sheri Dillon first highlighted that federal financial
conflict laws do not legally apply to the president. However, she explained,

Mr. Trump would take steps to avoid such conflicts. First, he would pass control of the Trump Organization to his eldest two sons, Donald Jr. and Eric. The Trump Organization would hire watchdogs to review possible conflicts. Trump himself would not view the company's detailed financial reports. The Trump Organization would not engage any "new" foreign deals—a step away from a position he took just a month earlier, when the president-elect promised that his company would do "no new deals" of any sort—and hotel profits coming from foreign governments would go to the coffers of the Treasury. On the press conference table sat stacks of manila folders, purportedly containing many relevant documents and representing the sophistication and complexity of the plan. Reporters were not permitted to inspect the contents.

After Trump announced his plan to avoid financial conflicts of interest by naming his children to run his business, Walter Shaub, the director of the Office of Government Ethics, publicly critiqued the plan in an effort to pressure the president-elect to do more. Shaub pulled no punches:

> I think *Politico* called this a "half-blind" trust, but it's not even halfway blind. The only thing this has in common with a blind trust is the label, "trust." His sons are still running the businesses, and, of course, he knows what he owns. His own attorney said today that he can't "un-know" that he owns Trump Tower. The same is true of his other holdings. The idea of limiting direct communication about the business is wholly inadequate. That's not how a blind trust works. There's not supposed to be any information at all.

Shaub noted that although divestiture is costly, it is the price of public service and a sacrifice many public servants have made upon entering office. He said, "I don't think divestiture is too high a price to pay to be the President of the United States of America."

Armed with the moral high ground but no enforcement authority,

Shaub resigned. He believed that given the Trump administration's resistance to ethics oversight, he could do more outside government to strengthen the ethics regime than he could as director of OGE. In the summer of 2018, the Trump administration's White House ethics lawyer Stefan Passantino resigned; later reports suggested that his departure was spurred by the administration's disregard for ethics regulations and norms. Without confirming his motivations directly, Passantino later conceded that "being the Trump ethics guys is not all roses" and that the administration's sense that it should not merely accept norms and was there to "overturn the apple cart" stood, as Passantino put it, "exactly, diametrically opposed to [his] mandate" as an ethics official.

Trump's failure to divest, or at least to put his assets in a truly blind trust—the original ethical sin of his administration—is in some ways his largest bet and the one that matters most to him. He bet that political outrage over his conflicts of interest would abate over time. And he appears to have been right on that score. He also bet that the courts and the Constitution wouldn't stop him. The judiciary moves at its own glacial pace, so the results of that gamble are yet to be seen. Even if a court were to order him to divest at some point years into his administration, Trump would be in no worse a position than when Shaub first begged him to give up his business for the sake of the country. Congress, the entity that could more quickly respond to Trump's dare, has, as of this writing, not held a hearing on the subject.

Perhaps no building stands as a better symbolic monument to the dare than the Trump International Hotel in Washington, D.C. The hotel, which occupies the Old Post Office Pavilion at 1100 Pennsylvania Avenue in Northwest Washington, has a less recognizable address than does its neighbor a few blocks north at 1600 Pennsylvania, but it is perhaps a better representation of the current president. The building, which was the district's largest working post office until 1914, is owned by the federal government, and its tower is a local landmark in Washington. Back in 2012, amid some controversy, the General Services Administration awarded the Trump Organization a bid to develop the space into a hotel. The hotel opened thirteen days before Donald Trump was elected President of the United States. That is, when Trump took the oath of office promising to preserve and protect the Constitution, he did so down the street from a building owned by the government he would head, the government that leased to him a building at which anyone with a working credit card—including any foreign government—could pay him personally $600 per night for a room. The figure itself is telling. The Trump Hotel had originally planned to charge a little over $400 for the average room, but it raised its rates shortly after the inauguration. Throughout Trump's presidency, the hotel has charged more than its competitors despite a substantially lower occupancy rate, apparently tacking on a presidential premium.

Once the purview of the wonkiest of government lawyers, the emoluments clauses are having their fifteen minutes of fame thanks to the president's dares. As with other ethics laws, the foreign emoluments clause was drafted in response to a scandal. When Benjamin Franklin departed France, King Louis XVI gave Franklin a portrait of himself encrusted with 408 diamonds. It struck the founders that avoiding extravagant gifts from foreign governments was probably necessary to keep public officials virtuous and free of conflicted loyalties. Ironically, in the past, presidents have had to confront the foreign emoluments clause because of their perceived virtue. Three presidents have been awarded the Nobel Peace Prize while in office—Teddy Roosevelt, Woodrow Wilson, and Barack Obama. When Obama won the prize—which included $1.4 million in cash—he sought guidance from the Office of Legal Counsel about the money. The office produced a thirteen-page memorandum concluding that the foreign emoluments clause did apply to the president, that the prize was in fact an emolument, but that the awarding committee did not qualify as a foreign government. Thus Obama was entitled to accept it without congressional permission. Obama did so and distributed the money to ten charities. Roosevelt and Wilson also accepted their awards without asking

Congress. Roosevelt donated his prize money to charity but kept the gold medal to "hand it on to [his] children as a precious heirloom." Wilson may have just pocketed the cash.

There is little risk of Donald Trump's being awarded the Nobel Peace Prize anytime soon, though he has reportedly exerted great effort in attempting to convince foreign leaders to nominate him. Instead, it is Trump's extensive international business dealings that have put a spotlight on the foreign emoluments clause in particular, with scholars dividing on whether the provision technically prohibits him from operating and profiting from his international business.

Trump's attorneys argued in a white paper that "neither the Constitution nor federal law prohibits the President or Vice President from owning or operating businesses independent of their official duties." They reasoned that these transactions cannot constitute "presents" because the Trump Organization receives fair market value, and that they are not "emoluments" because the original public meaning of "emolument" was "a payment or other benefit received as a consequence of discharging the duties of an *office*." They have argued the same in court, so far to little avail. Critics fear that Trump is inappropriately profiting from the presidency because foreign officials, wanting to ingratiate themselves with him, stay at his hotels. And there is plenty of evidence that he is, in fact, profiting from the proximity of this property to his presidency. Numerous press reports have indicated that the Trump Organization broadly has not fared well during his presidency. *The Washington Post*, for example, has reported that Trump's luxury hotels in New York and Chicago are both suffering: "Revenue at both properties dropped noticeably as Trump's political career took off. The decreases have stirred tensions in the buildings and left many investors worried that the Trump brand may be curdling in the liberal cities where Trump built much of his empire." But the D.C. hotel has thrived, as foreign governments—among others—have made a point of using it as a way to cozy up to the president. For instance, shortly after Trump's election, lobbyists representing the government of Saudi Arabia spent more than $270,000 on rooms at the D.C. hotel in the span of three months. In 2018, the Philippine embassy held an event commemorating the anniversary of its independence at the hotel, coincidentally at the same time that country's government was seeking to negotiate a new trade agreement with the United States. The government of Kuwait has for three years running held its National Day celebration at Trump's hotel. Turkey and other countries have made a point of using the hotel as well.

At the Trump Hotel, domestic emoluments questions mirror the foreign emoluments concerns. Just as a foreign government can funnel money to the president through the hotel, so too can any U.S. state government. The domestic emoluments clause prevents the president from receiving anything beyond his salary either from the United States or from any individual state. It is designed to prevent the president from profiting from the office and also to prevent Congress and state governments from effectively bribing him. How many state governments are paying for events at the hotel by way of currying favor with its owner? The State of Maine, for one, paid for forty rooms over a two-year period for the governor and his staff, to the tune of $22,000.

The courts have moved slowly on emoluments matters, and it remains unclear whether the Constitution will ultimately be understood to tolerate this sort of thing or forbid it. That said, the courts have moved. In one lawsuit, a federal district court has found that members of Congress have standing to raise the issue, but, as of this writing, the court has not reached the merits of it. A different court found that the governments of Maryland and the District of Columbia have standing to raise the problem, that they "have plausibly alleged that the President has been receiving or is potentially able to receive 'emoluments' from foreign, the federal, and state governments in violation of the Constitution" and blocked an immediate appeal of that question and allowed discovery to go forward. A federal appeals court reversed this ruling. All these rulings will face continued challenges.

There is a reason that this is the first time courts are deciding these emoluments questions, and the reason is that prior presidents actually cared about not breaching the Constitution. They didn't issue Trump-like dares. When Reagan was elected, he solicited extensive legal opinions on how to resolve the matter of his California state pension. California state law dictated that Reagan, as a former state employee, be paid a pension, but Reagan didn't want to improperly receive money from a state. Ultimately, the government lawyers concluded that because the pension was not discretionary, it did not qualify as an emolument.

Trump hasn't bothered to seek legal opinions from the government on his manifold emoluments concerns, save for one. In the Old Post Office Building lease between the Trump Organization and the General Services Administration, there is a provision that no elected official may be party to or benefit from the lease in any way. Trump was not a government official when he signed the lease, but what happened when he won the election? He apparently wasn't interested in leaving the answer to this question to chance. Seven and a half hours after his inauguration, he installed a new acting head of the GSA—unusual speed for a relatively minor public post. Just over two months later, the GSA declared that Trump was in "full compliance" with the lease, despite the apparent conflict with its terms. In clearing the conflict, the GSA conferred an extraordinarily valuable benefit by saying that the president got to keep making money off his lease with the federal government. An Inspector General report released two years later concluded that GSA officials had improperly ignored constitutional questions related to the lease, failed to seek appropriate guidance from the Office of Legal Counsel, and that "GSA's decision-making process related to [Trump's] possible breach of the lease included serious shortcomings."

The Trump Hotel is one building. Whether the business arrangements in question violate the Constitution is a question that will ultimately be decided in litigation. But the conflicts are real, whether legal or not. Imagine them multiplied over the president's hundreds of other business interests around the globe and across the United States. Imagine the incentive to join the Mar-a-Lago Club or the Bedminster golf resort, putting tens or hundreds of thousands of dollars into the president's personal pockets by way of dining with him regularly. Bill Clinton rightly got in trouble for letting campaign donors stay in the Lincoln Bedroom. The scandal seems like amateur hour by comparison. The donors and the donations were all disclosed. The money went to party committees, not to Clinton personally. Today, all over the world, people can give President Trump money: small amounts, large amounts, and giant amounts. They can give it not to his campaign, but to his personal business. These payments are not disclosed.

And Trump can give what are effectively political contributions to himself too. The supposedly nonprofit Trump inaugural committee paid an astonishing $1.5 million to the president's hotel, including $700,000 for event space at a rate of $175,000 per day. The committee did this despite internal objections that this price was far above market rate. "These events are in [the president-elect's] honor at his hotel and one of them is for family and close friends," one staffer wrote in concern at the time. "Please take into consideration that when this is audited it will become public knowledge."

It *has* become public knowledge. And once again, the President of the United States is daring us to do something about it.

Trump's ethics dare extends to his administration. The president controls ethics across the executive branch in two ways: by staffing the government and by fostering an ethical executive branch culture and punishing violations. Recognizing the power of staffing, the Constitution divides the responsibility between the president and Congress. The so-called appointments clause of the Constitution gives the president the power, with the advice and consent of the Senate, to appoint "Ambassadors, other public Ministers and Consuls, Judges of the supreme Court, and all other Officers of the United States, whose Appointments are not herein otherwise provided for, and which shall be established by Law."

Hamilton believed that the senatorial role in appointments "would be an excellent check upon a spirit of favoritism in the President, and would tend greatly to prevent the appointment of unfit characters from State prejudice, from family connection, from personal attachment, or from a view to popularity." It's a good theory. And in the past, presidents who were careless or corrupt in staffing practices ultimately paid a price. Harry Truman's legacy was marred by the numerous scandals caused by appointing ethically deficient people to important offices. The political scientist James Barber writes that Truman's "personal physician played the commodities market, then lied about it to Congress; his Appointments Secretary went to jail for fixing a tax case; one of his secretaries accepted an $8,500 mink coat; his military aide saw nothing wrong with accepting the gift of not one, but seven deep freezers. It was a ragtag crew, a buzzing clot of 'five-percenters' and 'influence peddlers' flitting around Washington making arrangements for a price." Trump may ultimately pay an enormous price for the lax ethical standards he has set and the wholly inadequate vetting of nominees. But so far, staff ethics have been just another dare. Scandal after scandal has beset cabinet officials and White House staff alike, and Trump stands by people until doing so is no longer tenable—and then seemingly takes no lesson from the experience as to future hires.

During the transition, the director of OGE sent a letter to Senators Chuck Schumer and Elizabeth Warren warning that not all of Trump's nominees had submitted the paperwork required for the legally mandated ethics review. A large number of consequential—and controversial—confirmation hearings were scheduled in the absence of these reviews. OGE cautioned that the schedule would not allow sufficient time to complete them; this was especially true considering the complex financial backgrounds of Trump's "billionaire cabinet" and the necessity for highly detailed scrutiny of such individuals as the ExxonMobil CEO Rex Tillerson, who would go on to be confirmed as secretary of state. Usually the Senate refuses to schedule confirmation hearings until ethics reviews are complete, both so that members are fully informed in their votes and because the confirmation process serves as important leverage in ensuring full compliance. Once a nominee is confirmed by the Senate, there is little incentive for the individual to fully comply with ethics disclosure in a timely way, especially regarding potentially controversial issues. No matter, Trump forged ahead. He figured the Senate would confirm his people anyway. Again, he was right.

On multiple occasions since, cabinet officials have been able to remain in their posts through disqualifying ethics scandals only because a different cabinet official's ethics scandal was currently occupying the front page. Whether it's Tom Price, Scott Pruitt, Ryan Zinke, or Wilbur Ross, a culture of noncompliance with ethics norms has made noncompliance tolerable—or, at least, widened the window for it. The difference between Trump and Truman, however, is that Trump doesn't seem to care.

Other presidents have on occasion flagrantly challenged the boundaries of ethical governance. In 1960, President-elect John F. Kennedy infuriated many in Washington and across the country when he announced that he would appoint his younger brother Bobby Kennedy to serve as attorney general. Bobby Kennedy was thirty-five at the time, and he counted counsel to two Senate committees as nearly the whole of his legal experience. In short, he was utterly unqualified for the post. With the Kennedy experience as background, incidents of nepotism at post offices led Congress to pass the modern federal anti-nepotism statute, signed into law in 1967 by Lyndon Johnson. The broad law forbids "public officials"— expressly including the president—from appointing, employing, or in any way promoting family members to federal positions over which the official exercises jurisdiction or control.

The precise contours of the law are contested. But presidents since have largely refrained from testing its boundaries. Hillary Clinton's policy role in the Clinton White House on health-care matters represents something of an exception. In 1993 President Clinton named his wife as the unpaid chairperson of the President's Task Force on National Health Care Reform. In a lawsuit over the application of the Federal Advisory Committee Act to the task force, the D.C. Circuit Court of Appeals noted in an aside that it doubted that the anti-nepotism law applied to positions in the White House, as the White House might not qualify as an "agency" within the meaning of the anti-nepotism statute. But this is far from settled law.

Some argue, as the D.C. Circuit suggests, that the anti-nepotism statute bars relatives only from paid positions.

Once again, Trump has responded to legal uncertainty with a flamboyant dare: a wholehearted embrace of nepotism that simply challenges the political culture to restrain him if it can.

On this point, Trump has not been honest. He initially claimed that he would not appoint his children to any official administration role. But by December 2016 the president-elect's spokespeople began floating alternatives. Kellyanne Conway went on MSNBC's *Morning Joe* to explain that "the anti-nepotism law apparently has an exception if you want to work in the West Wing, because the president is able to appoint his own staff." As we have seen, nepotism was once a common practice in the White House back when presidents had to personally pay their own staffs. Once the White House staff was paid for by the Treasury, however, the notion of the taxpayers paying the president's family members became so unseemly that the practice significantly diminished. At least until Trump.

Just after his inauguration, the Justice Department's Office of Legal Counsel issued an opinion concluding that the federal anti-nepotism law did not prevent hiring family members to serve as White House staff. The opinion, following the D.C. Circuit's logic in a different case, explained that the law prevents nepotism in the staffing of "executive agencies" and that the White House is not, as a technical legal matter, an executive agency.

In the end, Trump brought not only his son-in-law, Jared Kushner, to the White House as a senior adviser but his daughter Ivanka Trump as well. Neither Jared nor Ivanka has any particular background or talents in their areas of assigned responsibility—consequential national interests ranging from domestic family leave policies to federal government infrastructure to Middle East peace.

Nor have Jared and Ivanka divested from their own business interests. Both have committed multiple ethics violations—from promoting their businesses in office to filing incomplete financial disclosures and untruthful security clearance forms. But then again, why should they bother with the rules? The president himself hasn't divested his assets. And he certainly isn't going to enforce the rules against his own children. In fact, he is willing to overturn the rules on behalf of his family. In early 2019 it emerged that the president had personally—over the objections of his intelligence community, his White House counsel, and his chief of staff—granted his son-in-law a top secret security clearance, which Kushner had previously been denied.

A culture of ethics is a fragile thing. It begins with the law, but it doesn't end there. The space the law leaves for self-dealing and graft, either by choice or because of the nature of the presidential office, is vast. And if a president makes a decision to exploit that space rather than prudentially protecting it—to push every line rather than drawing lines that set confidence-building boundaries, to dare the public rather than reassuring the public—the law will not substitute for political pushback as a remedy. The culture of ethics will decay. The decay begins at the head and spreads downward. If the president doesn't actually divest, why should anyone else? If the president's children aren't punished for ethical violations, why shouldn't others break the same rules with impunity? If cabinet officials keep their jobs despite scandals, why should those serving beneath them fear losing their own?

Thus far, Trump's bet has paid off to an astonishing degree. Nobody has taken up his dares. Congress has done little, though it may be beginning to stir. The courts, limited by the slow pace of litigation and legitimate substantive and procedural legal barriers to action, offer little short-term relief. So far, anyway, the only real pushback has come from prosecutors and state attorneys general who have probed the conduct of his campaign and foundation. And it has come from a dogged and relentless press, which has accomplished a great deal of disclosure—disclosure that, in turn, gives rise to the possibility of political response. As other billionaires eye the presidency, it's not hard to imagine them following the example of minimal ethical compliance and preserving their business entanglements. Contrary to former OGE director Shaub's admonition, as far as some very rich people were concerned, divestment has, in fact, been too high a price to pay for the presidency. Now, it seems, it doesn't need to be paid after all. As Trump has set the presidency to protecting his personal business interests and dared the polity to stop him, the polity has responded with a shrug. Perhaps a disgusted shrug, but a shrug nonetheless.

SEVEN

"The power to protect the guilty"

CORRUPTING JUSTICE

DONALD TRUMP HAD WAITED A LONG TIME FOR THIS MOMENT. The November 2018 midterm election campaign was over, and Democrats were riding an electoral backlash against the president to reclaim control of the House of Representatives. Now it was time: within twenty-four hours of the polls closing, the president fired Attorney General Jeff Sessions.

Sessions had been an early supporter of Trump's candidacy; as senator from Alabama, he'd given the long-shot candidate his first senatorial endorsement. And Trump had rewarded the early loyalty by announcing

Sessions as his pick to be attorney general less than two weeks after the election. But the honeymoon was short-lived; Trump regretted his choice almost immediately, and he wasn't shy about saying so. He also wasn't shy about saying why: he had a vision of how the Justice Department was supposed to work, and Sessions hadn't served that vision.

The trouble began in Sessions's very first month in office. That month, the new attorney general committed the unforgivable sin of recusing himself from oversight of the Russia investigation. It didn't matter to Trump that Sessions's recusal was in line with the counsel of career government attorneys and was required under Department of Justice conflict regulations. In the run-up to Sessions's announcement of recusal, Trump launched an aggressive campaign to convince him to ignore what the attorney general himself viewed as clear requirements to step aside. The president directed White House counsel Don McGahn to call Sessions and urge him to reverse his decision. When Sessions told McGahn that he intended to follow the rules, the White House ratcheted up the pressure; McGahn spent the day calling the attorney general's personal counsel, his chief of staff, and Senate majority leader Mitch McConnell, and he called Sessions personally twice more. McGahn's calls were not the only ones Sessions received that day from White House advisers lobbying against his recusal. But Sessions held firm. On March 2, 2017, the Justice Department announced that the attorney general had stepped aside from all matters related to the 2016 elections, including the Russia investigation. Not only was Sessions recused and thus unable to—as Trump understood the matter—"protect" Trump from the investigation; he also now stood in the way of Trump's ability to find someone who would.

The president was furious. He raged in the Oval Office at McGahn for his failure to prevent Sessions's recusal, saying, "I don't have a lawyer." It didn't matter that Trump himself had nominated the deputy attorney general, Rod Rosenstein, who, once confirmed, would serve in Sessions's place on the Russia probe. All that mattered was that Sessions had rendered himself useless for purposes of watching Trump's back. When the attorney general announced his recusal, McGahn backed off, and the Office of the White House Counsel gave the instruction that no one should have contact with Sessions on the matter, noting "serious concerns about obstruction." That weekend, however, the president pulled Sessions aside at Mar-a-Lago and pressured him to reverse the recusal. He would repeat the request at some later point, calling Sessions at home to press it. Still, the attorney general refused to change his mind.

In May, when FBI director James Comey refused to tell a congressional committee that the president wasn't under investigation, Trump fumed against Sessions, saying, "This is terrible Jeff. It's all because you recused . . . I appointed you and you recused yourself. You left me on an island. I can't do anything." Two weeks later, when Rosenstein appointed Special Counsel Robert Mueller, the president again directed his fury at Sessions, saying, "You were supposed to protect me" and insisting that Sessions resign. The next day, Sessions handed over a resignation letter, but Trump aides prevailed on him to refuse it. Still, Trump held on to the letter for two weeks before returning it with the note "Not accepted."

The next month, Trump again tried to convince Sessions to unrecuse himself, this time by attempting to send a message through his former campaign manager, Corey Lewandowski. After following up in July with Lewandowski—who never delivered the message—the president gave an unplanned interview to *The New York Times* complaining that had he known the attorney general would recuse himself, he "would have picked somebody else" for the job. A few days later, Trump tore into Sessions on Twitter, criticizing "our beleaguered A.G.," as he put it, for failing to aggressively investigate his former opponent Hillary Clinton. Behind the scenes, he was again demanding that Sessions resign.

This time, Congress took notice of the warning shots against Sessions and actually mobilized to deter another firing of senior law enforcement leadership. Republican senator Lindsey Graham—who had not yet become Trump's chief Senate ally—shot back, saying that if Trump fired the attorney general, there would be "holy hell to pay." And for a while Trump backed down. It wasn't until February 2018 that he resumed his public campaign, tweeting "Why aren't Dem crimes under investigation? Ask Jeff Sessions!" and a week later calling Sessions's handling of spurious allegations of FISA abuse "DISGRACEFUL!" Trump's rage at Sessions burst into public occasionally over the spring and summer, typically in the form of a dyspeptic tweet.

By August, he would be restrained no more. That month, he tweeted invective at the attorney general almost a dozen times and, in interviews, accused him of incompetence. Rumors of Sessions's imminent dismissal swirled, but the attorney general stubbornly tolerated the public humiliation and abuse. The president's aides scrambled to control the fallout, warning the president that firing Sessions should wait until after the November 2018 midterm elections. Graham himself offered the compromise. He no longer threatened "holy hell" but instead pronounced that Trump was "entitled to [have] an attorney general he has faith in." He added, "That's an important office in the country, and after the election, I think there will be some serious discussions about a new attorney general."

The message was clear. Trump could fire Sessions, but not before the midterms. So Trump fulminated and tweeted and waited. Then, finally, the election came, and the very next day, the president demanded and received Sessions's resignation. Trump also announced that—rather than following the ordinary succession rules, whereby the deputy attorney general would become the acting attorney general—he was bypassing Rosenstein to name Sessions's chief of staff, Trump loyalist Matthew Whitaker, to the acting post.

Sessions's ultimate sin had been not the recusal itself, but the attitude that lay behind it: the belief that the attorney general has a higher duty than deploying the power of the Justice Department on behalf of Trump. In Sessions's case, it took the recusal for Trump to see that attitude in a man he thought was a loyal supporter. But the die had been cast much earlier—the night Trump won the election—for FBI director James Comey, who was never part of the team. Unlike the attorney general, the FBI director serves a ten-year term, by statute. In creating a limited tenure that outlasts any individual president, Congress had sought to thread a needle—insulating the director from too much presidential pressure without rendering him or her excessively powerful with the lengthy tenure that characterized the bad old days of J. Edgar Hoover. Although the president could fire an FBI director, there was an overwhelmingly strong norm against doing so absent serious misconduct. What is obvious now but was less clear at the time is that a conflict between Trump and Comey was inevitable—a clash between the very cores of the two men. One man represented the personalization of the powers of the presidency, the belief that the executive branch should serve his interests and vanity. The other represented the long American tradition of investigative and prosecutorial independence, the conventional presidency's expectation that law enforcement has a function and a mission separate from politics and separate from serving those in power. Trump was not a competent exemplar of the personalization of presidential power, and Comey may have been an imperfect champion of the tradition he sought to defend. But they were both committed to their roles.

Authoritarian government can nowhere abide independent law enforcement. The authoritarian leader simply has to get control over the coercive apparatus of the state. He has to do so for both defensive and offensive reasons. The defensive side is that he needs to prevent that independent law enforcement apparatus from being arrayed against him, his family, his friends, and his supporters. The offensive side is that he needs to use it against his foes and those who would challenge him.

The law enforcement professional in a liberal democratic society, by contrast, cannot abide political interference or direction. Doing so makes her into a kind of janissary, which is the antithesis of the idea of the impartial application of the law. Although the federal law enforcement officer is part of the president's administration, she swears her own oath to the Constitution, and her oath is not a personal one to the leader. Using her powers to target the president's foes or to protect the president's friends is understood as a form of corruption. Jeff Sessions and Jim Comey are very different people, but ultimately their firing offense was the same: they were going to play by the rules—rules that the president found threatening.

Trump and Comey might have coexisted, at least for a while longer, under less fraught and personal conditions—that is, conditions not defined by the ongoing investigation of Russian electoral interference in the circumstances of Trump's election and the larger morass of allegations touching the new president and his intimates. Without the Russia investigation, it might have taken a while before Trump felt the need to interfere directly with the conduct of an investigation, and perhaps he wouldn't have minded quite so much when Comey proved unmovable on such substantive matters. One can imagine, under other circumstances, a frayed relationship that didn't quite reach the breaking point. As it was, however, the clash came quickly, and it was ferocious when it came.

Well before Trump's election, the country saw a lively debate about "tyrant-proofing" the White House, a debate that focused almost entirely on policing the margins of the president's powers. Privacy advocates rushed to warn that surveillance law was ripe for presidential abuse and that the National Security Agency could be loosed on American citizens; civil libertarians suggested that Americans rethink the president's unconstrained military authorities. Writing in *The Atlantic*, Conor Friedersdorf asked, "Under current precedent, the commander in chief can give a secret order to kill an American citizen with a drone strike without charges or trial. Should Donald Trump have that power?" Friedersdorf went on:

> Before moving into a new house, parents of small children engage
> in child-proofing. Before leaving the White House, Obama should
> engage in tyrant-proofing. For eight years, he has evinced a high
> opinion of his own ability to exercise power morally . . . You'll be

gone soon, Mr. President, and for all our disagreements, I think your successor is highly likely to be less trustworthy and more corruptible than you were.

Such critiques, however, missed something fundamental about the American presidency—and about Trump. Only in *House of Cards* would Trump get into the Oval Office and immediately begin plotting which Americans to take out with a drone. It's true that the Bush administration, in the crisis environment after September 11, authorized NSA surveillance activity that stretched—and, in some cases, broke—the law. Yet this does not mean that Trump could normalize tyranny in the face of an NSA bureaucracy that, the table-pounding of civil libertarians aside, really does follow the rules. Nor did Trump try to do so.

Indeed, the soft spot in the federal government—as Trump understood, even if his detractors did not—was not the NSA; it was not any of the programs the agency's prolific leaker, Edward Snowden, had revealed; it was not the drone program. The soft spot, the least tyrant-proof part of the government, turned out to be the U.S. Department of Justice and the larger law enforcement and regulatory apparatus of the U.S. government.

Here's the problem: Without control of the Justice Department, the would-be tyrant's tool kit is radically incomplete. He can make trouble for people by using the IRS or regulatory powers, but unless he can threaten the deployment of the state's truly coercive powers, he's mostly just talking. He is also vulnerable, as Trump has always been, to investigation himself. It is the Justice Department that controls the federal power to prosecute people; its various components control major investigative capabilities too. And even when it can't initiate a criminal probe, the Justice Department has civil enforcement powers—the ability to sue.

To the aspiring strongman who admires Vladimir Putin and Recep Tayyip Erdoğan and Kim Jong Un and Mohammed bin Salman, an independent Justice Department presents both an unacceptable threat and a colossal missed opportunity.

From a democracy-protection point of view, of course, the Justice Department in the wrong hands is an exceptionally dangerous instrument. In a famous speech to the U.S. attorneys in 1940, Attorney General Robert Jackson—who was soon to be named to the Supreme Court—explained the reason. It is a speech, ironically, that Trump's former deputy attorney general, Rod Rosenstein, has sometimes quoted publicly:

> Law enforcement is not automatic. It isn't blind. One of the greatest difficulties of the position of prosecutor is that he must pick his cases, because no prosecutor can even investigate all of the cases in which he receives complaints. If the Department of Justice were to make even a pretense of reaching every probable violation of federal law, ten times its present staff will be inadequate. We know that no local police force can strictly enforce the traffic laws, or it would arrest half the driving population on any given morning. What every prosecutor is practically required to do is to select the cases for prosecution and to select those in which the offense is the most flagrant, the public harm the greatest, and the proof the most certain.
>
> If the prosecutor is obliged to choose his cases, it follows that he can choose his defendants. Therein is the most dangerous power of the prosecutor: that he will pick people that he thinks he should get, rather than pick cases that need to be prosecuted. With the law books filled with a great assortment of crimes, a prosecutor stands a fair chance of finding at least a technical violation of some act on the part of almost anyone. In such a case, it is not a question of discovering the commission of a crime and then looking for the man who has committed it, it is a question of picking the man and then searching the law books, or putting investigators to work, to pin some offense on him. It is in this realm—in which the prosecutor picks some person whom he dislikes or desires to embarrass, or selects some group of unpopular persons and

then looks for an offense, that the greatest danger of abuse of prosecuting power lies. It is here that law enforcement becomes personal, and the real crime becomes that of being unpopular with the predominant or governing group, being attached to the wrong political views, or being personally obnoxious to or in the way of the prosecutor himself.

A prosecutor—and, by extension, a tyrant who directs that prosecutor—can harass or target almost anyone and can often do so without violating any law. She can also protect from investigation those she cares about personally or politically, creating a powerful instrument of impunity for those who do her bidding. This defensive side of the abuse of law enforcement often gets overlooked. But cultivating impunity for friends is actually key to building autocracy—the carrot of support that accompanies the stick of opposition. David Frum, writing about Viktor Orbán's Hungary, describes it as the essential element to Orbán's undermining of democracy: "Day in and day out, the regime works more through inducements than through intimidation. The courts are packed, and forgiving of the regime's allies. Friends of the government win state contracts at high prices and borrow on easy terms from the central bank. Those on the inside grow rich by favoritism; those on the outside suffer from the general deterioration of the economy. As one shrewd observer told me on a recent visit, 'The benefit of controlling a modern state is less the power to persecute the innocent, more the power to protect the guilty.'"

To abuse the Justice Department for defensive purposes, to prevent it from investigating one's friends and family and supporters, one needs only to hold its collar. But one needs a tight grip on that collar—either leverage or a political ally willing to put loyalty over his oath. The Mueller report describes how the White House aides Reince Priebus and Steve Bannon became alarmed to learn that the president was holding on to Sessions's unaccepted resignation letter back in May 2017; they feared, as Mueller describes it, "that it could be used to influence the Department of Justice." Priebus said that the letter in Trump's pocket "would function as a kind of 'shock collar' that the president could use any time he wanted," and it meant that Trump "had 'DOJ by the throat.'" Aware of the potential for abuse, the pair endeavored to retrieve the letter from the president.

To abuse the Justice Department for offensive purposes, to use it as an instrument of repression against one's enemies, requires something more: the ability not merely to hold the collar but also to direct an attack. Bringing a meritless, politically motivated case is pretty hard to do; judges and juries offer genuine protections, after all, and they do not look kindly on weak cases with a vindictive sheen. But prosecutors don't actually need to indict a person in order to cause serious problems. They need only open an investigation; that alone can be ruinous. And the standards for doing so, for what is called "predication" in a criminal investigation, are not all that high. The fabric of American federal law—criminal and civil law alike—is so vast that a huge number of people and institutions of consequence are ripe for some sort of meddling from authorities. This is not hard to do, and the abusive official doesn't even need to win in order to succeed.

The Justice Department has institutional defenses against this sort of thing, but they are notably and perhaps surprisingly weaker and less formal than, say, the much-feared intelligence community's institutional defenses against abuses. These defenses mostly do not reside in statute or in the complex oversight structures that civil libertarians complain are not restrictive enough in the case of NSA. They reside in the so-called Levi Guidelines, internal rules that set the standards for when and against whom the FBI can open an investigation. They reside in certain normative rules about contacts between the Justice Department and the White House. Most important, they reside in the behavioral expectations of a lot of replaceable people who have taken their own oaths of office. They reside in an institutional culture at the Justice Department that values the independent and apolitical administration of justice. This is actually a powerful set of constraints, but consequentially these are not legal constraints.

There are good reasons why the country has left itself vulnerable to high-level prosecutorial abuse. The justice system actually depends on prosecutorial discretion for a lot of good things. It is what prevents the mechanical application of the law in a fashion that would itself be tyrannical. It is what allows focus on the most important offenses. It is what allows the justice system to be nimble, targeting drug cartel crimes in the 1980s and 1990s and shifting to terrorism and internet crimes in the subsequent decade. The law can be slow to change. The political system's enforcement priorities, by contrast, can shift much more quickly; think of how attitudes toward nonviolent drug offenses have changed over the past decade much faster than the laws on the subject. Prosecutorial discretion allows flexibility even in the absence of legislative change that can be slow and difficult. Any attempt to completely eliminate our vulnerability to high-level prosecutorial abuse also risks grave damage to the legal system.

But once again, an important element of our system presupposes a president who is fit to oversee it. It's a bit like nuclear launch authority, which ultimately depends on presidential wisdom and virtue to garner the benefits of flexibility and limit the dangers. The combination of broad prosecutorial discretion with a relationship between the White House and the enforcement apparatus that is regulated almost entirely by norms is a delicate business. In Trump's hands, it's a loaded gun. It is precisely the kind of feature of the presidency one would want to tyrant-proof, because there are really only two things standing between Trump and the offensive and defensive uses of the criminal enforcement authorities of the United States: a culture and people.

Trump went to war against both.

Whether out of candor or—more likely—out of bombastic ignorance, Trump has never made the slightest pretense of respecting his highest prosecutors' autonomy. The most remarkable feature of his behavior toward law enforcement is how overt it is. Where midcentury presidents struck a pose of virtue in public and quietly tolerated or encouraged abuses, Trump openly calls for the abuses. Indeed, as his interactions with Sessions show, he gets indignant that they are not occurring. He thus not only merely assaults the specific norm itself; he is openly hostile to the value of nonpartisan and apolitical law enforcement that the norm seeks to protect. Trump's behavior toward his law enforcement apparatus must count among his gravest breaches of the traditional presidency's expectations.

During the campaign, he presided over crowds that chanted about his opponent, "Lock her up!" He talked routinely, while campaigning and after his ascension, about supposed crimes by his political opponents on which the FBI and Justice Department should be focused. And, as the Mueller report describes, he also ordered abusive investigations in private, including asking Sessions, on multiple occasions, to investigate Hillary Clinton. In one December 2017 meeting, Trump told Sessions that if he unrecused himself and directed an investigation of Clinton, he would "be a hero," at the same time saying, with an implied wink, "Not telling you to do anything. [Alan] Dershowitz says POTUS can get involved . . . I'm not going to do anything or direct you to do anything. I just want to be treated fairly." Trump routinely accuses enemies of crimes and just as routinely objects to prosecution of his allies. He comments regularly on pending investigations, often based on no information other than what he has apparently seen conspiracy-minded commentators say on television. He attacks by name individual law enforcement officers and Justice Department officials—both career officials and those of his own appointment. He persistently reserves the right to pardon suspects who are either under indictment or facing possible charges. He likewise dangles the possibility of firing or interfering with both the prosecutors investigating him and the officials who supervise those investigations. He publicly entertains the possibility of revoking the security clearances of sitting career officials in an effort to impede their ability to work.

In these actions, as well as in repeated public statements in which he makes plain his wish to deploy law enforcement both defensively and offensively, he actually reveals a coherent theory of justice. Commentators sometimes analogize Trump's attitude to that of authoritarian rulers or, at a smaller scale, mobsters. But Trump's theory of justice actually has a very old pedigree. Indeed, as long as Western thought has considered the question of what justice is, it has had to confront Trump's vision.

Book I of Plato's *Republic* deals with the definition of justice. In it, the very first conception of justice addressed by Socrates comes from a man named Polemarchus, who posits that "justice is helping friends and harming enemies." This is the vision Trump is embracing when he asserts baldly and regularly the propriety of his directing the Justice Department to go after his enemies and protect his friends. "I have absolute right to do what I want to do with the Justice Department," he has said.

And though Trump's vision of justice was repudiated by Socrates in ancient Greece and remains repugnant today to professional law enforcement, on this specific structural constitutional point—rather uncomfortably—Trump is not entirely wrong. The idea of what is colloquially called "law enforcement independence" is not intuitive—and in some important respects it is not even quite correct. The Constitution has no concept of the law enforcement function as independent from the broader executive power wielded by the president. The attorney general is a job created by Congress, not by the Constitution. The Justice Department, which the attorney general now heads, was also created by Congress and only came into existence many decades after the Constitution was ratified. More than one hundred of the Justice Department's leading officers are also appointed by the president with the advice and consent of the Senate—and a great many lesser officers by the president's administration alone. To describe the law enforcement apparatus as "independent" of the president in any sense is a bit of a constitutional and legal myth. That independence is certainly not a matter of law. Structurally and constitutionally, the Justice Department and its components—as we discussed earlier—are merely exercising delegated powers of the president himself.

The description is also not obviously democratically appropriate. If the public expects the Justice Department and the FBI to be "independent," whom are voters to hold accountable for major investigative foul-ups? Whom do they blame for investigations that do not come to appropriate fruition or for investigations that, say, do not take place at all? Conversely, whom do they blame for investigative abuses when they take place? Structurally, legally, and democratically, it arguably makes more sense for the president to be directly accountable for law enforcement's conduct, and thus to be involved in supervising it.

Yet despite this, a remarkably strong norm has developed—gradually and over a long period of time—in which presidents respect the prosecutorial autonomy of the Justice Department and the autonomy of its investigative units as well. There is a pervasive myth that this norm is purely a creature of the post-Watergate era—something that developed in the wake of Richard Nixon's and J. Edgar Hoover's abuses. But the roots of the norm are far older than that. It developed for a variety of reasons, not the least of which was the country's far-flung geography. And it reflects a careful integration of the structural constitutional concerns that militate toward presidential control—the call of presidential and democratic accountability—with important values such as the depoliticization of law enforcement and the impartial administration of justice.

The norm is a complicated one, whose precise texture has shifted over time. But the basic contours of it today are reasonably easy to sketch: presidents exercise policy control over the Justice Department, but they generally refrain from getting involved in specific investigative matters, which they leave to the appointees they select. When these two principles collide and broad issues of presidential or national policy hinge on investigative matters, communications between the White House and the Justice Department are carefully structured to get the White House the information it needs while preserving the investigative autonomy of the department. Successive prior administrations have thus promulgated policy memos limiting contacts between the department and the White House to certain subjects, certain situations, and certain offices.

It wasn't always this way. Historically, early presidents sometimes took direct roles in law enforcement operations. George Washington, for example, personally ordered the prosecution of people associated with the Whiskey Rebellion in 1792. He wrote to Alexander Hamilton directing "the Attorney General to attend the Circuit Court in York Town, and see that the Indictments are legally prosecuted and properly supported."

The following year, Washington stepped in more deeply. In a move that foreshadows in some respects Trump's attempts to persuade Comey to drop the investigation of General Michael Flynn, Washington wrote to the Pennsylvania district attorney, directing him to drop two indictments of people whom he deemed—as Trump would later put it—good guys. "Whereas it appears to me, from the representation of several respectable persons, and from sundry affidavits, that William Kerr and Alexander Beer, who were lately indicted in the Circuit Court of the United States, holden in the Town of York, in the State of Pennsylvania, for a riot, were innocent of the offence, with which they stand charged . . . ," he wrote, "I do hereby instruct you forthwith to [drop] the indictment aforesaid: and for so doing let this be filed as your warrant."

Washington's two immediate successors also got involved in specific law enforcement operations. Adams, for example, personally ordered the prosecution of William Duane, the editor of the famed Republican newspaper *Aurora*, under the notorious Sedition Act after the Federalist Senate demanded it. He wrote in 1800 to Charles Lee, the relevant district attorney, that Congress had passed a resolution asking that he "instruct the proper law officers, to commence & carry on a prosecution against [Duane] for certain false, defamatory, scandalous & malicious publications, in the said newspaper [which] tend[ed] to defame the Senate of the United States & to bring them into contempt & disrepute, & to excite against them the hatred of the good people of the U.S." Adams concluded: "In compliance with this request, I now instruct you Gentlemen to commence & carry on the prosecution accordingly."

The following year, Thomas Jefferson—who had assumed the presidency in the meantime—ordered the case dropped. In a letter to Edward Livingston, he explained,

The President is to have the laws executed. He may order an offence then to be prosecuted. If he sees a prosecution put into a train which is not lawful, he may order it to be discontinued and put into legal train. I found a prosecution going on against Duane for an offence against the Senate, founded on the Sedition act. I affirm that act to be no law, because in opposition to the Constitution; and I shall treat it as a nullity wherever it comes in the way of my functions. I therefore directed that prosecution to be discontinued & a new one to be commenced, founded on whatsoever other law might be in existence against the offence.

Jefferson also got intensely involved in the treason trial of his former vice president, Aaron Burr—and not just because the court issued a subpoena for the president's own testimony and documents. In a string of letters in 1807, Jefferson directed that transcripts of the trial be taken and sent to him. He asked that prosecutors refrain from citing the landmark case of *Marbury v. Madison,* which he loathed, and in fact asked "to have it denied to be law." He personally interviewed a witness, held out the possibility of a pardon for him, and then wrote a letter directing how this witness—and others—should be handled.

As Bruce A. Green and Rebecca Roiphe note in a lengthy history of presidential relations with the Justice Department, Jefferson "also ordered a Connecticut district attorney to bring a federal common law criminal case against Federalist printers who had called the President immoral, but then ordered the district attorney to drop the case when it became clear that the defendants were planning to put on evidence that Jefferson seduced a woman."

In 1827, Attorney General William Wirt actually wrote a legal opinion in the civil context, affirming the president's authority to order that a case be dropped. "I entertain no doubt of the constitutional power of the President to order the discontinuance of a suit commenced in the name of the United States in a case proper for such an order," he wrote. If the suit were meritless, for example, and "wholly unfounded in law" such as would amount to harassment of a defendant, whom it would expose to "needless annoyance and expense," he wrote, "I should consider the President not only authorized, but required by his duty, to order a discontinuance of such vexation; for it is one of his highest duties to take care that the laws be executed, and, consequently, to take care that they be not abused by any officer acting under his authority and control to the grievance of the citizen." Even back then, however, Wirt noted that the matter was fraught. The power to intervene in suits, he wrote, "is a high and delicate one, and requires the utmost care and circumspection in its exercise; and I could never advise its exercise in any case in which a court" had considered a case as having merit.

Andrew Jackson was particularly aggressive in supervising law enforcement, and his attorney general—Roger Taney—followed up on Wirt's opinion, in 1831, with a strong statement of presidential authority: "Assuming that the district attorney possesses the power to discontinue a prosecution, the next inquiry is, Can the President lawfully direct him, in any case, to do so?" Taney answered, "I think the President does possess the power. The interest of the country and the purposes of justice manifestly require that he should possess it; and its existence is necessarily implied by the duties imposed upon him in that clause of the constitution before referred to, which enjoins him to take care that the laws be faithfully executed."

Even in more recent years, the direct involvement of presidents in investigative or prosecutorial matters has not been unheard of—and has not always been improper—for the simple reason that lines between investigative interests and policy interests are not always clear, and investigations often implicate high interests of national policy that presidents simply cannot avoid. In the aftermath of the September 11 attacks, for example, President George W. Bush could not avoid allocating responsibility for the campaign against Al Qaeda among the military, the intelligence community, and law enforcement. This inevitably involved some degree of deciding how to weigh law enforcement interests against other, competing interests. Was it more important to interrogate Khalid Sheikh Mohammed or to prosecute him? And if it was important to do both, which should come first in sequential terms? To decide which agency should have custody over such high-value detainees required presidential involvement in law enforcement matters. After all, to put such people in the hands of the CIA implied that they would, at least at the outset, receive no trial. To put them in the hands of the military would mean that they would be tried, if at all, by military commission. To transfer them to the Justice Department would mean a civilian trial in federal court. And who but the president can decide between the competing interests of his own cabinet departments? When President Bush moved Khalid Sheikh Mohammed and thirteen other detainees in CIA custody to Guantánamo in 2006, he personally announced that he had transferred them there to face trial by military commission. And he specifically asked Congress for the authority to hold military commission trials to make this possible.

The story did not end there. When President Obama decided to shutter Guantánamo, his attorney general, Eric Holder, announced that five of the September 11 conspirators would be moved to New York to be tried in federal court. Obama had made a point of not getting involved in this decision, but he was kept informed of it. The reporter Daniel Klaidman recounts a conversation between Obama and Holder when the two men presided together over a July 4 celebration and the attorney general advised the president of his inclination to try Mohammed in federal court. Obama responded, "It's your call. You're the attorney general." But the decision, once public, blew up in the administration's face, with many members of Congress vociferously opposing any plan to bring Guantánamo terrorism suspects to New York. In response to the public outcry and the congressional opposition, Obama acquiesced to Guantánamo remaining open, and Holder was forced to conclude that the detainees would be tried by military commission there.

These actions were not unprecedented. During World War II, when Adolf Hitler had sent a group of saboteurs to American shores, they were quickly rounded up, and President Franklin Delano Roosevelt personally ordered that they be tried by military commission, not in civilian courts. Roosevelt actually went further, prescribing not merely the forum for trial, but the availability of capital punishment. As the legal scholar Jack Goldsmith recounts, "When Roosevelt learned of the saboteurs' capture, he insisted to [Attorney General Francis] Biddle that they be tried by a military court where ordinary procedural niceties would not stand in the way, justice would be swift, and the death sentence could be imposed." And when the Supreme Court stepped in to hear the case, Roosevelt suggested to Biddle that he might defy a court order if the court didn't let him have his way. "I want one thing clearly understood, Francis," he said. "I won't give them up . . . I won't hand them over to any United States marshal armed with a writ of habeas corpus. Understand?" Biddle understood, and so did the Supreme Court, which upheld the military commission.

Another example of overt presidential involvement in pending criminal matters came under President Obama when the administration negotiated a spy swap with Moscow for a group of Russian spies who had been arrested and charged. Obama personally approved the deal, which cut short the criminal proceedings. The ten Russian agents were given a hasty plea deal and put on a plane so they could be exchanged in Vienna for Western agents locked up by the Russians.

Presidents have other ways of getting involved in criminal investigative matters. Some are subtle, quiet signals of approval or disapproval, requests for information that may be proper in and of themselves but also show interest in particular matters, or policy directives that are not specific to individual investigations but may have predictable effects on known cases. There are also overt interventions in the form of public statements. While the Paul Manafort jury was deliberating in the former campaign manager's tax evasion and fraud case, Trump's public comments—that the defendant "happens to be a very good person" and that "it's very sad what [prosecutors have] done to Paul Manafort"—were far from the first time a president has commented on a pending matter. Richard Nixon famously commented on the guilt of Charles Manson, saying during his trial that he "was guilty, directly or indirectly, of eight murders without reason." (The White House quickly retracted Nixon's statement.) While the FBI was still investigating Hillary Clinton's conduct regarding her private email server, Obama made public remarks that seemingly exonerated her. He also made public comments about Khalid Sheikh Mohammed's execution while Mohammed's case was pending; prejudicial remarks by both Bush and Obama and their staffs prompted litigation over whether such comments, given the president's status as commander in chief of the military hierarchy, precluded a fair trial.

And then, of course, there is corrupt and covert interference, which has happened too. Richard Nixon famously sought to have the CIA pressure the FBI to bring the Watergate investigation to a close. He demanded IRS investigations of people he perceived as political enemies. And he was not alone in these abuses. His predecessors Lyndon Johnson and John F. Kennedy and Franklin Roosevelt had all engaged in political spying on domestic foes. And none of them was above unleashing the law enforcement apparatus of the country against people who were not in favor. To some degree, these abuses were a creature of the FBI's first director, J. Edgar Hoover, who used the agency to spy on, harass, and blackmail people, often for the benefit of those above him. In the FDR administration, Hoover was particularly active in wiretapping the president's foreign policy critics, including Charles A. Lindbergh and the New York office of the America First Committee, one of the leading isolationist organizations. Decades later, under the Kennedy and Johnson administrations, Hoover's FBI both wiretapped the telephone lines of Martin Luther King, Jr., and later conducted a sustained covert campaign against him. President Johnson used the FBI to wiretap the Mississippi Freedom Democratic Party at his own party's convention in 1964, and also had it investigate members of Barry Goldwater's staff.

In many such instances, presidents were passive beneficiaries of Hoover's conduct. But there were also cases in which presidents were more active participants in the use of law enforcement against their enemies.

According to memos written by Hoover in 1936, FDR specifically requested that the FBI investigate suspected communist and fascist organizations to acquire "general intelligence information," taking special care to ensure that very little was committed to writing. This unwillingness to create a historical record suggests that, even as methods of surveillance were used, there was a sense that such interference on the part of the president would not be well received by the public, either at the time or in posterity. Similarly, Kennedy and his brother Bobby Kennedy relentlessly pursued the Teamsters union leader Jimmy Hoffa. The vendetta between the brothers and Hoffa began when President Kennedy was still a senator and Bobby served as counsel to the so-called McClellan Committee, which was charged with investigating racketeering and labor mismanagement. Bobby Kennedy's relentless hatred of Hoffa followed him to the Justice Department when he became attorney general. Hoover did not share the Kennedys' interest in Hoffa, preferring to focus on what he perceived to be the threat from domestic communists. Proceeding without the assistance of the FBI, Kennedy set up a so-called Get Hoffa Squad, consisting of more than twenty prosecutors.

All of which is to say that the tradition of prosecutorial and investigative autonomy is impure—impure because it developed slowly, impure because it has important exceptions, impure because law enforcement can sometimes be abusive and legitimately require political oversight, and impure because the principle has often been honored in the breach.

Yet with all that conceded, it is simply not true that the norm is solely a post-Watergate creation or a wholly modern graft onto our expectations of the executive branch. The modern norm is a relatively recent iteration of a much older idea that has deep roots in liberal political theory: law enforcement does not serve the will of those in power. The ultimate evidence that the values the norm seeks to protect are older, much older, than the specific norm itself is that none of the presidents who benefited from Hoover's misconduct or ordered political investigation did so openly. They had shame about it because it was already disreputable.

The origins of the more exacting modern proscription of political interference with law enforcement lie at least in part in the country's geographic spread, which inhibited centralization of power. While the president had the formal authority to direct the conduct of individual criminal prosecutions and occasionally did so, day-to-day prosecutorial decisions had to be made by what were then called district attorneys—now called U.S. attorneys—not centrally. Distances were too large. Many cases were too local to warrant involvement by the central government. So while presidents could order cases brought or dropped, or even involve themselves in directing which cases their prosecutors should or should not cite, they generally didn't. Prosecutorial autonomy developed because most places were far from Washington.

What's more, federal criminal law for much of the country's early history was a kind of dead zone. Most law enforcement took place at the hands of local officials under state law. A lot of prosecutions were actually private actions brought by individual citizens. Although highly local actions can be abusive too, the diffusion of prosecutorial power tends to mitigate concerns about centralized authoritarianism. A great deal of federal law enforcement, such as it was, related to revenue crimes and slave catching.

Beyond the U.S. Marshals Service's limited activity—primarily retrieving fugitives, often under the Fugitive Slave Act—and some postal inspectors, there was no federal law enforcement agency. The U.S. Secret Service was created in the immediate aftermath of the Civil War to deal with counterfeiting. But the FBI did not come into existence until the early twentieth century. Only during Reconstruction, as the federal government developed the need to enforce federal law in the South, did Congress even establish the Justice Department. So one reason the norm of investigative and prosecutorial noninterference developed is that there wasn't that much federal law enforcement to interfere with.

The establishment of the Justice Department created a measure of centralization, putting geographically dispersed U.S. attorneys under the authority of the attorney general and building a bureaucracy of enforcement.

Paradoxically, it also helped reinforce the developing norm. This was, after all, a period of professionalization. The idea, write Green and Roiphe, was that "a centralized law department would not only preserve quality and efficiency, but also prevent cronyism and draw on professionalism to prevent both political and personal incentives from perverting criminal justice."

By the time Robert Jackson gave his famous speech to the U.S. attorneys, quoted earlier, the idea that law enforcement should behave apolitically was sufficiently a point of orthodoxy that it suffuses the entire speech. Consider, for example, that when Jackson describes "the most dangerous power of the prosecutor" as the ability to "pick people that he thinks he should get, rather than cases that need to be prosecuted," he is describing a *danger*, not a virtue. When he worries that the prosecutor could target "some person whom he dislikes or desires to embarrass, or selects some group of unpopular persons and then looks for an offense," he is describing a nightmare scenario, not an aspiration. And when he describes the ultimate nightmare, it is that "the real crime becomes that of being unpopular with the predominant or governing group, being attached to the wrong political views, or being personally obnoxious to or in the way of the prosecutor himself." This was 1940, long before many of the abuses cataloged by the Church Committee report in 1976, and already one can see the modern orthodoxy—of which a measure of investigative and prosecutorial autonomy is an inherent corollary—substantially congealed. Jackson does not need to take the time to explain that these nightmares are nightmares rather than happy daydreams. He assumes, correctly, that the U.S. attorneys will share his premise.

But Trump, quite openly, does not share it.

Watergate and the Church Committee—by laying bare the extent to which successive presidents had sometimes undermined this premise in secret—triggered the development of more specific policies designed to protect the premise. One of them was the limits on White House–Justice Department contacts. Another was the promulgation of the Levi Guidelines, which prevented the FBI from investigating people in the absence of an appropriate factual predicate for the investigation. Importantly, however, because of the structure of the executive branch, none of these policies bind the president, though they profoundly influence the traditional understanding of how presidents do and should behave.

Trump's war against the orthodox understanding of federal law enforcement seems to proceed from an actual perplexity at the expectation that anyone in power might not use his authority as Polemarchus urges: to reward friends and punish enemies. When Trump talks about his relationship with the Justice Department and the FBI, he sounds genuinely confused at the expectation that he would not direct specific investigations, call off others, and generally involve himself at the policy level only. When he's not actively chafing at the restrictions, he's saddened by them, sounding almost wistful at the powerful instrument he has but cannot deploy. In one 2017 interview, Trump told a radio talk show:

> You know, the saddest thing is, because I am the President of the United States, I am not supposed to be involved with the Justice Department. I'm not supposed to be involved with the FBI. I'm not supposed to be doing the kind of things I would love to be doing and I am very frustrated by it. I look at what's happening with the Justice Department, why aren't they going after Hillary Clinton with her emails and with her dossier, and the kind of money . . . I don't know, is it possible that they paid $12.4 million for the dossier . . . which is total phony, fake, fraud and how is it used? It's very discouraging to me. I'll be honest, I'm very unhappy with it, that the Justice Department isn't going . . . maybe they are but you know as president, and I think you understand this, as a president you're not supposed to be involved in that process. But hopefully they are doing something and at some point, maybe we are going to all have it out.

It was a statement of remarkable candor: Trump declared it "the saddest thing" that he could not call up an investigation of his political opponent. He said he would "love to be doing" things with the FBI and the Justice Department—things that defy more than a century of public expectation of the president—and declared himself "very frustrated" and "very unhappy" that he can't manage to do them. He said with bold frankness that he would like to be able to interfere with ongoing investigations. He declared himself a corrupt actor who believes that the FBI and the Justice Department should be at his beck and call for political purposes. And he also declared himself hemmed in, meaningfully constrained, and unable for some reason to do those things he so wants to do. In May 2019 Trump declared that it would be "appropriate" for him to ask the attorney general to investigate the son of former vice president Joe Biden, who happened to be the front-runner in the Democratic presidential primary.

Trump's failure—so far, anyway—to get the Justice Department under control has not been for lack of trying. His remarkable campaign against the norm of investigative and prosecutorial autonomy began only days after he took office, when he summoned Comey for their private dinner at the White House and sought a pledge of his loyalty. This dinner initiated the campaign whose full scope, as it pertains to the Russia investigation at least, is the subject of Volume II of the Mueller report. Comey, in public statements and to Mueller, describes a series of private interactions in which Trump lobbied him to drop the investigation of Flynn, called him to ask him to announce publicly that Trump was not under investigation, and tried to cultivate what Comey regarded as a patronage relationship with him. The Mueller report finds that Comey's account is credible, while the president's denials of it are not. The private side of the war did not end with Comey's firing. As we have seen, Trump's public fury when Sessions recused himself from the Russia probe was only a shadow of his private rage, and it went on until Sessions was removed. Trump pressured both Rosenstein and Andrew McCabe—who succeeded Comey as acting FBI director—on specific matters as well. As noted in chapter 3, at one point he directed McGahn to order the firing of Special Counsel Robert Mueller, though McGahn would not carry out the order. When

Trump fired Sessions and replaced him with Matthew Whitaker, he asked Whitaker to exercise control over the Southern District of New York investigation of his payments to women he had slept with.

But Trump's war has involved a public campaign as well as a private one. It's not just the serial tweets that sometimes name individual law enforcement officials, or the now-routine public statements decrying the Russia investigation as a "WITCH HUNT," or demanding prosecution of Comey or Clinton, or declaring individual FBI officials a "disgrace." Trump is not the first president to have his lawyers on television regularly attacking federal law enforcement, though he is the first to do so himself on a near-daily basis. His campaign has also included the recruitment of the investigative apparatus of allied congressional committees to harass federal law enforcement officers of his own administration. It is not clear whether the congressional Republicans who deployed their committees against Mueller, Rosenstein, and the line agents and lawyers who worked the Russia probe—at least until the election cost them congressional control—did so at Trump's behest or merely on their own initiative and to his pleasure. What is entirely clear is that Trump's campaign to control federal law enforcement and protect himself from it had a substantial congressional element, in which the House Intelligence Committee, the House Oversight Committee, and the House Judiciary Committee under Republican leadership all harassed and threatened officials whom Trump wished to neutralize but could not muster the political will to remove from office. Trump, in turn, gave cover to those efforts, which were so convenient to his interests. Congressional Republicans went so far as to threaten to impeach Rosenstein over their demands for documents, and Trump himself encouraged those demands over the strident objections of his own intelligence and law enforcement leadership.

The campaign has been persistent. With the possible exception of hostility to foreigners and immigrants and the press, it is one of the few truly consistent themes of Trump's presidency. And it reflects a genuine vision too, albeit one sharply at odds with the traditional presidency's settled understanding of appropriate conduct. It is a vision that almost perfectly inverts the orthodox understanding articulated by Jackson in his famous speech. It is a vision, to rewrite Jackson's speech, in which the Justice Department picks not those cases in which the offense is the most flagrant, the public harm the greatest, and the proof the most certain, but those cases that most assist and least inconvenience power. It is a vision in which the prosecutor should pick people whom she thinks she should get because getting that person would make the president happy; it is a question of picking the man and then searching the law books or putting investigators to work to pin some offense on him. Trump evidently believes that law enforcement is personal and that the real crime is being unpopular with the predominant or governing group, being attached to the wrong political views, or being personally obnoxious to or in the way of the president himself.

It is only by understanding Trump's vision of law enforcement as an actual vision that one can understand his apparent fixation on former Attorneys General Eric Holder and Bobby Kennedy in relation to his anger at Sessions. In a tense conversation with McGahn over Sessions's recusal decision, the Mueller report recounts, Trump said that Holder had protected Obama, and Bobby Kennedy had protected his own brother as well: "You're telling me that Bobby and Jack didn't talk about investigations? Or Obama didn't tell Eric Holder who to investigate?" Days later, while alone with Sessions at Mar-a-Lago, Trump brought up Holder and Kennedy again. And in his public comments he was even clearer as to what he meant by the comparison, telling *The New York Times*,

> I don't want to get into loyalty, but I will tell you that, I will say this: Holder protected President Obama. Totally protected him. When you look at the I.R.S. scandal, when you look at the guns for whatever, when you look at all of the tremendous, ah, real problems they had, not made-up problems like Russian collusion, these were *real* problems. When you look at the things that they did, and Holder protected the president. And I have great respect for that, I'll be honest, I have great respect for that.

Although Trump's admiring comments about Bobby Kennedy have some basis in fact, he creates an imaginary Holder to put on this particular pedestal. Holder may have been a political ally of Obama's, but the evidence that Obama was actually in need of legal protection, or that Holder acted as attorney general to protect him, is altogether lacking. But Trump's admiration, in any event, is for a deeply corrupt vision. It's admiration for an executive branch without professionalism. It's admiration for law enforcement as nothing more elevated or noble than expression of the will and interests of those in power. It's admiration for a vision of law enforcement in which those in power, as Frum puts it, "protect the guilty."

As of this writing, it is unclear how successful Trump will be in supplanting the orthodox vision of the role and function of federal law enforcement with this corrupt one. The damage to the institutions of the Justice Department and the FBI in terms of personnel lost to resignation or firing, diminished morale and prestige, and degradation of culture has been substantial. It is by no means irreparable, however. Institutional culture is a stubborn thing. And the institutions have shown remarkable resilience. As we have seen, Sessions did not unrecuse himself, and even the most loyal of Trump allies such as Lewandowski did not pass along Trump's messages to him. The investigations that so offended the president did not cease. They were, to the contrary, robust. Bannon turned out to be right when he warned the president that he could fire Comey but he couldn't fire the FBI. Trump's efforts to trigger investigations of his foes have, despite his persistence and commitment, mostly failed.

At the same time, there have been cracks. Under pressure from the president, the Justice Department has released unprecedented quantities of highly sensitive material about a pending investigation to overtly partisan congressional committees. Political considerations have certainly influenced the FBI's handling of high-profile personnel matters. The president's serial naming of individual law enforcement officers has ruined people's careers and stoked congressional investigations already fired up to protect the president and discredit those investigating him.

Perhaps most important of all is Trump's simple demonstration of the idea that a president can involve himself in specific law enforcement decisions and not face immediate and catastrophic political consequences. If the next president decides that she too wants to jettison the FBI director and pick her own, Congress will be hard-pressed to object. Trump has put on the table a radical departure from the orthodox understanding of the proper role of the president's political preferences in law enforcement investigations and prosecutorial decisions. Whether Trump's conduct ultimately reinforces the orthodox understanding, erodes it, or upends it entirely will be largely a function of the extent to which the political system tolerates or punishes him for it.

EIGHT

"A TOTAL POLITICAL WITCH HUNT!"

INVESTIGATING THE PRESIDENT

O N THE MORNING OF APRIL 18, 2019, ATTORNEY GENERAL Bill Barr gathered reporters at the Justice Department for a hastily arranged press conference. Nearly a month earlier, Special Counsel Robert S. Mueller III had given Barr the findings of his investigation into Russian interference in the 2016 election, and now it was time for Mueller's report to be made public. The reporters filling the pressroom that morning seemed perplexed as to why exactly Barr had summoned them. No one in the press had yet seen Mueller's more-than-four-hundred-page report. Weeks earlier, Barr had released a summary letter announcing that the report's "principal conclusions" cleared the president of conspiracy and did not reach a conclusion on obstruction of justice, and he had refused to elaborate further in the ensuing media frenzy. The report, he seemed to say, would speak for itself. So why call the press now, just hours before reporters and members of the public would finally have a chance to read it for themselves?

In some respects, it was a miracle that they were even there. Throughout the Mueller investigation, it had been a matter of doubt whether the special prosecutor would be able to complete his probe. The president had openly contemplated shutting it down and pardoning its subjects. That he had not done so, that the country had reached this day of accountability even after the Russia investigation had led to the firings of Comey and Sessions and that Mueller's account would now become public, was no small matter.

Perhaps it was to make that bitter pill easier for the president to swallow, perhaps it was out of sincere fidelity to the party line, perhaps it was out of rank cynicism, but the attorney general had a bone to throw to the president. Publicly and formally, and in his capacity as the nation's chief law enforcement officer, Barr was going to read the report in the light most favorable to Trump. In his summary letter released weeks prior, Barr had said that the Mueller investigation "did not find that the Trump campaign or anyone associated with it conspired or coordinated with Russia in its efforts to influence the 2016 U.S. presidential election." Barr's earlier summary had also said that the special counsel "did not draw a conclusion—one way or the other—as to whether" the president had committed the crime of obstruction of justice, adding that the report did not resolve the "'difficult issues' of law and fact concerning" the president's actions and intent. Since Mueller had declined to render a traditional prosecutorial judgment, Barr said that he was bound to offer his own conclusion that the president had not committed any crimes.

At the press conference, Barr went further, offering variants of the president's "no collusion" mantra. He adopted a decidedly exculpatory and justifying attitude toward the president's often hostile interactions with the investigation, noting with a tone of righteousness that "the President was frustrated and angered by a sincere belief that the investigation was undermining his presidency, propelled by his political opponents, and fueled by illegal leaks."

Barr knew that when the report became public that day, it would indeed speak for itself. At some level, he must have also known that the story it would tell was quite different from the one presaged by his rendition of it. To Barr's credit, he hadn't tried to bury the truth through redactions. Although there were quite a few of those, enough of the document was legible for it to tell the story Mueller meant to tell. It was a story that rendered Barr's summary absurd.

For even though the investigation had not found evidence to support a charge of criminal conspiracy on the part of Trump campaign officials, it described in excruciating detail a candidate—and a campaign—aware of the existence of the Russian plot to criminally interfere in the U.S. election for the purpose of supporting Trump, who welcomed the Russian efforts and encouraged and delighted in the assistance, and who brazenly and serially lied to the American people about the existence of the foreign conspiracy. The report spent more than a hundred pages chronicling the campaign's and the Trump Organization's many contacts with individuals tied to the Russian government, contacts they had repeatedly and strenuously denied having.

The special counsel had not rendered a judgment on whether the president committed the crime of obstruction—considering himself bound by Department of Justice guidance that a sitting president cannot be indicted and believing it unfair to formally accuse someone he could not charge. But the report described a president who, on numerous occasions, engaged in conduct calculated to hinder a federal investigation. It laid out multiple instances in which the president's conduct seemed to meet every statutory element of criminal obstruction of justice, and, in at least some of those instances, it noted no persuasive constitutional or factual defense for what the president did. The report tiptoed right up to the line of accusing the president of committing a crime, leaving the final conclusion on that score to Congress in the immediate term and to prosecutors in the longer term after Trump's tenure in office ends.

Barr could spin to match the president's talking points all he liked, but he could not change the reality at hand. The report Barr released, as an officer of the executive branch, told devastating truths about Donald Trump. And Trump let him do it.

As Barr announced at the press conference, the president hadn't asserted executive privilege to prevent public disclosure of any material in the report, though he subsequently asserted it aggressively with respect to Congress. More fundamentally, he hadn't told Barr not to give it to Congress or not to make it public. At the end of the day, after two years of the president yowling about "witch hunts," his own attorney general told the public what the hunt had found.

Ten days before he swore his oath of office, Trump first described the scandal that would consume his early presidency as a "WITCH HUNT." On January 10, 2017, *BuzzFeed News* published the document that became known as the "Steele dossier," following earlier CNN reporting on the material. In response, Trump tweeted, "FAKE NEWS—A TOTAL POLITICAL WITCH HUNT!" A few days earlier, Trump had been briefed on the dossier by then FBI director James Comey in their first encounter, when the intelligence community leadership came to Trump Tower to brief him more generally on Russian interference in the 2016 election. In the wake of the briefing, Trump's nerves were apparently raw, and not just because of the suggestion in the dossier that his campaign had been colluding with the Russians. As Comey later described the encounter, Trump was especially offended by the suggestion that he would need to use prostitutes, as Steele alleged he did in a Moscow hotel in 2013. At the briefing itself, "He ... strongly denied the allegations, asking—rhetorically, I assumed—whether he seemed like a guy who needed the services of prostitutes," Comey later wrote.

Comey had a rude surprise of his own the day of that first meeting. After hearing reports about Russian intervention in the election, the president and his aides did not even wait for the law enforcement and intelligence professionals to leave the room before pivoting to political optics. "They had no questions about what the future Russian threat might be. Nor did they ask how the United States might prepare itself to meet that threat," he wrote. "Instead, with the four of us still in our seats . . . the president-elect and his team shifted immediately into a strategy session about messaging on Russia. About how they could spin what we'd just told them." Left alone with the president-elect to brief him on the Steele material, with Trump growing more and more defensive, Comey felt the need to reassure the incoming president. "We are not investigating you, sir," he said.

Comey's reassurance was accurate, but Trump's spidey sense that the FBI's interest in matters Russia boded ill for him was not wrong either. By the time Trump and Comey met, the FBI already had begun electronic surveillance of the former Trump campaign adviser Carter Page, and there was an active investigation of his former campaign chairman Paul Manafort as well. Within a few weeks of Comey's briefing to Trump, the bureau would interview another former campaign adviser, George Papadopoulos, who would make statements he would later acknowledge to be false. And the bureau was drawing closer to its fateful interview with Michael Flynn, the interview in which Flynn would make false statements to which he would later plead guilty. By March 2017, Comey—in cooperation with the Justice Department—acknowledged publicly to Congress that the FBI was investigating links between the Trump campaign and Russian electoral interference.

Comey continued to reassure Trump that the FBI was not investigating him, a fact that Trump repeatedly pressured Comey to make public. But by May of the president's first year in office, that reassurance was no longer true: Trump was very much a subject of the FBI's scrutiny. By then, the president had fired Comey, and the FBI had opened both a criminal investigation of possible presidential obstruction of justice and a counterintelligence investigation of Trump. When Mueller was appointed as special counsel shortly thereafter, he took over the obstruction line of inquiry as well as the underlying Russia investigation.

The day after Mueller's appointment, Trump tweeted, "This is the single greatest witch hunt of a politician in American history!" By the time of Barr's press conference, the phrase had become a kind of mantra. As of this writing, Trump has used it on Twitter alone more than two hundred times.

Donald Trump is not the first American president to see his administration dogged by investigation almost from the start. Bill Clinton saw special counsel investigations follow almost his entire period in office, and his predecessor—George H. W. Bush—had a special prosecutor investigation that began during his predecessor's administration and continued throughout his four years in office. Nor is Trump the first president to be elected under circumstances that many people regarded as raising questions about his legitimacy as president: both Rutherford B. Hayes and George W. Bush were famously elected in contests in which electoral votes were disputed and in which many voters doubted the integrity of the mechanisms by which the political system resolved those disputes. Trump is not even the first president whose political enemies suspect that he is in the thrall of a foreign power. In the early years of the republic, the Jeffersonians earnestly believed the Federalists to be shills for Great Britain, while the Federalists believed Thomas Jefferson to be under French influence.

But Trump is the first president whose presidency, from the beginning, has been dominated by scandal, investigation, and the president's response to both. Unlike Richard Nixon, for whom Watergate arose only during his campaign for reelection and whose first term was defined by other things, Trump has never served a single day in office without *l'Affaire Russe* hanging over his head, first in the form of unanswered questions, then in the form of the investigation, and after that in the form of Congress and the public wrestling with the special counsel's findings. The Mueller probe also spurred other inquiries that outlived it, including investigations in the Southern District of New York related to Trump's involvement in alleged campaign finance violations and irregularities in the conduct of his inaugural committee. Neither the elder Bush nor even Clinton saw his presidency defined by investigation the way Trump's has been by the Russia probe and its offshoots. The elder Bush's presidency, while it inherited the Iran-Contra probe, was never seriously threatened. For its part, the Clinton presidency, though it was plagued by a series of shape-shifting investigations, confronted a serious threat from investigators for just over a year in his second term. And while George W. Bush and Hayes faced questions about the circumstances of their elections, those questions did not touch either man's personal conduct or trigger lengthy investigations.

The Trump presidency, by contrast, presents a kind of perfect storm: a presidency under investigation from the outset, in which the investigation implicated the circumstances of the man's elevation to the office, directly concerned his personal probity and behavior, and was wrapped up in suspicions that the president was knowingly or unknowingly compromised by a hostile foreign power. Although the Mueller report's conclusions alleviate the very worst fears one might have of Trump's acting as a witting Russia agent, it by no means put to rest all concerns about his relationship with Vladimir Putin and Russia, and it actively exacerbates other concerns, particularly on the obstruction side. There has been nothing like this set of circumstances since the dawn of the American republic.

If the spectacle of an attorney general releasing a report that is devastating to the president he serves (and written by the department he supervises) while characterizing that report in a fashion that facilitates the president's spin seems confusing, there are reasons for that. One of them is that the President of the United States is a unique subject for a criminal investigation; he or she is differently situated in important respects from all other people who interact with federal investigators and prosecutors. At the most basic level, the president cannot be subjected to criminal investigation at all without to some degree consenting to being investigated. He may call the proceedings a witch hunt, as Nixon did before Trump. She may rail against the unfairness of it all or allege misconduct on the part of her prosecutors. As we discussed in chapter 3, however, the president presides as the head of a unitary executive. This means that when push comes to shove, the federal prosecutors who would lead any such investigation are executive branch officials who ultimately work for the president. So, although Congress and state authorities can investigate the president against his will, if federal law enforcement officials set their authorities against the president, it is because he is allowing them to do so. A president truly willing to prevent an investigation of himself at all costs could order senior officials not to proceed, could fire those officials who refused the order, and could replace them with ones who would comply. This ability to direct and fire his own prosecutors is the envy of every other criminal subject in the country, none of whom is also the boss of the FBI agents and prosecutors who interview, investigate, and litigate against them.

Beyond the blunt power to stop an investigation to which he or she does not consent, the president has other unique tools available to frustrate it. For example, he has the power to pardon other investigative subjects who might give evidence against him in exchange for leniency. No other person, no matter how powerful, has this authority to remove the pressure when federal prosecutors squeeze a witness. Thus, to the extent that witnesses have cooperated with Mueller or with prosecutors in the Southern District of New York against Trump, it's partly because Trump has permitted those offices to put pressure on those witnesses—pressure he in fact has the power to alleviate but chooses not to.

As the Mueller report recognized, the president also cannot be indicted while he or she remains in office. Whether this restriction is a matter of constitutional law is a contested question among scholars and practitioners. As a functional matter, however, the answer to the theoretical question doesn't matter much, since the long-standing position of the executive branch is that a sitting president is immune from criminal prosecution. Whether correct or not, this position binds all executive branch officials, which is to say that it binds anyone actually capable of bringing a federal criminal case against a president. So the president doesn't merely have the power to order around his own prosecutors and remove them if they disobey; he not only has the power to pardon other witnesses whom they pressure or threaten. He also is uniquely invulnerable to the core punitive and coercive sanction that a criminal investigation is designed to produce, at least in the short term.

And as Trump has shown with his "witch hunt" tweets, and as we discussed at length in chapter 4, the president has the power to speak. It is true that all criminal subjects have a right to speak out against their investigators. But no other has the capacity to launch the kind of sustained public relations campaign that a president does, particularly when that president has a Twitter following in the tens of millions and an allied coalition of ideologically aligned media amplifiers and congressional allies keen to deploy their own powers to boost the president's signal.

It's a powerful combination of tools, one you might think would convey a kind of impunity, rendering the president in a meaningful sense immune to criminal investigation—if not quite above the law in theory, at least unthreatened by the law in practice. Certainly it is a state of affairs that strikes many other democracies as bordering on the insane. To guard against precisely this risk, those countries have structured law enforcement entities to be independent of their executives. It is a matter of no small irony that the president's closest foreign political ally, Israeli prime minister Benjamin Netanyahu, has faced his own series of investigations at home—investigations that as of this writing he has been unable to impede, which culminated in Israel's attorney general recommending his criminal indictment. But as we discussed in prior chapters, the president's control over law enforcement is an inherent feature of the American unitary executive. And though it's true that the system risks placing the president above the law, in practice it doesn't actually work out that way.

In reality, presidents have a weaker hand than their formal powers would suggest, and presidents have generally consented to investigations that inconvenience them, sometimes even catastrophically. Richard Nixon's downfall in the Watergate scandal still serves as the dominant cultural and legal reference point for investigations of the president. And Watergate remains as of this writing the only time in American history that a presidency has been effectively ended by an investigation, one that the president was ultimately unable to control.

The reason presidents are less free in practice than they might appear in theory is that even the most brazen have been politically constrained in their response to investigations—constrained by public opinion, constrained by Congress, and constrained by the threat of impeachment. Presidents consent to their own investigation not because they are public-spirited or because they have nothing to hide. They consent because they make the judgment that the consequences of the failure to do so are likely to be worse than the consequences of permitting an investigation to proceed. Blocking an investigation, even if done by means entirely within the president's lawful powers, might trigger an impeachment. Pardoning clearly guilty witnesses for wholly self-interested reasons might do the same, or it might provoke electoral retribution against the president's own party. And an element of the oath of office probably creeps in as well: politicians who aspire to govern sometimes have inhibitions about torching the instrumentalities of governance and law enforcement.

But consider for a moment the assumptions behind this elaborate system. Only two things backstop the expectation that presidents must consent to their own investigation at the hands of their own branch of government: electoral accountability and structural separation of powers. The ability to investigate and hold a president accountable for serious wrongdoing—which is critical to the health of the nation—is thus guaranteed only by a series of norms and by political deterrence of the violation of those norms. The nation has entrusted, in other words, the protection and observance of these norms to the very person who is to be investigated. And to make sure he or she acts appropriately, it has created a system of threats that have to be backed up in order to be effective. It is a sort of Fabergé egg of democratic accountability, and it is in Trump's hands for safekeeping for the present.

All of which raises some pretty basic questions: What if the president takes the sort of "I dare you" approach that Trump brings to all ethics matters? What if, in the face of breaches of norms and expectations of presidential conduct, Congress shows itself unwilling to back up those norms and expectations with meaningful threats? And what if the president's poll numbers are stubbornly resilient in the face of disastrous performance?

Criminal investigations of the president are a comparatively new feature of the American constitutional system, dating essentially to Watergate. The components of this feature, however, are much older. Political scandal and suspicions of misdeeds by the president and his coterie are, of course, as old as politics. Congressional investigations of executive conduct date back as early as the George Washington and John Adams administrations, and criminal investigations of conduct surrounding the president—including activity in the White House itself—are old as well. As such, the need for the peculiar institution of the special prosecutor—called in various iterations a "special counsel" or an "independent counsel"—as an arrangement to insulate the integrity of an investigation from political influence, developed relatively early. Tensions between presidents and the special prosecutors they tolerate—or do not tolerate—are as old as the latter institution's various forms.

In the early republic, the notion of a criminal investigation of the president was all but unthinkable. To the extent that scandals were investigated, they were investigated by Congress, not by any criminal investigator. And they typically focused on executive branch officials rather than the president himself. Federal criminal law was scant, in any event, so remedies tended to be political, not criminal. The history of early scandals, therefore, tends to be a history of either Congress leveraging its power against presidential administrations and demanding answers or, just as often, presidents holding their own officials accountable.

George Washington was shocked to learn in 1795 of the supposed betrayal of his secretary of state, Edmund Randolph. An intercepted letter suggested that Randolph was secretly working for, and demanding payments from, France. After personally confronting Randolph with the letter and watching his reaction, Washington received Randolph's resignation.

The congressional power to investigate executive branch conduct also saw its origins in the Washington administration, with the St. Clair disaster, in which a U.S. military force under General Arthur St. Clair was routed by Indian armies in what is now Ohio. In response, the House of Representatives took the position that the House could serve as an investigative body, and it took the matter on. As Matthew Waxman has written,

> Exercising oversight authority, the House of Representatives convened a committee to investigate St. Clair's military debacle. Washington and his cabinet considered carefully whether they were required to submit to the committee, especially conscious that they were setting precedent here with respect to congressional requests for documents. They decided that they were obliged to comply with the inquiry because the investigation flowed from Congress's powers. They further agreed that, although in other circumstances it would be proper to withhold some requested documents, Washington should furnish them in this case . . . Saint Clair and Secretary of War Henry Knox also testified. The investigatory committee ultimately pinned blame for the calamitous operation not on St. Clair personally but on the nascent War Department.

During the John Adams administration, members of Congress believed that Adams was lying about the famous XYZ Affair—in which the French foreign minister sought bribes from American diplomats as a condition of receiving the American delegation, thus touching off the so-called Quasi-War with France. But it was Congress, not any special counsel, that demanded and secured the disclosure of the dispatches from the commissioners, revealing that Adams, in fact, was telling the truth about his diplomats' actions. During the Zachary Taylor administration, Secretary of War George W. Crawford pushed the Treasury Department to pay threefold interest on a large debt owed to a Georgia family, and he pocketed half of it—nearly $100,000—himself. Congress investigated the scandal, which dogged the remainder of Crawford's tenure, but the matter was never fully resolved.

It was the corruption of the Ulysses S. Grant administration, which coincided with the early development of federal law enforcement, that provoked the first recognizably modern presidential scandal, complete with a special prosecutor, criminal misconduct in the White House itself, tensions between prosecutors and a president who felt harassed by them, presidential testimony in a criminal proceeding, and even the removal of the special counsel for an excess of independence. The corruption around Grant—himself by most accounts an honest man with a surfeit of faith in the scoundrels around him—was legendary and diverse, but the Whiskey Ring scandal was unique in provoking an actual criminal investigation that touched upon conduct within the White House.

The Whiskey Ring was a network of corrupt distilleries that used a relatively crude scheme to evade federal taxes. The distillers would underreport their output, thus fraudulently minimizing tax liability, and then pay off federal inspectors in the Treasury Department who came to verify their claims. They also had extensive contacts in the political echelons, and they financed Republican politicians, including Grant himself. One of their sources, who tipped them off about coming raids, was Grant's personal secretary and close friend, a man named Orville Babcock.

At the broadest level, Grant consented to the investigation of the Whiskey Ring, which was the personal crusade of his Treasury secretary, Benjamin Bristow. When Bristow and his solicitor, Buford Wilson, briefed the president on the incipient investigation, Grant pledged his cooperation. He later famously declared in a handwritten note, "Let no guilty man escape if it can be avoided—Be specially vigilant—or instruct those engaged in the prosecution of fraud to be—against all who insinuate that they have high influence . . . to protect them." And the investigation that ensued was remarkably productive, netting 350 indictments, including of participants who had been Grant's friends and political supporters. Grant even grudgingly allowed the indictment of Orville Babcock, at whose trial he testified by deposition. Grant vouched for Babcock and tried to have the allegations against him reviewed by a military panel instead of a court.

The special prosecutor Grant appointed in the case, however, a former senator named John Henderson, proved a little too independent. Henderson, the first special prosecutor in the country's history, refused to turn over his material to the military panel, and moved to indict Babcock. The final straw was when Henderson, at a separate Whiskey Ring trial, asked at an oral argument, "What right has the President to interfere with the honest discharge of the duties of a Secretary of the Treasury? None, whatsoever." Grant, in response, had Henderson removed, and a different special prosecutor tried Babcock, who was eventually acquitted with help from Grant's own testimony. In contrast to modern times, when the firings of Special Prosecutor Archibald Cox and FBI director Comey have provoked political firestorms, Grant's removal of Henderson actually received the backing of his cabinet and did not result in a major backlash. This undoubtedly reflects the fact that the norms of the modern presidency's interactions with law enforcement were still in their infancy. It also may reflect the fact that Henderson's comments in the case were genuinely disrespectful of the actual executive branch hierarchy, in which the president does, in fact, have the right to direct the conduct of the secretary of the Treasury. It probably also reflects the fact that Grant was politically popular.

In other respects, however, Grant's handling of the Whiskey Ring scandal presages important aspects of the modern confrontation between presidents and their prosecutors. Grant tolerated the investigation, but he also hated it and bristled at it as it got closer to him. In a detail with peculiarly Trumpian echoes, when there were reports that investigators might be focusing on his son and brother, Grant demanded that those reports be publicly rebutted. He was also infuriated by the practice Trump would later call "flipping" witnesses. At one point Grant actually had the attorney general advise U.S. attorneys in the Midwest against letting witnesses cooperate in exchange for immunity. To Wilson, he complained, "When I said let no guilty man escape, I meant it, and not that nine men should escape, and one be convicted." The Whiskey Ring episode also poisoned Grant's relationship with Bristow, who resigned, faulting Grant, as he wrote in his letter of resignation, for "withdrawal of your confidence & official support." At the end of the day, Grant consented to the Whiskey Ring investigation, but only grudgingly and only because he had no other choice.

The president's consent to a wide-ranging investigation by special prosecutors of executive branch wrongdoing turns out to be more easily obtained when the president isn't being asked to allow investigation of his own government but of that of his dead predecessor. Dead presidents, after all, don't fire special prosecutors, nor do they issue untoward orders or pardon those who remain loyal to them. So when President Warren Harding died of a heart attack in San Francisco in 1923, he probably smoothed the way for the Teapot Dome investigation, the first corruption investigation to imprison a member of the cabinet. Teapot Dome involved a kickback scheme in which Interior Secretary Albert Fall granted no-bid oil leases on federal lands in Wyoming and California in exchange for bribes. Revelations of the scheme, which emerged only after Harding's death, were the result of a surprisingly dogged and tenacious congressional investigation. As the damning facts came out, the new president, Calvin Coolidge, didn't resist the appointment of a special prosecutor to examine the matter; in fact, in an innovation, he proposed two of them, one Democrat and one Republican, to work together on it. And in contrast to both prior and subsequent special prosecutor investigations, he sought specific legislation to authorize the appointments, which proceeded by presidential nomination with the advice and consent of the Senate. Coolidge's first nominees encountered Senate resistance, but his second efforts bore remarkable fruit. A then-obscure Republican lawyer named Owen Roberts—who later rode the fame of the Teapot Dome investigation to become a Supreme Court justice—and a former Democratic senator named Atlee Pomerene were confirmed by the Senate in February 1924. And, although Alexander Hamilton had warned against dividing executive authority, Pomerene and Roberts worked remarkably well together, securing indictments against Fall and against the men who bribed him. Fall was convicted for receiving the bribes, though the men who offered the bribes were acquitted. The former attorney general, Harry Daugherty, was never charged with involvement in the Teapot Dome affair, though he was indicted and acquitted in a separate property fraud scheme. Prior to Watergate, Teapot Dome was the country's most notorious political scandal, and the successful use of the special prosecutor almost certainly provided the template for Watergate when that scandal broke half a century later.

Watergate profoundly changed the way Americans understand presidential scandal and the investigation of it. For one thing, the investigation was not simply, as with Teapot Dome, an investigation of corrupt activity at the senior levels of government or, as with the Whiskey Ring, an investigation of corrupt activity in the White House and by people close to a president. Watergate involved corrupt activity *by the president himself,* and thus involved ultimately a criminal investigation *of the president.* That had never happened before, and it raised acutely the question of whether a president would or must consent to an executive branch investigation not merely of those around him, but of himself—one that could lead to his own impeachment or even criminal prosecution. A separate novel feature was the sheer scope of the presidential criminality. Richard Nixon turned out to be not just a very uncommon criminal himself, but also one who surrounded himself with others. His senior White House staff, attorney general, and campaign staff all went to prison in connection with the Watergate scandal. What's more, his vice president, Spiro Agnew, was forced to step down in a plea bargain in connection with a separate bribery and extortion scandal that just happened to erupt at the same time. And

Watergate, of course, turned out to be the tip of a very large iceberg of spying scandals involving the intelligence community, scandals that continued to unfold throughout the 1970s.

The degree to which the president's personal conduct was directly at issue in the Watergate investigation, along with the particularly bad nature of that conduct, made the question of presidential consent to the investigation especially fraught. Nixon's consent was an open question, particularly when—in the Saturday Night Massacre—he fired Special Prosecutor Archibald Cox and also lost the attorney general and the deputy attorney general, who both refused to carry out the order to fire Cox and subsequently resigned or were fired, respectively. Nixon very much sought to obstruct the investigation of Watergate: the "smoking gun" tape depicted an instruction by the president to his chief of staff to have the CIA intervene to get the FBI to back off the investigation of the break-in at the Democratic campaign headquarters. Nixon also sought to obstruct the separate investigation of Agnew. The statement that he consented to the investigation that ultimately brought him down is thus perhaps a bit mischievous.

But it's also, in important respects, true. Although Nixon sought to obstruct the investigation in any number of ways and did fire Cox, in the end he had to tolerate it. He was politically constrained by the threat of impeachment from ever actually shutting it down. And he had to replace Cox with a prosecutor—Leon Jaworski—who continued the investigation with even stronger protections for his independence of action than Cox had.

It was the fear of being seen as obstructing the investigation that prevented Nixon from destroying the incriminating Oval Office tapes. He knew the recordings would be damning, but he developed a different strategy for preventing their publication. The Harvard law professor Philip Heymann, who worked with Cox, has argued that Nixon knew that, though he might be able to create enough smoke to avoid formal charges, if he was perceived as hindering the investigation, he'd never "convince the many doubters that he hadn't engaged in an illegal cover-up." Heymann writes that, for Nixon's purposes,

[a] Supreme Court decision that an overriding national interest in secrecy—expressed legally as an executive or national security privilege—protected him from having to reveal what had happened in the White House would be much better. [Nixon] could describe withholding the tapes as a matter of a President's "responsibility" to say nothing in order to protect our national security and to maintain badly needed Presidential powers to consult close aides. Thus, declining to reveal their content would quite possibly seem simple patriotism in those years of Middle-East wars, changed relations with Russia, and opening to China. Stated more broadly, the President's argument in the courts would be that no single-focused interest in the Watergate break-in and its aftermath—or of practically any single crime—was as important as protecting the conditions of privacy that all presidents require in order to exercise the many grave responsibilities of their office. Without protection of the secrecy of his conversations by executive and national security privileges, the tail of a minor case of burglary would be wagging the dog of ensuring the nation had a functioning chief executive.

In other words, Nixon's play was formally to consent to be investigated and then couch attempted obstruction as a defense of the office of the presidency rather than one of self-preservation. But it was Nixon's technical, formal consent to the investigation that proved pivotal to the Supreme Court's holding in the landmark tapes case, which ultimately triggered the president's resignation. One of the many novel questions the Watergate scandal raised was whether and under what circumstances the executive branch could litigate against itself. If the executive is unitary, after all, how can a prosecutor who works for the president ask a court to force that president to give up evidence? Isn't the handling of the tapes merely an internal executive branch dispute? The court resolved this critical threshold question of its own jurisdiction over the matter with reference to Nixon's consent to the investigation. The court explained that

> the Attorney General has delegated the authority to represent the United States in these particular matters to a Special Prosecutor with unique authority and tenure. The regulation gives the Special Prosecutor explicit power to contest the invocation of executive privilege in the process of seeking evidence deemed relevant to the performance of these specially delegated duties.

The court went on to reason that "so long as this regulation is extant, it has the force of law":

> It is theoretically possible for the Attorney General to amend or revoke the regulation defining the Special Prosecutor's authority. But he has not done so. So long as this regulation remains in force, the Executive Branch is bound by it, and indeed the United States, as the sovereign composed of the three branches, is bound to respect and to enforce it.

In other words, the president has the power to get rid of the office of special prosecutor or to limit the prosecutor's power to demand evidence by instructing the attorney general to issue an order to him or by altering the regulation, if not by a direct exertion of power himself. But as long as Nixon didn't do so, he effectively consented to Jaworski's choices as to how to investigate and litigate, including against the president himself. The entire authority of the Supreme Court to hear the Nixon tapes case hinged on this point. The president was permitted to use blunt—and thus highly visible—instruments, such as firing people or rescinding the regulations. He could refuse to consent to an investigation outright and suffer the political consequences. But he could not formally consent to it and then work to impede it while shirking accountability for his actions.

Again, Nixon's consent did not emerge from any public-spiritedness on his part. He initially tried to ride out the investigation, and his supporters stood by him through much of it. Had the tapes not materialized, Nixon might well have survived Watergate. By the time the crisis over the tapes reached the point of litigation, Nixon knew that the cost of withholding his consent outright would at least be risking removal from office. Yet he still fired Cox. His consent to the investigation after this attempt to shut it down was the sort of consent one gives with a gun to one's head. He could provoke a constitutional confrontation he could not win by shutting down the investigation, by refusing to comply with the Supreme Court's ruling, by pardoning the Watergate felons, or by otherwise exerting some of the rawest powers of the presidency—and he would go down in the flames of immediate congressional response. Or, in the alternative, he could submit to the slow, steady progression of the investigation and fight it in litigation and in the public relations arena. For all his criminality and his experimentations and flirtations with refusing his consent altogether, Nixon ultimately chose the latter course, and when he lost the political clout to continue the fight on those terms, he resigned. He did not burn the house down, though he may have doused it in kerosene and walked out holding a lit match.

The fallout from Watergate has conditioned every subsequent investigation of a president. Watergate, for starters, established that removal was not merely a theoretical possibility but could actually result from a combination of criminal process and impeachment. It established, as the above-quoted passage from *United States v. Nixon* held, that at least under certain circumstances, a special prosecutor could actually litigate against the President of the United States—which is to say that a finger of the executive branch could attack the head that supposedly controls it. It limited the executive privilege a president could assert in such litigation.

More fundamentally, it established a certain public expectation that a presidential scandal would be investigated as a criminal matter, not merely dealt with as a political matter. As such, it shifted the locus of investigation of presidential scandal from Congress to the executive branch. Ironically, at the very time the country grew worried about "the imperial presidency" and the growth of presidential power, it migrated the power to investigate the president from a coordinate branch of government into the executive branch itself. And finally, the response to Watergate included attempts to codify in statute some of these principles and expectations, specifically the 1978 law that came to be known as the "independent counsel" law.

For as long as it remained on the books, the independent counsel law reduced the necessity of presidential consent. It created an automatic trigger for the appointment of a special prosecutor whenever the evidence or allegation reached a certain minimum level of credibility; it gave the power to name the prosecutor to a panel of judges; it removed the attorney general from the line of command in supervising that prosecutor, giving the special prosecutor "full power and independent authority" to stand in for the attorney general in matters within his or her jurisdiction; and it limited the circumstances in which the special prosecutor could be fired to situations of "good cause" and gave the prosecutor an appeal mechanism to review his or her dismissal. The independent counsel law caused a proliferation of special prosecutor investigations, not just against presidents but against any number of lower-level officials covered by its terms. It dogged three successive administrations—those of Ronald Reagan, George H. W. Bush, and Bill Clinton. At the presidential level, Reagan and Bush dealt with the Iran-Contra investigation, and Clinton confronted the Starr investigation, which began as a probe of an Arkansas land deal and ended in Clinton's impeachment over lies and obstruction of justice in connection with the Monica Lewinsky affair.

In different ways, all three presidents pushed back against the independent counsels who investigated them: Bush Sr., at the end of his presidency, pardoned a group of Iran-Contra figures. Clinton engaged in protracted litigation with Kenneth Starr's team over a wide variety of issues and ran a public campaign of delegitimization against Starr and his witnesses. Reagan sought to have the independent counsel law thrown out on constitutional grounds, supporting Supreme Court litigation to invalidate the law altogether. All three presidents chafed at the law and did a lot of complaining about the behavior of the special prosecutors who served under it.

But if the independent counsel provisions diminished the necessity of presidential consent to investigations, they did not eliminate it entirely. Firing Lawrence Walsh, the Iran-Contra prosecutor, or Kenneth Starr was never seriously contemplated; indeed, even as the Reagan administration sought to have Walsh's independent counsel role thrown out by the courts, it concurrently appointed him as a special prosecutor under the old regulatory system so the investigation would continue even if the legal challenge prevailed. The expectation that a criminal investigation was a necessary part of resolving an allegation of impropriety against a president was, after Watergate, so deeply embedded in public expectations of ethics in government that using the power of the president to prevent an investigation from happening was simply not an option. Presidents could complain about independent counsels, but those same presidents would sign legislation reauthorizing the offending law; indeed, Reagan signed reauthorizations in 1983 and 1987, and in 1994 Clinton signed the law under which the Starr investigation then proceeded.

At the time of the Starr investigation, when Clinton's defenders made all sorts of allegations against Starr and his prosecutors, one of the present authors pointed out that, in a meaningful sense, Clinton was consenting to Starr's activity. In a *Washington Post* op-ed written in 1998, he described the Clinton position about Starr—that "the independent counsel is a menace to the public whom our victim-in-chief is stoically suffering, but a menace that . . . he is powerless to stop"—as a "compound falsehood." The article noted that even if "Starr were the runaway, out-of-control prosecutor the White House describes," the president could simply direct the attorney general to fire him, consistent with the independent counsel law. And while "firing Starr would, of course, have unpalatable political overtones emanating from the Saturday Night Massacre during Watergate," the law expressly allowed that Starr could be fired "only by the personal action of the Attorney General and only for good cause." Even as Starr spent months preparing an impeachment referral against Clinton, Clinton never attempted to shut down the investigation.

Another important development during this period was completion of the pattern, hinted at in Watergate, in which congressional investigation of executive branch misconduct became subservient to executive investigation of itself. In Teapot Dome, the criminal investigation grew out of congressional investigation. During Watergate, prosecutors and congressional investigators shared the task of probing the scandal. By the time of the Iran-Contra scandal more than a decade later, the form of shared responsibility persisted, but the reality did not; congressional investigations took place, but Walsh's investigation dominated. Indeed, the congressional investigations brought the enterprise of dual-branch investigation into some disrepute by granting limited immunity to two key figures— Oliver North and John Poindexter—in a fashion that later caused the D.C. Circuit Court of Appeals to throw out convictions obtained by Walsh.

To some degree, this pattern simply reflected the fact that the executive branch has more powerful investigative tools than does the legislature: better and more numerous investigators, more refined forensic capacities, and authorities better tailored for forcing witness cooperation. Investigation is something the executive branch does routinely and well. It is something the legislative branch does less routinely—and less well. The legal tools to help investigators get information are mostly designed for the executive. Congress cannot obtain wiretap or surveillance orders, and it's not geared up to enforce even the subpoenas it has the power to issue. Congress doesn't have a crime lab or evidence facilities. The more complicated and technical investigations became, the less plausible an actor Congress thus was to perform them.

Congress, of course, could have developed some of these capabilities. To this day it retains substantial investigative authorities of its own; it can hold hearings, conduct interviews, and subpoena documents and testimony. It is possible to imagine a world in which Congress could conduct thorough investigations on its own without relying on the executive branch, though perhaps not investigations with the power or sophistication of the executive branch. It might hire independent, professional staff and delegate subpoena and other powers to that staff. But there are limits to what Congress can do here, at least without making dramatic statutory changes. And Congress hasn't gone that route, in any event. Instead, it let its own investigative powers atrophy, and that habit became self-perpetuating. Deferring to the executive gave rise to habits of deferring—which is to say habits of Congress not doing its own work.

By the time of the Lewinsky matter, Congress didn't even try to do its own investigation. It simply waited on the sidelines for the criminal process to spoon-feed it a factual record. The Lewinsky scandal broke in January 1998, yet Congress did nothing until the Starr Report arrived in September 1998, almost nine months later. Congress effectively treated Starr, an executive branch official, as its own impeachment investigator. Even after Starr's referral, congressional investigation added virtually no information of its own.

In other words, by the time of the Starr investigation, what the president was being asked to consent to was something quite beyond a criminal investigation of executive branch conduct involving people close to him, as happened in the Whiskey Ring. It even went beyond the president's being forced to tolerate a criminal investigation of himself under threat of impeachment, as in Watergate. Clinton effectively tolerated an executive branch officer, under the cloak of a criminal investigation, being converted into an impeachment investigator on behalf of the legislative branch. The criminal probe in the Lewinsky matter was not a pretext, in the sense that there were, in fact, live criminal questions that ultimately required dispositions. Those questions, however, were very much secondary matters. The principal question was always one of impeachment. And the criminal probe thus provided plausible cover for the executive branch to perform the legislative branch's investigation on its behalf.

Concern over the risks inherent in this reality did not detain many commentators during the Clinton scandals, perhaps because nobody was truly afraid that Clinton would prevent Starr from doing his work. But the concern grows acute when there is a genuine worry that a president will not tolerate an executive branch investigation—and Congress does not bother to do one of its own.

When the independent counsel law expired at the end of 1999, by agreement of both parties it was allowed to die. The independent counsel regime had profound constitutional difficulties, notwithstanding the Supreme Court's having upheld it; but its ultimate problem was a related set of policy difficulties. It created prosecutors who were simply too independent. The institution, having now gored both Republican and Democratic administrations, no longer had a constituency. And so the current special counsel regulations were promulgated in its place. These regulations create a prosecutor within the Justice Department with some independence, but this prosecutor does report to the attorney general.

Still, the expectations that developed in the wake of Watergate and that came to be embodied in the independent counsel law did not die. The expectation that the criminal process is the principal means of investigating presidential misconduct—indeed, the expectation that the legislature will defer to and work off the record established by prosecutors—is plainly visible in the legislative deference to the Mueller investigation. Over two years of Republican control of the Congress, only the Senate Select Committee on Intelligence saw fit to investigate Russian interference in the 2016 election in a serious bipartisan fashion, and no committee in either house of Congress publicly took on questions of Trump's conduct a sustained way. The attitude of Republicans was either to claim to await Mueller's findings—only to be largely silent when they finally came—or to preemptively seek to discredit them. There was no move to put congressional investigation at the center of the accountability process. Democrats decried the lack of investigation, and while they began pursuing a more energetic investigative agenda after taking control of the House of Representatives in January 2019, they still voiced significant deference to Mueller's fact-finding, if not to his conclusions. The locus of the investigation was always within the executive branch, and the initial legislative reaction to Trump's conduct hinged entirely on the findings generated by that investigation, not on the findings of any investigation conducted by Congress itself.

When the Mueller report finally came, it demonstrated extraordinary wrongdoing on the part of the president but made no explicit accusations of criminality—a combination that seemed to baffle congressional Democrats. Their bewildered early response stemmed from the degree to which they had invested in the special counsel and the criminal process the disposition of questions that are ultimately not criminal in character: What should Congress do in response to the president's conduct? What legislation should it pass? What pressure should it bring to bear on Trump to change or cease objectionable behaviors? Should it ultimately tolerate his conduct? The Mueller report offered many facts, but no answers.

This is because the special counsel regulations ultimately don't bear the weight being put on them especially well. A criminal investigation, after all, is not a truth commission. A criminal investigation is not conducted in public, and it usually yields a public record only when someone is indicted or pleads guilty. Moreover, by its nature, it has to be concerned with crimes, not political misdeeds. And giving a reporting function to a prosecutor beyond the strict accounting of indictable criminality is always a dicey proposition—as became especially evident in the context of the Starr investigation. Starr was criticized for sharing too much in his report, but the converse risk is also present: the risk of a prosecutor sharing too little. Mueller determined that because he was unable to indict the sitting president consistent with the Department of Justice guidance, it would be improper for a prosecutor to accuse the president of a crime the prosecutor could not charge or even to "apply an approach that could potentially result in a judgment that the President committed crimes." If he had been able to say that the president had *not* committed crimes, Mueller wrote, he would have done so. In other words, by Mueller's read, a criminal investigation of the president can only exonerate the president and cannot accuse him. Having laid bare his conundrum, Mueller declared that he was creating a record for prosecutorial assessment when the president leaves office and can theoretically be indicted, thus leaving the matter in Congress's hands in the short term.

Essentially, there's a profound mismatch between the type of investigation the executive conducts—a criminal probe—and the ultimate remedy available to Congress. Impeachment, after all, is not a criminal remedy. And it is not available only for crimes. The great constitutional scholar Charles Black, Jr., proved this point in three pithy sentences: "Suppose a president were to move to Saudi Arabia, so he could have four wives, and were to propose to conduct the office of the presidency by mail and wireless from there. This would not be a crime, provided his passport were in order. Is it possible that such gross and wanton neglect of duty could not be grounds for impeachment and removal?" Relying on the executive branch for an impeachment investigation risks limiting impeachment to the subject matters the executive branch investigates. And a prosecutor cannot investigate the broader and far more important question of whether the president behaved in a wholly unacceptable fashion with regard to federal law enforcement.

Most fundamentally, putting so much weight on the criminal process made the question of Trump's consent to the investigation the whole ball game. Because, unlike Starr, Mueller was not protected by the independent counsel law. So to the extent that Congress vested in him, through its own inaction and deference, the power to conduct its impeachment investigation, it was very much betting that the president would allow that investigation to go forward.

There are profound dangers in Congress's letting the executive— which is to say the president—do Congress's investigations on its behalf, particularly when you're dealing with an investigation of the president personally. Yes, proceeding in this fashion gives the legislature the benefit of the executive's superior investigative tools. But it also creates a kind of variation of the Fort Knox problem, one in which all the investigative capacity and all the investigative fruits are in the hands of the investigative subject. It puts an immense premium on the question of the president's consent to the investigation—and willingness to not impede it or corrupt it—making Congress's own constitutional functions not a backstop for the norms of presidential consent, but a kind of hostage to presidential compliance with those norms. After all, if the only thing that protects the norm of presidential consent to and noninterference with investigations is the threat of impeachment, and Congress has subcontracted its impeachment investigation to the very executive branch officer whose independence is supposed to be guaranteed by the threat of impeachment, then Congress is not functioning as a coordinate branch of government enforcing the norm. It is functioning as a supplicant, asking the executive for the benefit of the norm and entirely dependent on executive good faith for compliance. This is corrosive stuff for a system built on separated powers. The idea of a unitary executive, after all, relies on the idea that the executive has watchers in other branches. It relies on the idea that the executive fears those actors. And it relies on the idea that such fear deters bad behavior.

Trump's ultimate consent to the Mueller investigation leaves a complicated legacy. On the one hand, he did permit the investigation to proceed to its conclusion. Trump did not fire his prosecutors, at least not those directly responsible for the investigation. Nor did he prevent either Mueller or the prosecutors of the Southern District of New York from taking investigative steps they deemed appropriate. And, strangely enough given his public posture, Trump cooperated to a considerable degree with the witch-hunters, making large volumes of material available to investigators and largely not resisting efforts to interview White House staff. He mostly did not assert privileges preventing key staff from speaking to

Mueller, and he provided written answers to some limited questions. Indeed, to the extent that he has refused cooperation in practice, Trump's refusal has largely taken the form of the assertion of nonfrivolous legal entitlements—for example, his claim that prosecutors cannot compel him to sit for an interview. Such claims are, to be sure, legally contestable, but they are not different in kind from the claims of other presidents who have confronted investigative demands from prosecutors in circumstances in which pushback could be supported with plausible legal arguments.

All of this is not to say that Trump entirely gave his consent to be investigated. Rather, as the Mueller report describes, the president tried to withhold his consent a number of times and by a number of means. As we saw in the prior chapter, the president waged a large-scale campaign to get a grip on those who would investigate him. And, of course, Trump did order White House counsel Don McGahn to have Mueller removed as special counsel—but McGahn decided he would rather resign than carry out the order. In addition to pressuring Sessions to undo his recusal in the Russia investigation, Trump also reportedly pressured his replacement Whitaker to get control over the investigation in the Southern District of New York, suggesting a similar intention to deny his consent to those inquiries.

Trump also publicly threatened to go much further. He has not pardoned anyone connected to investigations of himself, but he has repeatedly and publicly entertained the idea, and his suggestion that he would "take care" of those who remained loyal to him may have injured the Mueller investigators. The Mueller report documents Trump's overtures through his private counsel toward Michael Flynn, Paul Manafort, and Michael Cohen in an apparent effort to prevent their cooperation with federal law enforcement. Both Flynn and Cohen decided to come clean anyway, but Manafort breached his plea agreement and lied to prosecutors. In other words, the president allowed prosecutors to apply pressure to Manafort, but then worked behind the scenes and in public to use the powers of his office to undermine that pressure. So to say that Trump "consented" to the

Mueller investigation by formally allowing it to proceed to its completion elides important facts. He tried to stop it, but couldn't. He sought to limit its jurisdiction and failed. And he tried actively to coax witnesses not to help. He was, at the end of the day, thwarted in his efforts to stymie the Mueller probe—both by his personal incompetence and by disobedient staff who refused to carry out his orders. Such consent, if consent it represents, is only de facto. Trump's public stance has been emphatically to reserve the right to block investigation of himself. In the end, the limited consent he granted to Mueller continues to raise the question of whether he will consent to investigations to which he is subject in the future. So the risk remains that Trump will eventually decide to call the bluff of Congress and the public. From the beginning, he has demonstrated in incremental ways that he can get away with plenty that prior presidents wouldn't have dared to attempt—for example, firing the FBI director and then the attorney general and openly admitting that both actions were related to the Russia investigation. In both cases, Congress tolerated the move.

The findings of the Mueller report are themselves a challenge to Congress. We do not know what Congress will ultimately do in response; as of this writing the House of Representatives and the White House are sparring over a variety of subpoenas and document production demands, and an impeachment process is under way on other matters. If the legislative branch ultimately decides to tolerate Trump's obstructive conduct as described in the report, then Trump might well conclude that Congress will tolerate direct efforts to stop investigations in the future. And he would be quite reasonable to reach precisely that conclusion. In short, Trump's interactions with investigators—as described by Mueller and as seen in his conduct with respect to other investigations—have deeply tested the question of whether Congress would, in fact, enforce the norms surrounding investigation of the president with its impeachment and removal power. Trump's radical proposition is that the president need not observe these norms. He has advanced this idea in dozens of comments. And Congress has not responded with a clear message that if he did not honor them, it would end his presidency.

There is a grave risk in Congress's not drawing clear lines of consequences and accountability on this point. It is the risk of deterrence failure. Trump has repeatedly engaged in activity that should have antagonized an institution that has the power to destroy his presidency but has long-cultivated habits of slumber. The question is whether that entity will now awaken to insist that presidents permit investigations of themselves. Or will it roll over, mutter something disapproving, and go back to sleep?

NINE

"Without deliberation . . . or appreciation of facts"

THE CONDUCT OF FOREIGN AFFAIRS

THE MORNING OF DECEMBER 19, 2018, DAWNED WITH ALMOST no one expecting a U.S. withdrawal of military forces from Syria. Bashar al-Assad wasn't expecting it in Damascus. Vladimir Putin wasn't expecting it in Moscow. American allies worldwide were not expecting it. And almost nobody within the U.S. government was expecting it either.

Plenty of controversy had long attended the two thousand or so American troops serving in the country, and many people opposed the military engagement in the region more generally. But whatever problems they perceived, few analysts or political figures were recommending a sudden announcement of a quick withdrawal as the answer. The American presence, after all, had been key to rolling back the gains of the Islamic State, and it had, to some degree, restrained Turkey in its interactions with Kurdish forces and Russia and the Assad regime in their brutal victory in the country's civil war. Virtually no one was arguing that creating a sudden vacuum in the region would help matters.

It's safe to say that Trump awoke on December 19 facing no pressure to announce a major policy shift that had significant implications for allies and the stability of an unstable ecosystem, much less any pressure to do so without doing advance work to alert partners and allow them to prepare.

The week prior, however, on December 14, Turkish president Recep Tayyip Erdoğan had reached Trump by phone and complained of the U.S. presence in the country and its continued support of Syrian Kurdish fighters. As *The Washington Post* later recounted, Trump responded, "You know what? It's yours." He added: "I'm leaving."

The matter stayed quiet over the next few days until the president suddenly took to Twitter to declare in a series of tweets that the United States had "defeated ISIS in Syria, my only reason for being there" and that it was "time to bring our great young people home." The military let it be known that the president had ordered that the withdrawal be completed within thirty days.

The response from U.S. allies was swift and alarmed. "For now of course we remain in Syria," said France's European affairs minister Nathalie Loiseau. "The fight against terrorism is not over." A British defense official shared one of Trump's triumphant tweets about the defeat of ISIS, adding, "I strongly disagree." Kurdish forces, whom Turkey would likely menace without the U.S. presence, declared that Trump's decision would "lead to a state of instability and create a political and military void in the region."

Domestically, even staunch Trump defenders expressed opposition.

Lindsey Graham fretted that the announcement had "rattled the world" and declared that there was bipartisan support for the president to reverse course. When Vice President Pence went to Capitol Hill to meet with congressional Republicans on the matter, "virtually everyone who spoke, spoke in opposition to the decision," as Senator Marco Rubio put it. The Republican-controlled Senate even passed a measure rebuking the president.

The only prominent Republican who spoke up in favor of the president's action domestically was the famously anti-interventionist senator Rand Paul. Internationally, Trump's biggest supporters were Russian president Putin and Turkish strongman Erdoğan.

The biggest blow, however, came from within the president's own cabinet. In a terse letter of resignation, Secretary of Defense James Mattis—the only member of Trump's cabinet with a truly independent and bipartisan reputation—wrote, "Our strength as a nation is inextricably linked to the strength of our unique and comprehensive system of alliances and partnerships." The storied former U.S. Marine general declared, "We must be resolute and unambiguous in our approach to those countries whose strategic interests are increasingly in tension with ours." And he stated that his "views on treating allies with respect and also being clear-eyed about both malign actors and strategic competitors are strongly held and informed by over four decades of immersion in these issues." He was stepping down, he concluded, because the president has "the right to have a Secretary of Defense whose views are better aligned with" his own. The clear implication was that, unlike Mattis, the president did not believe in the country's alliances or in being "clear-eyed about both malign actors and strategic competitors." Shortly thereafter, the State Department's special envoy on ISIS matters, Brett McGurk, announced that he was hastening his planned departure, later criticizing the president's "snap decision" that, McGurk wrote, "was made without deliberation, consultation with allies or Congress, assessment of risk, or appreciation of facts."

Trump appeared caught off guard at the shock his announcement generated. True to form, he came out swinging with personal attacks against

Mattis and McGurk. And he objected to the idea that his decision had come without warning. "Getting out of Syria was no surprise," he tweeted indignantly. "I've been campaigning on it for years, and six months ago, when I very publicly wanted to do it, I agreed to stay longer."

In an important sense, Trump was right on this point. When he hadn't been promising that he would "utterly destroy ISIS," he had often promised to avoid overseas deployments and expressed frustration at the existing commitments in Afghanistan and Syria and Iraq. His desire to disentangle the United States from its various military commitments overseas was certainly no secret. And it was broadly consistent with the growing anti-interventionist strain in both political parties. Obama too, after all, had been publicly opposed to unnecessary military engagements in the Middle East. And Trump's skepticism of U.S. intervention overseas, which often sounded more like the traditional left than like his own party, had tapped into a latent strain of conservative skepticism of an assertive U.S. presence abroad.

On the other hand, his administration, with its usual lack of message coherence, had been busily sending precisely the opposite signals in the weeks just before Trump's sudden withdrawal announcement. So the announcement came not only over the objections of all of his most senior advisers, but also as a 180-degree reversal of everything his administration had been saying up until the moment at which he changed course.

Trump's announcement of the Syria withdrawal isolates some of the distinctive features of his style of foreign policy decision-making, a style that presents a deep challenge to the way the traditional presidency thinks about foreign affairs. The traditional presidency, after all, values consistency of messaging in foreign policy, predictability, process-driven reliability with allies, and clear signals to foes; it emphasizes impersonal representations of national interests that don't change all that much as new figures come upon and leave the scene. Despite this preference for stability, the presidency faces the fewest constraints in the area of foreign affairs, making it the zone most susceptible to presidential personalization, to someone new coming in and throwing decades of conventional wisdom out the window just because he or she feels like it. And that's what Trump has done. His exercise of the foreign policy authorities of the presidency embraces a decision-making style based on his highly impulsive personality and his rejection not just of process but also of unwelcome information. It is primarily conditioned by the interpersonal interactions between Trump and his counterparts. And Trump often—though certainly not always—sets his unusual deployment of these powers toward substantive goals that are openly defiant of policy positions supported by a strong bipartisan consensus, at least among elites and foreign policy professionals. Foreign policy thus presents a dramatic case study for the expressive presidency—a realm in which the constraints are least tight and the stakes can be the highest. It is the arena in which the president's word is most easily made flesh, which is what the expressive presidency is really all about.

The Syria announcement was a perfect storm, combining virtually all the salient features of Trump's foreign policy decision-making. It was impulsive, blindsiding both allies and senior officials of his own administration. It was highly personal, elevating presidential instinct and opinion over any policy process and treating a major geopolitical concession as if it were a matter to be arranged with a friend on the phone. And it flew in the face of a strong political consensus—not, in this case, a consensus that American troops should be in Syria, but a consensus that, whatever their proper place in that conflict-ridden country, this was no way to get them out.

Predictably, the announcement touched off months of chaos and conflicting statements from the administration and the president himself. The thirty-day withdrawal deadline came and went. U.S. troops remained on the ground in Syria until—as this book was going to press in October 2019—the cycle repeated itself and Erdoğan persuaded Trump to abandon the Kurds to a Turkish military onslaught.

The Syria pronouncement was not the first time the distinctive features of Trump's foreign policy decision-making dovetailed in dramatic fashion. At the Helsinki summit with Putin, Trump had generated outrage across the political spectrum with his extemporaneously accommodationist stance toward the Russian leader. He about-faced from threatening North Korea with the "fire and fury" of nuclear annihilation to holding chummy summits with Kim Jong Un in Singapore and Vietnam and the demilitarized zone after the dictator won him over with what Trump later called "love letters." In doing so, Trump went against a strong bipartisan consensus that opposed making concessions to the North Koreans in the absence of tangible, measurable, and verifiable commitments. And in his repeated threats to abandon the NATO alliance and allies in Asia, he threatened one of the bedrock premises of post–World War II foreign policy across administrations of both parties.

Foreign policy is particularly vulnerable to the expressive presidency because it is where the presidency is least constrained by law and cumbersome regulatory schemes and where bureaucratic processes are most easily waved away. The president's leeway is certainly not absolute. Congress has legislative and appropriations authorities that both meaningfully shape American foreign policy and constrain presidential action. Trump has sometimes struggled with these, as when Congress passed by veto-proof majorities a law strengthening sanctions against Russia that the president opposed—effectively forcing it on him. To prevent the president and his then secretary of state, Rex Tillerson, from gutting the foreign assistance budget, Congress also stepped in, funding activity over the new administration's objections. And the president is also hemmed in by legally binding treaty commitments with actors all over the world. A president's foreign policy actions are, in any number of ways, checked by other actors.

Yet they are far less checked than his or her actions in the domestic sphere. In this sense, foreign policy is the place where the expressive presidency is potentially the most expressive and where it poses the highest stakes. In domestic affairs, most presidential authority flows from delegated congressional authority. For example, Congress has the power to regulate such things as telecommunications or environmental protec-

tions, and it creates federal agencies to execute its will; the president simply manages those agencies. The president has no independent authority
to investigate crimes beyond the power Congress gives him or her by making certain activity criminal in the first place. The president has no power
to collect taxes beyond the laws Congress passes levying them. And the
president has no power to regulate, say, drug safety, beyond that which
Congress creates. Most, though not all, domestic presidential power is
ultimately delegated congressional power.

By contrast, in foreign policy, a great deal of the president's power
flows directly from the Constitution itself; congressional enactments
are comparatively sparse. There is no comprehensive regulatory regime
directing how U.S. relations with, say, Brazil or France should operate—
though relations with countries like Cuba and Iran do have an overlay of
statutory sanctions. Given the relative freedom, it's no surprise that presidents who feel frustrated by the constraints of domestic policy often turn
their focus to foreign policy.

How the executive came to enjoy so free a hand in foreign affairs is
the subject of many volumes of scholarship. For its part, the Constitution actually spends relatively few words on the president's foreign
policy responsibilities. It makes her commander in chief of the military.
It gives him the power, with the advice and consent of two-thirds of the
Senate, to make treaties. It gives her the authority, with the Senate's
consent, to appoint ambassadors to other countries. It gives him the
power to "receive Ambassadors and other public Ministers" from other
countries. And it, more generally, vests in her "the Executive Power"—a
clause that is understood by some scholars, though not all, to fill in gaps.
That's it.

The hitch is that each of these powers contains multitudes, or at least
has come to contain multitudes through accretion over generations of
practice by presidents. The power to make treaties is the power to negotiate with other countries, and that power to negotiate has evolved over the
centuries to include the authority to make agreements that are something

less than treaties but that still guide and bind U.S. action in critical respects. The Iran nuclear deal is one famous recent example of this, but hundreds of so-called executive agreements with other countries exist in wide-ranging areas. The power to negotiate is also the power to make demands, to make promises, to explore arrangements that might or might not lead to treaties. It is, broadly speaking, the power to engage other countries in diplomacy.

The power to receive ambassadors has come to be understood as the power to recognize other governments and their claims—the power, for example, to move the embassy in Israel from Tel Aviv to Jerusalem and the power to withdraw recognition of Venezuelan president Nicolás Maduro and grant that recognition to an opposition leader who claims the presidency. And, of course, the commander in chief power has come to include the authority to order U.S. troops into combat around the world, to threaten the use of force, and to wake up one morning and announce a withdrawal from Syria that nobody was expecting.

The other hitch is that on top of these constitutional powers, Congress has added layer upon layer of statutory authority that empowers the president further. Federal statutes give the president, for example, wide authority over who can come into the United States—authority very much in play when Trump issued the travel ban. They give her power to designate foreign non-state groups as terrorist organizations and to impose criminal penalties on those who give "material support" to such groups. They give him powers to impose economic sanctions on countries and individuals. They give her the power to impose tariffs. They give him the power to declare national emergencies and to take a raft of actions pursuant to such declarations. They give her a plethora of other powers as well. And since 2001, Congress has also authorized the president to use "all necessary and appropriate force" to respond to September 11, a delegation of authority that has been interpreted to authorize sprawling counterterrorism operations all over the world.

This aggregation of power to the executive was not intended by the founders, yet it was driven by some of the features of the executive that they designed quite intentionally. Foreign affairs are that area in which what Alexander Hamilton called "energy" is most obviously useful and "decision, activity, secrecy, and despatch" most necessary. Hamilton's point was that those features are more likely to be present in a process led by one person than in a process led by many people. Over time, acting on that same assumption, the larger, less organized group—Congress—has handed over great responsibility to the "single" body of the executive.

A great many scholars find this migration of power alarming, and some find the premise flawed as well. Arthur Schlesinger's famed work on the subject, *The Imperial Presidency*, argues that Vietnam proved wrong the assumption that "foreign policy must be trusted to the executive" and that "the traditional arguments in favor of presidential supremacy—unity, secrecy, superior expertise, superior sources of information, decision, dispatch—turned out to be immensely overrated." Unity may have existed in the 1790s, Schlesinger argued, but it "was an illusion in the vast and refractory executive branch of the 1970s." Leaks made executive secrecy a kind of joke. The arguments Hamilton and John Jay advanced in *The Federalist Papers*, he writes, "applied . . . a good deal more to their own time than to the nuclear age." All that remained in the modern era "was the mystical assumption that the Presidency was more likely to be right than the Congress." Of course Trump, with his active contempt for intelligence information and his chaotic style, rather bolsters Schlesinger's skepticism about Hamilton's premises. Yet rightly or wrongly, those premises have shaped the allocations of foreign policy decision-making.

And the modern president's preeminence in foreign affairs has its defenders too. The Supreme Court famously declared the president to be the "sole organ of the federal government in the field of international relations" and noted that "he, not Congress, has the better opportunity of knowing the conditions which prevail in foreign countries, and especially is this true in time of war. He has his confidential sources of information. He has his agents in the form of diplomatic, consular and other officials."

Modern presidents have the power to do a great deal more than the founders—even Hamilton—ever imagined. This is not Donald Trump's fault. It is a condition he inherited. But it is a condition that makes the presidency especially vulnerable to a mercurial personality like his in the domain of foreign affairs.

The foreign affairs power, as personalized by Trump, also dovetails mischievously with another outlying feature of his deployment of presidential power. Foreign policy is an area of presidential responsibility that is largely composed of the activity Trump prefers above all others: talking.

Foreign policy and domestic affairs are profoundly different in this respect. Whereas administering domestic policy is inseparable from the details of implementing complex programs—actions that tend to take place through legislative engagement and agency-level implementation of regulations and laws—in foreign relations, making an announcement or having a phone call often *is* the policy. When the president, for example, declares that the United States will use military force to defend European allies, the articulation of that commitment—at least if other countries believe it—is policy-making. Conversely, when the president publicly casts doubt on whether U.S. forces will defend allies, that speech is also policy. Other countries respond to it and take action on the basis of it. The president can get on the phone with a dictator and have a conversation and then hang up and order a withdrawal of U.S. forces from a foreign deployment, and that order will be carried out—at least if he doesn't change his mind. No lawsuit will interfere. A great many foreign policy actions, distilled to their core, boil down to someone—either the president or someone acting on his behalf—saying something, either publicly or privately. Sending an aircraft carrier group to a location in the world in a fashion that might be provocative is almost the prototypical kinetic action. But ordering that to happen as commander in chief is, in essence, the president saying something. This is why, to go back to an example cited in chapter 3, it was so important to White House aides to remove letters from Trump's desk; stopping him from saying things was a way of stopping bad things from happening. The president writing a letter saying that he was withdrawing from the trade agreement with South Korea *was* a withdrawal from it. Stop the letter, and you stop the withdrawal.

This is also true when the president is exercising powers delegated by Congress. The means of executing that authority is often just saying things. The act of imposing sanctions, issuing tariffs, or declaring national emergencies amounts to the president announcing that he or she has concluded something. The language of countless statutes is explicit in conveying authority to the president to do things by saying things.

Another reason why foreign policy is particularly vulnerable to presidential mouthing off is that so much of U.S. power internationally rests on confidence. Presidential statements that erode this confidence have an operational quality even when they do not trigger any specific exertion of governmental power. A president who repeatedly suggests that NATO is obsolete helps make NATO obsolete, for the simple reason that NATO's strength stems from certainty among both allies and adversaries that the U.S. security umbrella in fact extends across the alliance. Staff can try to manage the president's relationship with NATO through manipulations, such as those we described John Bolton undertaking in chapter 3, but when a president raises questions about whether the United States really will defend its allies, it encourages rivals to challenge those allies and encourages allies to seek alternatives to alliance with the United States. An immense amount of foreign policy comes down to talking and being believed when one talks. And it is for precisely this reason that in the foreign policy domain, presidents and their representatives have tended to be very careful with what they say.

Back in 1950, Harry Truman's secretary of state Dean Acheson gave a speech defining an American "defensive perimeter" in the Pacific that ran "along the Aleutians to Japan and then [went] to the Ryukyus" and from "the Ryukyus to the Philippine Islands." This line excluded South Korea and Taiwan from the realm of U.S. military protection, an omission Acheson had intended as an effort to build support for a Korean economic aid bill. But when North Korea crossed the 38th parallel six months later, critics pointed to this speech—rightly or wrongly—as the United States having signaled to Pyongyang that it wouldn't defend South Korea. The criticism may well have been unfair, but the episode demonstrates that speaking carelessly can have supremely high stakes in foreign policy. Even Acheson's carefully prepared remarks went sideways; Trump's lies and ill-considered, shoot-from-the-hip statements carry greater risks. If the president declares repeatedly that he is going to build a wall on the southern border, saying it does not give him the authority to do it. It doesn't give him the money to do it. These still have to be wrangled from Congress, which has great substantive control over border policy and even greater control over the appropriation of funds. By contrast, if the president gets on the phone with his Mexican counterpart and demands that Mexico pay for the wall, as Trump has also done, that speech alone is operational. Mexico reacts to it. Countries don't have the luxury of treating presidential speech as though it didn't happen.

This idea that presidential words are operational as foreign policy casts a troubling light on the exchange between Secretary of State Mike Pompeo and Senator Bob Menendez at the Senate Foreign Relations Committee hearing described in chapter 3. Recall that in this exchange, Pompeo was bluntly, if momentarily, honest about the fact that he does not regard offhand statements by President Trump as U.S. foreign policy. When called on the matter, Pompeo had to backtrack. But the exchange raises an important set of questions: When speech constitutes policy, and policies can set off currency free falls and diplomatic incidents and even wars, how is anyone to know which statements by the president to take seriously? Countries around the world are struggling with this question every day of Trump's challenge to the traditional presidency.

Historically speaking, foreign policy by means of presidential statement is more the norm than the exception. George Washington's famed Neutrality Proclamation in 1793 was little more than the eighteenth-century equivalent of a tweet. The Monroe Doctrine was, likewise, articulated in President James Monroe's 1823 State of the Union message to Congress. What would become a foundation of decades of U.S. policy toward the activities of the imperial powers within what it considered its sphere of influence was really just a president talking. These statements are in every respect different from Trump's shooting off a tweet, except in the one critical sense—that they are formally exactly the same. They are presidents articulating what the United States will and will not do with respect to the other countries with which it needs to interact.

But if foreign policy by presidential statement is common in American history, even inevitable and organic to the conduct of foreign relations, the manner in which Trump has wielded this power is unlike anything the country has ever seen.

Consider the degree to which his foreign policy is driven by his impulsiveness. Generally speaking, presidents are deliberative people who care to understand what they are doing. Beyond their inbred fear of bringing the country and their own reputations to ruin, a number of interrelated factors have restrained presidential impulsiveness over the history of the American presidency.

One is the combination of geography and technology. The oceans are big. Particularly in the age before transoceanic telecommunications, it took time for presidential decisions to make their way to Europe and for information to make its way back. Consequently, actual presidential involvement in major foreign policy decisions was far more attenuated than it is today. Ambassadors had delegated authorities to make representations on many critical matters without waiting to hear from Washington, so when the president sent a delegation to negotiate a treaty, he was at the mercy of the negotiators he sent, having limited ability to communicate once they had left. These deals were take-it-or-leave it propositions. In theory, the president or the Senate could reject them, but neither had the technical capacity to micromanage the negotiating process in a fashion that imbued it with their own personality quirks. And impulsive presidential personalities had less capacity to cause problems when messages were transported by ship and horseback before the telegraph, then the telephone, radio, and television permitted direct exchanges with other leaders and communication with the public unmediated by staff.

Staff has also played a role in tempering presidential impulsiveness. History is replete with examples of presidential explosions of rage that never translated into policy because orders were slow-walked or because staff talked presidents down from rash judgments.

One thus scans history in vain for Trump-like examples of presidential impulsiveness in major foreign affairs decisions. There are, to be sure, examples of presidents so ideological on an important point that they pursue it bullheadedly and stick with it long after its folly is clear. Thomas Jefferson came into office in 1801, for example, committed to shrinking the young navy—notwithstanding the country's recent serious naval confrontation with France and the ongoing maritime tensions with Great Britain. As president, Jefferson developed a loony scheme in which the entire coast of the United States would be defended with 188 small boats—called gunboats—so he sought funding from Congress to build such boats while neglecting the navy's larger ships. Even as tensions with Britain heated up over the succeeding years, neither Jefferson nor his successor, James Madison, engaged in basic military planning or preparedness for what would become the War of 1812. Madison actually sought a declaration of war against the world's leading military power in the absence of a real army at a time when British naval ships outnumbered American ones by hundreds.

But if Jefferson's and Madison's handling of the run-up to the War of 1812 was ideological and incompetent, it was in no sense impulsive. Madison engaged in lengthy diplomacy before finally going to Congress for a war declaration. There was no point at which either man woke up one morning and turned U.S. policy on its head.

Most major foreign policy decisions, particularly fateful ones, are the polar opposite of impulsive. The Mexican-American War was deliberately engineered by President James Polk, who had campaigned on the promise to annex Texas. This engineering involved lies, along with a military incident specifically provoked in order to justify war, but it was the result of a strategic vision.

Similarly, in the mythology of history, America's entry into the Spanish-American War has an impulsive quality—triggered by the explosion of the *Maine* in Havana's harbor in February 1898 following months of "yellow journalism" about Spanish barbarities in Cuba—but the reality is rather different. Between the explosion aboard the *Maine* and the actual declaration of war was more than two months of intensive investigation and negotiation. Even Nixon's famous "madman theory" of negotiation with the communist bloc did not involve *actual* madness; the idea of the theory, which predated Nixon's emotional difficulties late in his presidency, was that the North Vietnamese and Soviet governments should *believe* him unbalanced—thus making them more apt to make concessions in negotiations out of fear of what he would do.

Trump's impulsiveness is also an outlier in areas less momentous than the great decisions of war and peace. There really aren't notable cases where, say, Millard Fillmore woke up on the wrong side of the bed and took a fateful action or when Grover Cleveland adopted retaliatory trade sanctions against an ally because its leaders said something about him he didn't appreciate. The Miller Center at the University of Virginia, as part of its extensive compilation of historical materials concerning the presidency, offers summaries of the foreign policy actions of each of the country's forty-four pre-Trump presidents. None of them describes any incident remotely as impulsive as Trump's tweets about North Korea or his Syria announcement or his comments at Helsinki. The presidential historian Michael Beschloss writes, "For most of American history, Presidential impulses would have been restrained by aides, friends, party leaders and/or Members of Congress. Presidents thought of themselves as making decisions as part of a team and were usually wary of launching major surprises."

Trump, of course, does not think of himself as part of a team. Rather, he engages with the powers of his office on highly individual and personal terms, and foreign policy is no exception. On the campaign trail, in a kind of parody of the madman theory, he repeatedly and explicitly promised to be impulsive and erratic in foreign policy. "We must as a nation be more unpredictable," he said. "We are totally predictable. We tell everything. We're sending troops. We tell them. We're sending something else. We have a news conference. We have to be unpredictable. And we have to be unpredictable starting now." Trump was speaking in the narrow context of not signaling our military intentions to our adversaries, ISIS specifically, but he has never hidden his impulsiveness. He made clear that he didn't want to listen to generals; he knew more about ISIS than they did. He made clear that he trusted his gut more than he trusted his advisers. His campaign actively promised that he would shoot from the hip. Unlike in Nixon's case, however, Trump's promise to be unpredictable was no ruse. It was an honest account of his personality as an actor on the world stage.

This impulsiveness is visible even—perhaps especially—in trade policy, one of the areas where Trump's policy views are most consistent and coherent, and one of the areas in which he can at least tentatively claim some measure of political success. The foreign policy establishment, after all, has consistently warned of economic catastrophe as a result of Trump trade policies, but the catastrophes haven't materialized. Indeed, Trump's hard line toward China has materially moved the consensus in both parties toward a more assertive posture. There is, in short, a genuine policy vision here, unlike in many areas.

Yet even where Trump has sincere policy commitments—whose merits we leave to others to evaluate—he governs in eruptions. It is notable that most of the reported incidents in which staff have secreted letters off Trump's desk, discussed earlier, have involved efforts to head off some precipitous trade action. Not all of these efforts have succeeded. One result has been the slapping of tariffs on imported steel and aluminum under a law designed to protect national security—tariffs that apply even to such staunch military allies as Canada. Other results have been threats to blow up NAFTA and serial offense to European allies. The point here is not that Trump's policy is wrong; we are not trade experts. The point, rather, is that the mode of its delivery is highly discordant with the manner in which the traditional presidency exercises the office's foreign policy powers. The traditional presidency eschews the emotionalism in which Trump revels.

Presidential emotionalism is risky stuff and tends to end badly. The Iran-Contra affair had roots in Ronald Reagan's emotional response to U.S. hostages held in Lebanon, a response that partakes of aspects of Trumpian impulsivity. In 1985 Reagan met with the families of hostages held by Iranian proxy forces. Prior to this meeting, writes the Reagan biographer Lou Cannon, aides had prevented the president from talking with these families "partly to spare him from emotionally trying encounters and partly to prevent him from making unwise commitments." As Robert McFarlane, Reagan's national security adviser, wrote of the meeting with the hostages' families, "Everyone who worked with Ronald Reagan was acutely aware of his great concern for the fate of the seven men held hostage in Beirut in the summer of 1985." The meeting left Reagan shaken, and Cannon concludes that his "personal feelings about freeing these hostages was the principal cause, though not the only one, for his enthusiastic pursuit of the Iran initiative." Indeed, in the wake of the meeting with the families, Reagan grew deeply committed to freeing the remaining hostages in Lebanon. And this obsession with freeing them led him to authorize what became the opening of a secret channel with the Iranians and the trading of arms for hostages—though Reagan convinced himself that he was not trading arms for hostages. Meanwhile, former secretary of state George Shultz later wrote, the "Iranians must have learned . . . that the president would do just about anything to get the hostages released."

But even this sort of emotionalism is quite distinct from the personalization and impulsivity we see from Trump. Reagan didn't think he could sweet-talk the Iranians into being our friends. And he did not suddenly decide to trade arms for hostages; nor did the project proceed from some rash public statement made on the spur of the moment. In fact, as a covert action, it was done in secrecy over a protracted period of time. Reagan drifted into the action as a result of a strong emotional reaction of which he couldn't rid himself. The emotional impulse of the moment, in other words, turned out to be more than an impulse. It became, even on consideration, an overriding policy objective even if it was one about which Reagan could not level with himself or the public.

Trump, in addition to his impulsiveness, dramatically differs from other presidents in his tendency to reduce foreign policy engagements to interpersonal dealmaking. He expresses great pride in his personal prowess in this area, and he consistently boils down U.S. relations with other countries to the individual rapport between him and some foreign counterpart. His focus on whether we are getting a good deal or a bad deal seems to relate less to the United States' long-term strategic interests with respect to a country and more to who is solicitous of him personally—the North Koreans and the Saudis, for example—and who is not—say, the British and the Canadians and, most particularly, the Germans. Sometimes this instinct clashes with other strongly held prior commitments, particularly in the area of trade. For example, his deep, long-standing suspicion of China on trade matters is sometimes mitigated by his having an apparently good personal relationship with Chinese leader Xi Jinping. In such cases, the bilateral relationship tends to teeter from expressions of warmth to expressions of hostility and confrontation.

More generally, Trump's outsize confidence in his ability to conduct diplomacy entirely through personal rapport merges with his love of theatrics, and this tends to produce major meetings from which he anticipates great things because of his ability to "get along" with authoritarian dictators. Prior to Trump's second summit with Kim Jong Un, the administration simply had not advanced the negotiations to the point where a "good deal" was a plausible outcome; yet the president seemed to believe that what mattered most was that he and Kim got along and that an agreement would therefore materialize. When Trump's personal charisma proved insufficient to overcome three-quarters of a century of hostility and mistrust— when he could not achieve in a few conversations the denuclearization of the Korean Peninsula—the summit in Hanoi was hastily concluded without any agreement. Nor did a subsequent photo op of the two leaders in the demilitarized zone produce any kind of breakthrough.

Prior presidents have sometimes taken personal approaches to foreign policy. Franklin Roosevelt developed a strong rapport with Joseph Stalin ahead of the Yalta summit, and Richard Nixon developed a relationship with Mao Tse-tung. But those relationships weren't treated as the essence of either Soviet-American or Sino-American relations; they merely facilitated the work conducted by armies of diplomats behind the scenes.

A final distinctive element of Trump's exercise of foreign policy authorities is one not of form, but of substance. Trump pursues a foreign policy agenda that, at least in some areas, dramatically disrupts what had been matters of consensus.

This is not necessarily a bad thing. Part of the reason people voted for Trump was the promise that he would shake things up or even burn them down when necessary; many Americans have become suspicious of centrist policies that they feel don't serve their interests, which they perceive to be forced on them by a bipartisan foreign policy establishment out of touch with their concerns. This establishment is internationalist in orientation, believes in free trade, and is more prone to interventionism than is the general public. And critiques of it are common on the political right and the political left. Obama himself felt hemmed in by this consensus in some areas. The merits of any specific policy position aside, it is legitimate for Trump to be a dissenter from orthodoxies, to run against them, and to govern based on his own beliefs rather than those of the self-appointed guardians of orthodox foreign policy wisdom. Defying conventional wisdom can be good.

For better or worse, it is highly unusual for presidents to act dramatically and repeatedly in the face of relative consensus. Presidents sometimes must act *across* deep ideological divisions; they sometimes have to move relatively entrenched public and political opinion. But they seldom serially defy broad ideological agreement; they seldom pursue policies for which virtually nobody is arguing. This is partly because, even in foreign policy, presidents still need to build support in Congress if they want such things as funding or military authorization or if they want to avoid legislation designed to frustrate their objectives. And presidents want to get reelected, or, if barred from reelection, they want to prevent voter retaliation against their political parties. Trump, however, acts in the face of developed consensus frequently and on basic issues—as when he doubts that NATO is important or that Kim Jong Un's regime is an international menace or that Putin's Russia is a dangerous adversary. Trump doesn't generally attempt persuasion on these points; there is no real effort to convince even his own political party on the substantive merits. He instead bullheadedly adopts a view and relies on Republicans not opposing him too actively on it.

This really hasn't happened before. Consider the most politically divisive war in American history (other than the Civil War), the War of 1812. The vote in favor of the declaration of war against Great Britain was along party lines in both houses of Congress, the only time in history that has happened. As the war dragged on, it even provoked serious talk of secession by the New England states, which opposed the war because of its devastating consequences for trade with England. But President James Madison had the backing of a majority of both houses of Congress, which did vote for the war. The same is true of Lyndon Johnson during the Vietnam War. That war sparked, of course, great controversy, but the Gulf of Tonkin Resolution, which authorized it, passed nearly unanimously. And though history remembers the anti-war protest movement, much of the political pressure Johnson faced came from the other direction. Johnson may have dragged the country into Vietnam through deceit, but the political ranks came willingly. Making foreign policy within the boundaries of already accepted opinion is more the norm than the exception. There are, to be sure, times when presidents have to shift a relatively well-developed consensus before they can pursue their chosen policy. By most accounts, Franklin Delano Roosevelt wanted to get involved in World War II some time before U.S. public opinion would tolerate it. And Nixon wanted an opening with China at a time when this was quite unthinkable in many political circles. But Nixon didn't simply declare he was doing it over objections; he spent years laying the groundwork for the change and convincing people to abandon the orthodoxy.

To be clear, not all of Trump's major foreign policy decisions fly in the face of a broad ideological consensus. The decisions to withdraw from the Iran nuclear deal and the Paris climate accord were both supported by large swaths of the political right and may well have happened even under a more mainstream Republican president. And though some of Trump's trade moves have had the air of a temper tantrum, his suspicion of free trade is certainly shared by many Americans on both the left and the right. Concern that the United States not be overly accommodating toward China is a point with a broad constituency as well. So when Trump acts to impose tariffs on China, he is not acting in the face of a consensus. He's taking a side in a debate. Ditto Trump's decision to move the U.S. embassy in Israel from Tel Aviv to Jerusalem. Here, Trump was actually executing on a long-standing U.S. policy that Congress had endorsed and that prior presidents—while candidates—had promised, only to back off later when in power. In this case, Trump can be said to have represented faithfully a policy that a large number of actors purported to endorse but did so either insincerely or without the courage of their convictions.

That said, Trump's instincts and decisions very often go against the thinking of both major political parties. Neither party's leadership is notably skeptical of NATO or inclined to give Vladimir Putin the benefit of the doubt. Of course, Trump is sometimes able to shift the thinking of his party. Because of his consensus-busting, many more Trump supporters admire Russia today than before he began expressing admiration for Putin. In January 2019, twenty-two conservative members of the House actually voted against a resolution expressing support for NATO and seeking to make it difficult for Trump to withdraw from it. These members never would have supported such a resolution at any time previously.

This tendency of some politicians, pundits, and citizens to fall in line behind whatever position Trump adopts—irrespective of prior political convictions—tends to mask the degree of Trump's ideological deviation. In some cases, of course, his success in shifting his party's views reflects the hitherto unnoticed fragility of the consensus. This is clearly true in the case of trade and matters of globalization, where Washington elites have long tended to confuse an elite consensus behind trade liberalization with a broader public consensus that really does not exist. It may also be true, to some degree, with respect to U.S. commitments to its allies, where the internationalist commitments of the foreign policy establishment have always been stronger than those of the public at large. Still, Trump has had an impact even when the preexisting consensus was not especially fragile. There was never before much pro-Russian sentiment on the American right. And it was certainly not the case that many conservatives favored overt displays of chumminess with Kim Jong Un.

One extreme example of this ideological innovation is Trump's evident solicitude for authoritarian dictators. U.S. support for allied dictators is nothing new and certainly not outside of any bipartisan normalcy, yet the degree of overt affection Trump has shown for foreign dictators—indeed, his active preference for them over elected leaders of democratic allies—is wildly outside the conventional U.S. approach to autocratic allies, much less to autocratic rival and enemy states. The White House's response to the murder of the journalist Jamal Khashoggi by Saudi operatives in the kingdom's consulate in Istanbul defied an understanding across much of the American political spectrum about how the country should respond to such an outrage. The White House considered how to respond for several days before deciding to adopt a credulous posture toward Saudi lies about the matter and to proceed deferentially toward a regime that had just dismembered a journalist who resided in the United States. In addition to his embrace of Putin, his "love" for Kim Jong Un, and his protection of the Saudi prince Mohammed bin Salman, Trump has lavished praise on figures such as Erdoğan of Turkey, Hungary's Viktor Orbán, and the Philippines' leader Rodrigo Duterte. Trump speaks of foreign tyrants with apparent jealousy, once quipping that he wished "my people" would "sit up at attention" in his presence the way the oppressed North Koreans do with their leader. Trump adopts this posture even where it confers on him no political benefit—indeed, even where it inflames the belief that he is in Putin's pocket. The president could do a great deal to allay concerns that he is somehow compromised by Russia by simply adopting a traditional Republican stance toward Putin. His approach of overt pandering is so baffling and contrary to his own political interests that, however sincerely it may reflect his views, it could not be better calculated to excite suspicions by seeming to defy innocent explanation.

Trump's penchant for leaping to the end of the ideological bell curve extends even into the most sensitive and dangerous areas, where the call of stability and consensus is strongest. Several months before Trump's election, the MSNBC television host Joe Scarborough revealed that in a one-hour briefing with a foreign policy expert, Trump had repeatedly asked what the point of having nuclear weapons was if the country couldn't use them. This raised unnerving questions as to whether he understood the difference between nuclear and conventional weapons and whether he recognized or valued the number of human lives at stake. Reasonable minds differ about disarmament, proliferation, and deterrence policy; reasonable minds in the modern era do not differ about whether the point of having nuclear weapons is to use them. To the contrary, they agree that the point of having them is to hope, in the most profound possible sense, to never need to use them.

In the United States, there have traditionally been dramatic political consequences for anyone perceived as deviating from this fundamental view. During the 1964 presidential campaign, Johnson's opponent Barry Goldwater suggested that "defoliation of the forests by atomic weapons" could halt supplies from North Vietnam. Goldwater later insisted that he opposed using nuclear weapons in Southeast Asia, but the damage was done. Johnson and the Democrats hammered him as an extremist itching for nuclear confrontation. The Democratic response to Goldwater's slogan "In your heart, you know he's right" was "In your guts, you know he's nuts." The famous "daisy ad," in which a shot of a little girl counting flower petals morphs into one of an atomic explosion, ended with Johnson's voice-over: "These are the stakes. To make a world in which all of God's children can live, or to go into the dark. We must either love each other, or we must die."

Goldwater lost in a landslide. But Trump won. In *The Imperial Presidency*, Schlesinger writes that "presidential supremacy in foreign affairs had worked well enough when the electoral process sent men of intelligence, restraint and constitutional sensitivity to the White House." He argued that the lesson of the 1970s was that "the electoral process was not infallible" in this regard. And yet Schlesinger's examples and those of the intervening decades pale in comparison to what we see in Trump. Other presidents have not behaved like Trump, because their personalities were nothing like Trump's: their knowledge base was deeper, their work ethic stronger, their engagement with and use of their staffs more productive, and their egos better regulated. They did not behave the way Trump does, because they were less impulsive, less emotionally transparent, and better insulated from and within situations where impulsiveness carried potentially devastating consequences.

Yet, at least as of this writing, Trump has gotten away with it. He has not provoked a military confrontation with North Korea; in fact, tensions on the Korean Peninsula are notably less than they were when he took office. Russia has not invaded any additional neighbors; nor has it won sanctions relief from the United States. NATO has not fallen apart. The disasters that many devotees of the foreign policy consensus had predicted have not materialized either. Moving the embassy to Jerusalem was going to provoke an intifada—and didn't. Blowing up the Iran deal was going to precipitate a crisis—and hasn't so far. Trump's trade policies were going to lead to economic ruin—and haven't so far. And Trump has had successes, the territorial defeat of ISIS most notably, though his impulsive withdrawal has now endangered even that. The problems that Trump's management of foreign policy have generated have been corrosive of America's position in the world, and they have cheered American adversaries. But at least as we finish this book (and with the caveat that things could change), they have mainly proved manageable to date—more manageable than the consensus he has so often defied would have led one to expect.

This reflects, to some degree, the extent to which the United States is locked in a complex web of relationships that are less dependent on personalities than we sometimes imagine. But it also reflects a number of oddities in the way different institutional actors respond to Trump.

Many foreign interlocutors, particularly allies, have adopted a posture closely akin to that of congressional Republicans, who simply ignore what the president says and focus instead on what the United States does. Like members of Congress who pretend not to have seen presidential tweets and focus on his implemented policy actions, allied governments often avoid responding to presidential statements that would trigger major international incidents if uttered by any prior president. A president's foreign policy statements matter, but only if they are taken seriously. This actually has worked a surprisingly high percentage of the time—particularly because Trump's own government behaves similarly. It's relatively easy for NATO allies to pretend that Trump isn't threatening to jettison the alliance when his senior aides openly contradict his skepticism about it. For U.S. interlocutors, one strategy for managing Trump, in short, has been to rely on the decidedly non-unitary features of the Trumpian executive—to ignore, to the extent possible, presidential statements unless and until they are actually operationalized as policy by others, and to manage the engagement with the United States on a track separate from the relationship with its head of state.

The strategy has proved a useful stopgap, but it functions merely as a holding action; it's a strategy for waiting Trump out, not a strategy for engaging the United States, or its presidency, over time. In any event, it works only to a point. After all, in the long run, foreign militaries cannot deal with Mattis instead of Trump; the James Mattises eventually get frustrated and leave. Nor can foreign countries ignore forever the impulsive threats to impose tariffs; one day, a letter may not get removed from the president's desk and those threats will appear in the form of an order actually imposing such tariffs. They cannot entirely ignore the constant threats to NATO, for many countries rely on NATO for their very existence—and Russia might come to believe that NATO is a paper tiger.

More generally, the erosion of American prestige, the diminishing of the confidence of its allies and the fear of its adversaries, and the lessened desire on the part of other countries to work with the United States together represent a price that, even absent a specific catastrophe, gets paid over time. It gets paid when other countries hedge their bets with China because the United States is not a reliable partner. It gets paid when other countries do not want to follow when the United States chooses to lead.

And, of course, it gets paid in moments of crisis, and crises inevitably come. In crisis moments, after all, the executive is always unitary. It snaps back to that Hamiltonian form, its great virtue being the ability to act with energy. In that moment of crisis, everyone around the world will know they are dealing with a highly impulsive individual who makes decisions with proud ignorance, without consultation or regard for consequences—an individual who makes decisions that lie wholly outside traditional expectations of American behavior.

TEN

"It squints towards monarchy"

THE KINGLY POWERS

O N THE MORNING OF JANUARY 10, 2019, THE PRESIDENT SPOKE with a gaggle of reporters as he crossed the South Lawn to board his helicopter. Negotiations over funding for Trump's border wall had broken down the previous day, and a reporter asked the president if he planned to declare a national emergency in order to access funding that Congress was refusing to authorize. The president answered:

> I have the absolute right to declare a national emergency. The lawyers have so advised me. I'm not prepared to do that yet. But if

I have to, I will. I have no doubt about it; I will. I have the absolute right to declare. This was passed by Congress . . . Other Presidents have used it. Some fairly often. I have the absolute right to declare a national emergency.

It wasn't the first time the president had claimed an "absolute right" to do something. In May 2017, in response to revelations that he had impulsively divulged highly classified intelligence to Russian officials in the Oval Office, he took to Twitter to declare he had "the absolute right" to share the information. In December 2017, when pressed on whether he would order the Justice Department to reopen the Hillary Clinton email matter, the president told reporters from *The New York Times*, "I have absolute right to do what I want with the Justice Department." In June 2018, when the *Times* reported on a letter Trump's attorneys had sent to the Special Counsel's Office claiming the president's authority to pardon anyone, including potentially himself, Trump doubled down, tweeting in a fit of pique, "I have the absolute right to PARDON myself." In April 2019, Trump tweeted that the United States "has the absolute legal right to have apprehended illegal immigrants transferred to Sanctuary Cities."

The president was not wholly wrong in these bombastic claims. Although legal scholars have long debated whether a president can pardon herself, and though the ability to declare a national emergency is a statutory authority that falls somewhat short of absolute, the president was certainly correct that he has broad powers in these areas. If self-pardoning is a bridge too far, the president does have the right to pardon the federal crimes of anyone else, save in matters of impeachment. And as we discussed in chapter 7, as a formal constitutional matter, his right to direct the Justice Department is pretty clear. When it comes to sharing classified intelligence with adversaries on a whim, the president does have total and unqualified authority.

There is, indeed, a specific set of presidential powers that are not checked, powers characterized by total, unreviewable, and wholly personal presidential control. Those powers can fairly be described as absolute. And while they are far from the mightiest powers the president holds, they are ones that Trump—perhaps unsurprisingly—holds very dear.

Trump discovered these powers quite early. In August 2017—seven months into his presidency—Hurricane Harvey was bearing down on Texas. The media carried wall-to-wall coverage of the storm, which was the most substantial hurricane to make landfall in the United States in more than a decade. It was the first significant natural disaster to test the new administration, but on the evening of August 25, the White House was occupied with other matters: the president had suddenly announced his pardon of Joe Arpaio, a former Arizona sheriff who had become a symbol of the hard-line immigration stance embraced by Trump's most ardent supporters.

The president's critics swiftly accused him of using the hurricane as cover for a shameful move while the press was focused elsewhere. In the White House, the president's aides certainly saw the Friday late-night news dump in the midst of a national emergency—a genuine one, not a contrived one for invocation of presidential emergency powers—as a way to avoid negative coverage. Trump, however, had a different calculation in mind, or so he later professed. He insisted that he had timed the announcement to the hurricane, not in order to bury it, but rather to amplify the attention. As he told reporters, "Actually in the middle of a hurricane . . . I assumed the ratings would be far higher than they would be normally."

Trump had been publicly mulling over a pardon for Arpaio weeks before the announcement. He told Fox News in an interview earlier that month that he was "seriously considering" it, saying that Arpaio "has done a lot in the fight against illegal immigration. He's a great American patriot, and I hate to see what has happened to him."

What had "happened to" Arpaio was that a federal judge found him in criminal contempt of court. Back in 2011, when Trump's presidential ambitions were little more than a late-show punch line, a federal court had enjoined Arpaio from stopping and detaining individuals simply because he suspected they were in the country illegally. Immigration violations are generally treated as a civil, not a criminal, offense, and in any event the Constitution prevents officers from stopping individuals where there is no reasonable suspicion of their having violated federal or state law. Arpaio had made little secret of the fact that the practices of his department were based on racial profiling, and he did even less to hide his personal animus toward Latinos. Faced with the court's edict, Arpaio didn't stop. He violated the order again and again. The court found him in civil contempt, noting that in addition to ongoing violation of the injunction, he had lied to the court and obstructed its orders. Eventually the judiciary had enough and took the unusual step of finding Arpaio to be in criminal contempt—a charge that carried six months in jail.

Trump didn't seem to care about any of that. Arpaio was an early political ally who had endorsed Trump's presidential campaign and later even provided event security for his rallies. Trump made clear that he liked the guy; the pardon rewarded his loyalty and support. The president, before Arpaio's conviction, had actually pressed the White House counsel and attorney general on whether he could have the case against Arpaio dropped. The pair pushed back and suggested that a pardon after the fact was an alternative more squarely within the president's powers. After the conviction, with Trump clearly contemplating the pardon, commentators warned that pardoning Arpaio would be controversial and could spark political and even legal challenge.

Trump decided to do it anyway, putting his "I dare you" principle to work once again.

The immediate response was outrage among Democrats and finger-wagging from moderate Republicans in Congress. Arpaio's home state senators were the strongest Republican voices against the pardon: Senator Jeff Flake said he wished that Trump had allowed the legal process to play out. The state's senior senator, John McCain, said that pardoning a remorseless Arpaio "undermines [Trump's] claim for the respect of rule of law." However, most congressional Republicans—those best positioned to impose some actual costs on the White House—simply shrugged. Legal scholars could complain that this particular use of the pardon undercut the constitutional role of the judicial branch by preventing a court from enforcing its orders in the face of flagrant defiance by a powerful elected official. Commentators could rail against Arpaio's blatant racism and abuse of power against vulnerable minorities. But for all the fury and disapproval, no one could actually do anything about the pardon, even if they wanted to.

Article II, Section 2 of the Constitution grants the executive the power "to grant Reprieves and Pardons for Offenses against the United States, except in Cases of Impeachment." Scholars debate the margins of this power—the question of the self-pardon, for example. But Trump's pardon of Arpaio—abusive though it was—didn't lie at the outer edges of his authority; it lay at the core. Just as there was no question that Trump had the power to fire James Comey, there was no question that Trump had the authority to extend clemency to Arpaio; there was no question that nobody could review the action or second-guess it legally; and there was no question that the action couldn't be undone after the fact. Trump's critics could howl and scream about the lack of process, about the brazen abusiveness of the pardon, and about its hostility to the judicial process. But no court could block it. Unlike in so many other instances, Trump simply decided something and then it was done.

Having discovered the clemency power, Trump quickly became enamored of it, like a child with a cherished new toy. He brought it up in interviews and solicited ideas for new names from his supporters and others. He suggested that he might commute the sentence of the disgraced former Illinois governor Rod Blagojevich, who had been a contestant on Trump's reality television show, and Martha Stewart, who starred in a spin-off version of the series. The families of felons rushed to Fox News to plead their case directly to its most prominent viewer.

And Trump started using it, issuing a spree of pardons to favored actors, including the right-wing pundit Dinesh D'Souza, who had violated campaign finance law, and former vice presidential aide Lewis "Scooter" Libby, who had been convicted of lying about his role in the disclosure of the identity of a CIA officer during the Bush administration. In a dig at Hillary Clinton and her staff's handling of classified material, he pardoned a former navy sailor who had pleaded guilty to illegally retaining classified material from a submarine; Trump had once tweeted about the case. At the urging of the reality TV star Kim Kardashian West, he commuted the life sentence of a drug offender named Alice Marie Johnson. And he commuted the sentences of Oregon ranchers convicted of burning federal lands and an Iowa kosher meatpacking executive who had employed hundreds of undocumented aliens and had been convicted of financial fraud. At the urging of Sylvester Stallone, he gave a pardon posthumously to the African American boxing champion Jack Johnson, who had been convicted in 1913 of transporting a white woman across state lines "for immoral purposes." He pardoned a soldier convicted in military proceedings of killing an Iraqi prisoner while in a combat zone. He pardoned the convicted fraudster Conrad Black, who had previously written a book praising Trump's presidency. He pardoned Patrick Nolan, a former Republican legislator and conservative activist who had pleaded guilty to racketeering in the 1990s.

Trump hinted at more ominous pardons, dangling clemency before those individuals implicated in the special counsel investigation into Trump's own presidential campaign and poised to cooperate in exchange for reduced sentences. The power to do something, after all, inherently includes the power to promise to do it, threaten to do it, or hint that one might do it. According to the Mueller report, Trump did not merely dangle pardons publicly; as we've seen, his lawyers hinted privately to Paul Manafort and Michael Cohen that they would be taken care of if they did not cooperate with Mueller. The president told Michael Flynn to stay strong and had messages passed to Flynn that he was a hero and that Trump cared about him.

Later, in 2019, the president denied reports that he had offered a DHS official a pardon if he got into trouble following Trump's orders to close the border to asylum seekers; other allies attempted to spin Trump's comment as a possible joke. Offering to pardon an official in order to convince him or her to disregard the law would seem to be the very antithesis of the constitutional command that the president shall take care that the laws be faithfully executed. And, of course, there was the suggestion that Trump might pardon himself.

There is a reason why Trump became so besotted with the pardon power, but it isn't the degree of power conveyed by the authority. After all, the power to grant clemency to one person or to some group of people pales in comparison with the ability to command the world's greatest military. It pales in comparison with the ability to veto legislation. And it pales in comparison with the power to name Supreme Court justices. Nor was Trump attracted to the pardon power because of its benevolence. Notwithstanding the benediction given at his rainy inauguration—"God blesses those who are merciful . . ."—the president's trademark is not mercy, but holding grudges and settling scores.

Rather, it is the unreviewable, unilateral *nature* of the power that so attracted Trump. Here he had found an executive power that looked more like the authority wielded by a monarch than by a president. Trump had been frustrated in so many areas by how much process policy-making requires and by how energetically the courts reviewed presidential actions, yet here was a power that is unchecked and process-free, in which his personal judgment and action is all there is. Here was a power that actually reflected the way Trump imagined the rest of the presidency would work and had felt frustrated when he'd discovered that it did not. He had apparently imagined being president as something like being king; he would wave his hand, his rhetoric suggested, and things would happen by sheer application of his will. The reality of the presidency had been something else entirely: building legislative consensus was difficult, acting in the absence of legislation had a way of provoking judges, and even foreign policy required convincing people. With the pardon power, though, Trump suddenly found an area in which his word did operationalize as law—an arena in which he could behave like a king.

The president's kingly powers are actually not limited to pardons, so he didn't stop there. In July 2018 Trump figured out a novel way to target some of his higher-profile critics by going after their security clearances. Senator Rand Paul had suggested to Trump that he revoke the security clearance of former CIA director John Brennan, and when then press secretary Sarah Huckabee Sanders was asked about the president's view at a White House press conference, she was ready for the question. "Not only is the president looking to take away Brennan's security clearance," she said, reading from prepared notes, "he's also looking into the clearances of [James] Comey, [James] Clapper, [Michael] Hayden, [Susan] Rice, and [Andrew] McCabe. The president is exploring the mechanisms to remove security clearance because they've politicized and, in some cases, monetized their public service and security clearances."

What constituted such politicization and monetization? Sanders made clear that she was talking about nothing more than political criticism: "Making baseless accusations of improper contact with Russia or being influenced by Russia against the president is extremely inappropriate. And the fact that people with security clearances are making these baseless charges provides inappropriate legitimacy to accusations with zero evidence."

Several weeks later, the White House issued a statement in the name of the president announcing that he had, in fact, revoked Brennan's clearance. The statement was actually dated just a few days after Sanders's original announcement, but it wasn't released until mid-August 2018 in an apparent effort to divert a damaging news cycle dominated by coverage of revelations from a former Trump aide's tell-all book. The statement contained a number of broadsides against Brennan but once again stated baldly that the revocation action was based on his having leveled what Sanders characterized as "unfounded and outrageous allegations—wild outbursts on the internet and television—about this administration."

The response to the president's action was swift and powerful—at times even moving. Admiral William McRaven, who oversaw the U.S.

Joint Special Operations Command during the period of the raid that killed Osama bin Laden and had always been resolutely apolitical, penned an opinion article in *The Washington Post* asking Trump to revoke his clearance too. Calling Brennan "one of the finest public servants I have ever known," he wrote, "I would consider it an honor if you would revoke my security clearance as well, so I can add my name to the list of men and women who have spoken up against your presidency."

Many others spoke out with McRaven, but the cumulative response was entirely rhetorical. Congress, perhaps unsurprisingly, did nothing. And although many analysts expected that Brennan would challenge the action against him, he ultimately did not try to sue. Brennan could have tried to take aim at some element of the process used against him, but in reality there wasn't much to do. Although the action was wholly unprecedented and wholly inappropriate, it was almost certainly within the president's power. Security clearances, and indeed the ability to designate information as classified in the first instance, flow from the president's constitutional authority as commander in chief. Since 1940, when Franklin Delano Roosevelt issued the first executive order on classification, presidents have regulated classification by that means. Prior to that, classification decisions were treated as a military matter. The Supreme Court articulated the principle clearly in 1988, however, writing in a case called *Department of the Navy v. Egan* that the president's "authority to classify and control access to information bearing on national security and to determine whether an individual is sufficiently trustworthy to occupy a position in the Executive Branch that will give that person access to such information flows primarily from this constitutional investment of power in the President, and exists quite apart from any explicit congressional grant." In other words, when it comes to security clearances, the president giveth and the president taketh away.

The additional public acts of revocation against people like Comey and Rice and Hayden never materialized, but they were beside the point. By doing it once, Trump had demonstrated that he could; what had been an

unthinkable abuse was suddenly thinkable. And by threatening to do it repeatedly, he had leveraged that single act for maximum communicative—
and intimidation—value.

The president is unconstrained not just in stripping security clearances,
but in granting them as well. On the last day of February 2019, *The New York
Times* reported that the prior May, President Trump had discarded concerns from the CIA and FBI, and overruled his own White House counsel
and chief of staff, to order that his son-in-law, Jared Kushner, be granted a
top secret security clearance. The intelligence community and Trump's top
staffers had all warned that based on the evidence, Kushner was not suit-
able to be trusted with highly sensitive national security information. The
chief of staff at the time, John Kelly, had been so disturbed by the episode
that he wrote a contemporaneous memo to document the order.

For many individuals steeped in the bureaucratic niceties of the classified world, the report of Trump's involvement confirmed a lingering
suspicion. Kushner had been dogged by questions regarding his security
clearance since the earliest days of the administration, when his wife's
father had thumbed his nose at anti-nepotism rules to install Kushner in
the West Wing as a senior adviser. The red flags had been almost too numerous to count. Kushner's business owed more than a billion dollars on
one of its properties, offering an obvious point of leverage. Indeed, immediately following Trump's election, Kushner had raised eyebrows by meeting
with Chinese nationals with whom he was negotiating a business venture.
During the transition, Kushner attempted to establish a back channel with
the Kremlin, using secure lines at the Russian embassy instead of those the
U.S. government could provide. Then he'd failed to disclose on his security
clearance paperwork not only that fact but also numerous other foreign contacts. At the White House, he'd taken on a wide-ranging and highly sensitive Middle East portfolio, and his close personal relationship with Saudi
Crown Prince Mohammed bin Salman had come under increasing scrutiny.
Reports came out that the National Security Council was alarmed to discover that Kushner was engaged in contact with multiple foreign officials

without coordinating through that office, as is the ordinary procedure. This combination did not go unnoticed by foreign intelligence services.

In February 2018, *The Washington Post* reported that U.S. intelligence had earlier picked up chatter among foreign officials discussing ways to "manipulate" Kushner "by taking advantage of his complex business arrangements, financial difficulties and lack of foreign policy experience." The process for adjudicating access to classified information is thorough and exacting, with multiple layers of review by career officials searching for any sign of a threat. And so Kushner's background investigation had dragged on for nearly a year with no end in sight. Eventually even his interim clearance was downgraded to lesser access.

Then, suddenly, in May 2018, Kushner was granted a full top secret clearance. Everything was aboveboard, the White House insisted. Sources "familiar with the matter" made a point of telling the major papers that the permanent clearance was "granted by career White House and intelligence officials after the completion of his FBI background check." These sources even pointed to the observance of this rigid process as vindication, evidence that Kushner was no longer any kind of focus of the special counsel's investigation and that it should clear any suspicion regarding his conduct. Kushner's lawyer, Abbe Lowell, underscored the point in a statement that Kushner's "application was properly submitted, reviewed by numerous career officials and underwent the normal process."

But none of that was true. The process hadn't cleared Kushner; it had concluded that he posed too great a threat. It took nearly a year before the public learned not only that Trump had personally intervened—in the face of contrary recommendations at the highest levels—to order that Kushner be given a clearance but also that the administration had been lying to the public about it ever since. The administration's response? Counselor to the president Kellyanne Conway went on Fox News and declared that while the White House wouldn't discuss security clearances, "I will tell you the president has the absolute right to do what was described."

It was the equivalent of a child's taunt, but Conway was at some level correct. Just as he'd been able to pardon Arpaio, just as he had the power to take away Brennan's clearance, the president did have the authority to overrule his own staff and the intelligence community to grant his son-in-law access to the nation's most consequential secrets. For that matter, he also has an absolute right to give a security clearance to Kim Jong Un or Chinese leader Xi Jinping or Ayatollah Khamenei in Iran if he feels so inclined. What went unaddressed in Conway's response is that "can" is not the same as "should," though the only mechanism the founders had for distinguishing between the two—the oath of office—has to be felt as a burden by the president in order to do its work of distinguishing. If the president doesn't feel some difference between self-dealing and working on behalf of the public interest, if she experiences her powers as monarchical prerogatives there for personal grandeur and benefit, the distinction between what she may do and what she ought to do becomes one without meaningful difference.

As a general matter, the American presidency was crafted in reaction to, not in imitation of, European monarchies. In *Federalist* 69, Alexander Hamilton defended at length the Constitution's proposed presidency from suggestions of monarchical power. In that essay, "The Real Character of the Executive," Hamilton makes the case that despite some surface appearances, the American president is almost entirely dissimilar to a monarch. "The President of the United States would be an officer elected by the people for FOUR years; the king of Great Britain is a perpetual and HEREDITARY prince," he wrote, though he had earlier advocated for lifetime tenure and lost. The president is "amenable to personal punishment and disgrace; the person of the other is sacred and inviolable." The president has only a qualified veto that can be overridden, while the king's veto is absolute. The president is commander in chief of the military, but only Congress can declare war and raise a military; the king, by contrast, has both, along with the power to raise an army. The president has real checks on his power to appoint officers and judges. The president lacks all sorts of powers to regulate commerce that the king has, which the

Constitution gave to Congress. The president "has no particle of spiritual jurisdiction; the other is the supreme head and governor of the national church!" Both are executives, Hamilton argues, but there the resemblance ends: "What answer shall we give to those who would persuade us that things so unlike resemble each other? The same that ought to be given to those who tell us that a government, the whole power of which would be in the hands of the elective and periodical servants of the people, is an aristocracy, a monarchy, and a despotism."

Hamilton was right, but he was only *mostly* right. Patrick Henry, the preeminent anti-Federalist, warned of the perils of "a great and mighty President, with very extensive powers—the powers of a King." Henry did not allege an outright coronation in the Constitution; rather, he spoke of "an awful squinting; it squints towards monarchy . . . Your President may easily become King." And if Hamilton was correct that the president is ultimately very different from a monarch, Henry was right that the Constitution left certain residual monarchical powers in the presidency. It did so on purpose. One need not even squint especially hard to see these residues. They are the set of unreviewable executive powers committed exclusively to the president, the areas in which the Constitution does not merely fail to constrain but expressly delegates exclusive power to the president.

What one might call the kingly powers bring together in one place many of the themes we have discussed in prior chapters. The kingly powers are easily deployed for the expressive purposes so central to Trump's conception of the presidency. They are, or can be, processless—areas in which the president can simply act. Relatedly, they are the powers in which the executive is most unitary, most personal. When the president issues a pardon or makes a unilateral decision regarding who gets access to classified information, the rest of the executive branch falls away. He is just a man. These powers are also fully deployable in service of Trump's primitive conception of justice—rewarding friends and punishing enemies. They can be used, or threatened, to frustrate investigations that loom over him or his family. They can be used to excite his base and anger his political critics.

They are deeply enmeshed with his revolutionary conception of presidential speech. Their exercise is one of the purest expressions of the presidential oath, which is the only thing that meaningfully limits them.

And Trump, in his oathless presidency, is advancing a simple proposition with respect to the kingly powers: he will use them, and threaten their use, for no public purpose other than crude personal expression, base messaging, the sabotage of critics, and self-protection in the face of investigations. He will abuse them openly, flagrantly, flamboyantly. He will promise to abuse them regularly, thus leveraging them for additional communicative power. He will use them in a fashion that dares the public to do anything about it, secure in the notion that there is very little the public can do.

As time went on, Trump discovered other authorities in which the action of the president is not subject to meaningful review or constraint. The man who made "You're fired!" a slogan of his television show discovered that, although hiring senior officials often required Senate consent, firing them never did. When asked to explain the firing of Comey, Sanders noted that the president "has the authority to hire and fire" and therefore, she claimed, "he doesn't have to justify his decision." The Comey firing was only the beginning of a wave of dismissals that has crashed over the administration since then. In fashions often calculated to maximize humiliation, Trump dismissed a secretary of state, an attorney general, a White House counsel, and a White House chief of staff; he bullied a national security adviser, another chief of staff, and a homeland security secretary into resigning.

As the Brennan and Kushner examples show, he also discovered control over classified information—and not only by granting or withholding clearances. If anyone else cleared for access to such highly classified information had blurted information about Israeli operations against the Islamic State to Russian officials in the Oval Office, it would have been an actual crime; as president, however, Trump could do it with impunity. He later discovered that he could order information released to the public, as when he threatened to declassify highly sensitive intelligence materials related to the Russia investigation that Trump's defenders among congressional Republicans sought from the Justice Department and the FBI.

When Congress sought to investigate the matter of Jared Kushner's clearance—as well as to investigate reports that Trump had similarly intervened to grant his daughter, Ivanka, a clearance too—the White House took the position that, given the exclusive and unreviewable nature of the president's authority in this area, even the power of oversight itself is limited. White House counsel Pat Cipollone wrote in a letter to Representative Elijah Cummings, chairman of the House Committee on Oversight and Reform, "It is clearly established as a matter of law that the decision to grant or deny a security clearance is a discretionary function that belongs exclusively to the Executive Branch." The committee, he argued, "has not explained any potential legislation that Congress could legitimately enact to alter the standards or the process that the Executive Branch follows for granting clearances to the President's closest advisors in the Executive Office of the President." Hence, Cipollone rejected what he termed the committee's "radically intrusive demands for the individual background files on its list of selected individuals."

Congress itself has granted the president some quasi-kingly powers, authorities that are not exclusive and unreviewable in the constitutional sense, but have become nearly so as a result of sweeping delegations of power to the executive in statute. The so-called emergency powers fall into this category. For example, Congress has supplemented the president's inherent authority over border protection with sweeping legislative grants of power in the event of a national emergency. When Trump claims the "absolute right to declare a national emergency," he is referring not to the Constitution, but to the broad statutory language that essentially gives him the discretion to determine what, exactly, qualifies as an emergency. And indeed the law doesn't say anything about what substantively constitutes a national emergency or otherwise limits the president in making a frivolous declaration. Other presidents were too prudent to suggest that such a statute gave them an absolute right, as that would have opened them up to claims of abuse. But Trump isn't the slightest bit concerned with such suggestions. He has the power to act; doing so appeals to him, and so he will.

In theory, this statute could be changed and limited. And unlike true kingly powers, the president's action under it is subject to judicial review. But in forcing the question by declaring a specious national emergency in response to Congress's refusal to appropriate money for his border wall, the president proved how slack the reins really are. When bipartisan majorities in both houses tried to exert the power Congress had reserved to itself—passing a resolution of disapproval to essentially invalidate his emergency declaration—Trump vetoed that resolution. And Congress couldn't muster the votes needed to override the veto. Having given up the power, the legislature couldn't get it back.

The kingly powers are not the make-or-break powers of a presidency. The framers of the Constitution knew better than to allow the president unfettered control over the most important activities of government. In the hands of a reckless person, however, they permit a great deal of mischief, both in their exercise and in their dangling. When exercised for reasons of vanity or narcissism or temper tantrum or corruption, they can play an important spoiler role, frustrating the legitimate investigative functions of government, making public what should be secret or secret what should be public, or protecting the favored guilty from accountability. They are also the powers that remain to a president once he or she has failed at the hard task of more traditional governance. Building legislative coalitions is hard work, after all, as is policy development. The kingly powers, by contrast, are always there, and their availability does not depend on the competence of the person who wields them. Presidential power may be, as Richard Neustadt put it, the "power to persuade," but the kingly powers do not depend on persuasion; the idiot monarch wields them as surely as does the wise and decent one.

Of the kingly powers, the pardon and clemency authority stands out for the clarity and explicitness of its remit—which is discussed in, not inferred from, the Constitution itself—and the extent to which the founders actively theorized it and, along the way, recognized and accepted its risks. It thus most clearly highlights the aberration that Trump's use of the power represents.

Perhaps not surprisingly, the power's lineage traces directly back to the British Crown. The concept of pardons long predates the establishment of European monarchies, but it is the distinct pardon of the English kings—in purpose, administration, and potential for abuse—that arrived in the New World. In seventeenth-century Europe, the king's pardon was, as the philosopher Kathleen Dean Moore puts it, a royal gift "analogous in theory and practice to divine grace." Kings didn't have to provide any particular justification for granting pardons, and they routinely did so, not out of mercy or justice, but to reward friends and punish enemies and "to populate their colonies, to man their navies, to raise money, and to quell rebellions." The British Crown, writes another scholar, delegated "full and absolute" pardon power to the governors of the American colonies.

Despite trends among the early states toward vesting some or all of the pardon power in legislatures—a reflection of the post–Revolutionary War suspicion of powerful executives—the American framers adopted the British model and granted the power exclusively to the president. As a result, the Supreme Court has interpreted the presidential pardoning power as commensurate with that of the English Crown. As Chief Justice John Marshall wrote, "We adopt their principles respecting the operation and effect of a pardon, and look into their books for the rules prescribing the manner in which it is to be used."

Yet even as the founders agreed to vest the clemency power in one man, they disagreed on its purpose. In debates over the Constitution, James Iredell took the view that the purpose of the pardon was to restore justice where the law produced an unjust result. There might be occasions in which a person violates the letter of the law, but the circumstances require mercy, he argued. An "inflexible adherence" to the law might itself "be the cause of very great injustice." In this view, the purpose of pardons are justice and mercy.

Hamilton was sympathetic to the view that pardons could prevent a justice "too sanguinary and cruel," yet the great theoretician of executive authority also made a different argument for granting the executive an unfettered pardon authority. He noted that it preserved the ability to offer pardons to rebels "in seasons of insurrection and rebellion" in order to "restore the tranquility of the commonwealth." In other words, one key purpose of pardons is to allow the executive to sidestep the justice system when doing so is necessary for the greater good of the nation.

Hamilton's instrumental view of the pardon proved correct right away and over the long term. Some of George Washington's earliest uses of the power were to pardon participants in the Whiskey Rebellion in 1795. Somewhat ironically, Hamilton, who so forcefully argued for the utility of pardons in preserving the peace, had urged Washington to deal aggressively with the rebels as a demonstration of the power of the federal government. Washington ultimately chose restraint, making a point of explaining in his State of the Union address that he believed it "consistent with the public good" that he should "mingle in the operations of Government every degree of moderation and tenderness which the national justice, dignity, and safety may permit."

The presidents who followed Washington each used pardons to serve their own visions of the interests of state. Like Washington, John Adams pardoned participants in a rebellion in Pennsylvania, and James Madison agreed to pardon an unsavory group of pirates in exchange for their assistance to General Andrew Jackson during the War of 1812.

Half a century later, Abraham Lincoln employed mass amnesty of Confederates at the end of the Civil War. In an echo of this action more than a century later, Jimmy Carter issued a mass pardon of draft resisters in the aftermath of the Vietnam War. Truman, Carter, Clinton, and Obama all granted clemency of one sort or another to Puerto Rican terrorists in efforts to reconcile with nationalists on the island. Ronald Reagan commuted the life sentence of a foreign spy in exchange for the return of U.S. prisoners abroad; these types of hostage exchanges are often a fraught endeavor when it comes to public opinion. In the wake of World War I, Warren Harding grew concerned about the sedition conviction of the socialist leader Eugene Debs, who was serving a ten-year prison sentence for anti-war agitation. Clemency for Debs was not a popular proposition, particularly in Harding's political camp, but Harding commuted his sentence once Germany had ratified the peace treaty ending the war. John W. Dean writes that "Debs and others imprisoned because of the war were lingering remnants of events [Harding] wanted behind the nation."

For his part, Trump has used the pardon power not on the model of either Iredell's or Hamilton's high-minded visions, but rather as a reflection of the crude vision of justice he shares with many entitled rulers. Certainly there was no great reason of state to take any of the clemency actions Trump took in his first two years. And while the posthumous pardon to Jack Johnson and the commutation of Alice Marie Johnson's sentence do fall into the tradition of using the pardon power to alleviate injustice, the pardons of Arpaio, D'Souza, and Libby do not. True, a case for mercy is an inherently subjective judgment; who is deserving of it is a judgment peculiarly dependent on the individual personality of the bearer of mercy and his or her conception of justice. And Libby's case had been a cause célèbre among some conservatives for a long time. But Trump has never disguised his view that an individual's solicitude for the president personally determines that person's merit. So, while we have no doubt that the president managed to whip himself into the belief that these prosecutions had been, as he put it in the Arpaio case, "unfair," his apparent view of fairness is heavily conditioned by self-interest.

Indeed, with Trump, there is generally no attempt to distinguish the public interest from the man's own personal interests. Even when he articulates a public interest basis for an action, he does so with a kind of wink, under the amorphous guise of fairness and unfairness, which seems to translate roughly into whom he likes and dislikes. "He was treated very unfairly by our government!" Trump tweeted of D'Souza, whom the White House claimed was "a victim of selective prosecution for violations of campaign finance laws." About Libby, the president said, "For years I have heard that he has been treated unfairly." The idea of "unfairness" here seems to denote little more than inconvenience to Trump's political supporters—or inconvenience to people from whom Trump would garner political support for his association with them. The veneer of an actual public interest grows thinner still with the pardons Trump dangles: his former national security adviser, set to cooperate with prosecutors against him, has been treated unfairly, as has his former campaign manager, at the very time Manafort was contemplating a plea deal. The subtext, not even especially hidden, is that people who stay loyal might get a pardon too. As Mueller wrote, "Evidence concerning the President's conduct towards Manafort indicates that the President intended to encourage Manafort to not cooperate with the government . . . The evidence supports the inference that the President intended Manafort to believe that he could receive a pardon, which would make cooperation with the government as a means of obtaining a lesser sentence unnecessary."

There's another factor at work here as well: one suspects that Trump's conception of justice in these cases was also heavily conditioned by the desire to "own the libs." That is, part of the attraction of the pardon power was precisely the anger it would generate among his own political opponents. Many presidents have used the pardon power despite the fact that it would anger people. Trump, however, seems to enjoy its use precisely *because* it angers people. And though national reconciliation was certainly among the high-minded original justifications for the pardon power, infuriating political enemies was just as certainly not. In this sense, Trump's use of the kingly powers should be understood as closely related to his peculiar form of presidential speech; and in that framework, as we discussed in chapter 4, divisiveness is actually a positive thing, as it tends to energize his own political supporters and thus hold together the narrow political coalition on which he depends.

In thinking about Trump's use of the pardon itself and of the other powers where he is least constrained, the debate among the founders over the pardon power is significant in another respect: it reflects the founders' calculations of which risks to accept in the final Constitution.

As with other powers, the potential for abuse is highest when the executive has sole and unfettered control. Steadfast in his faith that elections would produce just rulers, Hamilton argued that the gravity of the responsibility will inspire the executive to use the pardon power judiciously:

> The reflection that the fate of a fellow-creature depended on [the President's] sole fiat would naturally inspire scrupulousness and caution; the dread of being accused of weakness or connivance, would beget equal circumspection . . . It is not to be doubted that a single man of prudence and good sense is better fitted, in delicate conjunctures, to balance the motives which may plead for and against the remission of the punishment, than any numerous body whatever.

When Hamilton refers to a "single man of prudence and good sense," he is describing a person possessing a certain measure of civic virtue, a certain capacity for moral and political reflection—a person capable of swearing an oath seriously and having it weigh upon him or her.

Other framers were far more circumspect, shrewdly anticipating someone like Trump. Edmund Randolph warned that the "prerogative of pardon in these cases was too great a trust. The President may himself be guilty. The Traytors may be his own instruments." Randolph, as we saw in chapter 8, ironically later came under suspicion for an untoward liaison with France. But at the convention, he proposed an amendment that would prevent pardons for treason. In the debates, George Mason put a finer point on the peril: "The President of the United States has the unrestrained power of granting pardons for treason; which may be sometimes exercised to screen from punishment those whom he had secretly instigated to commit the crime, and thereby prevent a discovery of his own guilt." The founders were aware of other potential abuses as well. The English kings offered plenty of examples; mentions of pardons in exchange for compensation are found as early as the laws of Henry I in the twelfth century.

Yet ultimately, the convention delegates were persuaded by the Hamiltonian position that the pardon should be minimally restrained. They considered and rejected proposals to grant the Senate consent power over pardons, and they rejected Randolph's proposal to exclude treason as a pardonable offense. This stands in contrast with other, similar debates. The convention debated making the presidential veto absolute but instead settled on a legislative override. And it debated allowing the executive an unfettered hand in making appointments, but was ultimately convinced to condition such selections on the advice and consent of the Senate. Notwithstanding the many possible pitfalls, the only explicit limitations that were placed on the pardon was that it applied only to federal—not state— offenses and that it could not be used in cases of impeachment.

Ironically, it is the very prerogative nature of the pardon, its kingliness, that has made it scary to most modern presidents. Pardons are a politically risky endeavor, for presidents have nobody to hide behind when they issue them. Presidents can blame their legislative failures on Congress or on individual legislators. A policy disaster even within the executive branch normally takes place at the agency level, so the president can assign blame there. But a pardon uniquely belongs to the president himself, and the political accountability for it rests always with him.

What's more, pardons seldom result in substantial political benefit: they can yield a grand gesture, but giving indulgences to criminals has not proved especially rewarding for modern presidents. The result has been that the power has been in decline in recent decades. Barack Obama was something of an exception here, using clemency energetically as a policy instrument against excessive drug sentencing. But most recent presidents have used the power sparingly and been deeply cognizant of its political risks. At a time when scholars generally are anxious about the growth of presidential power, many have concluded that the real problem with this most plenary of presidential authorities is not that modern presidents use the pardon power abusively, but that they don't use it enough.

Presidents have actually developed means of making the pardon power a little less kingly—mostly through bureaucratization, the creation of process around this most personal feature of the presidency as a way of creating distance between the president and the power's exercise. No president has ever attempted to delegate the pardon authority outright—and it's doubtful that he could lawfully do so—but the Office of the Pardon Attorney at the Department of Justice generally reviews applications and makes recommendations regarding the outcome.

The first pardon attorney was appointed during the Benjamin Harrison administration in 1891. It is, in part, a bureaucratic necessity; it applies a disciplining process to the hundreds of applications for clemency submitted each year. The vast majority of pardons and commutations go unnoticed by the public, unless the recipient is somehow notable or the circumstances controversial. But the Office of the Pardon Attorney does not simply serve a process function; it serves a legitimizing function as well. A Justice Department recommendation that a pardon be issued or not issued pursuant to a set of neutral criteria creates a presumption of legitimacy. It also gives the president something to point to in order to blunt political criticism.

Conversely, when presidents depart from the process, they often find themselves in trouble. Notably, in 1999 President Bill Clinton disregarded the Justice Department process in issuing pardons to members of a Puerto Rican nationalist group imprisoned on terrorism convictions. Clinton relied on the advice of his White House counsel, and the individuals in question did not even submit clemency applications. Critics alleged that the pardon was an attempt to woo voters for his wife's future Senate campaign.

Likewise, in 2008 President George W. Bush sent a warrant of clemency to the Justice Department for nineteen people. The next day, he directed the pardon attorney not to "execute and deliver" the pardon for one of them, Isaac Toussie, after it was discovered that Toussie's father had made large political contributions to Republicans, raising questions about whether he had effectively purchased the pardon. The Toussie application had been reviewed not by the pardon attorney, but by the White House counsel. Bush directed the Office of the Pardon Attorney to conduct its own assessment before making a recommendation. Having created a problem by circumventing the office, Bush returned to the process to restore legitimacy.

But the constraints of the Office of the Pardon Attorney are, in reality, a fiction. Unlike other areas where executive branch process has become so integral to presidential decision-making that courts can no longer be expected to defer to presidential actions that entirely flout it, the pardon process is a thin procedural gloss on what remains an intimate and personal presidential power. Courts have held that the president is not required to abide by the process or even review the office's recommendations. In other words, it constrains the president only when he wants it to.

And constraint is precisely what Trump does not tolerate; he rejects process of all kinds, as we have seen. None of his clemency actions appear to have gone through the conventional pardon process. He seems entranced by pardons precisely because they and the other kingly powers are the closest thing the real presidency offers to actual government by tweet. Virtually alone among modern presidents, Trump is happy to be out on the limb where these powers put him. He prefers it there because that is where the presidency is most expressive.

And leveraging the expressive value of presidential acts is always Trump's most visible priority. One critical feature of his exercise of the kingly powers is that the power to act conveys the power to dangle the action, or threaten it. With normal presidential powers, those meaningfully constrained by actors outside the executive branch, the power to dangle is limited. Trump, after all, can threaten to veto legislation, but a veto presupposes that legislation passes in the first instance, and in any event, Congress can override a veto. He can threaten to name Jeanine Pirro or Rudy Giuliani to be attorney general, but the Senate would likely not confirm either one. But the threat to exercise one of the kingly powers has only political blowback as constraint. Normal presidents may be leery of dangling actions they won't really take; bluffing, like lying, erodes presidential credibility, after all. But Trump, judging from his public statements, very deeply doesn't care about his credibility. And he often revels in negative reaction, so blowback to a dangled pardon or security clearance revocation delights him.

The result is that while Trump's actual deployment of the kingly powers has been limited, he has used the power to dangle them constantly. He dangled pardons for those caught up in the Mueller investigation—from Paul Manafort to Michael Flynn. He threatened to fire Mueller and Rod Rosenstein and others on a semi-regular basis. And he has likewise threatened to release classified material as part of his political war against the investigations of him. He has exercised the powers themselves just often enough to force the public not to consider these threats as mere noise.

And the constraint on such behavior is politics alone—the willingness of other actors to respond and of the public to recoil at the evident flouting of the oath of office. To the extent that the Supreme Court has ever read a limitation into the pardon authority, it was in a 1927 decision authored by Justice Oliver Wendell Holmes, who wrote, "A pardon in our days is not a private act of grace from an individual happening to possess power. It is part of the Constitutional scheme. When granted, it is the determination of the ultimate authority that the public welfare will be better served by inflicting less than what the judgment fixed." The suggestion that the president isn't permitted to exercise the pardon power *against* the public welfare seems like more of a constraint than it is. He alone, after all, is the arbiter of what that interest might be. This binds the pardon power and the other kingly powers particularly closely to the oath of office and the more general expectation that presidents will act in good faith. At the end of the day, after all, the crux of the definition of an abusive exercise of the kingly powers comes down to the question of good faith: Does the president believe that a pardon, or a release of classified material, or the granting of a clearance, or the disclosure of sensitive information to a foreign actor is in the public interest? Does she believe it is a faithful execution of her office? Or is she acting for some other reason?

Trump is certainly not the first president to wield these powers in a fashion that reasonable people suspected was more self-interested than public-spirited. Consider Bill Clinton's last-minute pardon of the fugitive Marc Rich—and his own half brother, Roger. Many people suspected that George H. W. Bush's pardon of six people implicated in the Iran-Contra scandal was closer to political self-dealing than to good faith. Even pardons smiled upon by history were suspect in their time. When Gerald Ford pardoned Richard Nixon, the act was deeply unpopular, despite Ford's clear articulation of his belief that the pardon was necessary for the nation to move forward. Many members of the public could never shake the suspicion that the act was part of a trade or a deal to facilitate Nixon's resignation. But Trump's flamboyance about the self-interested nature of his use of the kingly powers is new. He's doing this corruptly, and he wants you to know it.

The notion that kingly powers are legitimately deployable for wholly self-interested reasons finds its ultimate expression in Trump's insistence on the right to pardon himself. He seems to see these powers in a largely defensive context, as a set of tools to be used to protect himself from investigation and accountability. The power to fire is the power to decapitate or influence an investigation of himself. The power to strip people of security clearance is the power to punish critics, both inside and outside of government, whom he loathes because of their comments and actions in the context of the Russia scandal. The power to release classified material is the power to defend himself with strategic information disclosures by allies on Capitol Hill. And the power to pardon is the power directly to frustrate criminal prosecutions and to signal to those who might cooperate that the president can make their problems go away. In this context, it makes all the sense in the world that Trump will not forswear the ultimate abuse of the pardon power. If the definition of "unfairness," after all, is inconvenience to those who support Donald Trump, who has been treated more unfairly than he has?

"A man unprincipled in private life desperate in his fortune, bold in his temper"

THROUGHOUT MUCH OF THE 2016 PRIMARY SEASON, IT WAS completely unthinkable that Donald Trump could obtain the presidential nomination of a major political party—but he did. And until a little after 9:00 p.m. on November 8, 2016, it was unthinkable that he could actually be elected president.

Everyone knew how election night 2016 was going to go: Hillary Clinton was going to win. The evening's coverage would be devoted to tallying the margins of victory, as Republican senator Lindsey Graham's prediction from months earlier would finally come true: "If we nominate Trump, we will get destroyed . . . and we will deserve it." But as the evening wore on and the key states were too close to call, cable news pundits began to furrow their brows and the tone turned sharply from jocular to serious. The unthinkable was suddenly being thought.

At 10:39 p.m., the networks projected that Trump had won the swing state of Ohio and, minutes later, Florida as well. By the time Trump clinched Pennsylvania, his win was all but inevitable, but an ashen John Podesta, Clinton's campaign manager, still took the stage in the Javits Center in New York in a weak attempt to rally the troops: "Let's get these votes counted and let's bring this home."

Then, at 2:30 a.m. eastern standard time, the networks called Wisconsin and its ten electoral votes. It was over; the magic number, 270 electoral votes, had been reached. Donald J. Trump had been elected president.

The certainty of Trump's defeat had been so widespread that the polling website FiveThirtyEight took heat during the election run-up for being too conservative in its estimates against him. It had put Clinton's odds of victory at 70 percent, not 80 percent or 90 percent. The suggestion that Trump had close to a 30 percent likelihood of becoming president struck many observers as too absurd to entertain. Unthinkability is a powerful drug.

As we finish writing this book in the fall of 2019, we do not know a lot of things that readers will know by the time anyone reads it. We do not know who will emerge as the Democratic front-runner to challenge Trump. While an impeachment process is under way, we do not know whether the Democratic majority in the House of Representatives will ultimately seek to impeach the president or, if it does so, what misconduct will serve as the basis for the action. We do not know the full extent of new scandals emerging from the Trump administration or what additional abuses might be revealed. Yet even with all the uncertainty of the current moment, the unthinkability of Trump's reelection has become an unmistakable feature of public commentary on his presidency. It shows up everywhere—in the evident relief on the part of many pundits at Trump's negative approval ratings, in the strategy on the part of allied governments to try to wait out this episode in American history, in the January 2019 assumption-laden celebrations that the country had made it "halfway." It shows up when an analyst like Jack Goldsmith writes a lengthy magazine article with what he terms a "relatively hopeful" analytical core—that "the Constitution has prevented presidential law-breaking, and that most of Trump's norm violations will not persist"—predicated entirely on the explicit assumption that Trump's presidency "will continue to fail and that he will not be reelected." The article mentions only at the end, and only as a caveat, that "if Trump succeeds and makes it to a second term, his norm-breaking will be seen to serve the presidency more than it does today. If that happens, the office will be forever changed, and not for the better."

Trump's reelection is not unthinkable. A major-party candidate for president always has a significant chance of winning. An incumbent to the office of the presidency always has a chance of winning reelection. *Always.* This is especially true when the economy has performed well and unemployment is low, both of which conditions exist as we write. Nor is Goldsmith understating the stakes, even if he mentions them only in passing. At stake in Trump's reelection is whether the American electorate wants the institution of the presidency to be changed forever.

Changing the presidency is not necessarily a bad thing. The office has changed a great deal over the past two centuries, as we have seen in this book. Not all customs are good; not all new things are bad. And there is a lot more flexibility in public understanding and expectations of the office than much of the current commentary suggests. Some presidents have ignored deeply held expectations about the office in deliberate efforts to change them. In some cases, the norms have been simply allowed to change. In others, political conditions have given rise to new, more elaborate constraints. As we have seen, for example, Teddy Roosevelt tested and Woodrow Wilson then shattered the nineteenth-century expectations of presidential speech, replacing it with a twentieth-century norm of presidents speaking directly to the public. There are subtler and more complex evolutions over time as well. In the past, the process of nominating and confirming federal circuit court judges involved a great deal more presidential deference to the senators in whose states judges would serve. The tradition known as "senatorial courtesy" dated back to George Washington with respect to executive appointments and had long dominated lower court appointments too. But that didn't stop President Jimmy Carter from consciously dismantling the norm with respect to circuit judges—a step he took in the name of increasing diversity on the bench. His successor, Ronald Reagan, capitalized on the demolished norm in order to appoint more ideologically conservative judges. The presidency changed because presidents acted to change it, and the existing norms went undefended.

Conversely, sometimes the breach of a norm leads to a reparative process, in which the political system does seek to shore up the norm. The normative expectation that a president would not serve more than two elected terms also dated from Washington's precedent. While not law, it functionally constrained the office—until, of course, it didn't. After Franklin Delano Roosevelt won a third term and then a fourth, Congress passed the Twenty-Second Amendment, which declares, "No person shall be elected to the office of the President more than twice." The states ratified the amendment in 1951, and thus the broken norm was healed permanently by the most formal constitutional mechanism available.

We have argued in this book that the best way to understand Trump's violations of the normative expectations of the traditional presidency is as a series of proposed changes to the office, a series of changes that collectively reflect a wholly new vision of the office and its powers. The question at stake in his reelection is whether the country wishes to incorporate both this larger vision of an expressive presidency and some or all of Trump's specific innovations into the common law of the presidency or whether it wishes to repudiate them and make them disreputable.

The United States has had bad presidents, and along with its lousy presidents, the country has developed a number of different means of addressing the bad apples. In his recent book, *How to Get Rid of a President*, David Priess notes, "Through design or improvisation, presidents have been (or can be) ousted by voters, rejected by their own parties, removed in place by opponents or subordinates, dismissed preemptively, displaced by death, taken out by force, declared unable to serve, or impeached and removed."

The Trump era has inspired a renewed debate over the mechanisms, wisdom, and purpose of impeachment. As we finish this book, much about the impeachment process remains unknown. What we do know is that in November 2020 the electorate will once again choose a president and that reelecting Trump is preponderantly likely to be an option on the ballot. And though impeachment is a dramatic power, elections are by far the most important tool for getting rid of presidents, in terms of both routine occurrence and the populace's ability to reject innovations the president in question has proposed. A president impeached and removed is the subject of a palace coup of sorts; the will of the people is actually overturned. But a president repudiated at the polls is rejected by the same electorate that installed him. And a president who proposes innovations to the office and faces electoral rejection finds those innovations much more squarely rejected than does a president impeached and removed for specific acts of misconduct that may not implicate those larger proposed innovations.

Conversely, reelection is a ratification. It is one of two key means by which the public accepts proposed innovations to the presidency by occupants who defy expectations of presidential conduct—the other one being adoption of those innovations by successors. Reelection is the means by which the country distinguishes good change from bad change. It's the means by which the electorate decides which presidents are Andrew Johnsons and James Buchanans, mere blips in the office, and which are Woodrow Wilsons and Franklin Delano Roosevelts, who transform the presidency forever.

The election of a demagogue was not unthinkable to the founders. James Madison famously warned that "enlightened statesmen will not always be at the helm," and, as we noted in chapter 4, Alexander Hamilton presciently warned of a Trump-like figure—"unprincipled in private life desperate in his fortune, bold in his temper"—coming to power by "flatter[ing] and fall[ing] in with all the non sense of the zealots of the day."

But, having recognized the risks, the founders placed a remarkable faith in the belief that presidential elections would produce wise and judicious executives. As a principal protection, they designed the Electoral College to filter out public passions and ensure that only nonpartisan statesmen would attain the presidency, while still ensuring at some level that the choice would be—in Madison's words—the choice of the people at large. The problem is that many founding-era assumptions about presidential selection proved wrong. The president, in fact, turned out to be not a nonpartisan statesman, but a product of political factions the founders did not foresee. The office relatively quickly came to be won through what can only be deemed the practice of precisely the "popular arts" the founders disdained. And the Electoral College did not work as an assembly of independent minds. Electors now vote mechanically in favor of the winner of their state's popular vote, leaving the Electoral College as a meaningless check on the possibility of a wholly unfit person attaining the presidency. The American electoral system effectively prevented the emergence of someone like Trump for so long not because of the Electoral College's supposed anti-populism, but because the political parties themselves played something of the anti-populist filtering role that the founders imagined being played by the Electoral College. The parties did not nominate candidates far outside the strictures of the traditional presidency. But the parties' filtering role has weakened in recent years as the political parties themselves have weakened and their internal nominating processes have become more democratic. Their weakening left the American tradition oddly vulnerable at once to both populism and potential counter-majoritarianism; it is now possible for a populist demagogue to obtain the nomination of a major party and then win the Electoral College without a popular majority.

This is precisely what happened in 2016. As ballots were counted in the days after the election, Clinton surged ahead in the popular vote;

she ultimately bested Trump's tally by nearly three million votes. A few members of the Electoral College launched a campaign to convince their fellow electors to disregard the popular votes in their respective states and to become "faithless electors" by casting a ballot for someone other than Trump. They called themselves the "Hamilton Electors" in a nod to *Federalist* 68. In the end, only seven electors broke with their obligations, and ironically, the majority of those came from Clinton-backing states. In an intense irony, the masses actually got it right in decisively rejecting a populist demagogue they believed unfit for office, while the Electoral College—fashioned to defend the country from such a man's election by just such electoral masses but now enfeebled by a populist fear of counter-majoritarian institutions—ushered him into office. And there is a real risk that the gulf will widen in 2020 and Trump will lose the popular vote by larger margins but still win the Electoral College.

The American presidency is a package deal. You can't have its nimbleness and capacity for decisive action without its potential for misuse and its dependency on good faith. You can't have its unity without its capacity for impunity. You can't have its independence without its capacity for going rogue. What ultimately disciplines it is the need to go back to the electorate every four years for ratification.

That necessity offers the country the opportunity to correct errors, even grave errors. But it also carries the risk of ratification of error and incorporation of error into the dense fabric of public expectations. Reelection conveys the unambiguous message that a president's behavior, his fundamental conduct of the office and use of his powers, is tolerable. It is a statement that the public trusts this person, who took the oath of office once, to do so again.

All of which raises, as an initial matter, the question of whether the current electorate does trust Donald J. Trump to take the oath of office once again. It raises the question of what Trump's reelection would be ratifying. It raises the question of whether the public accepts as tolerable a purely expressive presidency. It raises the question of whether it accepts a presidency devoid of process and fundamentally about the vanity of an individual. It raises the question of whether it accepts a presidency in which the cabinet manages the president rather than the president managing his staff. It raises the question of whether it accepts a presidency pervasively predicated on lies and proudly unethical in its conduct of routine affairs. It raises the question of whether it accepts a presidency that imagines law enforcement as a shield for allies and an instrument of power against enemies. It raises the question of whether it accepts a presidency that does not consent to scrutiny of its conduct. And it raises the question of whether it accepts a presidency that conducts foreign policy on the basis of whim and tantrum. These are the questions that Trump's reelection puts before voters.

To ask these questions plainly is also to answer them, but that is the easy part—intellectually, if not politically. The immediate task will be actually effectuating Trump's exit from office, should the voters reject him. Given Trump's public statements on the subject, it is not too paranoid to wonder whether Trump would be inclined to graciously concede an election he lost, without attempting to raise questions as to the legitimacy of his defeat. The history of contested elections in this country is a complicated one, and a person like Trump could inflict grievous wounds to the office on his way out the door. Suffice it to say that a transition *from* Trump will be a difficult one indeed.

Even assuming that it goes reasonably smoothly, there will still be hard questions to ask about the background conditions that left the polity willing to put such a man in such an office. And there will be questions to ask about the damage Trump managed to do and how to repair it, how to reestablish expectations he has shattered. And there will be questions about how much work law can do—and what sort of law can do that work—to codify those expectations in actionable rules for the future.

In other words, even if voters reject Trump, the work of defending the presidency is not done. The hard part is the question of what needs to happen after that.

The day Trump loses his reelection bid—if, indeed, he does lose—and the day he leaves office, the argument that his bark was worse than his bite will have its day. Yes, he made a lot of noise and was very unpleasant, but he did not in fact inflict nearly as much damage as alarmists suggested. In this argument, which already has a certain currency, the presidency itself has proven stronger than Trump; to the extent that it couldn't tame him while he was in office, it waited him out. During that time, the country's institutions weathered the storm and held. The Department of Justice hasn't started broadly investigating and prosecuting the president's political opponents and appears to have largely held off Trump's attempts to influence its work. The intelligence community hasn't abandoned its mission and descended into partisanship and politics. The country hasn't gone to war with North Korea or Iran. Its international alliances are bruised, but they have survived. So there's really not that much to repair.

The new president will arrive on the scene, and everything will snap back to normal. The new president will be scrupulous about telling the truth; he or she will not merely abide by ethics rules but will do so demonstratively; he or she will respect facts and process. And the world will again be as it once was. President Trump will not be unthinkable, but the memory of him primarily will serve as a warning of what happens when a leader tempts fate and defies the rules. The work of reform and repair will thus be relatively easy, a matter of reminding people of the cautionary tale the Trump administration represents. The presidency snapped back after Andrew Johnson. Why not after Trump?

The problem with this rosy scenario is that it ignores the background conditions that led to a Trump presidency being possible in the first place. Andrew Johnson was never elected, after all; Abraham Lincoln died. But Trump *was* elected president. He is a creature of a fierce, modern political polarization that will not go away just because he leaves the scene. He didn't create it; it created him. Trump is a product of a drive to beat the other side at any and all costs, a willingness to suspend rules of fair play—rules of accepted political conduct and rules of basic decency—if doing so will help defeat the other side. He is a product of an era of political tribalism, where you know which team you're on and then figure out what you think about a given issue, rather than the other way around. The presidency, at least if Americans aspire for it to represent national leadership—rather than leadership of one faction in its war with the other—needs better defenses against this ambient political environment.

This is particularly true because there is reason to worry that the damage Trump has inflicted on the office and its institutions is greater than it will appear on the day he leaves office and countless Americans breathe a sigh of relief at their deliverance. Mostly the damage lies in thinking the unthinkable and speaking it aloud and trying it out. No, the Justice Department didn't prosecute Trump's enemies, but Trump talked about it constantly, and talking about it legitimizes it. He fired an FBI director and an attorney general for not putting the Justice Department and its investigative apparatus at his disposal. Is the lesson future presidents will learn from this never to do such things—or merely to do them a little more quietly? Yes, the intelligence community may have remained resolutely apolitical, but the commitment of its congressional overseers to impartial oversight crumbled utterly, and a president resolutely and publicly rejected the very idea of apolitical intelligence. Should Americans imagine that a long-term presidential disinformation campaign undertaken in partnership with major media organizations will have no demonstration effect for future presidents? To be sure, American alliances have survived, but should Americans really imagine that the word of the presidency means what it did internationally only recently? Most broadly, Trump has demonstrated what an oathless presidency looks like. In an atmosphere of intense polarization, in which hating and defeating the other side is the only virtue, it seems reasonable to expect that even in failure, aspects of this experiment will influence future presidents. And it seems imprudent to bet against some enterprising politician attempting a more sophisticated Version 2.0 of the entire undertaking.

In other words, a new president who arrives in office promising to respect pre-Trump norms will not be enough. If a first step is rejecting and repudiating Trump himself and facilitating his actual exit from office, the second key step is fortifying the presidency's institutional protections using well-designed laws. This project will necessarily weaken, to some degree, the traditional unity and energy in the executive branch. As in the period after Watergate, there will be a calibration necessary here, one limited by the Constitution as well as by genuine need for a presidency capable of nimble action. Whatever the solution may be, it is not to paralyze the office.

But there is a limit to what legal reforms, as essential as they are, can really do. Because the foundational problem is not ultimately one that can be addressed in law. No law, after all, can make the president mean the oath he or she swears. And however many worthy laws Congress passes to restrict in the future this or that abuse committed by Trump in the past, the person unconstrained by his or her oath will find ways to abuse the mammoth powers of the presidency. If Trump showed anything about presidential power, it was that the core powers of the office—the ones Congress cannot do much about—are themselves powerful instruments when abused. Where the defect truly is what James Comey called "the nature of the person," law cannot fix it.

And this leaves us with a lacuna in the defense of the presidency. The defeat and removal of Trump is a necessary condition for that defense, but it is also an insufficient condition; his replacement with someone genuinely committed to observing the norms of the traditional presidency is a necessary condition, but it too is insufficient; legal reforms are necessary, yet they are insufficient as well.

All of which returns us to the place where we began, the oath of office, for it was precisely this lacuna that the founders tried to fill with a script: a promise to "faithfully execute" the law and to "preserve, protect and defend the Constitution," rooted in a shared agreement to be part of a common political system. It was a promise that bound the swearer of the oath to the whole polity by acknowledging obligation not merely to those who supported him but also to those who did not.

If Americans do not somehow insist that this promise be a sincere one, the rest of the system will not work. The norms will not hold. The laws will all be paper tigers. The polarization will generate more and cleverer Trumps and counter-Trumps, and the political system will not stop them, because people won't actually want it to—or they won't want it enough. They will just want their demagogue to prevail over the other side's demagogue.

Which is to say, the president's promise is not the only one that counts here. This country asks public officials—not only the president but all federal employees—to swear an oath of office as they enter government service. It asks members of the military to swear an oath of enlistment. And it asks new American citizens to swear an oath of allegiance at their naturalization ceremonies. None of those oaths are scripted in our founding document, and each one varies a bit to suit its purpose, but they all share a common refrain: "I will support and defend the Constitution and laws of the United States of America against all enemies, foreign and domestic; . . . I will bear true faith and allegiance to the same." This is how we bring in new citizens, because this is the fundamental compact of a constitutional republic; it's the obligation natural-born citizens already have.

To support and defend the Constitution means to support and defend its institutions. The American presidency, for all its paradoxes, is an office that has served this nation well, but today the presidency itself needs a champion—someone who will not merely take and mean that oath, but will stand for and argue for and represent the values Trump has attacked. If Americans wish to preserve and protect the presidency, they must not forget that this defense is not a passive endeavor.

POSTSCRIPT

A S THIS BOOK WAS GOING TO PRESS IN THE FALL OF 2019, A new scandal erupted over President Trump's interactions with the president of Ukraine. As we write, the House of Representatives has launched what appears to be a fast-moving impeachment inquiry. New information is spilling out daily. Public support for impeachment, and even removal from office, is rising in the polls. And although the wall of Trump's support among Republican voters and elected officials is holding for now, cracks are starting to form.

By the time you read this brief postscript, you will know a great deal more about this matter than we do as we write it. At the very least, you will know more about what occurred when the Trump administration and the president's personal lawyer sought to recruit the government of Ukraine to investigate the family of one of Trump's political opponents in advance of the 2020 presidential election. You will certainly know more about the impact of the affair on the Trump presidency. You may even know whether it triggers the beginning of that presidency's crumbling—or if it turns out to be just another blip from which Trump recovers and restores the erratic equilibrium in which his presidency chronically resides.

Despite the present uncertainty, *l'Affaire Ukrainienne* warrants a few observations—not just because of its apparent magnitude and political implications but also because of its relationship to the thesis we have developed in these pages. This is a capstone scandal, combining the many abusive features of the personalized, expressive presidency that we have discussed. We have argued that Trump is proposing a fundamentally new vision of executive power in the American political system, one that sublimates the presidency's core management functions and public service dimensions to the personal interests of the officeholder and to the expressive aspects of the office. Each chapter examines this theme in particular contexts, with attention to particular presidential authorities and responsibilities. In Trump's phone call with his Ukrainian counterpart and related efforts, and in the aftermath of their revelation, all these themes come together: one scandal unites them all.

As we noted in the introduction, Trump has rarely had to exceed the limits of executive power in order to abuse his office. Rather, he has inflicted damage again and again by personalizing and abusing powers that the presidency clearly possesses. The Ukraine affair conforms to this template. Though the details are still emerging, it is already clear that the president employed the foreign policy authorities of his office to pressure a foreign government into using its law enforcement apparatus to generate dirt on a U.S. citizen in order to benefit Trump politically. Trump did so personally in his phone call with Ukrainian president Volodymyr

Zelensky; he did so through his private attorney; and he did so through the State Department and other administration officials. In these events, one can point to no specific deployment of a presidential power that exceeds the plain boundaries of Trump's authority. If Trump had undertaken the same acts for some public-spirited reason, each might individually be construed as a defensible exercise of presidential power. Leaning on a foreign leader is diplomacy, after all, and diplomacy sometimes takes the form of explicit quid pro quo. Seeking international law enforcement cooperation on matters of public policy is not especially unusual. Delaying aid as a form of leverage to achieve a policy objective is the ordinary rough-and-tumble of international politics. What makes this scandal a scandal is not the specific powers that Trump deployed, but that he deployed them in the service of purely self-interested, private concerns.

Here we see again the salience of the oath of office, as we discussed in chapter 1. Trump's conduct is scandalous, not just because of what he did but because he so clearly did not do it to "faithfully execute the Office of the President of the United States" or to "preserve, protect and defend" the U.S. Constitution and the interests of the nation. As we have argued, the presidential oath is not a mere formality or an expression of hazy benevolence; it is a foundation of our political system, the feature of the presidency that embeds in it a requirement of good faith and civic virtue.

The episode also illustrates the near-total collapse of executive branch process, our subject in chapter 2. In a normal presidency, a request for international law enforcement cooperation would run through the Justice Department and the State Department. By contrast, in his phone call with Zelensky, Trump urged a foreign head of state to meet with his personal lawyer, Rudy Giuliani, and to contact the attorney general, William Barr, directly. Barr quickly made it known that he was unaware of Trump's having mentioned him on the call and the Justice Department asserted that it was not involved in the matter. When it came to the law enforcement and investigative concerns of the United States in its interactions with foreign partners, it appears that it was not the attorney general—or any other government policy maker or official, in fact—who represented the executive branch. Instead, it was the president's private emissary. Indeed, Giuliani appears to have been pervasively involved in all aspects of the effort to pressure Ukraine, and his activities certainly provoked profound anxiety among State Department and White House officials. The State Department was attempting to carry out the official U.S. policy of providing Ukraine with support to help the country hold off Russian occupation of its territory. But that policy and process was in tension with the president's desired result, so Trump circumvented official channels by involving his personal lawyer. In some core sense, the president has the power to do this. As we have seen, the use of process is ultimately optional. Just as Trump can send his son-in-law to negotiate Middle East peace, so too can he send Giuliani to strong-arm Ukraine—as he did.

There is a close connection between the president's rejection of process and his rejection of facts that cause him inconvenience. In the case of Ukraine, Trump's decision to hold up aid was not driven by any executive branch fact-finding or policy deliberation. There is, after all, no need for such deliberation or fact-finding when the considerations are of a personal and political nature and do not relate to conventional policy judgments at all. This is another case of the president using the executive branch not to understand or respond to the realities of the world, but rather to conform the world to his desired reality. In his first week in office, Trump wanted to have had the largest inaugural crowd ever, so he demanded that the government produce pictures proving it was so, and he demanded that his press secretary say it was so. In the summer of 2019, the president wanted evidence from Ukraine to undermine the assessment that Russia interfered in the election that brought him to power. It was irrelevant that the U.S. intelligence community had insisted that the Russians did just that—indeed, that the Justice Department had asserted in an indictment that it could prove this beyond a reasonable doubt. Nor did it matter that Trump's own aides repeatedly advised him that his alternative theory of Ukrainian involvement was nothing more than an oft-debunked conspiracy theory. In the same vein, Trump wanted evidence to support his belief that Joe Biden had urged the firing of a Ukrainian prosecutor in order to protect his son, Hunter. And so Trump demanded these things—this time not from his own hapless staff, but from a dependent foreign government that was desperate for military assistance.

The Ukraine tale might seem too sinister for Daniel Drezner's toddler-in-chief thread, but the same infantile presidential management style we discussed in chapter 3 is at work here as well. Texts and testimony from foreign policy officials tasked with implementing U.S. policy on Ukraine have the tone of frustrated capitulation one might associate with an exhausted caregiver. Just give him what he wants, U.S. officials told the Ukrainians, and we can all get to the important business at hand. Many a parent has joked about the necessity of bribery with toys and treats when it comes to managing small children; it's less amusing when the bribe in question involves launching an abusive government investigation in exchange for antitank missiles. But the dynamic is the same; as with the exhausted parent, we see the weary necessity of picking one's battles. There is a bitter irony here for Trump too, to the extent that *l'Affaire Ukrainienne* becomes the transformative scandal of his presidency. How many times has Trump been thwarted by aides who've ignored his demands and thus saved him from his own worst impulses? Here they acceded to his wishes—and he is paying the price.

Indeed, the price of Trump's abandonment of process constraints in this affair will be high, as it leaves him particularly exposed now that the story has emerged. Had he delayed military aid following some ordinary interagency review, there would be an administrative record for him to hide behind, even if his own motivations were impure. In the moment, the president may have found the ability to take direct action empowering. After all, he could simply overrule hundreds of people below him, send off his lawyer to advance his goals, and then get on the phone to personally make his demands. But this approach left him no fig leaf. He cannot now feign ignorance or noninvolvement. As Trump once said in dismissing the importance of State Department positions, "The one that matters is me."

And predictably, as we also discussed in chapter 3, such gross failures of process have led people to take matters into their own hands—to disunity within the executive branch. The scandal began to unfold when a whistle-blower—still unidentified as of this writing—followed instructions from the House Intelligence Committee and filed a complaint with the inspector general of the intelligence community, who then formally notified Congress. This is, of course, the proper channel through which to air such concerns. But it nevertheless speaks to an executive branch that is in conflict with itself. A great many people within the government appear to have spoken to the whistle-blower, who recorded a broad array of those staff concerns in his complaint. As the matter became public, officials also began leaking prolifically, often to express their anxieties about what the administration and the president were doing—and even ended up testifying over White House objections. Those anxieties stem from the fact that the executive branch was formally pursuing one policy on Ukrainian aid—with the bipartisan support of Congress—while the president was directing a different one behind the scenes for entirely self-interested reasons.

Trump's peculiar style of presidential speech, discussed in chapter 4, also plays a role in the Ukrainian scandal. It is perhaps not a surprise that, in an hour of sudden crisis, Trump has stuck rigorously with language that has worked well for him to date. Indeed, it would have been surprising had he *not* defaulted to arguing by repeated assertion that the Zelensky conversation was "beautiful" and "perfect," had he *not* attacked the whistle-blower as a spy and traitor, and had he *not* grafted onto this new scandal the same epithets he developed for the Russia investigation. It would have been surprising had he *not* flooded the airwaves with his own repetition of verbal leitmotifs he created for the new occasion or adapted from the earlier one: that there was no quid pro quo, that he was fighting corruption, that it was all "The Greatest Witch Hunt in the history of our Country!" And it would have been more surprising still had he *not* taken to Twitter to attack House

Intelligence Committee chairman Adam Schiff and *not* stood on the White House lawn to double down on the impropriety of his request to Ukraine by publicly asking China to investigate the Bidens as well. Trump's supporters also returned to their familiar defenses of his speech. Senator Marco Rubio, for example, suggested that Trump's on-camera request of China was not serious, but an attempt to troll the media. And many Republicans avoided questions by pretending not to have read the call memorandum or seen the president's tweets or heard his public comments.

The Ukrainian scandal also reflects Trump's propensity to lie, our subject in chapter 5. On its own, Trump's insistence that there was nothing untoward about his interaction with Zelensky and the surrounding machinations might be dismissed as reflecting his genuine conviction that he'd done nothing wrong. His repeated contention, however—that his concern in pressuring Ukraine was simply to combat "corruption"—is impossible to take seriously. Nor is it possible to give credit to his suggestion that he withheld aid in order to protest Europe's lackluster commitment to Ukraine. Trump has never shown interest in corruption in Ukraine, or anywhere else, in any context other than that of targeting his political opponents and their families. If his true concern were Europe's commitment to Ukraine, demanding investigations from Zelensky is unrelated to the matter.

Because the White House has thoroughly decimated its reserve of credibility, the public and the media have largely refused to credit these pretextual justifications. And Trump's evolving story has placed his Republican defenders in an untenable position as well; his surrogates spent days arguing that his phone call with Zelensky did not really concern investigating the Bidens—only to have Trump turn around and declare he'd sought exactly that and wanted the same from China. Ironically, Trump has actually lied less about the Ukrainian scandal than about prior matters. This may be because he is apparently unashamed of his conduct, and also because Giuliani went on CNN to first deny that he had asked the Ukrainians to investigate the Bidens, only to spill the beans minutes later, practically shouting the admission: "Of course I did!"

The scandal further reflects, if perhaps only in a glancing fashion, Trump's monetization of the presidency, which we've discussed in chapter 6. On the phone call, Zelensky made a point of telling Trump that he had stayed in Trump Tower on his last visit to New York. One can only imagine how many times foreign leaders have similarly felt compelled to tell Trump that their countries' delegations have frequented his properties. Perhaps more galling is the hypocrisy of it all. Trump accuses Biden's son of leveraging his father's status as vice president for personal enrichment—even as Trump personally has leveraged his office to enrich himself and his family, and his own children run a business that overtly trades on the president's name for foreign and domestic dollars alike.

In chapter 7 we discussed Trump's propensity to deploy law enforcement authorities against his political enemies. In l'Affaire Ukrainienne, we see the export of that propensity into the foreign policy arena. Setting aside questions of explicit quid pro quo, the president unambiguously requested that Zelensky investigate the Bidens. In the domestic context, in order to protect civil liberties and prevent the government from spying on its political foes, a framework of formal executive guidelines controls the manner in which law enforcement can open investigations. Those guidelines spell out the legitimate bases for launching probes; needless to say, the political advantage of those in power isn't one of them. Trump's attempt to use the presidency's foreign policy powers to pressure another government to open an investigation into an American citizen for political reasons represents the same attempted abuse of investigative powers that we've seen in his efforts to pressure the Justice Department domestically.

Although certain processes exist in international law enforcement cooperation to prevent such abuses, they are more primitive than the comparable domestic safeguards, and they are easier to circumvent. And here Trump ignored them completely. He wasn't asking foreign partners to share information pursuant to a mutual legal assistance treaty, which is something an ordinary president might do—or, to be precise, something the Departments of Justice and State might do under an ordinary president. Nor was he encouraging foreign prosecutions for important policy reasons in a case in which the United States lacked jurisdiction but had some significant policy interest, which is also something an ordinary president might do. He was, rather, asking a foreign sovereign to go after his enemies in exactly the way he expects to use his own sovereign power to go after his enemies. The fact that Trump may believe conspiracy theories does not change the reality that he's wielding presidential power to deputize foreign governments as opposition researchers for his campaign.

This should not come remotely as a surprise. As we've discussed in chapter 7, this is the same substantive demand Trump has made of his own law enforcement apparatus almost since the day he assumed office. Can anyone truly believe that, having demanded loyalty from his first FBI director and having asked him to drop the investigation of former national security adviser Michael Flynn, having berated his first attorney general for refusing to seize control of the Russia investigation and launch investigations of Hillary Clinton, and having serially attacked and forced out much of the Justice Department's and FBI's senior leadership, Trump would now shrink at recruiting foreign law enforcement to aid him politically?

On a more positive note, the Ukrainian scandal takes the history of presidential investigations we discussed in chapter 8 into a new realm. In that chapter, we noted how the Trump-era Congress has failed to conduct its own investigations—though this represents the culmination of a long-term trend rather than an entirely novel development. When it comes to the factual inquiries associated with its impeachment function, Congress has largely relied on executive branch officials who are dependent on presidential consent to conduct the very probes on which the core questions of impeachment hinge. This abdication of responsibility has had consequences. It's notable that the president's conversation with Zelensky took place on the day after Special Counsel Mueller testified before Congress. In other words, as soon as the media proclaimed that Mueller's lackluster performance was the end of Democrats' hope of impeaching Trump over the Russia investigation, the president immediately turned around and again invited a foreign power to interfere in a U.S. election—a testament to the proposition that the failure to enforce norms of behavior encourages their further violation. When this recidivism came to light several months later, Congress didn't push for the Justice Department to appoint a new special prosecutor. Although there was some outrage that the Justice Department refused to even investigate the president's actions as a possible criminal law violation, a remarkable thing happened at the same time: Congress simply began investigating by itself, an action that didn't require Trump's consent. He could not fire those in charge of this inquiry. And within a remarkably short period of time, having taken responsibility for its own investigative functions, the House had forced the release of the White House's call memo and the whistle-blower's complaint, and it had garnered cooperation from key witnesses. It remains to be seen as of this writing whether the White House will cooperate with congressional investigators in any way and, if not, whether Congress will seek to compel cooperation by litigation or merely treat noncompliance as an impeachable offense in its own right.

These events may seem to resemble an inverted version of the XYZ Affair in the John Adams administration. There, Congress asserted its investigative prerogatives because it suspected that a French diplomat had been soliciting bribes from the United States in exchange for receiving the U.S. delegation that had come to Paris. Today, the president of the United States stands accused of, among other things, refusing to meet with a Ukrainian delegation at the White House unless Ukraine first greased his palm by launching an investigation into his adversaries—what one State Department official called Trump's "deliverable."

Perhaps Congress was emboldened to act owing to the misconduct previously uncovered by the Mueller investigation. The fact that Congress had already soft launched an impeachment inquiry probably made it easier to take the more dramatic—if procedurally symbolic—step of announcing a formal proceeding. Perhaps the Ukrainian affair was merely the sledgehammer that broke the camel's back. But in important respects, the most significant feature of the Ukrainian scandal is that it spurred Congress to at last take full responsibility for the investigation of the Trump administration's misdeeds. There would be no more outsourcing of this work to executive branch agencies, special counsels, or even the press. Whatever the outcome of its efforts, a legislative coalition committed itself to accountability.

At its core, *l'Affaire Ukrainienne* is, of course, a foreign policy scandal. Trump's actions have consequences for the United States' geopolitical standing and its relationships with allies, as well as for the people of Ukraine and other countries. In chapter 9 we noted that foreign policy, as a constitutional matter, is the area in which a president is least constrained—and thus where Trump's impulsive and erratic style can be most consequential. Here it would be generous to describe Trump's demands of Zelensky as impulsive; in fact, there is considerable evidence that Trump planned his demand regarding the Bidens in advance. Indeed, from Trump's point of view, this request appears to have been the entire purpose of the call, and both sides had done preparatory work on the assumption that Trump would make it. That said, if the demand itself was not impulsive, the call was certainly erratic, reflecting the same unfocused improvisation we described in chapter 9. The call memorandum released by the White House—a quasi-transcript of the conversation—does not reflect a president who is working from organized materials prepared by a staff in advance. In it, Trump bounces from subject to subject, heedless not only of the impropriety of his requests but also of the degree to which his most important claims are conspiracy theories wholly unsupported by facts.

The other salient feature of Trump's foreign policy decision-making outlined in chapter 9 is his tendency to deviate from substantive consensus views of the United States' international interests. The Ukraine call illustrates this vividly. Trump is maneuvering in a manner that plainly conflicts with whatever bipartisan consensus might exist concerning appropriate policy. American politicians and policy analysts may disagree about the wisdom of providing aid or military assistance to Ukraine; to our knowledge, however, nobody has argued for making such aid contingent on Ukrainian willingness to involve itself in favoring one candidate over another in the domestic politics of the United States. And though Congress has vested the executive with some discretion concerning when to transmit appropriated funds—and in some cases has even tolerated delaying funds as diplomatic leverage—nobody argues that congressionally appropriated funds should be used to extort personal political favors from foreign leaders.

But this appears to be exactly what occurred here. Following the release of the call transcript, the White House and its defenders insisted that it did not reflect a quid pro quo. Yet the attendant circumstances drip with the conditionality of the provision of much-needed aid for Ukraine on the provision of dirt about the Bidens. Text exchanges between U.S. diplomats in the period surrounding the call are frank about the matter. Wrote one worried diplomat, "Are we now saying that security assistance and WH meeting are conditioned on investigations?" That is, of course, precisely what the administration was saying.

It was partially as a consequence of the brazenness of what had happened—and Giuliani's public admission of it—that the weight of Trump's defense has rested not on factual denial but on the assertion of prerogative. This assertion is close kin to the kingly powers we discussed in chapter 10. Trump has not denied that he had these interactions with Zelensky, that he leaned on him to investigate Joe and Hunter Biden, or that he held up aid while doing so. Rather, he has asserted both the rightness of his doing these things and his entitlement to do them. And he has done this, almost inevitably, using the precise language he always deploys when invoking the kingly powers: "As the President of the United States, *I have an absolute right*, perhaps even a duty, to investigate, or have investigated, CORRUPTION, and that would include asking, or suggesting, other Countries to help us out!" (emphasis added).

Once again, Trump is not entirely wrong in his assertion of power. As with so many things this president does, the ultimate abusiveness lies not in exceeding the boundaries of presidential authority. There is, after all, no doubt that the president has the right to raise the need to combat corruption with a foreign leader. There is no doubt that the president in fact has the authority to condition aid to a foreign country on some extrinsic factor. There really is no doubt generally that the president has the raw power to do the things he did. Likewise, there is no doubt that the president has the authority to store records of communications with foreign officials on highly classified servers, as the White House did here. But the classification authority—which is near absolute—is intended to protect national security interests, not to conceal presidential wrongdoing. As with the firing of James Comey, the dangling of pardons to those who might cooperate against him, and so many other actions, the assertion of a right to do something does not answer the more fundamental question of the propriety of doing it. And just as Trump has the "absolute right" to wield his powers abusively, Congress has the absolute right to hold him accountable for his exercise of those powers—as it has now begun to do.

At least in this regard, we can hope that Trump's transgressive vision of the presidency has finally met its match. If only belatedly, the Ukraine affair seems to have given a shock to the constitutional system—a shock that may at last jolt it into functioning as the founders imagined it would.

NOTES

Introduction: "It's MODERN DAY PRESIDENTIAL"

3 *not the worst weather*: According to presidential lore, President William Henry
Harrison caught a cold that became pneumonia while giving a lengthy inaugural
address on a cold, wet day; Harrison died several weeks later, though modern analysts regard his death as more likely the result of enteric fever from unsanitary
conditions at the White House than a sickness from the weather at his swearing-in.
For an account of the traditional understanding of Harrison's death and for the re-
visionist understanding of it, see Jane McHugh and Philip A. MacKowiak, "Death
in the White House: President William Henry Harrison's Atypical Pneumonia,"
Clinical Infectious Diseases 59, no. 7 (October 1, 2014): 990–95, https://doi.org/10
.1093/cid/ciu470.

3 *William Howard Taft's inauguration*: An account of the weather at Taft's inauguration is included in the diary of Fred W. Carpenter. "Diary Entry of Fred W. Carpenter, March 4, 1909," the Papers of William Howard Taft, available at www.loc.gov/resource/msspin.pin3602/?st=gallery. See also Andrew Glass, "Taft Inaugurated as 27th U.S. President, March 4, 1909," *Politico*, March 4, 2019, www.politico.com/story/2019/03/04/this-day-in-politics-march-4-1909-1198775.

3 *the day that Donald J. Trump became the forty-fifth President*: For weather conditions on Inauguration Day, see Angela Fritz, "Inauguration Day Was the 4th Warmest on Record, and Mildest Since 1989," *Washington Post*, January 20, 2017, www.washingtonpost.com/news/capital-weather-gang/wp/2017/01/20/inauguration-day-weather-is-dreary-and-wet-heres-the-forecast-timeline-updates/.

3 *had only sparse crowds*: For an account of the crowd-size controversy at Trump's inauguration generally, see Lori Robertson and Robert Farley, "The Facts on Crowd Size," FactCheck.org, January 23, 2017, www.factcheck.org/2017/01/the-facts-on-crowd-size/. For images of the crowd size along the inaugural parade route specifically, see Sarah Frostenson, "Photos: President Trump's Inaugural Parade Attracted Relatively Few People," *Vox*, January 20, 2017, www.vox.com/policy-and-politics/2017/1/20/14342688/photos-trumps-inaugural-parade-small-crowd. See also Jen Kirby, "President Donald Trump Stays Mostly Inside the Car During the Inaugural Parade," *New York*, January 20, 2017, http://nymag.com/intelligencer/2017/01/along-the-route-of-trumps-inaugural-parade.html; Kalhan Rosenblatt, "Inaugural Parade Route Appears Empty in Some Areas," NBC News, January 20, 2017, www.nbcnews.com/card/inaugural-parade-route-appears-empty-some-areas-n709906.

4 *hushed and somber tones*: For examples of the tone of 2017 Inauguration Day coverage, see NBC News, "The 58th Presidential Inauguration of Donald J. Trump (Full Video)," available at https://youtu.be/prd2RfhF1tM; contrast with coverage of 2009 Inauguration Day, CBS News, available at https://youtu.be/l9sRI3aZFlo. See also Hadas Gold, "Media Coverage Muted on Eve of Trump's Swearing In," *Politico*, January 19, 2017, www.politico.com/story/2017/01/inauguration-coverage-difference-233861, noting the sense in the media that Trump's "inauguration feels different [from Obama's], and it's been reflected in the coverage." See also later accounts describing a somber mood in the press tents at Trump's inauguration. See, e.g., Justin Peters, "What Was the Mood at the Inauguration Press Tents? Quiet and Sad," *Slate*, January 20, 2017, https://slate.com/news-and-politics/2017/01/what-was-the-mood-at-the-trump-inauguration-press-tents-quiet-and-sad.html.

4 *"some weird shit"*: Multiple people reported hearing Bush say "That was some weird shit" after he left the dais, though it is unclear whether he was referring to the overall event or to Trump's inaugural address. See Yashar Ali, "What George W. Bush Really Thought of Donald Trump's Inauguration," *New York*, March 29, 2017, http://nymag.com/intelligencer/2017/03/what-george-w-bush-really-thought-of-trumps-inauguration.html. The former president has never sought to clarify what

precisely he was referring to; he has also never denied the comment or suggested that it was taken out of context.

4 *"American carnage"*: See the president's inaugural address, available at www .whitehouse.gov/briefings-statements/the-inaugural-address/.

4 *the living former U.S. presidents attended the event*: For the presence of living former presidents save George H. W. Bush, see Brian Naylor, "Hillary and Bill Clinton to Attend Trump Inauguration," NPR, January 3, 2017, www.npr.org/2017 /01/03/508072518/hillary-and-bill-clinton-to-attend-trump-inauguration.

4 *"Crooked Hillary"*: See, for example, Maggie Haberman, "Donald Trump, in Upstate New York, Tries Another Label for Hillary Clinton," *New York Times*, April 16, 2016, www.nytimes.com/politics/first-draft/2016/04/16/donald-trump-in -upstate-new-york-tries-another-label-for-hillary-clinton/.

4 *"Lock her up!"*: See, for example, Nick Gass, "'Lock Her Up' Chant Rules Republican Convention," *Politico*, July 20, 2016, www.politico.com/story/2016/07/rnc -2016-lock-her-up-chant-hillary-clinton-225916.

4 *could not even bring themselves to shake hands*: Andrew Prokop, "Hillary Clinton and Donald Trump Didn't Shake Hands at the Debate," *Vox*, October 9, 2016, www.vox.com/2016/10/9/13222118/debate-donald-trump-hillary-clinton -handshake.

4 *speculated that the Clintons might not attend*: For an example of speculation regarding Clinton attendance, see Tara Palmeri, "Carter Is Only Former President to RSVP for Trump's Inauguration," *Politico*, December 22, 2016, www.politico .com/story/2016/12/trump-inauguration-presidents-232937.

4 *"honor our democracy and its enduring values"*: Hillary Clinton, Twitter, January 20, 2017, https://twitter.com/HillaryClinton/status/822472212569616385. Clinton wrote, "I'm here today to honor our democracy & its enduring values. I will never stop believing in our country & its future. #Inauguration."

5 *The inauguration prayers*: The text of the Reverend Samuel Rodriguez's prayer can be found at www.cnn.com/2017/01/20/politics/donald-trump-inauguration -samuel-rodriguez/index.html.

5 *Trump's wife, Melania, held two Bibles*: Erin McCann, "The Two Bibles Donald Trump Used at the Inauguration," *New York Times*, January 18, 2017, www.ny times.com/2017/01/18/us/politics/lincoln-bible-trump-oath.html.

6 *pose as role models*: For example, a January 2018 Quinnipiac University poll found that 90 percent of Americans believe it is "important . . . that a president be a good role model for children." The same poll found that 67 percent of Americans did not think that President Trump is one. The poll is available at https://poll.qu.edu /images/polling/us/us01252018_uboe26.pdf/.

6 *boasting of marital infidelity*: See, for example, the transcript of his comments made to Billy Bush on a hot mic in the *Access Hollywood* tape, while he was married to Melania, available here: www.nytimes.com/2016/10/08/us/donald-trump-tape -transcript.html. He also boasts of affairs with married women in Donald Trump and Kate Bohner, *The Art of the Comeback* (New York: Times Books, 1997), 116:

"If I told the real stories of my experiences with women, often seemingly very happily married and important women, this book would be a guaranteed bestseller."

6 *belittling political opponents with lewd insults*: The New York Times developed an interactive tool that shows the insults Trump has hurled at candidates for office, politicians, the news media, and others. See Jasmine C. Lee and Kevin Quealy, "The 598 People, Places and Things Donald Trump Has Insulted on Twitter: A Complete List," *New York Times*, last updated May 24, 2019, www.nytimes.com /interactive/2016/01/28/upshot/donald-trump-twitter-insults.html.

6 *namesake charitable foundation*: It was well known before the election that the Trump Foundation was something other than a charitable mechanism by which Trump gave away his own money. See David A. Fahrenthold, "How Donald Trump Retooled His Charity to Spend Other People's Money," *Washington Post*, September 10, 2016, www.washingtonpost.com/politics/how-donald-trump -retooled-his-charity-to-spend-other-peoples-money/2016/09/10/da8cce64 -75df-11e6-8149-b8d05321db62_story.html.

6 *finding ways to avoid paying taxes*: Trump famously said this during a debate with Hillary Clinton. See Daniella Diaz, "Trump: 'I'm Smart' for Not Paying Taxes," CNN, September 27, 2016, www.cnn.com/2016/09/26/politics/donald-trump -federal-income-taxes-smart-debate/index.html.

7 *treated in depth elsewhere*: See, for example, John Judis, *The Nationalist Revival: Trade, Immigration and the Revolt Against Globalization* (New York: Columbia Global Reports, 2018); William A. Galston, *Anti-Pluralism: The Populist Threat to Liberal Democracy* (New Haven, CT: Yale University Press, 2018); Yascha Mounk, *The People vs. Democracy: Why Our Freedom Is in Danger and How to Save It* (Cambridge, MA: Harvard University Press, 2018).

7 *306 electoral votes*: While Trump won states controlling 306 electoral votes, only 304 electors ultimately cast their votes for him. See House Congressional Record, Vol. 163, no. 4, 115th Cong., 1st Session, H185–190, available at www .congress.gov/115/crec/2017/01/06/CREC-2017-01-06-pt1-PgH185-8.pdf.

7 *"virtue or morality is a necessary spring of popular government"*: Washington in his 1796 farewell address to the nation said, "It is substantially true, that virtue or morality is a necessary spring of popular government. The rule, indeed, extends with more or less force to every species of free government. Who, that is a sincere friend to it, can look with indifference upon attempts to shake the foundation of the fabric?" The text of the address is available at www.mountvernon .org/education/primary-sources-2/article/washingtons-farewell-address -1796/.

7 *"the only foundation of republics"*: The full quotation reads, "The Form of Government, which you admire, when its Principles are pure, is admirable indeed. It is productive of every Thing, which is great and excellent among Men. But its Principles are as easily destroyed, as human Nature is corrupted. Such a Government is only to be supported by pure Religion, or Austere Morals. Public Virtue can-

not exist in a Nation without private, and public Virtue is the only Foundation of Republics." Letter from John Adams to Mercy Otis Warren, April 16, 1776, available at https://founders.archives.gov/documents/Adams/06-04-02-0044.

7 *"virtue and honor" were the "foundation of confidence"*: The full quotation reads, "The institution of delegated power implies, that there is a portion of virtue and honor among mankind, which may be a reasonable foundation of confidence; and experience justifies the theory. It has been found to exist in the most corrupt periods of the most corrupt governments." Alexander Hamilton, *Federalist* 76.

7 *"society cannot exist unless"*: Edmund Burke, "A letter from Mr. Burke, to a member of the National Assembly in answer to some objections to his book on French affairs," 1791, available at https://quod.lib.umich.edu/e/ecco/004804929.0001 .000?rgn=main;view=fulltext. Burke, an Anglo-Irishman, was an influential contemporary of the American founding fathers.

8 Can He Do That?: The podcast home page appears at www.washingtonpost.com /podcasts/can-he-do-that/. The introductory trailer, in which the quoted language appears, is available at www.washingtonpost.com/podcasts/can-he-do -that/introduction-to-the-podcast/.

9 *swear an oath of office*: U.S. Constitution, Article II, Sections 1 and 3.

9 *"new birth of freedom"*: Abraham Lincoln, the Gettysburg Address, November 19, 1863.

9 *"shithole countries"*: See Josh Dawsey, "Trump Derides Protections for Immigrants from 'Shithole' Countries," *Washington Post*, January 12, 2018, www .washingtonpost.com/politics/trump-attacks-protections-for-immigrants-from -shithole-countries-in-oval-office-meeting/2018/01/11/bfc0725c-f711-11e7-91af -31ac729add94_story.html.

9 *imagined that the office would tame him*: See, for example, Nouriel Roubini, "The Oval Office Will Tame President Donald Trump," *Guardian*, November 11, 2016, www.theguardian.com/business/2016/nov/11/oval-office-will-tame-us -president-donald-trump.

10 *Mueller's final report*: The redacted Mueller report, entitled "Report on the Investigation into Russian Interference in the 2016 Election," was released on April 18, 2019, and is available at https://assets.documentcloud.org/documents /5955249/Report.pdf.

10 *such as the size of his inauguration crowd*: See Glenn Kessler, "Spicer Earns Four Pinocchios for False Claims on Inauguration Crowd Size," *Washington Post*, January 22, 2017, www.washingtonpost.com/news/fact-checker/wp/2017/01/22 /spicer-earns-four-pinocchios-for-a-series-of-false-claims-on-inauguration -crowd-size/.

10 *the so-called pivot*: For an appropriately derisive summary of such talk, see Ezra Klein, "There Is No Trump Pivot, and There Never Will Be," *Vox*, September 22, 2017, www.vox.com/policy-and-politics/2017/9/22/16346904/there-is-no-trump -pivot-there-never-will-be.

12 *Jack Goldsmith's blunt assessment*: Jack Goldsmith, "Will Donald Trump Destroy

the Presidency?" *Atlantic*, October 2017, www.theatlantic.com/magazine/archive /2017/10/will-donald-trump-destroy-the-presidency/537921/.

12 *he's no Woodrow Wilson*: In his academic career, prior to becoming president, Wilson authored multiple works critiquing the structure of American government: *Congressional Government* (1885) and *Constitutional Government of the United States* (1908).

13 *"MODERN DAY PRESIDENTIAL"*: Donald J. Trump, Twitter, July 1, 2017, https://twitter.com/realdonaldtrump/status/881281755017355264.

13 *rally for a Republican congressional candidate*: A video of this rally is available at www.c-span.org/video/?c4787611/saccone-rally-comments-speech.

14 *Lincoln unilaterally suspending habeas corpus*: Lincoln issued a series of orders suspending habeas corpus during 1861, beginning with an April 27 order to General Winfield Scott authorizing the suspension of habeas corpus between Washington and Philadelphia. When Chief Justice Roger Taney wrote in *Ex parte Merryman* that the suspension of habeas corpus was an exclusively congressional power, Lincoln famously defended his action in a July 4 address to Congress, asking, "Are all the laws but one to go unexecuted, and the Government itself go to pieces lest that one be violated?" See Ex parte Merryman, 17 F. Cas. 144 (1861), and "Message to Congress in Special Session," July 4, 1861. Suspension of habeas corpus is today understood nearly universally as a congressional, not an executive, power.

14 *Truman trying to seize the steel mills*: See Executive Order 10340, Signed April 8, 1952, 17 FR 3139, April 10, 1952, and Youngstown Sheet & Tube Co. v. Sawyer, 343 U.S. 579 (1952).

14 *presidents over time going to war on their own*: For a detailed discussion of the evolution of presidential war powers absent congressional declarations, see Arthur M. Schlesinger, Jr., *The Imperial Presidency* (New York: Houghton Mifflin, 1973).

14 *Roosevelt threatening to pack the Supreme Court*: When a conservative majority in the Supreme Court struck down New Deal legislation, Roosevelt introduced a plan to pack the court with additional justices. The plan was laid out in the Judicial Procedures Reform Bill of 1937, introduced on February 5, 1937, and discussed in a fireside chat the next month. See Franklin D. Roosevelt, "Fireside Chat, March 9, 1937," available at www.presidency.ucsb.edu/node/209434. The court-packing plan failed, partly because the court's treatment of New Deal legislation shifted. The Supreme Court's perceived capitulation to political pressure is commonly known as "the switch in time that saved nine."

14 *electoral rebuke Republicans suffered*: For example, in the 1974 midterm election following Nixon's resignation, Democrats made substantial gains in both the House and the Senate, and in the 1976 presidential and congressional election, Jimmy Carter defeated Gerald Ford and the Democrats retained control of both houses of Congress. See *Vital Statistics on Congress*, Brookings Institution, available at www.brookings.edu/wp-content/uploads/2016/06/Vital-Statistics -Chapter-2-Congressional-Elections.pdf.

14 *enthusiastic remarks in favor of torture*: See, for example, Maggie Haberman, "Warning of U.S. Attacks, Donald Trump Advocates Allowing Torture," *New York Times*, March 22, 2016, www.nytimes.com/politics/first-draft/2016/03/22 /warning-of-u-s-attacks-donald-trump-advocates-allowing-torture/.

14 *possibility of intelligence abuses*: See, for example, Andy Greenberg, "Imagine If Donald Trump Controlled the NSA," *Wired*, October 19, 2016, www.wired.com /2016/10/imagine-donald-trump-controlled-nsa/. Trump's loose talk contributed to such concerns. For example, in explaining to voters that he was not involved in the DNC hack, he famously said at a 2016 rally, "Probably it was China or somebody else. Might be a 400-pound person sitting in bed," but he also said of the hacking, "I wish I had that power. Man, that would be power." See Nick Gass, "Trump on Russia Hack: 'I Wish I Had That Power,'" *Politico*, July 27, 2016, www .politico.com/story/2016/07/donald-trump-russia-china-hackers-226312.

14 *what he might do with drones*: See, for example, Tom Watts, "Here's What a Donald Trump Drone Program Could Look Like," *Business Insider*, September 20, 2016, www.businessinsider.com/donald-trump-drone-program-preview-2016-9.

14 *"bad dudes" he might bring to Guantánamo*: For Trump's comments about bringing "bad dudes" to the detention facility in Cuba, see "Trump to Load Up Guantanamo Bay with 'Some Bad Dudes,'" Reuters, February 23, 2016, www .reuters.com/video/2016/02/23/trump-to-load-up-guantanamo-bay-with-som ?videoId=367501571.

14 *interrogation policy didn't change*: See, for example, Gina Haspel's testimony before the Senate Select Committee on Intelligence, May 9, 2018, on her confirmation as CIA director, where she stated, "The U.S. government has a clear legal and policy framework that governs detentions and interrogations. Specifically, the law provides that no individual in U.S. custody may be subjected to any interrogation technique or approach that is not authorized by and listed in the Army Field Manual," and "CIA will not restart such a detention and interrogation program."

14 *"wires tapped"*: Donald J. Trump, Twitter, March 4, 2017, https://twitter.com /realDonaldTrump/status/837989835818287106.

14 *about the "unmasking"*: Donald J. Trump, Twitter, June 1, 2017, https://twitter .com/realDonaldTrump/status/870234811616677889.

15 *key intelligence authority*: Donald J. Trump, Twitter, January 11, 2018, https:// twitter.com/realdonaldtrump/status/951431836030459905. For our discussion of this particular episode, see Susan Hennessey and Benjamin Wittes, "Trump Tweets Against a Key National Security Priority," *Lawfare*, January 11, 2018, www.lawfareblog.com/trump-tweets-against-key-national-security-priority.

15 *"the executive Power"*: U.S. Constitution, Article II, Section 1.

15 *power to "appoint . . . Officers of the United States"*: U.S. Constitution, Article II, Section 2.

15 *authority to pardon people*: U.S. Constitution, Article II, Section 2.

1. "I do solemnly swear": The Oath

17 *travel ban*: See Executive Order 13769, "Protecting the Nation from Foreign Terrorist Entry into the United States," 82 FR 8977, January 27, 2017, www.federalregister
.gov/documents/2017/02/01/2017-02281/protecting-the-nation-from-foreign
-terrorist-entry-into-the-united-states. See also Executive Order 13780, "Protecting the Nation from Foreign Terrorist Entry into the United States," 82 FR 13209,
March 6, 2017, www.federalregister.gov/documents/2017/03/09/2017-04837
/protecting-the-nation-from-foreign-terrorist-entry-into-the-united-states. The
orders that were the subject of the litigation would be superseded by a third presidential directive on travel restrictions for foreigners. See White House Proclamation, "Presidential Proclamation Enhancing Vetting Capabilities and Processes for
Detecting Attempted Entry into the United States by Terrorists or Other Public-
Safety Threats," September 24, 2017, www.whitehouse.gov/presidential-actions
/presidential-proclamation-enhancing-vetting-capabilities-processes-detecting
-attempted-entry-united-states-terrorists-public-safety-threats/.

17 *many disparaging statements*: See, for example, Jenna Johnson and Abigail
Hauslohner, "'I Think Islam Hates Us': A Timeline of Trump's Comments About
Islam and Muslims," *Washington Post*, May 20, 2017, www.washingtonpost
.com/news/post-politics/wp/2017/05/20/i-think-islam-hates-us-a-timeline-of
-trumps-comments-about-islam-and-muslims/.

18 *the department wrote*: See Brief for Appellants, International Refugee Assistance
Project v. Trump, No. 17-1351 (4th Circuit, March 2017), available at https://
assets.documentcloud.org/documents/3524359/Doj-Brief-ca4-20170324.pdf.

18 *The department's invocation of Trump's oath*: For a discussion of the Justice Department's written submission regarding Trump's oath and the deviation from
prior precedent, see Quinta Jurecic, "Did the Justice Department Just Admit
Doubts Over Trump's Oath?" *Lawfare*, March 26, 2017, www.lawfareblog.com
/did-justice-department-just-admit-doubts-over-trumps-oath.

19 *ruling doge died in Renaissance Venice*: See Edward Muir, *Civic Ritual in Renaissance Venice* (Princeton, NJ: Princeton University Press, 1981), 268.

19 *before a president takes office*: U.S. Constitution, Article II, Section 1.

20 *"take Care that the Laws be faithfully executed"*: U.S. Constitution, Article II, Section 3.

20 *the presidential oath barely appears in Supreme Court case law*: Very few references
to the presidential oath appear in Supreme Court opinions. One recent attempt
to bring the presidential oath before the Supreme Court involved a suit in December 2008 to prevent Chief Justice John Roberts from requiring that Barack
Obama say "so help me God" at the end of his oath, though that phrase is not
included in the Constitution text. The suit was dismissed in D.C. federal district
and appellate courts, and the Supreme Court denied certiorari. See Newdow v.
Roberts, No. 09-5126 (D.C. Circuit, May 2010).

20 *the subject of extensive scholarly literature*: There are some notable exceptions to

this. The political scientist and legal scholar Matthew A. Pauley chronicles much of the scholarship on the question of the presidential oath in his book *I Do Solemnly Swear: The President's Constitutional Oath: Its Meaning and Importance in the History of Oaths* (Lanham, MD: University Press of America, 1999). We have incorporated much of that work in the discussion that follows.

20 *The founders specifically considered the presidential oath*: See Benjamin Wittes and Quinta Jurecic, "What Happens When We Don't Believe the President's Oath?" *Lawfare*, March 3, 2017, www.lawfareblog.com/what-happens-when-we-dont -believe-presidents-oath.

20 *describes the coronation oath of the English kings*: Edward Corwin, *The President: Office and Powers, 1787–1984* (New York: New York University Press, 1984), 69.

21 *considered the purpose of the oath*: Joseph Story, *Commentaries on the Constitution of the United States* (Durham, NC: Carolina Academic Press, 1987), 545.

21 *the promise of faithful execution*: Andrew Kent, Ethan J. Leib, and Jed Handelsman Shugerman, "Faithful Execution and Article II," *Harvard Law Review* 132 (June 2019): 2118–20, available at http://dx.doi.org/10.2139/ssrn.3260593. Kent and his coauthors write that scholars "have not uncovered any clear precedents or determinate meaning of this language." Prior usage of similar language was "almost entirely religious" in character. See p. 2137.

22 *the power to veto legislation*: U.S. Constitution, Article I, Section 7.

22 *commander in chief of the military*: U.S. Constitution, Article II, Section 2.

22 *impeachable for bribery*: U.S. Constitution, Article II, Section 4.

22 *take care clause*: U.S. Constitution, Article II, Section 3.

22 *recognized that oaths did not provide a sufficient condition*: In *Federalist* 18, James Madison offered the ancient Greek republics of the Amphictyonic council as an "instructive analogy" for the embryonic United States, noting that the members "took an oath mutually to defend and protect the united cities, to punish the violators of this oath, and to inflict vengeance on sacrilegious despoilers of the temple." Madison noted that "upon paper, this apparatus of powers" should be sufficient, especially since the "Amphictyons had in their hands the superstition of the times, one of the principal engines by which government was then maintained" and had sworn an oath to "use coercion against refractory cities" when necessary. But, as Madison also pointed out, the oath was not enough for holding a government together; his point was that even the Amphictyonic council oath could not preserve the structure of the ancient confederacy in the absence of sound constitutional structures. Madison may have been dismissive of the ancient beliefs of the Greek city-states as reflecting the "superstition of the times," but he recognized the value of the exercise as well.

23 *impulsively added "so help me God"*: Michael Riccards, *A Republic, If You Can Keep It: The Formation of the American Presidency: 1700–1800* (Westport, CT: Greenwood Press, 1987), 73–74, quoted in Pauley, *I Do Solemnly Swear*, 109.

23 *pleaded with secessionists*: Abraham Lincoln, inaugural address, March 4, 1861, available at www.presidency.ucsb.edu/documents/inaugural-address-34. The full

quotation reads: "In your hands, my dissatisfied fellow-countrymen, and not in mine, is the momentous issue of civil war. The Government will not assail you. You can have no conflict without being yourselves the aggressors. You have no oath registered in heaven to destroy the Government, while I shall have the most solemn one to 'preserve, protect, and defend it.'"

23 *Hobbes had argued*: Hobbes writes that "all therefore that can be done between two men not subject to Civill Power, is to put one another to swear by the God he feareth: Which *Swearing*, or OATH, is a *Forme of Speech, added to a Promise; by which he that promiseth, signifieth, that unlesse he performe, he renounceth the mercy of his God, or calleth to him for vengeance on himselfe*. Such was the Heathen Forme, *Let* Jupiter *kill me else, as I kill this Beast*. So is our Forme, *I shall do thus, and thus, so help me God*. And this, with the Rites and Ceremonies, which every one useth in his own Religion, that the feare of breaking faith might be the greater." Thomas Hobbes, *Leviathan*, ed. Ian Shapiro (New Haven, CT: Yale University Press, 2010), 87. A modern adaptation of this passage is quoted in Pauley, *I Do Solemnly Swear*, 34.

23 *Jeremy Bentham, a contemporary of the founders*: Jeremy Bentham, *Rationale of Judicial Evidence*, quoted in Pauley, *I Do Solemnly Swear*, 28.

23 *the way we form a social contract*: Pauley writes of Hobbes's view, "That is the sort of oath, sanctioned by fear of the consequences of breaking it, that brings natural man out of the state of nature by means of the *first* social covenant or compact." See Pauley, *I Do Solemnly Swear*, 34.

23 *the founders made*: Pauley, *I Do Solemnly Swear*, 158.

23 *Sanford Levinson*: Sanford Levinson, *Constitutional Faith* (Princeton, NJ: Princeton University Press, 1988), 55.

24 *Robert Livingston*: See George Washington, first inaugural address, *Records of the United States*, April 30, 1789, available at www.archives.gov/legislative/features /gw-inauguration.

24 *Supreme Court justice William Cushing administered the oath*: Pauley observes that the norm of the chief justice of the Supreme Court administering the oath of office, which began when Oliver Ellsworth swore in John Adams, may have endured for subsequent presidents because the chief justice possesses a "dignity that is above partisanship." See Pauley, *I Do Solemnly Swear*, 246.

24 *Sarah Hughes*: See "Lyndon B. Johnson being sworn in as President by Federal District Judge Sarah T. Hughes aboard the Presidential plane, as wife Lady Bird, former First Lady Jacqueline Kennedy, and others look on," 1963, Library of Congress, available at www.loc.gov/item/98504395/.

24 *Roosevelt met a federal district judge*: Theodore Roosevelt, *An Autobiography* (New York: Charles Scribner's Sons, 1921), 349.

24 *first presidential oath on April 30, 1789*: For a description of Washington swearing his oath and a discussion of his personal sincerity and the degree to which he meant his oath sincerely, see Pauley, *I Do Solemnly Swear*, 108–109.

24 *Washington wrote to a friend*: Washington wrote, "My movements to the chair of Government will be accompanied with feelings not unlike those of a culprit

who is going to the place of his execution: so unwilling am I, in the evening of a life nearly consumed in public cares, to quit a peaceful abode for an Ocean of difficulties, without that competency of political skill, abilities & inclination which is necessary to manage the helm. I am sensible, that I am embarking the voice of my Countrymen and a good name of my own, on this voyage, but what returns will be made for them: Heaven alone can foretell. Integrity & firmness is all I can promise—these, be the voyage long or short, never shall forsake me although I may be deserted by all men." Letter from George Washington to Henry Knox, April 1, 1789, available at https://founders.archives.gov/documents/Washington /05-02-02-0003.

25 *Fisher Ames of Massachusetts*: Woodrow Wilson, "The First President of the United States," *Harper's New Monthly Magazine*, Vol. 93, November 1896.

25 *second inaugural*: George Washington, second inaugural address, March 4, 1793, available at http://avalon.law.yale.edu/18th_century/wash2.asp.

25 *Johnson spoke of taking his oath*: For Johnson's comments on swearing his first presidential oath aboard Air Force One and his reaction to hearing Nixon swear his own oath, see Pauley, *I Do Solemnly Swear*, 5–6.

26 *It wasn't just the Democrats*: For a photograph showing the stricken faces of congressional Republicans at the moment of the oath, see Christopher Morris's headline image in a collection of inauguration photography from *Time* magazine: "Trump's First Day," image available at http.//time.com/president donald-trump -inauguration-day-photos/.

26 *doubt as to the integrity of his oath*: This chapter includes a number of passages that are adapted from Wittes and Jurecic, "What Happens When We Don't Believe the President's Oath?"

26 *questions about Obama's legitimacy to doubt his American birth*: For data on the prevalence of the false belief that President Obama was not born in the United States, including after Donald Trump repudiated his own birtherism, see Kyle Dropp and Brendan Nyhan, "It Lives. Birtherism Is Diminished but Far from Dead," *New York Times*, September 23, 2016, www.nytimes.com/2016/09/24 /upshot/it-lives-birtherism-is-diminished-but-far-from-dead.html.

26 *prevailed in the 2000 election*: A recount of votes in Florida, on which the 2000 presidential election turned, was ended—and the election thus decided in George W. Bush's favor—by a Supreme Court decision. Because Al Gore had won the popular vote, notwithstanding the Supreme Court ruling and resulting Electoral College vote, many Americans questioned the legitimacy of the ruling and of Bush's tenure. See Bush v. Gore, 531 U.S. 98 (2000).

27 *contested election of 1876*: Tilden won the popular vote, but votes in the Electoral College remained disputed among accusations of widespread voter fraud. The election was ultimately decided in Hayes's favor by a special election commission created by Congress. See William Rehnquist, *Centennial Crisis: The Disputed Election of 1876* (New York: Alfred A. Knopf, 2004).

27 *that triggered the South's secession*: For an account of President-elect Abraham

Lincoln's efforts to preserve the Union between his election and inauguration, see chap. 17 of Michael Burlingame, *Abraham Lincoln, A Life: Volume 1* (Baltimore: Johns Hopkins Press, 2009), 684–759.

27 *Herbert Hoover swore to "maintain" the Constitution*: The error was in Chief Justice William Howard Taft's recitation of the oath at Hoover's second inaugural, to which Hoover responded, "I do." Archival footage is available at www.youtube .com/watch?v=ctAKm9G8ji8. Ironically, just three days earlier, Taft had written to Hoover explaining the oath proceedings and quoting, accurately, the oath of office in full. See letter from William Howard Taft to Herbert Hoover, March 1, 1929, available at www.docsteach.org/documents/document/letter-from-chief -justice-william-howard-taft-to-president-herbert-hoover-regarding-the-oath-of -office.

27 *Nixon inserted an "and" that didn't belong*: Nixon swore to "preserve and protect and defend" the Constitution in 1973. Archival footage is available at www .youtube.com/watch?v=OguQMo34_Ck.

27 *At Obama's first inauguration*: See "Obama Retakes Oath of Office After Flub," Associated Press, January 21, 2009, www.nbcnews.com/id/28780417/ns/politics -white_house/t/obama-retakes-oath-office-after-flub/.

27 *promising to commit war crimes*: See Jenna Johnson, "Trump Says 'Torture Works,' Backs Waterboarding and 'Much Worse,'" *Washington Post*, February 17, 2016, www.washingtonpost.com/politics/trump-says-torture-works-backs-waterboard ing-and-much-worse/2016/02/17/4c9277be-d59c-11e5-b195-2e29a4e13425 _story.html.

27 *described the election*: Jeremy Diamond, "Trump: 'I'm Afraid the Election's Going to Be Rigged,'" CNN, August 2, 2016, www.cnn.com/2016/08/01/politics /donald-trump-election-2016-rigged/index.html.

27 *would not promise to respect the outcome if he lost*: Patrick Healy and Jonathan Martin, "Donald Trump Won't Say If He'll Accept Result of Election," *New York Times*, October 19, 2016, www.nytimes.com/2016/10/20/us/politics /presidential-debate.html.

28 *Comey would use this phrase*: For a full account of the events surrounding Comey's initial meeting with Trump, including the former FBI director's statements regarding his motivation for contemporaneously memorializing the interaction, see James Comey, Statement for the Record, Senate Select Committee on Intelligence, June 8, 2017, www.intelligence.senate.gov/sites/default/files/documents /os-jcomey-060817.pdf. See also "Full Transcript and Video: James Comey's Testimony on Capitol Hill," *New York Times*, June 8, 2017, www.nytimes.com /2017/06/08/us/politics/senate-hearing-transcript.html.

29 *also memorialized his conversations with Trump*: Andrew G. McCabe, "Every Day Is a New Low in Trump's White House," *Atlantic*, February 14, 2019, www .theatlantic.com/politics/archive/2019/02/andrew-mccabe-fbi-book-excerpt -the-threat/582748/.

30 *"presumption of regularity"*: For a discussion on the presumption of regularity in judicial review of the Trump administration's executive actions, see Note, "The Presumption of Regularity in Judicial Review of the Executive Branch," *Harvard Law Review*, June 8, 2018, available at https://harvardlawreview.org/2018/06/the-presumption-of-regularity-in-judicial-review-of-the-executive-branch/.

30 *The bureaucracy leaked*: For an analysis of leaks from the bureaucracy from the early period of the Trump administration, see Amanda Taub and Max Fisher, "As Leaks Multiply, Fears of a 'Deep State' in America," *New York Times*, February 16, 2017, www.nytimes.com/2017/02/16/world/americas/deep-state-leaks-trump.html.

30 *Judges refused to credit executive branch statements*: See, for example, the Ninth Circuit's ruling on the second version of the travel ban order in Hawaii v. Trump, No. 17-15589 (9th Circuit, June 12, 2017), pp. 41–51, available at https://cdn.ca9.uscourts.gov/datastore/opinions/2017/06/12/17-15589.pdf.

30 *the press often treated presidential statements as presumptively untrue*: Trump's dishonesty and the press's reaction to it is treated in depth in the fifth chapter of this book.

31 *In 1846, Enoch Lewis*: Enoch Lewis, *A Dissertation on Oaths* (Philadelphia: Hunt/Kite, 1838), 14–15, quoted in Pauley, *I Do Solemnly Swear*, 30.

32 *On Saturday, he traveled to the CIA*: See "Trump CIA Speech Transcript," CBS News, January 23, 2017, www.cbsnews.com/news/trump-cia-speech-transcript/

32 *"this was the largest audience to ever witness an inauguration"*: Statement by Press Secretary Sean Spicer, January 21, 2017, available at www.whitehouse.gov/briefings-statements/statement-press-secretary-sean-spicer/.

32 *"alternative facts"*: "Conway: Press Secretary Gave 'Alternative Facts,'" NBC's *Meet the Press*, January 22, 2017, www.nbcnews.com/meet-the-press/video/conway-press-secretary-gave-alternative-facts-860142147643.

32 *shared a side-by-side photograph*: See Michael D. Shear and Maggie Haberman, "Trump Called National Park Chief over Twitter Post on Inaugural Crowd," *New York Times*, January 26, 2017, www.nytimes.com/2017/01/26/us/politics/trump-inauguration-crowd-size-park-chief.html.

32 *the administration ordered*: On January 20, 2017, an internal email sent to National Park Service employees and shared with *Gizmodo* stated, "We have received direction . . . to immediately cease use of government Twitter accounts until further notice. PWR parks that use Twitter as part of their crisis communications plans need to alter their contingency plans to accommodate this requirement." See William Turton, "National Park Service Banned from Tweeting After Anti-Trump Retweets," *Gizmodo*, January 20, 2017, https://gizmodo.com/national-park-service-banned-from-tweeting-after-anti-t-1791449526.

32 *he described Trump's calling him*: After he left office, in a *Vanity Fair* interview, former chief of staff Reince Priebus gave his account of the president's response to the tweet shared by the National Park Service, and the president's

personal involvement in issuing the directive to cease use of Twitter to the Department of the Interior. See Chris Whipple, "'Who Needs a Controversy Over the Inauguration?': Reince Priebus Opens Up About His Six Months of Magical Thinking," *Vanity Fair*, March 2018, www.vanityfair.com/news/2018/02/reince -priebus-opens-up-about-his-six-months-of-magical-thinking,

2. "The President needs help": White House Decisions

35 *Trump had devoted the first week of his presidency*: See, for example, Julie Hirschfeld Davis and Matthew Rosenberg, "With False Claims, Trump Attacks Media on Turnout and Intelligence Rift," *New York Times*, January 21, 2017, www.nytimes .com/2017/01/21/us/politics/trump-white-house-briefing-inauguration-crowd -size.html; "Trump Pledges 'Major Investigation into Voter Fraud,'" BBC, January 25, 2017, www.bbc.com/news/world-us-canada-38746559; Shane Goldmacher and Matthew Nussbaum, "At CIA Headquarters, Trump Boasts About Himself, Denies Feud," *Politico*, January 21, 2017, www.politico.com/story/2017 /01/trump-cia-langley-233971.

35 *withdrawal from the Trans-Pacific Partnership*: See "Presidential Memorandum Regarding Withdrawal of the United States from the Trans-Pacific Partnership Negotiations and Agreement," January 23, 2017, www.whitehouse.gov /presidential-actions/presidential-memorandum-regarding-withdrawal-united -states-trans-pacific-partnership-negotiations-agreement/.

36 *first lawsuit as president*: See Complaint, Citizens for Responsibility and Ethics in Washington v. Donald J. Trump, No. 17-458 (SDNY, January 23, 2017), available at https://s3.amazonaws.com/storage.citizensforethics.org/wp-content/uploads /2017/03/23164833/EMOLUMENTS-COMPLAINT1.pdf.

36 *Keystone XL pipeline*: See "Presidential Memorandum Regarding Construction of American Pipelines," January 24, 2017, available at www.whitehouse .gov/presidential-actions/presidential-memorandum-regarding-construction -american-pipelines/.

36 *executive orders on his promised border wall*: See Executive Order 13767, "Border Security and Immigration Enforcement Improvements," 82 FR 8793, January 25, 2017, www.federalregister.gov/documents/2017/01/30/2017-02095 /border-security-and-immigration-enforcement-improvements; Executive Order 13768, "Enhancing Public Safety in the Interior of the United States," 82 FR 8799, January 25, 2017, www.federalregister.gov/documents/2017/01/30/2017 -02102/enhancing-public-safety-in-the-interior-of-the-united-states.

36 *Mexican president Enrique Peña Nieto*: See Azam Ahmed, "Mexico's President Cancels Meeting with Trump Over Wall," *New York Times*, January 26, 2017, www .nytimes.com/2017/01/26/world/mexicos-president-cancels-meeting-with -trump-over-wall.html.

36 *"Protecting the Nation from Foreign Terrorist"*: Executive Order 13769, "Protecting the Nation from Foreign Terrorist Entry into the United States," 82 FR 8977, January 27, 2017, www.federalregister.gov/documents/2017/02/01/2017

-02281/protecting-the-nation-from-foreign-terrorist-entry-into-the-united
-states.

36 *"total and complete shutdown of Muslims"*: Jenna Johnson, "Trump Calls for 'Total and Complete Shutdown of Muslims Entering the United States,'" *Washington Post*, December 7, 2015, www.washingtonpost.com/news/post-politics /wp/2015/12/07/donald-trump-calls-for-total-and-complete-shutdown-of -muslims-entering-the-united-states.

36 *insisted that the new policy was not a Muslim ban*: In a statement about the policy, the White House said, "To be clear, this is not a Muslim ban, as the media is falsely reporting. This is not about religion—this is about terror and keeping our country safe. There are over 40 different countries worldwide that are majority Muslim that are not affected by this order." See "President Donald J. Trump Statement Regarding Recent Executive Order Concerning Extreme Vetting," January 29, 2017, www.whitehouse.gov/briefings-statements/president-donald-j-trump-statement -regarding-recent-executive-order-concerning-extreme-vetting/.

36 *"This is the protection of the nation from foreign terrorist entry"*: "Secretary of Defense Ceremonial Swearing-In," C-SPAN, January 27, 2017, at timestamp 12:19, www.c-span.org/video/?422913-1/president-trump-signs-executive-action -calling-extreme-vetting-refugees.

36 *travel ban unleashed immediate chaos*: See, for example, Glenn Kessler, "The Number of People Affected by Trump's Travel Ban: About 90,000," *Washington Post*, January 30, 2017, www.washingtonpost.com/news/fact-checker/wp/2017/01/30/the -number-of-people-affected-by-trumps-travel-ban-about-90000/; "'My Family Was in Shock': The Harm Caused by President Trump's Executive Orders on Travel to the US," Amnesty International, May 2017, www.amnestyusa.org/wp-content /uploads/2017/05/my_family_was_in_shock_report.pdf; Joanna Walters, Edward Helmore, and Saeed Kamali Dehghan, "US Airports on Frontline as Donald Trump's Travel Ban Causes Chaos and Protests," *Guardian*, January 28, 2017, www .theguardian.com/us-news/2017/jan/28/airports-us-immigration-ban-muslim -countries-trump.

36 *order was signed without warning*: Report of the Office of the Inspector General, "DHS Implementation of Executive Order #13769 'Protecting the Nation from Foreign Terrorist Entry into the United States' (January 27, 2017)," U.S. Department of Homeland Security, January 18, 2018, available at www.oig.dhs.gov /sites/default/files/assets/2018-01/OIG-18-37-Jan18.pdf.

37 *order suspended all entry to the United States*: Executive Order 13769, "Protecting the Nation from Foreign Terrorist Entry into the United States," 82 FR 8977, January 27, 2017, www.federalregister.gov/documents/2017/02/01 /2017-02281/protecting-the-nation-from-foreign-terrorist-entry-into-the -united-states.

37 *Protests began at airports*: Michael D. Shear, Nicholas Kulish, and Alan Feuer, "Judge Blocks Trump Order on Refugees Amid Chaos and Outcry Worldwide," *New York Times*, January 28, 2017, www.nytimes.com/2017/01/28/us/refugees

-detained-at-us-airports-prompting-legal-challenges-to-trumps-immigration
-order.html.

37 *ACLU had petitioned a federal court*: Petition for Writ of Habeas Corpus and Complaint for Declaratory and Injunctive Relief, Darweesh v. Trump, et al., No. 17-480 (EDNY, January 28. 2017), available at https://assets.documentcloud.org /documents/3434634/Petition-for-Writ-of-Habeas-Corpus-on-Behalf-Of.pdf.

37 *federal judge in Virginia*: Temporary Restraining Order, Aziz v. Trump, et al., No. 17-116 (EDVA, January 28, 2017), available at https://assets.documentcloud .org/documents/3437770/Virgina-Ruling-TRO-Order-Signed.pdf.

37 *enforcement of the whole ban nationwide*: Order, State of Washington v. Trump, et al., No. 17-141 (W.D. Washington, February 3, 2017), available at https://assets .documentcloud.org/documents/3446215/Washington-v-Trump-Order.pdf.

38 *people who had helped U.S. forces in Iraq*: See David Zucchino, "Visa Ban Amended to Allow Iraqi Interpreters into U.S.," *New York Times*, February 2, 2017, www .nytimes.com/2017/02/02/world/middleeast/trump-visa-ban-iraq-interpreters .html.

39 *limited to a facial review of the order's text*: See Memorandum, "Re: Proposed Executive Order Entitled, 'Protecting the Nation from Foreign Terrorist Entry into the United States,'" Office of Legal Counsel, January 27, 2017, available at https://assets.documentcloud.org/documents/3442905/EO-Foreign-Terrorist -Entry.pdf.

39 *The Homeland Security Department was briefed*: The *New York Times* reported that Secretary John Kelly was being briefed by telephone when a participant on the call saw the president signing the order on television. See Michael D. Shear and Ron Nixon, "How Trump's Rush to Enact an Immigration Ban Unleashed Global Chaos," *New York Times*, January 29, 2017, www.nytimes.com/2017/01 /29/us/politics/donald-trump-rush-immigration-order-chaos.html.

39 *Neither the military nor the intelligence community*: See Shear and Nixon, "How Trump's Rush to Enact an Immigration Ban Unleashed Global Chaos"; John Wolcott and Julia Edwards Ainsley, "Trump's Go-To Man Bannon Takes Hardline View on Immigration," Reuters, January 30, 2017, www.reuters.com /article/us-usa-trump-immigration-bannon/trumps-go-to-man-bannon-takes -hardline-view-on-immigration-idUSKBN15E2TG.

39 *had counted on executive branch processes*: This meme showed up much more often as a hope than as a prediction. See, for representative examples, Nouriel Roubini, "The Oval Office Will Tame President Donald Trump," *Guardian*, November 11, 2016, www.theguardian.com/business/2016/nov/11/oval-office-will-tame-us-president -donald-trump; Roberta Rampton, "Trump Will Get Wake-Up Call When He Takes Office, Obama Says," Reuters, November 14, 2016, www.reuters.com/article /us-usa-trump/trump-will-get-wake-up-call-when-he-takes-office-obama-says -idUSKBN1390HL; Ezra Klein, "It's Now on America's Institutions—and the Republican Party—to Check Donald Trump," *Vox*, November 9, 2016, www.vox.com /policy-and-politics/2016/11/9/13570824/trump-wins-election-institutions;

Nicholas Kristof, "Gritting Our Teeth and Giving President Trump a Chance," *New York Times*, November 9, 2016, www.nytimes.com/2016/11/10/opinion/gritting -our-teeth-and-giving-president-trump-a-chance.html.

40 *Acting Attorney General Sally Yates*: The text of Yates's letter, dated January 30, 2017, is available via *The New York Times* at www.nytimes.com/interactive/2017 /01/30/us/document-Letter-From-Sally-Yates.html.

40 *Trump immediately fired Yates*: See "Statement on the Appointment of Dana Boente as Acting Attorney General," January 30, 2017, www.whitehouse.gov /briefings-statements/statement-appointment-dana-boente-acting-attorney -general/.

40 *After a federal appellate court enjoined its enforcement*: Per Curiam Order, State of Washington v. Trump, et al., No. 17-35105 (9th Circuit, February 9, 2017), available at https://cdn.ca9.uscourts.gov/datastore/opinions/2017/02/09/17-35105.pdf.

40 *the government withdrew the order*: For the government's withdrawal and replace- ment, see Executive Order 13780, "Protecting the Nation from Foreign Terrorist Entry into the United States," 82 FR 13209, March 6, 2017, www.federalregister .gov/documents/2017/03/09/2017-04837/protecting-the-nation-from-foreign -terrorist-entry-into-the-united-states. See also Glenn Thrush, "Trump's New Travel Ban Blocks Migrants from Six Nations, Sparing Iraq," *New York Times*, March 6, 2017, www.nytimes.com/2017/03/06/us/politics/travel-ban-muslim -trump.html.

40 *Supreme Court finally okayed*: Trump et al. v. Hawaii, No. 17-965, 585 US ___ (2018), available at www.supremecourt.gov/opinions/17pdf/17-965_h315.pdf.

41 *Civil service rules*: 5 U.S. Code Part III.

41 *Uniform Code of Military Justice*: 10 U.S. Code, Chapter 47.

41 *Administrative Procedure Act*: 5 U.S. Code, Chapter 5.

41 *statutory responsibilities that assign roles*: For example, the Foreign Intelligence Surveillance Act assigns specific responsibilities to Justice Department officials in the course of applying for orders for electronic surveillance. See 50 U.S. Code § 1804. More generally, 28 U.S. Code § 509 vests, with certain limited excep- tions, "all functions of other officers of the Department of Justice . . . in the Attor- ney General."

42 *after taking a walk around the White House grounds with a single aide*: Chuck Todd, "The White House Walk-and-Talk That Changed Obama's Mind on Syria," NBC News, August 31, 2013, www.nbcnews.com/news/world/white-house -walk-talk-changed-obamas-mind-syria-flna8C11051182.

42 *His advisers had no warning*: Roberta Rampton and Jeff Mason, "Obama's Syria De- cision: A Walk, a Debate, and a New Approach," Reuters, August 31, 2013, www .reuters.com/article/us-syria-crisis-obama-decision-idUSBRE98001520130901.

42 *when presidents have failed to run good processes*: For a discussion of the process surrounding the intelligence programs authorized following the September 11 attacks and the ensuing backlash, see chap. 5 of Jack Goldsmith, *The Terror Presi- dency* (New York: W. W. Norton, 2007), 141–76. See also chap. 6 of James Comey,

A Higher Loyalty: Truth, Lies, and Leadership (New York: Flatiron Books, 2018), 74–99.

42 *a senior CIA official told him*: Deputy CIA director Mike Morell, who was running the bin Laden team, told Obama, "The case for W.M.D. wasn't just stronger: it was *much* stronger" than the case that the figure in Abbottabad was, in fact, bin Laden. Mark Bowden, "The Hunt for 'Geronimo,'" *Vanity Fair*, November 2012, www .vanityfair.com/news/politics/2012/11/inside-osama-bin-laden-assassination -plot.

42 *authorized the bin Laden raid having heard*: Bowden, "The Hunt for 'Geronimo.'"

42 *to put together a coalition to confront Iraq*: Ambassador Dennis Ross, who served as the director of the State Department's Policy Planning Staff during the George H. W. Bush administration, gives a detailed account of the diplomatic exertion to respond to Saddam Hussein's aggression in Kuwait in chap. 4 of *Statecraft: And How to Restore America's Standing in the World* (New York: Farrar, Straus and Giroux, 2007), 73–99.

43 *radically divergent agendas*: For example, Hamilton and Jefferson disagreed sharply on foreign policy, as Ron Chernow explains in chap. 54 and elsewhere in his biography of Washington. Ron Chernow, *Washington: A Life* (New York: Penguin Books, 2010), 656–68.

43 *Washington eventually dismissed key cabinet members*: For an account of Washington's firing of Edmund Randolph, see Chernow, *Washington: A Life*, 732–36. Similarly, for an account of Adams firing Secretary of State Timothy Pickering and Secretary of War James McHenry, see David McCullough, *John Adams* (New York: Touchstone, 2011), 539.

43 *Washington tended to side with Hamilton*: See Chernow, *Washington: A Life*, 516–17, 648–50, 675–83, 742–44.

43 *there were only three cabinet-level departments*: See Chernow, *Washington: A Life*, 596.

43 *Only five more were added*: The Veterans Administration was created in 1930 and elevated to a cabinet-level position in 1988. See "History: Department of Veterans Affairs," available at www.va.gov/about_va/vahistory.asp. The War Department was replaced by the National Military Establishment in 1947, which was renamed the Department of Defense in 1949. See "About the Department of Defense (DOD)," available at https://archive.defense.gov/about/.

43 *reported to the Treasury Department*: Jed Shugerman writes, "In the very beginning, the Attorney General had no power over the district attorneys or their appointment process. In 1797, Congress gave the Comptroller of the Treasury significant prosecutorial authority over district attorneys in directing suits over revenue and debts. In practice, district attorneys were not really supervised at all. Active supervision was impossible over such long distances, with such limited transportation and communication." See Jed H. Shugerman, "The Creation of the Department of Justice: Professionalization Without Civil Rights or Civil

Service," *Stanford Law Review* 66: 131–32, available at https://ir.lawnet.fordham
.edu/cgi/viewcontent.cgi?article=1638&context=faculty_scholarship.

44 *David McCullough describes*: McCullough, *John Adams*, 509.

44 *reviewed all letters*: For all the anecdotes described in this paragraph save the one
involving Grover Cleveland, see Steven G. Calabresi and Christopher S. Yoo, *The
Unitary Executive: Presidential Power from Washington to Bush* (New Haven, CT:
Yale University Press, 2008), 41, 46, 66.

45 *And President Grover Cleveland*: John P. Burke, *The Institutional Presidency: Or-
ganizing and Managing the White House from FDR to Clinton*, 2nd ed. (Baltimore:
Johns Hopkins Press, 2000), 6.

45 *Washington personally led a column*: John C. Yoo, "George Washington and Executive Power," UC Berkeley Public Law Research Paper No. 1703014, 12–13,
available at https://ssrn.com/abstract=1703014 or http://dx.doi.org/10.2139
/ssrn.1703014.

45 *When Jefferson was president*: Burke, *The Institutional Presidency*, 3–4.

45 *It was not until 1857*: See Burke, *The Institutional Presidency*, 4.

45 *presidents paid staff out of their own pockets*: See Burke, *The Institutional Presidency*, 4.

45 *many presidents hired family members*: John Quincy Adams, Andrew Jackson,
John Tyler, Abraham Lincoln, Andrew Johnson, and Grant all hired their sons
as presidential staff. Washington, James Polk, and James Buchanan all employed
their nephews. See Burke, *The Institutional Presidency*, 4.

45 *as secretary of state in the Washington administration*: See "Department History,"
Office of the Historian, U.S. Department of State, available at https://history
.state.gov/departmenthistory/short-history/staffing.

45 *When the Treasury Department moved to Washington*: See Department of the Treasury, "Historic Offices of the Secretary of the Treasury," available at https://web
.archive.org/web/20190119211158/https://www.treasury.gov/about/history
/exhibition/Pages/Historic-Offices-of-the-Secretary-of-the-Treasury.aspx.

45 *In 1836 the department was split into six bureaus*: See "The Department
Reorganized—Again," Office of the Historian, U.S. Department of State, available at https://web.archive.org/web/20190425170614/https://history.state.gov
/departmenthistory/short-history/reorganized.

46 *sarcastic memo*: See Alvin S. Felzenberg, "The Transition: A Guide for the President-
Elect," *Hoover Policy Review*, October 1, 2000, www.hoover.org/research/transition
-guide-president-elect. Roosevelt appears to have shared the story of the four bears
in numerous public speeches. See, for example, an October 17, 1928, speech in Bing-
hamton, New York, available from the FDR Library at www.fdrlibrary.marist.edu
/_resources/images/msf/msf00266, in which he references having told the story at
many previous events.

47 *"administrative state"*: At his first speaking appearance during Trump's tenure
in office, Bannon told a group of conservative activists that the administration

would fight for the "deconstruction of the administrative state." See Philip Rucker and Robert Costa, "Bannon Vows a Daily Fight for 'Deconstruction of the Administrative State,'" *Washington Post*, February 23, 2017, www.washingtonpost.com /politics/top-wh-strategist-vows-a-daily-fight-for-deconstruction-of-the -administrative-state/2017/02/23/03f6b8da-f9ea-11e6-bf01-d47f8cf9b643 _story.html.

47 *Roosevelt was painfully aware*: Burke, *The Institutional Presidency*, 6–9.

47 *In 1937 the Brownlow Committee*: "Administrative Management in the Government of the United States," The President's Committee on Management, 1937, 5, available at https://babel.hathitrust.org/cgi/pt?id=mdp.39015030482726;view =1up;seq=1.

47 *Its recommendations . . . eventual bill*: Burke, *The Institutional Presidency*, 9–11.

48 *During the reorganization*: Burke, *The Institutional Presidency*, 12.

48 *Additional reforms followed*: For example, Justice Elena Kagan, while still a law professor, explained the Reagan-era reforms to the process by which the White House reviewed executive branch rulemaking. See Elena Kagan, "Presidential Administration," *Harvard Law Review* 114 (2001): 2245–78. Wrote Kagan, "Reagan . . . instituted, through two executive orders, a centralized mechanism for review of agency rulemakings unprecedented in its scale and ambition," p. 2277. She further wrote, "Executive Order 12,291, issued during Reagan's first month in office, established the system: the order required executive—but not independent—agencies to submit to OMB's Office of Information and Regulatory Affairs (OIRA) for pre-publication review any proposed major rule, accompanied by a 'regulatory impact analysis' of the rule, including a cost-benefit comparison."

48 *Congress created the National Security Council*: "The National Security Act of 1947," Public Law 80-253, July 26, 1947; 61 Stat. 496.

48 *By the early 1990s*: Those units were the National Security Council, the Office of Policy Development, the Office of Management and Budget, the Council of Economic Advisers, the Office of Science and Technology Policy, the Council on Environmental Quality, the Office of the U.S. Trade Representative, the Office of Administration, the Office of National Drug Control Policy, and the Office of the Vice President. See Burke, *The Institutional Presidency*, 14.

50 *Former New Jersey governor Chris Christie*: This episode is reported in Michael Lewis, *The Fifth Risk* (New York: W. W. Norton, 2018), 20–22.

50 *The reprieve turned out to be brief*: See Lewis, *The Fifth Risk*, 30–31. Trump's comment to Christie appears on p. 22.

50 *Meanwhile, voluminous Obama administration transition*: See Lewis, *The Fifth Risk*, 27, 38–39, 42, 90, 92, 160, 190.

50 *The Trump transition didn't even . . . when he said to Christie*: Lewis, *The Fifth Risk*, 35–36.

50 *As of the end of his first year in office*: Jan Diehm, Sergio Hernandez, Aaron Kessler, Tal Kopan, Curt Merrill, and Sean O'Key, "Tracking Trump's Nominations,"

CNN Politics, last updated December 31, 2017, www.cnn.com/interactive/2017 /politics/trump-nominations/.

50 *As of August 2019*: See "Tracking How Many Key Positions Trump Has Filled So Far," *Washington Post* in partnership with Partnership for Public Service, last updated August 5, 2019, www.washingtonpost.com/graphics/politics/trump -administration-appointee-tracker/database.

51 *"I like acting. It gives me more flexibility"*: Amanda Becker, "Trump Says Acting Cabinet Members Give Him 'More Flexibility,'" Reuters, January 6, 2019, www .reuters.com/article/us-usa-trump-cabinet-idUSKCN1P00IG.

51 *"The one that matters is me"*: See "Trump Talks Tax Cuts, Future of Immigration Reform," Fox News, November 2, 2017, at timestamp 7:30, available at www .youtube.com/watch?time_continue=1&v=EA2pH3CD5Ns.

51 *Major Garrett writes*: Major Garrett, *Mr. Trump's Wild Ride: The Thrills, Chills, Screams, and Occasional Blackouts of an Extraordinary Presidency* (New York: St. Martin's Press, 2018), 26.

51 *ban on transgender service members*: See Donald J. Trump, Twitter, July 26, 2017, available at https://twitter.com/realdonaldtrump/status/890193981585444864, https://twitter.com/realdonaldtrump/status/890196164313833472, https:// twitter.com/realdonaldtrump/status/890197095151546369. Trump wrote, consolidating his three tweets in one passage, "After consultation with my Generals and military experts, please be advised that the United States Government will not accept or allow . . . Transgender individuals to serve in any capacity in the U.S. Military. Our military must be focused on decisive and overwhelming . . . victory and cannot be burdened with the tremendous medical costs and disruption that transgender in the military would entail. Thank you." For reporting on the incident, see Julie Hirschfeld Davis and Helene Cooper, "Trump Says Transgender People Will Not Be Allowed in the Military," *New York Times*, July 26, 2017, www .nytimes.com/2017/07/26/us/politics/trump-transgender-military.html.

51 *the policy saw swift judicial rebuke*: See Memorandum Opinion, Jane Doe 1, et al. v. Donald J. Trump, No. 17-1597 (D.D.C., October 30, 2017), available at www.lawfareblog.com/document-dc-district-court-rules-transgender-military -service-member-ban; Order, Jane Doe 1, et al. v. Donald J. Trump, No. 17-1597 (D.D.C., December 11, 2017), available at www.lawfareblog.com/document-dc -district-court-denies-doj-motion-partial-stay-doe-v-trump.

51 *the military had to start over*: See "Presidential Memorandum for the Secretary of Defense and the Secretary of Homeland Security: Military Service by Transgender Individuals," March 23, 2018, available at www.lawfareblog.com /documents-new-trump-administration-policy-transgender-servicemembers.

51 *the litigation over the second version*: See Order, Jane Doe 2, et al. v. Patrick Shanahan, et al., No. 17-1597 (D.D.C., March 19, 2019), available at www.lawfareblog .com/document-judge-clarifies-preliminary-injunction-transgender-service-ban.

52 *Trump impulsively announced a meeting*: Peter Baker and Choe Sang-Hun, "With Snap 'Yes' in Oval Office, Trump Gambles on North Korea," *New York Times*,

March 10, 2018, www.nytimes.com/2018/03/10/world/asia/trump-north-korea.html.

52 *His announcement of the withdrawal of U.S. forces*: Paul Sonne, Josh Dawsey, and Missy Ryan, "Mattis Resigns After Clash with Trump Over Troop Withdrawal from Syria and Afghanistan," *Washington Post*, December 20, 2018, www.washingtonpost.com/world/national-security/trump-announces-mattis-will-leave-as-defense-secretary-at-the-end-of-february/2018/12/20/e1a846ee-e147-11e8-ab2c-b31dcd53ca6b_story.html.

52 *"malevolence tempered by incompetence"*: See Benjamin Wittes, "Malevolence Tempered by Incompetence: Trump's Horrifying Executive Order on Refugees and Visas," *Lawfare*, January 28, 2017, www.lawfareblog.com/malevolence-tempered-incompetence-trumps-horrifying-executive-order-refugees-and-visas.

53 *executive order to close the military detention facility*: See Executive Order 13492, "Review and Disposition of Individuals Detained at the Guantánamo Bay Naval Base and Closure of Detention Facilities," 74 FR 4897, January 22, 2009, available at www.federalregister.gov/documents/2009/01/27/E9-1893/review-and-disposition-of-individuals-detained-at-the-guantaacutenamo-bay-naval-base-and-closure-of.

53 *as Obama himself did*: Obama described part of the challenge in a February 2016 speech: "Unfortunately, during that period where we were putting the pieces in place to close it, what had previously been bipartisan support suddenly became a partisan issue. Suddenly, many you [*sic*] previously had said it should be closed backed off because they were worried about the politics. The public was scared into thinking that, well, if we close it, somehow we'll be less safe. And since that time, Congress has repeatedly imposed restrictions aimed at preventing us from closing this facility." See "Remarks by the President on Plan to Close the Prison at Guantanamo Bay," February 23, 2016, available at https://obamawhitehouse.archives.gov/the-press-office/2016/02/23/remarks-president-plan-close-prison-guantanamo-bay.

54 *journalist Bob Woodward recounts Reince Priebus's frustrations*: Bob Woodward, *Fear: Trump in the White House* (New York: Simon & Schuster, 2019), 144–45.

54 *"They were in their own silo"*: Woodward, *Fear*, 144.

54 *"No one could fire the family"*: Woodward, *Fear*, 144.

54 *"'You're a goddamn staffer!'"*: Woodward, *Fear*, 145.

55 *he also had dinner with his FBI director*: See James B. Comey, "Statement for the Record," U.S. Senate Select Committee on Intelligence, June 8, 2017, available at www.intelligence.senate.gov/sites/default/files/documents/os-jcomey-060817.pdf. See also Comey, *A Higher Loyalty*, 233–44. The Mueller report specifically notes that while the White House disputed Comey's story, "substantial evidence corroborates Comey's account of the dinner invitation and the request for loyalty." See "Report on the Investigation into Russian Interference in the 2016 Presidential Election," Vol. II, 35.

3. "This president runs this government": The Non-Unitary Executive

57 *Daniel Drezner tweeted*: Daniel W. Drezner, Twitter, April 25, 2017, available at https://twitter.com/dandrezner/status/856876322001432581.

57 *"Trump turns on the television"*: Ashley Parker and Robert Costa, "'Everyone Tunes In': Inside Trump's Obsession with Cable TV," *Washington Post*, April 23, 2017, www.washingtonpost.com/politics/everyone-tunes-in-inside-trumps-obsession -with-cable-tv/2017/04/23/3c52bd6c-25e3-11e7-a1b3-faff0034e2de_story .html.

58 *"Over time, Mr. Trump bridled"*: Glenn Thrush and Maggie Haberman, "Second Chance for 'Obamacare' Repeal. And for Reince Priebus," *New York Times*, May 5, 2017, www.nytimes.com/2017/05/05/us/politics/reince-priebus-health-care .html; Daniel W. Drezner, Twitter, May 5, 2017, https://twitter.com/dandrezner /status/860456460093992960.

58 *"Aides often leak stories"*: Stef W. Kight, "Trump 101: His Advisers Talk About Him Like He's a Child," *Axios*, May 7, 2017, www.axios.com/trump-101-his -advisers-talk-about-him-like-hes-a-child-1513302088-7d6d03f1-bf9d-4f88 -9679-37a54ce8f56a.html; Daniel W. Drezner, Twitter, May 7, 2017, https:// twitter.com/dandrezner/status/861342123341295616.

58 *Drezner wrote in an email*: Email from Daniel W. Drezner to Benjamin Wittes, August 10, 2018. Record on file with authors. Drezner develops these ideas at length in *The Toddler-in-Chief: What Donald Trump Teaches Us About the Modern Presidency* (Chicago: University of Chicago Press, forthcoming 2020).

60 *The Constitution creates a unitary executive branch*: See U.S. Constitution, Article II, Section 1: "The executive Power shall be vested in a President of the United States of America."

60 *The federal courts*: The structure of the federal judiciary is described in the U.S. Code at Title 28, Part 1.

60 *Congress has two chambers*: The bifurcation of Congress is established by the Constitution, Article I, Section 1. Article I, Section 5 grants each body of Congress the power to establish its own rules.

60 *funded and ran an opposition newspaper*: See Alvin Stephen Felzenberg, *The Leaders We Deserved (And a Few We Didn't)* (New York: Basic Books, 2008), 47.

60 *Lower executive branch officials*: For example, 10 U.S. Code § 8629 authorizes the secretary of the navy, "in any manner he considers proper, [to] buy the kind of fuel that is best adapted to the purpose for which it is to be used."

60 *civil servants are not appointed and removed*: For a discussion of the Civil Service Reform Act, which governs the circumstances under which civil servants can be dismissed or demoted, see Jared P. Cole, "The Civil Service Reform Act: Due Process and Misconduct-Related Adverse Actions," Congressional Research Service, March 29, 2017, available at https://fas.org/sgp/crs/misc/R44803.pdf.

60 *Presidential lack of control over the State Department*: See Laurence Silberman, "Toward Presidential Control of the State Department," *Foreign Affairs*, Spring

1979, available at www.foreignaffairs.com/articles/united-states/1979-03-01/toward-presidential-control-state-department.

61 *sudden hip-hop fame*: Lin-Manuel Miranda's musical *Hamilton*, based on Ron Chernow's biography of the founding father, has transformed Hamilton into a pop culture sensation.

61 *"Energy in the Executive"*: This discussion in full appears in Alexander Hamilton, *Federalist* 70.

62 *the war powers have migrated*: For a general account of the migration of war powers from the legislature to the executive, see Schlesinger, *The Imperial Presidency*. See also John Hart Ely, *War and Responsibility: Constitutional Lessons of Vietnam and Its Aftermath* (Princeton, NJ: Princeton University Press, 1993).

63 *Justice Antonin Scalia once famously wrote*: Morrison v. Olson, 487 U.S. 654 (1988).

63 *"In response to perceived abuses of executive power by the king"*: Michael Klarman, *The Framers' Coup: The Making of the United States Constitution* (New York: Oxford University Press, 2016), 213–18. Klarman's book includes an extended discussion of the convention debate over the relative merits of plural and unitary executive, from which the convention history and delegate quotes described here are drawn.

64 *in Israel*: See Basic Law: The Government, available at www.knesset.gov.il/laws/special/eng/basic14_eng.htm. Article 1 reads, generally, in an interesting contrast to Article II of the U.S. Constitution, "The Government is the executive authority of the State." Article 40(a), more particularly, reads, "The state may only begin a war pursuant to a Government decision." Under a law passed in 2018, the prime minister and defense minister alone, in "extreme circumstances," can authorize military action. See Isabel Kershner, "Israeli Law Vesting War Power in 2 Top Leaders Faces Criticism," *New York Times*, May 2, 2018, www.nytimes.com/2018/05/02/world/middleeast/israel-netanyahu-iran.html.

65 *unilaterally ordered a cruise missile strike*: See Michael R. Gordon, Helene Cooper, and Michael D. Shear, "Dozens of U.S. Missiles Hit Air Base in Syria," *New York Times*, April 6, 2017, www.nytimes.com/2017/04/06/world/middleeast/us-said-to-weigh-military-responses-to-syrian-chemical-attack.html.

65 *"a due dependence on the people"*: Alexander Hamilton, *Federalist* 70.

66 *Stephen Miller went on CBS's*: "Face the Nation Transcript February 12, 2017: Schumer, Flake, Miller," CBS News, February 12, 2017, available at www.cbsnews.com/news/face-the-nation-transcript-february-12-2017-schumer-flake-miller/.

66 *personally called the acting National Park Service director*: Shear and Haberman, "Trump Called National Park Chief over Twitter Post on Inaugural Crowd."

66 *"urgent directive"*: Lisa Rein, "Interior Department Reactivates Twitter Accounts After Shutdown Following Inauguration," *Washington Post*, January 21, 2017,

www.washingtonpost.com/news/powerpost/wp/2017/01/20/interior
-department-banned-from-twitter-after-retweet-of-smaller-than-usual-trump
-inauguration-crowd.

67 *he wasn't convinced that Russia had attempted to interfere*: See, for example, Karen
Yourish and Troy Griggs, "8 U.S. Intelligence Groups Blame Russia for Meddling, but Trump Keeps Clouding the Picture," *New York Times*, August 2, 2018,
www.nytimes.com/interactive/2018/07/16/us/elections/russian-interference
-statements-comments.html.

67 *he believed Russian president Vladimir Putin's denial*: See Peter Baker, "Trump and
Putin Have Met Five Times. What Was Said Is a Mystery," *New York Times*, January 15, 2019, www.nytimes.com/2019/01/15/us/politics/trump-putin-meetings
.html.

67 *calling the allegations a "hoax"*: On Trump's use of the term "witch hunt," see Dana
Milbank, "Trump Is Right. This Is a Witch Hunt!" *Washington Post*, March 18,
2019, www.washingtonpost.com/opinions/trump-is-right-this-is-a-witch-hunt
/2019/03/18/a2487b14-49bf-11e9-b79a-961983b7e0cd_story.html. See also
Larry Buchanan and Karen Yourish, "Trump Has Publicly Attacked the Russia
Investigation More Than 1,100 Times," *New York Times*, February 19, 2019, www
.nytimes.com/interactive/2019/02/19/us/politics/trump-attacks-obstruction
-investigation.html.

67 *top intelligence officials, however, contradicted him*: For a compilation of statements
by these officials, see Alex Potcovaru and Benjamin Wittes, "What They've Said
About Russian Election Interference," *Lawfare*, July 28, 2017, www.lawfareblog
.com/what-theyve-said-about-russian-election-interference.

68 *then FBI director James Comey testified*: "Full Transcript: FBI Director James
Comey Testifies on Russian Interference in 2016 Election," *Washington Post*,
March 20, 2017, www.washingtonpost.com/news/post-politics/wp/2017/03
/20/full-transcript-fbi-director-james-comey-testifies-on-russian-interference
-in-2016-election.

68 *later declared in a court filing*: Defendant's Motion for Summary Judgment, American Oversight v. DOJ, No. 17-718 (D.D.C., September 1, 2017), available at
www.documentcloud.org/documents/3985960-DOJ-Motion-for-Summary
-Judgment-in-Trump-Tower.html.

68 *after Haley announced that the United States would impose new sanctions*: See Peter Baker, "Trump Declines to Add Sanctions Against Russians, Contradicting
Haley," *New York Times*, April 16, 2018, www.nytimes.com/2018/04/16/us
/politics/trump-rejects-sanctions-russia-syria.html.

68 *statement was the result of "momentary confusion"*: See Kathryn Watson, "Nikki
Haley Responds to White House Claims: 'I Don't Get Confused,'" CBS News,
April 17, 2018, www.cbsnews.com/news/with-all-due-respect-i-dont-get-confused
-nikki-haley-says-of-russia-sanctions/.

68 *White House lent its support to the Saudi-led blockade*: Julian Borger, "Qatar

Blockade Exposes Rifts in Trump Administration's 'Peculiar' Foreign Policy," *Guardian*, June 24, 2017, www.theguardian.com/us-news/2017/jun/24/qatar -blockade-trump-administration-foreign-policy.

68 *Then defense secretary James Mattis quickly reassured the Qatari government*: Peter Beaumont, "US Signs Deal to Supply F-15 Jets to Qatar After Trump Terror Claims," *Guardian*, June 15, 2017, www.theguardian.com/world/2017/jun/15 /us-signs-deal-to-supply-f-15-jets-to-qatar-after-trump-terror-claims.

68 *Secretary of State Rex Tillerson cautioned the Saudis*: Daniel R. DePetris, "Rex Tillerson's First Big Test as Secretary of State Has Finally Come," *Quartz*, July 3, 2017, https://qz.com/1019149/qatar-rex-tillersons-first-big-test-as-secretary-of -state-has-finally-come/.

68 *When Turkish president Recep Tayyip Erdoğan won a referendum*: "Turkey Referendum: Trump Congratulates Erdogan," BBC News, April 18, 2017, www.bbc .com/news/world-europe-39626116.

68 *State Department noted "irregularities on voting day"*: James Masters and Kara Fox, "International Monitors Deliver Scathing Verdict on Turkish Referendum," CNN, April 18, 2017, www.cnn.com/2017/04/17/europe/turkey-referendum -results-erdogan/index.html.

69 *extended his congratulations to Philippine president Rodrigo Duterte*: David E. Sanger and Maggie Haberman, "Trump Praises Duterte for Philippine Drug Crackdown in Call Transcript," *New York Times*, May 23, 2017, www.nytimes .com/2017/05/23/us/politics/trump-duterte-phone-transcript-philippine -drug-crackdown.html.

69 *The State Department nonetheless released its human rights report*: See Ian Nicolas Cigaral, "State Department Report: EJKs Still 'Chief' Human Rights Concern in Philippines," *Philstar Global*, April 21, 2018, www.philstar.com/headlines /2018/04/21/1808082/state-department-report-ejks-still-chief-human-rights -concern-philippines. The executive summary of the State Department's 2018 Human Rights Report on the Philippines declares that "extrajudicial killings have been the chief human rights concern in the country for many years and, after a sharp rise with the onset of the anti-drug campaign in 2016, they continued in the reporting year, albeit at a lower level. From January to September 29, media chronicled 673 deaths in police operations suspected to be connected with the government's anti-drug campaign." U.S. State Department, *2018 Country Reports on Human Rights Practices: Philippines*, March 13, 2019.

69 *Organization for Security and Co-operation in Europe*: See Organization for Security and Co-operation in Europe, "Russia, Presidential Election, 18 March 2018: Statement of Preliminary Findings and Conclusions," March 19, 2018, available at www.osce.org/odihr/elections/russia/375670.

69 *White House staffers warned Trump*: See Carol D. Leonnig, David Nakamura, and Josh Dawsey, "Trump's National Security Advisers Warned Him Not to Congratulate Putin. He Did It Anyway," *Washington Post*, March 20, 2018, www.washingtonpost.com/politics/trumps-national-security-advisers-warned

-him-not-to-congratulate-putin-he-did-it-anyway/2018/03/20/22738ebc-2c68
-11e8-8ad6-fbc50284fce8_story.html.

69   *State Department spokeswoman at the time, Heather Nauert*: See Heather Nauert,
State Department Press Briefing, March 20, 2018, available at www.state.gov
/briefings/department-press-briefing-march-20-2018/.

69   *Trump infamously said that "both sides" were at fault*: "Full Transcript and Video:
Trump's News Conference in New York," *New York Times*, August 15, 2017, www
.nytimes.com/2017/08/15/us/politics/trump-press-conference-transcript
.html.

69   *military chiefs took to Twitter*: Dave Philipps, "Inspired by Charlottesville, Military Chiefs Condemn Racism," *New York Times*, August 16, 2017, www.nytimes
.com/2017/08/16/us/joint-chiefs-tweets-racism-charlottesville-veterans.html.

69   *Meanwhile, Haley and Attorney General Jeff Sessions*: For Haley's remarks, see
Sophie Tatum, "Nikki Haley to Staff on Charlottesville: 'We Must Denounce
Them at Every Turn,'" CNN, September 8, 2017, www.cnn.com/2017/09/08
/politics/un-ambassador-nikki-haley-charlottesville-email-state/index.html.
For Sessions's initial remarks, see Charlie Savage and Rebecca R. Ruiz, "Sessions
Emerges as Forceful Figure in Condemning Charlottesville Violence," *New York
Times*, August 14, 2017, www.nytimes.com/2017/08/14/us/politics/domestic
-terrorism-sessions.html. For Tillerson's remarks, see Anne Gearan, "Tillerson
Says Trump 'Speaks for Himself' on Values," *Washington Post*, August 27, 2017,
www.washingtonpost.com/news/post-politics/wp/2017/08/27/tillerson-says
-trump-speaks-for-himself-on-values.

70   *Gary Cohn, to the* Financial Times: "Transcript: Gary Cohn on Tax Reform
and Charlottesville," *Financial Times*, August 25, 2017, www.ft.com/content
/cb068f94-8915-11e7-bf50-e1c239b45787.

70   *Cohn's rebuke of the president*: Woodward, *Fear*, 250–51.

70   *President Obama's actions in dismissing General Stanley McChrystal*: See Michael
Hastings, "The Runaway General: The Profile That Brought Down McChrystal,"
Rolling Stone, June 22, 2010, www.rollingstone.com/politics/politics-news/the
-runaway-general-the-profile-that-brought-down-mcchrystal-192609/.

70   *McChrystal released a statement*: See "Obama Relieves McChrystal of Command,"
NBC News, June 23, 2010, www.nbcnews.com/id/37866754/ns/us_news
-military/t/obama-relieves-mcchrystal-command.

70   *President Harry Truman and General Douglas MacArthur*: Diary Entry of President Harry S. Truman, April 6, 1951, available at www.trumanlibrary.gov/li
brary/research-files/diary-entries-0.

71   *In firing MacArthur, he told the American people*: See "Statement and Order by the
President on Relieving General MacArthur of His Commands," April 11, 1951,
available at www.trumanlibrary.gov/library/public-papers/77/statement-and
-order-president-relieving-general-macarthur-his-commands.

71   *Pompeo was testifying before the Senate Foreign Relations Committee*: Senate Foreign Relations Committee hearing, July 25, 2018. Video of Pompeo's testimony

is available at www.c-span.org/video/?448677-1/secretary-pompeo-testifies
-russia-north-korea-summits.

75 *Trump ordered that Mueller be fired*: Mueller report, Vol. II, 84–85.

75 *Trump asked the attorney general*: Mueller report, Vol. II, 109.

75 *Mueller writes wryly*: Mueller report, Vol. II, 158.

75 *machinations of John Bolton*: Helene Cooper and Julian E. Barnes, "U.S. Officials Scrambled Behind the Scenes to Shield NATO Deal from Trump," *New
York Times*, August 9, 2018, www.nytimes.com/2018/08/09/us/politics/nato
-summit-trump.html.

76 *anonymous September 2018 op-ed in* The New York Times: Anonymous, "I Am
Part of the Resistance Inside the Trump Administration," *New York Times*, September 5, 2018, www.nytimes.com/2018/09/05/opinion/trump-white-house
-anonymous-resistance.html.

76 *It opens with Cohn*: See Woodward, *Fear*, Prologue, xvii–1. Another example from
a different walk of life came when the president's former personal lawyer, Michael
Cohen, pleaded guilty to criminal offenses involving payments during the 2016
campaign to women who claimed to have had sexual encounters with Trump. In
response, Trump tweeted, "Michael Cohen plead guilty to two counts of campaign
finance violations that are not a crime." See Donald J. Trump, Twitter, August 22,
2018, https://twitter.com/realDonaldTrump/status/1032260490439864320.
As the former FBI general counsel Jim Baker noted, this appears to be an interpretation of law by the president, whose views of the law have historically been
understood to bind the executive branch. Yet the executive branch seemed not
to take it as a binding interpretation of law. Asked Baker, "Are government attorneys now precluded from prosecuting anyone else who might have been involved in this conduct, including the president himself? Is the FBI precluded
from even investigating something that the president says is not a crime? Does
the U.S. attorney's office have to move to allow Cohen to withdraw his guilty plea
and have the court dismiss the information?" Or, in the alternative, he asked,
"will everyone in the Department of Justice simply ignore the president's tweet?"
See Jim Baker, "Donald Trump, Twitter and Presidential Power to Interpret the
Law for the Executive Branch," *Lawfare*, August 24, 2018, www.lawfareblog.com
/donald-trump-twitter-and-presidential-power-interpret-law-executive-branch.

77 *"We're not going to do any of that"*: Woodward, *Fear*, 147.

77 *Brad Berenson*: The conference "Institutionalizing the War on Terror Through
Congressional Legislation" was held on April 10, 2006, and was sponsored by
the American University Washington College of Law. Other panel members
included Amanda Frost, Jack Goldsmith, Jamin (Jamie) Raskin, David Rivkin,
and Benjamin Wittes; the discussion was moderated by Daniel Marcus.

78 *former director of national intelligence James Clapper*: Rachel Chason, "James Clapper Questions Trump's Fitness, Worries About His Access to Nuclear Codes,"
Washington Post, August 23, 2017, www.washingtonpost.com/news/morning

-mix/wp/2017/08/23/james-clapper-questions-trumps-fitness-worries-about
-his-access-to-nuclear-codes/.

79 *commentators tried to mute the reality*: See, for example, Julian Borger, "US Military Leaders Would Reject Illegal Order for Nuclear Strike, Senators Told," *Guardian*, November 14, 2017, www.theguardian.com/us-news/2017/nov/14/us-military-nuclear-weapons-strike-senate-trump.

4. "When a President speaks . . . it is for keeps": The Official Voice

81 *"Proclamation Against Crimes Against the Cherokee Nations"*: The text of George Washington's actual December 12, 1792, "Proclamation Against Crimes Against the Cherokee Nations" is available at https://millercenter.org/the-presidency/presidential-speeches/december-12-1792-proclamation-against-crimes-against-cherokee. For the Trumpian ad-lib, see "President Trump News Conference," C-SPAN, August 15, 2017, at timestamp 18:28, available at www.c-span.org/video/?432633-1/president-trump-there-blame-sides-violence-charlottesville&start=1091.

82 *More than seventy years later*: The text of the Gettysburg Address is available at http://rmc.library.cornell.edu/gettysburg/good_cause/transcript.htm. Then candidate Donald Trump's remarks at the 2015 Family Leadership Summit included the following regarding Senator John McCain, who was held as a prisoner of war in Vietnam for five years: "He's a war hero because he was captured. I like people that weren't captured." See "2015 Family Leadership Conference," C-SPAN, July 18, 2015 at timestamp 2:34:42, available at www.c-span.org/video/?327045-1/2015-family-leadership-summit&start=9269.

82 *In his first inaugural address in 1933*: Franklin D. Roosevelt's first inaugural address, delivered March 4, 1933, is available at www.presidency.ucsb.edu/documents/inaugural-address-8. For Trump's comments, see Tom Lutey, "Trump: 'We're Going to Win So Much, You're Going to Be So Sick and Tired of Winning,'" *Billings Gazette*, May 26, 2016, https://billingsgazette.com/news/state-and-regional/govt-and-politics/trump-we-re-going-to-win-so-much-you-re/article_2f346f38-37e7-5711-ae07-d1fd000f4c38.html.

82 *Announcing the dawn of the atomic age*: For Truman's statement, see "Statement by the President Announcing the Use of the A-Bomb at Hiroshima," delivered by President Harry Truman on August 6, 1945, available at www.presidency.ucsb.edu/documents/statement-the-president-announcing-the-use-the-bomb-hiroshima. Trump's addendum is adapted from his comments about ISIS. See Pamela Engel, "DONALD TRUMP: 'I Would Bomb the S— out of' ISIS," *Business Insider*, November 13, 2015, www.businessinsider.com/donald-trump-bomb-isis-2015-11.

82 *Ronald Reagan said to the Soviet leader*: President Reagan's speech at the Brandenburg Gate in Berlin, delivered June 12, 1987, is available at www.c-span.org/video/?110723-1/president-reagan-remarks-berlin-wall&start=711. The

relevant line appears at timestamp 11:58. The Trumpian addendum appeared in Trump's presidential campaign announcement, delivered June 16, 2015, at timestamp 48:03, available at www.c-span.org/video/?326473-1/donald-trump -presidential-campaign-announcement&start=2854.

83 *As he took the oath of office*: Trump's inaugural address, delivered January 20, 2017, is available at www.whitehouse.gov/briefings-statements/the-inaugural -address/.

83 *He is actually proud of it*: For the rally in Pennsylvania, see "President Trump in Moon Township, Pennsylvania," C-SPAN, March 10, 2018, at timestamp 1:04:30, www.c-span.org/video/?442305-1/president-trump-campaigns-rick-saccone -pennsylvania&start=3804. For Trump expressing pride on Twitter in his deviation from presidential rhetoric, see Donald J. Trump, Twitter, July 1, 2017, available at https://twitter.com/realdonaldtrump/status/881281755017355264.

83 *He has been warned repeatedly*: See, for example, Peter Nicholas, Michael Wursthorn, and Paul Kiernan, "As Market Rout Continues, Trump Stands Firm on Fed, Border Wall," *Wall Street Journal*, December 25, 2018, www.wsj.com /articles/as-market-rout-continues-trump-stands-firm-on-fed-and-shutdown -11545765737; Dana Bash, "President Urged to Stop Tweeting on Trump Tower Meeting," CNN, August 7, 2018, www.cnn.com/2018/08/06/politics/donald -trump-trump-tower-meeting/index.html; David A. Graham, "Trump's Dangerous Love of Improvisation," *Atlantic*, August 9, 2017, www.theatlantic.com /politics/archive/2017/08/get-on-board-the-trump-trane/536379/; Glenn Thrush and Peter Baker, "Trump's Threat to North Korea Was Improvised," *New York Times*, August 9, 2017, www.nytimes.com/2017/08/09/us/politics/trump -north-korea.html; Woodward, *Fear*, 238–44; and Matthew Nussbaum, "Trump and the Teleprompter: A Brief History," *Politico*, June 7, 2016, www.politico .com/story/2016/06/donald-trump-teleprompter-224039.

83 *wanting Osama bin Laden "dead or alive"*: Footage of Bush's controversial remarks to the press is available at www.youtube.com/watch?v=YFgn4EaCGQA.

84 *"Information of the State of the Union"*: See U.S. Constitution, Article II, Section 3.

84 *The veto power*: U.S. Constitution, Article I, Section 7.

84 *the bully pulpit*: The phrase "the bully pulpit" to describe the presidency is generally attributed to Theodore Roosevelt. A contemporary account of his use of the term appeared in the editorial "The Roosevelt Administration," *New York Times*, March 4, 1909. A digital edition of the editorial is available through the *New York Times* archives at www.nytimes.com/1909/03/04/archives/the-roosevelt -administration.html.

85 *"Rhetorical power is a very special case"*: Jeffrey Tulis, *The Rhetorical Presidency*, rev. ed. (1987; repr., Princeton, NJ: Princeton University Press, 2017), 203.

85 *In his famous 1960 book on presidential power*: Richard E. Neustadt, *Presidential Power and the Modern Presidents: The Politics of Leadership from Roosevelt to Reagan* (New York: Free Press, 1990 edition), 3–11.

86 *"Presidents preferred written communications"*: Tulis, *The Rhetorical Presidency*, 5–6.

87 *Tulis recounts a striking incident*: Tulis, *The Rhetorical Presidency*, 5.

88 *"The truth unquestionably"*: Alexander Hamilton, "Objections and Answers Respecting the Administration," August 18, 1792, available at https://founders .archives.gov/documents/Hamilton/01-12-02-0184-0002.

88 *"a dangerous ambition more often lurks"*: Alexander Hamilton, *Federalist 1*.

89 *"In the typical speech, Johnson"*: Tulis, *The Rhetorical Presidency*, 88.

89 *And Johnson was actually impeached for it*: The articles of impeachment against Andrew Johnson are available at www.senate.gov/artandhistory/history/common /briefing/Impeachment_Johnson.htm#7. See also Tulis, *The Rhetorical Presidency*, 87–93.

90 *Roosevelt did so cautiously*: See Tulis, "The Middle Way: Statesmanship as Moderation," *The Rhetorical Presidency*, 95–116.

90 *Wilson represented*: See Tulis, "The New Way: Leadership as Interpretation," *The Rhetorical Presidency*, 117–44.

90 *"new standards and new forms of address"*: Tulis, *The Rhetorical Presidency*, 132–33.

91 *Back when Washington and Adams gave their State of the Union addresses*: Tulis, *The Rhetorical Presidency*, 55–56.

91 *Wilson revived the live presidential speech*: Tulis, *The Rhetorical Presidency*, 133.

91 *Yes, Jefferson warned about impassioned orators*: Felzenberg, *The Leaders We Deserved*, 45.

91 *Wilson, by contrast, not only had*: James David Barber, *The Presidential Character: Predicting Performance in the White House* (Englewood Cliffs, NJ: Prentice Hall, 1972), 59, 113.

91 *Tulis presents striking data*: Tulis, *The Rhetorical Presidency*, 62–67, 139–44.

92 *A search through the entire nineteenth century*: The database of the American Presidency Project at the University of California, Santa Barbara, is available at www .presidency.ucsb.edu/advanced-search. Our search included the date parameters January 1, 1800, to December 31, 1899. It included the following twelve document categories: Fireside Chats, Inaugural Addresses, Interviews, Miscellaneous Remarks, News Conferences, Oral Addresses, Presidential Nomination Acceptance Addresses, Press Briefings, Saturday Addresses, Spoken Addresses and Remarks, Weekly Addresses, and Written Statements.

92 *Each modern president alone*: We repeated the search with the same twelve document categories but without the date restrictions and with restrictions to, in sequence, Presidents Obama, Bush, and Clinton. Barack Obama alone accounts for nearly 5,900 entries in the database using the same categories, George W. Bush more than 6,600, and Bill Clinton nearly 11,000. Focusing only on a narrower subset of purely oral communications, Obama alone still gave nearly 3,900 such public communications as president, according to the database.

92 *audience for presidential communications*: Tulis, *The Rhetorical Presidency*, 138–44.

92 *complexity level of presidential speech*: See Elvin T. Lim, *The Anti-Intellectual*

Presidency: The Decline of Presidential Rhetoric from George Washington to George W. Bush (New York: Oxford University Press, 2008), 19–39.

92 *the addresses came to involve less argument*: Lim, *The Anti-Intellectual Presidency*, 54–76. The quotation appears on p. 56.

93 *He aims to flood the zone*: In the afterword to the 2017 edition of *The Rhetorical Presidency*, Tulis terms this feature of Trump's demagogic style "proliferation"; the other two innovations, in Tulis's account, are "repetition" and "projection." The analysis of Trump is at pp. 224–37.

93 *he will never give up tweeting*: Bob Woodward reports in *Fear* that the president's aides have begged him to tone down his Twitter rhetoric. In one instance, he responded, "This is my megaphone." On another occasion he said, "This is who I am. This is how I communicate. It's the reason I got elected. It's the reason that I am successful." See Woodward, *Fear*, 205–206. Trump has said as much publicly. At the Freedom Inaugural Ball on January 20, 2017, the newly inaugurated Trump asked a cheering crowd of supporters, "Let me ask you, should I keep the Twitter going or not? Keep it going?" After applause and more cheers, he continued, "You know, the enemies keep saying, 'Oh, that's terrible,' but you know it's a way of bypassing dishonest media, right?" See "President Trump at the Freedom Inaugural Ball," C-SPAN, January 20, 2017, at timestamp 2:25, www.c-span .org/video/?422126-102/president-vice-president-attend-freedom-inaugural -ball&start=152.

94 *a string of messages notionally addressing Senate majority leader Mitch McConnell*: See Donald J. Trump, Twitter, August 10, 2017, https://twitter.com/realdonald trump/status/895686351529672704; Donald J. Trump, Twitter, August 10, 2017, https://twitter.com/realdonaldtrump/status/895599179522650112.

95 *some iteration or other of the "regular guy" test*: See, for example, Richard Benedetto, "Who's More Likeable, Bush or Kerry?" *USA Today*, September 17, 2004, https://usatoday30.usatoday.com/news/opinion/columnist/benedetto/2004 -09-17-benedetto_x.htm, citing a Zogby/Williams Identity Poll in which "57% of undecided voters would rather have a beer with" George W. Bush than with John Kerry; Monica Davey and Rick Pearson, "Bush, Gore Seek Aura of Regular Guy," *Chicago Tribune*, September 10, 2000, www.chicagotribune.com/news/ct -xpm-2000-09-10-0009100439-story.html.

95 *decision not to correct that limitation*: For "wires tapped," see Donald J. Trump, Twitter, March 4, 2017, https://twitter.com/realdonaldtrump/status /837989835818287106. Trump did delete the "covfefe" tweet, but he also pretended it was not an error; see Donald J. Trump, Twitter, May 31, 2017, https:// twitter.com/realdonaldtrump/status/869858333477523458; for the White House statement on the Khashoggi killing, see "Statement from President Donald J. Trump on Standing with Saudi Arabia," November 20, 2018, available at www.whitehouse.gov/briefings-statements/statement-president-donald-j-trump -standing-saudi-arabia/.

96 *If the traditional presidency expects*: The quotation "day which will live in infamy"

is from President Roosevelt's "Day of Infamy" address to Congress, December 8, 1941, available at www.c-span.org/video/?419693-1/president-roosevelts -day-infamy-address-congress; "ask not what your country can do for you" is from John F. Kennedy's inaugural address, January 20, 1961, available at www .jfklibrary.org/learn/about-jfk/historic-speeches/inaugural-address.

97 *Lyndon Johnson once responded*: Barber, *The Presidential Character*, 81, 84.

97 *Woodrow Wilson was more philosophical*: Barber, *The Presidential Character*, 62.

97 *Even the restrained Barack Obama*: "President Obama's Speech to the White House Correspondents' Dinner," C-SPAN, April 27, 2013, at timestamp 12:08, available at www.c-span.org/video/?312088-103/president-obamas-speech-white-house-cor respondents-dinner.

97 *Whether it's calling Senator Elizabeth Warren*: For Trump calling Warren "Pocahontas," see Donald J. Trump, Twitter, February 9, 2019, https://twitter.com /realdonaldtrump/status/1094368870415110145. For "little Adam Schitt," see Donald J. Trump, Twitter, November 18, 2018, https://twitter.com /realdonaldtrump/status/1064216956679716864. For "National Disgrace," see Donald J. Trump, Twitter, August 20, 2018, https://twitter.com/realdonaldtrump /status/1031505811074412544. For "low IQ" about an African American, see Donald J. Trump, Twitter, June 25, 2018, https://twitter.com/realdonaldtrump /status/1011295779422695424. For "enemy of the people," see Donald J. Trump, Twitter, February 17, 2019, https://twitter.com/realdonaldtrump/status/10971174 99336855553. For a personal attack on a career Justice Department official, see Donald J. Trump, Twitter, August 29, 2018, https://twitter.com/realdonaldtrump /status/1034821067423014913.

98 *"entitled to absolute immunity from damages liability"*: Nixon v. Fitzgerald, 457 U.S. 731 (1982).

99 *falsely suggest that individual American citizens are guilty of crimes*: Trump accused the former FBI counterintelligence official Peter Strzok of treason. See Rebecca Ballhaus, "Trump Accuses FBI Agent of 'Treason,'" *Wall Street Journal*, January 11, 2018, www.wsj.com/articles/trump-accuses-fbi-agent-of-treason -1515710206. He also suggested criminal conduct by Michael Cohen's father-in-law in a pair of December 2018 tweets. See Donald J. Trump, Twitter, December 3, 2018, https://twitter.com/realDonaldTrump/status/1069613383622803456, https://twitter.com/realDonaldTrump/status/1069614615510859776.

99 *"I know from experience that when a President speaks"*: Barber, *The Presidential Character*, 385.

99 *government lawyers argued that the tweet*: The legal arguments and authorities in this paragraph are made or cited in Defendant's Combined Memorandum in Opposition to Plaintiffs' Motion for Summary Judgment and Reply in Support of Defendant's Motion for Summary Judgment, James Madison Project, et al. v. Department of Justice, No. 17-597 (D.D.C., November 30, 2018), available at https://assets.documentcloud.org/documents/5396787/Reply-to-Opposition -to-Motion.pdf.

100 *Erica Newland*: Erica Newland, "I Worked in the Justice Department. I Hope Its Lawyers Won't Give Trump an Alibi," *Washington Post*, January 10, 2019, www .washingtonpost.com/opinions/i-worked-in-the-justice-department-i-hope-its -lawyers-wont-give-trump-an-alibi/2019/01/10/9b53c662-1501-11e9-b6ad -9cfd62dbb0a8_story.html.

100 *a New Yorker story that described how editors*: For the *New Yorker* story New-land describes, see Patrick Radden Keefe, "How Mark Burnett Resurrected Donald Trump as an Icon of American Success," *New Yorker*, January 7, 2019, www.newyorker.com/magazine/2019/01/07/how-mark-burnett-resurrected -donald-trump-as-an-icon-of-american-success.

102 *In his book* The Presidential Character: Barber, *The Presidential Character*, 7.

5. "An inexhaustible fund of political lies": The War on Truth

105 *Trump made what* The Washington Post *deemed*: Glenn Kessler, Michelle Ye Hee Lee, and Meg Kelly, "President Trump's List of False and Misleading Claims Tops 1,000," *Washington Post*, August 22, 2017, www.washingtonpost .com/news/fact-checker/wp/2017/08/22/president-trumps-list-of-false-and -misleading-claims-tops-1000/.

106 *the number reached two thousand*: Glenn Kessler and Meg Kelly, "President Trump Has Made More Than 2,000 False or Misleading Claims over 355 Days," *Washington Post*, January 10, 2018, www.washingtonpost.com/news/fact-checker/wp /2018/01/10/president-trump-has-made-more-than-2000-false-or-misleading -claims-over-355-days/.

106 *By September 2018*: Glenn Kessler, Salvador Rizzo, and Meg Kelly, "President Trump Has Made More Than 5,000 False or Misleading Claims," *Washington Post*, September 13, 2018, www.washingtonpost.com/politics/2018/09/13 /president-trump-has-made-more-than-false-or-misleading-claims.

106 *A mere 226 days after that*: Glenn Kessler, Salvador Rizzo, and Meg Kelly, "President Trump Has Made More Than 10,000 False or Misleading Claims," *Washington Post*, April 29, 2019, www.washingtonpost.com/politics/2019/04/29 /president-trump-has-made-more-than-false-or-misleading-claims.

106 *The Fact Checker*: The column, including the tagline, is available at www.washing tonpost.com/news/fact-checker/.

106 *standing in front of the CIA's hallowed memorial wall*: See "Remarks by President Trump and Vice President Pence at CIA Headquarters," January 21, 2017, avail-able at www.whitehouse.gov/briefings-statements/remarks-president-trump-vice -president-pence-cia-headquarters/.

107 *He lied about winning environmental awards*: Michelle Ye Hee Lee, "Trump's Unsupported Claim He Has 'Received Awards on the Environment,'" *Washington Post*, January 24, 2017, www.washingtonpost.com/news/fact-checker /wp/2017/01/24/trumps-unsupported-claim-he-has-received-awards-on-the -environment.

107 *lied about there having been millions of illegal votes*: Glenn Kessler, "Recidivism

Watch: Trump's Claim That Millions of People Voted Illegally," *Washington Post*, January 24, 2017, www.washingtonpost.com/news/fact-checker/wp/2017/01 /24/recidivism-watch-trumps-claim-that-3-5-million-people-voted-illegally-in -the-election.

107   *lied about two people being killed*: Michelle Ye Hee Lee, "Fact-Checking Trump's Rhetoric on Crime and the 'American Carnage,'" *Washington Post*, January 30, 2017, www.washingtonpost.com/news/fact-checker/wp/2017/01/30/fact-checking -trumps-rhetoric-on-crime-and-the-american-carnage.

107   *lied about receiving a unanimous endorsement*: Glenn Kessler, "President Trump's First Seven Days of False Claims, Inaccurate Statements and Exaggerations," *Washington Post*, January 27, 2017, www.washingtonpost.com/news/fact-checker /wp/2017/01/27/president-trumps-first-seven-days-of-false-claims-inaccurate -statements-and-exaggerations.

107   *lied about immigration vetting procedures*: On February 18, 2017, Trump said, "We've taken in tens of thousands of people. We know nothing about them. They can say they vet them. They didn't vet them. They have no papers. How can you vet somebody when you don't know anything about them and you have no papers?" Fact Checker writes, "Trump often claims there is 'no system to vet' refugees. The process actually takes two more years, after vetting that starts with the United Nations High Commissioner for Refugees and then continues with checks by U.S. intelligence and security agencies." See "100 Days of Trump Claims," *Washington Post*, www.washingtonpost.com/graphics/politics/trump -claims.

107   *lied about his executive orders*: "I just signed two executive orders that will save thousands of lives, millions of jobs, and billions and billions of dollars," Trump said on January 25, 2017, at the Department of Homeland Security. The Fact Checker responded: "Trump lauded two executive actions regarding immigration and border security, including building a wall along the border of Mexico. Again, the numbers appear to have little basis in reality." See Glenn Kessler, "President Trump's First Seven Days of False Claims."

107   *lied about saving money on some F-35 airplanes*: See Michelle Ye Hee Lee, "Trump's Claim Taking Credit for Cutting $600 Million from the F-35 Program," *Washington Post*, January 31, 2017, www.washingtonpost.com/news/fact-checker /wp/2017/01/31/trumps-claim-taking-credit-for-cutting-600-million-from -the-f-35-program.

107   *the Fact Checker staff realized it couldn't keep up*: The paragraphs are drawn from an author interview with Glenn Kessler on August 17, 2018. Audio and notes of interview on file with authors.

108   *to push Kessler past these reservations*: Glenn Kessler, "Not Just Misleading. Not Merely False. A Lie," *Washington Post*, August 22, 2018, www.washingtonpost .com/politics/2018/08/23/not-just-misleading-not-merely-false-lie.

108   *The database will continue*: Email from Glenn Kessler to Susan Hennessey, September 3, 2019. Record on file with authors.

108 *"Every president lies"*: Kessler interview, August 17, 2018.

109 *Quinta Jurecic warned*: Quinta Jurecic, "On Bullshit and the Oath of Office: The 'LOL Nothing Matters' Presidency," *Lawfare*, November 23, 2016, www .lawfareblog.com/bullshit-and-oath-office-lol-nothing-matters-presidency.

109 *distinguished from lying*: See Harry G. Frankfurt, *On Bullshit* (Princeton, NJ: Princeton University Press, 2005).

109 *Jonathan Swift penned a famous essay*: Jonathan Swift, "Political Lying," originally published in *The Examiner*, 1710. Republished in Henry Craik, ed., *English Prose* (New York: Macmillan, 1916), available at www.bartleby.com/209/633.html.

110 *documented seventy-seven instances*: Katelyn Polantz and Marshall Cohen, "The Mueller Report: A Catalog of 77 Trump Team Lies and Falsehoods," CNN, April 30, 2019, www.cnn.com/2019/04/30/politics/mueller-report-trump-team -lies-falsehoods/index.html.

110 *"Well, that's not a crime"*: Video of the relevant section of Barr's testimony is available at "Barr Hearing: Sen. Dianne Feinstein Questions Attorney General William Barr," YouTube, May 1, 2019, at timestamp 5:33, www.youtube.com/watch ?v=U7OkUFXJDqE.

111 *In a letter to Hamilton in 1788*: Letter from George Washington to Alexander Hamilton, August 28, 1788, available at https://founders.archives.gov/documents /Hamilton/01-05-02-0025.

111 *In 1832, a twenty-three-year-old Lincoln*: Abraham Lincoln, "Communication to the People of Sangamo County," March 9, 1832, available at https://quod.lib .umich.edu/l/lincoln/lincoln1/1:8?rgn=div1;view=fulltext.

112 *Jefferson once assured the president*: Letter from Thomas Jefferson to George Washington, September 9, 1792, available at https://founders.archives.gov /documents/Jefferson/01-24-02-0330.

112 *Alvin Felzenberg writes*: Felzenberg, *The Leaders We Deserved*, 47.

112 *"ought to be personally responsible for his behavior in office"*: Alexander Hamilton, *Federalist* 70.

113 *President George W. Bush's erroneous conviction*: A report by a special commission appointed to study the matter and headed by Judge Laurence Silberman and former senator Charles Robb found that President Bush received flawed intelligence over a long period of time in the President's Daily Brief. See "The Commission on the Intelligence Capabilities of the United States Regarding Weapons of Mass Destruction, Report to the President," March 31, 2005, p. 14, https://fas.org /irp/offdocs/wmd_report.pdf.

113 *honestly believed it and had reason to*: The Silberman-Robb report found that the intelligence failure of assessing weapons of mass destruction "was in large part the result of analytical shortcomings; intelligence analysts were too wedded to their assumptions about Saddam [Hussein]'s intentions. But it was also a failure on the part of those who collect intelligence—CIA's and the Defense Intelligence Agency's (DIA) spies, the National Security Agency's (NSA) eavesdroppers, and the National Geospatial-Intelligence Agency's (NGA) imagery

experts. In the end, those agencies collected precious little intelligence for the analysts to analyze, and much of what they did collect was either worthless or misleading. Finally, it was a failure to communicate effectively with policy makers; the Intelligence Community didn't adequately explain just how little good intelligence it had—or how much its assessments were driven by assumptions and inferences rather than concrete evidence." See Silberman-Robb report, p. 3.

114 *denials of intelligence findings about Russian hacking during the 2016 election*: See, for example, Yourish and Griggs, "8 U.S. Intelligence Groups Blame Russia for Meddling, but Trump Keeps Clouding the Picture."

115 *Elizabeth Drew*: Elizabeth Drew, *Washington Journal: Reporting Watergate and Richard Nixon's Downfall*, rev. ed. (New York: Overlook Duckworth, 2014), 70–71.

116 *Teddy Roosevelt was the first*: George Juergens, "Theodore Roosevelt and the Press," *Daedalus* 111, no. 4 (1982): 119.

116 *Woodrow Wilson held the first*: Martha Joynt Kumar, "Presidential Press Conferences: Windows on the Presidency and Its Occupants," White House Historical Association, May 16, 2011, www.whitehousehistory.org/presidential-press -conferences.

116 *Warren Harding and Calvin Coolidge*: Louis M. Lyons, "Calvin Coolidge and the Press," *Nieman Reports*, September 1964, https://niemanreports.org/articles /1964-calvin-coolidge-and-the-press/.

116 *Truman convinced reporters*: Kumar, "Presidential Press Conferences."

116 *"telling the truth slowly"*: Roger Simon, "Telling the Truth Slowly," *Chicago Tribune*, February 17, 1998, www.chicagotribune.com/news/ct-xpm-1998-02-17 -9802170125-story.html.

117 *she claimed to have heard from "countless" numbers of FBI personnel*: A transcript of Sanders's comments to the press on May 11, 2017, is available at www.white house.gov/briefings-statements/press-briefing-principal-deputy-press-secretary -sarah-sanders-homeland-security-advisor-tom-bossert-051117/.

117 *This obviously was not true*: See Nora Ellingsen, Quinta Jurecic, Sabrina McCubbin, Shannon Togawa Mercer, and Benjamin Wittes, "'I Hope This Is an Instance of Fake News': FBI Messages Show the Bureau's Real Reaction to Trump Firing James Comey," *Lawfare*, February 5, 2018, www.lawfareblog.com/i-hope -instance-fake-news-fbi-messages-show-bureaus-real-reaction-trump-firing -james-comey.

117 *She later told Mueller's office*: Mueller report, Vol. II, 72.

117 *Gerald Ford, notwithstanding executive privilege*: Statement of President Gerald Ford, House Committee on the Judiciary, Subcommittee on Criminal Justice, October 17, 1974, Gerald R. Ford Presidential Library, available at www .fordlibrarymuseum.gov/library/document/0019/4520699.pdf.

117 *George W. Bush campaigned on a promise to restore personal integrity*: See, for example, Frank Bruni, "Bush Calls on Gore to Denounce Clinton Affair," *New York*

Times, August 12, 2000, www.nytimes.com/2000/08/12/us/2000-campaign -texas-governor-bush-calls-gore-denounce-clinton-affair.html.

117 *"seriously, but not literally"*: The columnist Salena Zito defended Trump's false statement that "fifty-eight percent of black youth cannot get a job, cannot work," by saying that the claim "drives fact-checkers to distraction. The Bureau of Labor Statistics puts the unemployment rate for blacks between the ages of 16 and 24 at 20.6 percent. Trump prefers to use its employment-population ratio, a figure that shows only 41.5 percent of blacks in that age bracket are working. But that means he includes full time high-school and college students among the jobless. It's a familiar split. When he makes claims like this, the press takes him literally, but not seriously; his supporters take him seriously, but not literally." Salena Zito, "Taking Trump Seriously, Not Literally," *Atlantic*, September 23, 2016, www.theatlantic .com/politics/archive/2016/09/trump-makes-his-case-in-pittsburgh/501335/.

117 *that he would reinstate torture*: See Tom McCarthy, "Donald Trump: I'd Bring Back 'a Hell of a Lot Worse Than Waterboarding,'" *Guardian*, February 7, 2016, www.theguardian.com/us-news/2016/feb/06/donald-trump-waterboarding -republican-debate-torture.

117 *he might not concede the election if he lost*: Dara Lind, "Donald Trump: I'll Accept the Results of This Election—'If I Win,'" *Vox*, October 20, 2016, www.vox.com /policy-and-politics/2016/10/20/13347478/trump-concede-election.

118 *When he said "Second Amendment people" might do something*: Nick Corasaniti and Maggie Haberman, "Donald Trump Suggests 'Second Amendment People' Could Act Against Hillary Clinton," *New York Times*, August 9, 2016, www .nytimes.com/2016/08/10/us/politics/donald-trump-hillary-clinton.html.

118 *When he said he'd cover the legal fees of people who assaulted protesters*: Daniel White, "Donald Trump Tells Crowd to 'Knock the Crap out of' Hecklers," *Time*, February 1, 2016, http://time.com/4203094/donald-trump-hecklers/.

118 *When he urged Russia to find Hillary Clinton's missing emails*: Michael S. Schmidt, "Trump Invited the Russians to Hack Clinton. Were They Listening?" *New York Times*, July 13, 2018, www.nytimes.com/2018/07/13/us/politics/trump-russia -clinton-emails.html.

118 *Daniel Effron argues*: Daniel A. Effron, "Why Trump Supporters Don't Mind His Lies," *New York Times*, April 28, 2018, www.nytimes.com/2018/04/28/opinion /sunday/why-trump-supporters-dont-mind-his-lies.html.

119 *He lies about affairs*: Trump's first denial as president of the allegation that he had an affair with Stormy Daniels appears in a comment by his then personal attorney Michael Cohen to the *New York Daily News* in a story detailing Daniels's account of her interactions with Trump. See Chris Sommerfeldt and Denis Slattery, "Trump Allegedly Told Porn Star Stormy Daniels She Reminded Him of Ivanka During Affair," *New York Daily News*, January 17, 2018, www .nydailynews.com/news/politics/stormy-daniels-details-trump-romp-excerpts -2011-interview-article-1.3762149.

119 *He lies about lying about the affairs*: The president doubled down on his claim

that the accusation of an affair was false, including, for example, on Twitter, where he said that a reported settlement agreement with Daniels was "to stop the false and extortionist accusations made by her about an affair." Donald J. Trump, Twitter, May 3, 2018, https://twitter.com/realDonaldTrump/status /991994433750142976.

119 *He lies about the hush money he paid to cover up the affairs*: In comments to the press pool on Air Force One, Trump said he didn't know about the payments to Daniels or how Cohen got the money to pay her. See Julie Hirschfeld Davis, "Trump Denies Knowing of Any Hush Money Paid to Porn Actress," *New York Times*, April 5, 2018, www.nytimes.com/2018/04/05/us/politics/trump -stormy-daniels-hush-money.html.

119 *the president also dictates*: Mueller report, Vol. II, 101–103.

119 *He then lies about having dictated the lie*: Matt Apuzzo, "Trump Team Pushed False Story Line About Meeting with Kremlin-Tied Lawyer, Memo Shows," *New York Times*, June 4, 2018, www.nytimes.com/2018/06/04/us/politics/trump -mueller-falsehoods-tower-meeting.html.

119 *He lies about his willingness to release his tax returns*: Jill Disis, "All the Things Donald Trump Has Said About Releasing His Tax Returns," CNN Money, April 17, 2017, https://money.cnn.com/2017/04/17/news/donald-trump-tax-returns /index.html.

119 *He lied about his willingness to be interviewed*: Trump stated at a January 2018 press conference that he would testify under oath to Mueller's team. Video of the press conference is available at https://youtu.be/4t_W6ga9QWQ. By November, he had changed his tune. See Gabriel T. Rubin and Ryan Tracy, "Trump Says He Is Unlikely to Agree to Sit-Down Interview in Mueller Probe," *Wall Street Journal*, November 18, 2018, www.wsj.com/articles/trump-says-he-is -unlikely-to-agree-to-sit-down-interview-in-mueller-probe-1542562598.

120 *offered a blunt formulation of this defense*: Santorum made the remarks on February 27, 2019, on Anderson Cooper's CNN program. For a transcript of the episode, see http://edition.cnn.com/TRANSCRIPTS/1902/27/acd.01.html.

120 *Grover Cleveland hid his jaw cancer*: See, generally, Matthew Algeo, *The President Is a Sick Man: Wherein the Supposedly Virtuous Grover Cleveland Survives a Secret Surgery at Sea and Vilifies the Courageous Newspaperman Who Dared Expose the Truth* (Chicago: Chicago Review, 2011), and John Feerick, *The 25th Amendment: Its Complete History and Applications* (New York: Fordham University Press, 2014 edition), 11–14.

120 *Woodrow Wilson suffered a debilitating stroke*: See, for example, Feerick, *The 25th Amendment*, 14–16.

120 *to replace his sitting vice president with Harry Truman as a running mate*: Felzenberg, *The Leaders We Deserved*, 344.

121 *Kennedy outright denied that he had Addison's disease*: Richard Reeves, *President Kennedy: Profile of Power* (New York: Simon & Schuster, 1993), 24.

121 *Johnson's aides hid his incapacitating depression*: Robert Dallek, *Flawed Giant*:

Lyndon Johnson and His Times, 1961–1973 (New York: Oxford University Press, 1998), 282.

121 *Nixon's staff hid his alcoholism*: John A. Farrell, "The Year Nixon Fell Apart," *Politico Magazine*, March 26, 2017, www.politico.com/magazine/story/2017 /03/john-farrell-nixon-book-excerpt-214954; Eric Cortellessa, "How Leonid Brezhnev Almost Escalated the Yom Kippur War into a Nuclear Nightmare," *Times of Israel*, October 14, 2018, www.timesofisrael.com/how-leonid-brezhnev -almost-escalated-the-yom-kippur-war-into-a-nuclear-nightmare/.

121 *his personal physician*: For a copy of the letter, see Jessica Taylor, "Doctor: Trump Would Be 'Healthiest Individual Ever Elected' President," NPR, December 14, 2015, www.npr.org/2015/12/14/459700154/doctor-trump-would-be-healthiest -individual-ever-elected-president.

121 *personally dictated the entire letter*: Alex Marquardt and Lawrence Crook III, "Bornstein Claims Trump Dictated the Glowing Health Letter," CNN, May 2, 2019, www.cnn.com/2018/05/01/politics/harold-bornstein-trump-letter/index.html.

122 *White House physician Ronny Jackson*: Brett Samuels, "WH Doctor Credits 'Good Genes' for Trump's Excellent Health Despite Fast Food Diet," *The Hill*, January 16, 2018, https://thehill.com/homenews/administration/369216-white -house-doctor-credits-good-genes-for-trumps-excellent-health.

122 *whether a new White House physician had actually authored*: For example, James Hamblin in *The Atlantic* raised the prospect that "the authorship of this report is questionable." See James Hamblin, "Will Trump Live to 500?" *Atlantic*, February 15, 2019, www.theatlantic.com/health/archive/2019/02/trump -presidential-health-assessment/582919/.

123 *shot down a weather research plane*: Osgood Caruthers, "Soviet Downs American Plane; U.S. Says It Was Weather Craft; Khrushchev Sees Summit Blow," *New York Times*, May 6, 1960, https://archive.nytimes.com/www.nytimes.com /learning/general/onthisday/big/0501.html#article.

123 *When the Soviets revealed that they had both the plane and its pilot*: For Khrushchev's remarks to the Supreme Soviet, translated into English, see "Excerpts from Premier Khrushchev's Remarks on U.S. Jet Downed in Soviet," *New York Times*, May 8, 1960, https://timesmachine.nytimes.com/timesmachine/1960 /05/08/90661540.pdf.

123 *he considered resigning from office*: Eric Alterman, *When Presidents Lie: A History of Official Deception and Its Consequences* (New York: Penguin Books, 2004), 19.

123 *"inherent" right to lie*: Alterman, *When Presidents Lie*, 92.

123 *He later testified*: Sylvester's obituary in *The Washington Post*, published in 1979, recounts this testimony. It is available at www.washingtonpost.com /archive/local/1979/12/30/arthur-sylvester-78/5f916530-7226-41d8-ae18 -27ca69b0a525.

123 *Reagan's press secretary lied about the impending invasion*: Francis X. Clines, "A Reagan Press Official Resigns over Grenada," *New York Times*, November 1,

1983, www.nytimes.com/1983/11/01/world/a-reagan-press-official-resigns-over
-grenada.html.

123 *as did Carter's press secretary*: Helen Thomas, "Only Powell Admits Lying to
Press," UPI, April 23, 1982, www.upi.com/Archives/1982/04/23/Only-Powell
-admits-lying-to-press/4490388386000/.

124 *philosopher Sissela Bok*: Sissela Bok, *Lying: Moral Choice in Public and Private Life*
(New York: Vintage, 1999), 172.

124 *Cuban missile crisis*: Alterman, *When Presidents Lie*, 121.

124 *secretly supporting the coup against Ngo Dinh Diem*: For an account of Diem's
assassination and the Kennedy administration's involvement in it, see Howard
Jones, *Death of a Generation: How the Assassinations of Diem and JFK Prolonged
the Vietnam War* (New York: Oxford University Press, 2003).

124 *Johnson systematically sought to disguise*: Alterman, *When Presidents Lie*, 160–65,
199–201, 219–21.

125 *"credibility gap"—first coined around the time of the Cuban missile crisis*: The *Oxford
English Dictionary* attributes the original usage of the phrase "credibility gap" to
Senator Kenneth Keating in 1962. Available at www.oed.com/view/Entry/44108
?redirectedFrom=credibility+gap#eid8019302.

125 *Herb Klein, pledged*: See Jonathan Schell, "The Time of Illusion," *New Yorker*,
May 25, 1975, www.newyorker.com/magazine/1975/06/02/the-time-of-illusion.

125 *Polk used a purported attack*: Felzenberg, *The Leaders We Deserved*, 341.

125 *"tap dance, but never lie"*: Louis Jacobson, "Hope Hicks and the History of White
House 'White Lies,'" PolitiFact, March 1, 2018, www.politifact.com/truth-o-meter
/article/2018/mar/01/hope-hicks-and-history-white-house-white-lies/.

125 *serial denials*: See, for example, "Trump Says China Could Have Hacked Democratic Emails," Reuters, April 30, 2017, www.reuters.com/article/us-usa-trump
-russia-china-idUSKBN17W0N4.

126 *U.S. intelligence assessments*: Intelligence Community Assessment, "Assessing
Russian Activities and Intentions in Recent US Elections," Office of the Director
of National Intelligence, January 6, 2017, www.dni.gov/files/documents/ICA
_2017_01.pdf.

126 *"wires tapped"*: Donald J. Trump, Twitter, March 4, 2017, https://twitter.com
/realdonaldtrump/status/837989835818287106.

126 *a flurry of speculation*: See, for example, Charlie Savage, "What Can Be Gleaned
from Trump's Allegations of Wiretapping," *New York Times*, March 5, 2017, www
.nytimes.com/2017/03/05/us/politics/trump-phone-tapping-surveillance
-issues.html.

126 *in a court filing*: Defendants' Motion for Summary Judgment, American Oversight v. DOJ, No. 17-718 (D.D.C., September 1, 2017), available at https://assets
.documentcloud.org/documents/3985960/DOJ-Motion-for-Summary
-Judgment-in-Trump-Tower.pdf#page=4.

126 *thinly sourced conspiracy theories reported by disreputable*: The *Washington Post*

reported that a Breitbart article that circulated in the White House shortly before the tweet may have been what prompted the president's unfounded accusation. See Philip Rucker, Ellen Nakashima, and Robert Costa, "Trump Accuses Obama of 'Nixon/Watergate' Wiretap—but Offers No Evidence," *Washington Post*, March 4, 2017, www.washingtonpost.com/politics/trump-accuses-obama -of-nixonwatergate-wiretap--but-offers-no-evidence/2017/03/04/1ddc35e6-0114 -11e7-8ebe-6e0dbe4f2bca_story.html. See also Joel B. Pollak, "Mark Levin to Congress: Investigate Obama's 'Silent Coup' vs. Trump," Breitbart, March 3, 2017, www.breitbart.com/politics/2017/03/03/mark-levin-obama-used-police-state -tactics-undermine-trump/.

126 *prove false a single line about immigrants and terrorism*: Benjamin Wittes, "The Justice Department Finds 'No Responsive Records' to Support a Trump Speech," *Lawfare*, July 31, 2018, www.lawfareblog.com/justice-department-finds-no-responsive -records-support-trump-speech.

127 *Trump insisted that he had actually said Cook's last name*: See Jonathan Swan, "Trump Lied to RNC Donors About 'Tim Apple' Video," *Axios*, March 10, 2019, www.axios.com/trump-rnc-donors-apple-tim-cook-lie-2fd8b004-6fc3-4f81 -9eb0-3b92f3264ef1.html.

127 *He later tweeted that he had said Tim Apple*: Said Trump, "At a recent round table meeting of business executives, & long after formally introducing Tim Cook of Apple, I quickly referred to Tim + Apple as Tim/Apple as an easy way to save time & words. The Fake News was disparagingly all over this, & it became yet another bad Trump story!" Donald J. Trump, Twitter, March 11, 2019, https:// twitter.com/realdonaldtrump/status/1105109329290686464.

128 *"an orange jumpsuit"*: Woodward, *Fear*, 353.

130 *leaks about the president's calls with foreign leaders*: See, for example, Onur Ant, Nick Wadhams, and Selcan Hacaoglu, "Trump Says Turkey Can Easily Mop Up ISIS Remnants in Syria," *Bloomberg*, December 21, 2018, www.bloomberg .com/news/articles/2018-12-21/trump-call-that-went-rogue-hands-erdogan -surprise-win-on-syria. See also Leonnig, Nakamura, and Dawsey, "Trump's National Security Advisers Warned Him Not to Congratulate Putin. He Did It Anyway."

130 *leaks about his mood and private comments*: See, for example, Kevin Liptak, Jeff Zeleny, Dana Bash, Gloria Borger, Kate Bennett, Jeremy Diamond, Kaitlan Collins, Pamela Brown, Sarah Westwood, and Noah Gray, "Trump's Mood Takes a Foul Turn: 'He's Pissed—at Damn Near Everyone,'" CNN, November 15, 2018, www.cnn.com/2018/11/14/politics/donald-trump-mood-pissed-white-house -intrigue/index.html.

130 *leaks of sensitive national security information*: See, for example, Zeke Miller and Jonathan Lemire, "White House Issues Threat Over Leaked Trump Briefing Papers," Associated Press, March 22, 2018, www.apnews.com/341558b5904e4dc dac156244d7ebb11d.

130 *leaks about policy strategy*: See, for example, Nick Miroff, Dan Lamothe, and Josh Dawsey, "Trump Considering Plan to Ban Entry of Migrants at Southern Border, Deny Asylum," *Washington Post*, October 25, 2018, www.washingtonpost .com/politics/pentagon-plans-to-dispatch-800-more-troops-to-us-mexico -border-in-response-to-migrant-caravan/2018/10/25/6a121944-d868-11e8 -83a2-d1c3da28d6b6_story.html.

130 *about Trump's TV-watching habits*: See, for example, Maggie Haberman, Glenn Thrush, and Peter Baker, "Inside Trump's Hour-by-Hour Battle for Self-Preservation" *New York Times*, December 9, 2017, www.nytimes.com/2017/12 /09/us/politics/donald-trump-president.html.

130 *about disparaging comments and evaluations*: See, for example, Woodward, *Fear*, 357.

130 *about his legal strategy*: See, for example, Carol D. Leonnig, "A Beefed-Up White House Legal Team Prepares Aggressive Defense of Trump's Executive Privilege as Investigations Loom Large," *Washington Post*, January 9, 2019, www .washingtonpost.com/politics/a-beefed-up-white-house-legal-team-prepares -aggressive-defense-of-trumps-executive-privilege-as-investigations-loom -large/2019/01/09/066b8618-1045-11e9-84fc-d58c33d6c8c7_story.html.

130 *leaks of memos addressing a plan to stop leaks*: Chris Geidner, "Trump Administration Launches Broad New Anti-Leak Program," *BuzzFeed News*, September 13, 2017, www.buzzfeednews.com/article/chrisgeidner/trump-administration-launches -broad-new-anti-leak-program.

130 *when the president insisted that he was not involved*: Maggie Haberman, Michael S. Schmidt, Adam Goldman, and Annie Karni, "Trump Ordered Officials to Give Jared Kushner a Security Clearance," *New York Times*, February 28, 2019, www .nytimes.com/2019/02/28/us/politics/jared-kushner-security-clearance.html.

130 *"the incidence of official lying"*: Pozen writes, "There is an additional, more speculative sense in which leakiness may preserve the credibility of government, as well as the professional integrity of its employees: if it reduces the incidence of official lying." See David E. Pozen, "The Leaky Leviathan: Why the Government Condemns and Condones Unlawful Disclosures of Information," *Harvard Law Review* 127 (2013): 576, available at https://harvardlawreview.org/wp-content /uploads/pdfs/vol127_pozen.pdf.

130 *"Leakiness, in this context"*: Pozen, "The Leaky Leviathan," 576–77.

131 *"a pervasive culture of leaking may substitute"*: Pozen, "The Leaky Leviathan," 577.

131 *the president's norm violations are inspiring reciprocal violations*: Jack Goldsmith, "Will Donald Trump Destroy the Presidency?" *Atlantic*, October 2017, www .theatlantic.com/magazine/archive/2017/10/will-donald-trump-destroy-the -presidency/537921/.

132 *an episode described at length in the Mueller report*: Mueller report, Vol. II, 24–37.

132 *the calls had been scrutinized by counterintelligence investigators*: See the Mueller

report, Vol. II, 26: "Previously, the FBI had opened an investigation of Flynn based on his relationship with the Russian government."

132 *As Mueller recounts*: Mueller report, Vol. II, 26.

132 *Flynn later admitted as part of his plea agreement*: Statement of the Offense, U.S. v. Michael T. Flynn, No. 17-232 (D.D.C., December 1, 2017), available at www .justice.gov/file/1015126/download.

132 *press secretary Sean Spicer claimed*: Matthew Nussbaum, "A History of Explaining, and Defending, Michael Flynn," *Politico*, December 1, 2017, www.politico .com/story/2017/12/01/history-michael-flynn-explaining-defending-274792.

132 *Vice President–elect Mike Pence was sent out to CBS's* Face the Nation: The exchange between John Dickerson and the incoming vice president was as follows:

> DICKERSON: So did they ever have a conversation about sanctions ever on those days or any other day?
>
> PENCE: They did not have a discussion contemporaneous with U.S. actions on—
>
> DICKERSON: But what about after—
>
> PENCE: —my conversation with General Flynn. Well, look. General Flynn has been in touch with diplomatic leaders, security leaders in some 30 countries. That's exactly what the incoming national security advisor—
>
> DICKERSON: Absolutely.
>
> PENCE: —should do. But what I can confirm, having spoken to him about it, is that those conversations that happened to occur around the time that the United States took action to expel diplomats had nothing whatsoever to do with those sanctions.
>
> DICKERSON: But that still leaves open the possibility that there might have been other conversations about the sanctions.
>
> PENCE: I don't believe there were more conversations.

A complete transcript of Pence's interview is available at www.cbsnews.com/news /face-the-nation-transcript-january-15-2017-pence-manchin-gingrich/.

132 *Sally Yates later testified*: See "Full Transcript: Sally Yates and James Clapper Testify on Russian Election Interference," *Washington Post*, May 8, 2017, www .washingtonpost.com/news/post-politics/wp/2017/05/08/full-transcript-sally -yates-and-james-clapper-testify-on-russian-election-interference/.

133 *The Washington Post ran a story citing*: Greg Miller, Adam Entous, and Ellen Nakashima, "National Security Adviser Flynn Discussed Sanctions with Russian Ambassador, Despite Denials, Officials Say," *Washington Post*, February 9, 2017, www.washingtonpost.com/world/national-security/national-security-adviser -flynn-discussed-sanctions-with-russian-ambassador-despite-denials-officials -say/2017/02/09/f85b29d6-ee11-11e6-b4ff-ac2cf509efe5_story.html.

133 *the president, having been informed of the risk*: Whether Trump knew that Flynn was lying is not entirely clear. The Mueller report declares that Flynn lied within the administration, to Pence and others. See Mueller report, Vol. II, 29. At the same time, the report leaves some doubt as to whether the president knew the

substantive contents of Flynn's calls with Kislyak. "Flynn saw the President-Elect in person and thought they discussed the Russian reaction to the sanctions," Mueller writes, "but Flynn did not have a specific recollection of telling the President-Elect about the substance of his calls with Kislyak." See Mueller report, Vol. II, 26. What is clear is that the White House kept Flynn on and kept putting forth misinformation even after being warned that Flynn had not told the truth.

133 *Flynn was forced to resign*: Greg Miller and Philip Rucker, "Michael Flynn Resigns as National Security Adviser," *Washington Post*, February 14, 2017, www.washingtonpost.com/world/national-security/michael-flynn-resigns -as-national-security-adviser/2017/02/13/0007c0a8-f26e-11e6-8d72 -263470bf0401_story.html.

133 *"the devil be the father of lies"*: Swift, "Political Lying." Swift's reference is to John 8:44: "Ye are of *your* father the devil, and the lusts of your father ye will do. He was a murderer from the beginning, and abode not in the truth, because there is no truth in him. When he speaketh a lie, he speaketh of his own: for he is a liar, and the father of it." Book of John, Chapter 8, Verse 44, King James Bible.

133 *"But now ye seek to kill me"*: Book of John, Chapter 8, Verse 40, King James Bible.

6. "The love of power, and the love of money": Ethics in the White House

135 *Trump told an Irish television show*: "Colette Fitzpatrick Meets Donald Trump! | Ireland AM," Virgin Media Television, May 20, 2014, www.youtube.com/watch ?v=Hg-5KEt1Abg.

135 *telling the radio host Hugh Hewitt*: Hugh Hewitt, "Donald Trump on 2016 and Trolling the GOP," HughHewitt.com, February 25, 2015, www.hughhewitt.com /donald-trump-on-2016-and-trolling-the-gop/.

135 *in an interview with George Stephanopoulos*: "'This Week' Transcript: Donald Trump," ABC News, *This Week*, October 4, 2015, https://abcnews.go.com/Politics /week-transcript-donald-trump/story?id=34187405.

136 *he would "get them out at some point, probably"*: Maggie Haberman, "Donald Trump Says He'll Release His Tax Returns 'At Some Point,'" *New York Times*, February 22, 2016, www.nytimes.com/politics/first-draft/2016/02/22/donald -trump-says-hell-release-tax-returns-at-some-point/.

136 *But by February 2016*: Trump tweeted, "Just for your info, tax returns have 0 to do w/ someone's net worth. I have already filed my financial statements w/ FEC. They are great!" Donald J. Trump, Twitter, February 25, 2016, https://twitter .com/realDonaldTrump/status/702891487776866306.

136 *unable to do so while under audit*: In response to a debate question as to whether he was hiding something by not disclosing his tax returns, Trump said, "I get audited every year. I will absolutely give my return, but I'm being audited now for two or three years, so I can't do it until the audit is finished, obviously." See "The CNN-Telemundo Republican Debate Transcript, Annotated," *Washington Post*, February 25, 2016, www.washingtonpost.com/news/the-fix/wp/2016/02 /25/the-cnntelemundo-republican-debate-transcript-annotated.

136 *During a vice presidential debate in October 2016*: For a transcript of the October 4, 2016, debate, see Daniel White, "Read a Transcript of the Vice Presidential Debate," *Time*, October 5, 2016, available at http://time.com/4517096/vice-presidential-debate-kaine-pence-transcript/.

136 *every major-party presidential candidate*: Tom Kertscher, "Is Donald Trump the Only Major-Party Nominee in 40 Years Not to Release His Taxes?" PolitiFact, September 28, 2016, www.politifact.com/wisconsin/statements/2016/sep/28/tammy-baldwin/donald-trump-only-major-party-nominee-40-years-not/.

136 *"I am not a crook"*: Footage of the notorious remarks, delivered at a November 17, 1973, press conference, is available at www.youtube.com/watch?v=sh163n1lJ4M.

136 *commentators speculated*: See, for example, John Fund, "Trump's Refusal to Release Tax Returns Is a Ticking Time Bomb for the GOP," *National Review*, May 11, 2016, www.nationalreview.com/2016/05/donald-trumps-tax-returns-delegates-should-abstain-if-he-wont-release/.

137 *Mitt Romney, for example, called the failure*: Nick Gass, "Romney: Trump's Refusal to Release Tax Returns 'Disqualifying,'" *Politico*, May 11, 2016, www.politico.com/story/2016/05/mitt-romney-donald-trump-tax-returns-223088.

137 *White House counselor Kellyanne Conway announced*: Jim Zarroli, "Trump Aide Says He Won't Release Tax Returns, Claiming Most People Don't Care," NPR, January 22, 2017, www.npr.org/sections/thetwo-way/2017/01/22/511095966/trump-aide-says-he-wont-release-tax-returns-claiming-most-people-dont-care. The next day, Conway walked back the statement on Twitter, writing, "On taxes, answers (& repeated questions) are same from campaign: POTUS is under audit and will not release until that is completed. #nonews." Kellyanne Conway, Twitter, January 23, 2017, https://twitter.com/KellyannePolls/status/823515949068324864.

137 *the president's former lawyer*: Video of Cohen's testimony is available at "Michael Cohen Testimony Before House Oversight Committee," C-SPAN, February 27, 2019, www.c-span.org/video/?458125-1/michael-cohen-president-trump-he-racist-con-man-cheat.

137 *In April 2017 he tweeted*: Donald J. Trump, Twitter, April 16, 2017, https://twitter.com/realDonaldTrump/status/853595628655587334.

137 *a congressional committee has formally sought them*: Letter from Richard E. Neal to Charles P. Rettig, April 3, 2019, available at https://waysandmeans.house.gov/sites/democrats.waysandmeans.house.gov/files/documents/Neal%20Letter%20to%20Rettig%20%28signed%29%20-%202019.04.03.pdf.

137 *the Treasury Department refused the demand*: Letter from Steven T. Mnuchin to Richard E. Neal, May 6, 2019, available at https://assets.documentcloud.org/documents/5990994/Secretary-Mnuchin-Response-to-Chairman-Neal-2019.pdf.

138 *In May 2019 he defiantly tweeted*: Donald J. Trump, Twitter, May 11, 2019, https://twitter.com/realDonaldTrump/status/1127280257965412352.

139 *Benjamin Franklin warned*: "Convention Speech on Salaries," Papers of Benjamin Franklin, June 2, 1787, available via Yale University, http://franklinpapers.org/framedVolumes.jsp?vol=45&page=041.

139 *George Mason put it in somewhat starker terms*: "Notes of Robert Yates (June 23, 1787)," in Max Ferrand, *The Record of the Federal Convention of 1787*, Vol. 1 (New Haven, CT: Yale University Press, 1966), 391–92.

140 *ethics rules are about national security protections as well*: Susan Hennessey, "Ethics Rules Are National Security Rules," *Lawfare*, January 10, 2017, www .lawfareblog.com/ethics-rules-are-national-security-rules.

141 *"anti-corruption principle"*: Zephyr Teachout, "The Anti-Corruption Principle," *Cornell Law Review* 94 (2009); Zephyr Teachout, "Constitutional Purpose and the Anti-Corruption Principle," *Northwestern University Law Review* 108 (2014).

141 *opposing orientations*: Frank Lovett, "Republicanism," *Standard Encyclopedia of Philosophy*, ed. Edward N. Zalta, Summer 2008 Edition, available at https:// plato.stanford.edu/entries/republicanism/.

141 *"tempted by narcissism"*: Teachout, "The Anti-Corruption Principle," 375.

141 *James Madison famously opined*: James Madison, *Federalist* 51.

141 *The framers worried*: Zephyr Teachout describes in detail the framers' anxieties about corruption in "The Anti-Corruption Principle," 346–51, and documents the lengths the founders went to in order to prevent corruption in the executive at pp. 364–68.

142 *in part to prevent the executive from buying political loyalty*: Adrian Vermeule writes that "the Appropriations Clause . . . background is the similar concern of seventeenth- and eighteenth-century British Parliaments that an executive with access to the treasury as well as to offices could corrupt legislators and free itself from popular oversight." Adrian Vermeule, "The Constitutional Law of Official Compensation," *Columbia Law Review* 102 (2002): 509.

142 *legislative role in foreign affairs itself was designed*: Alexander Hamilton makes this argument with respect to the Senate's role in making treaties in *Federalist* 75.

142 *the Electoral College itself*: Alexander Hamilton, *Federalist* 68.

142 *foreign emoluments clause*: U.S. Constitution, Article I, Section 9.

142 *domestic emoluments clause*: U.S. Constitution, Article II, Section 1.

143 *government officials routinely moonlighted*: For an account of the history involving the Corwin episode, see Bruce Jennings and Daniel Callahan, *Representation and Responsibility: Exploring Legislative Ethics* (New York: Springer, 1985), 9.

143 *The Whiskey Ring*: Ron Chernow, *Grant* (New York: Penguin Press, 2017), 796–809.

143 *the Teapot Dome*: John W. Dean, *Warren G. Harding* (New York: Times Books, 2004), 155–60.

144 *Teapot Dome did, however, lead to*: George K. Yin, "Congressional Authority to Obtain and Release Tax Returns," *Tax Notes* 154, no. 8 (February 20, 2017), available at https://taxprof.typepad.com/files/154tn1013-yin.pdf#page=3. Writes Yin, "Several matters, including two involving possible conflicts of interest, helped bring the separation-of-powers imbalance to Congress's attention. During that period, Congress was investigating the Teapot Dome scandal—the alleged bribery of government officials in exchange for the leasing of public oil fields to private interests.

As part of its investigation, Congress sought from President Coolidge the tax returns of the alleged principals involved in the scandal, but the president initially resisted the request."

144 *In a special message to Congress, he explained*: Harry S. Truman, Special Message to the Congress Recommending Conflict-of-Interest Legislation, September 27, 1951, available at www.trumanlibrary.gov/library/public-papers/237/special-message -congress-recommending-conflict-interest-legislation.

144 *Ethics in Government Act of 1978*: 5 U.S. Code §§ 101, et seq.

145 *prosecution of Oliver North*: Lawrence E. Walsh, "U.S. v. Oliver North," in *Final Report of the Independent Counsel for Iran/Contra Matters. Vol. 1: Investigations and Prosecutions*, 105–22, August 4, 1993, available at https://archive.org/details /WalshReport/page/n57.

145 *conviction was later overturned*: U.S. v. Oliver L. North, 910 F.2d 843 (D.C. Circuit 1990).

145 *Though Bush pardoned*: David Johnston, "Bush Pardons 6 in Iran Affair, Aborting a Weinberger Trial; Prosecutor Assails 'Cover-Up,'" *New York Times*, December 24, 1992, https://archive.nytimes.com/www.nytimes.com/learning/general /onthisday/big/1224.html#article.

145 *he ordered the creation of uniform ethics rules*: See Executive Order 12674 as amended by Executive Order 12731, 81 FR 8008, originally issued April 12, 1989, available at www.justice.gov/archives/ncfs/page/file/761076/download. The rules are codified at 5 C.F.R. § 2635.101(b).

145 *Congress passed legislation prohibiting executive branch employees*: Jeffrey Green, "History of Conflicts Law," *Hamline Law Review* 26 (2003): 598. See also Nat'l Treasury Employees Union v. United States, 513 U.S. 454 (1994).

146 *Office of Government Ethics has indicated*: David H. Martin, "Letter to a Deputy DAEO," Office of Government Ethics, October 20, 1983, available at www.oge .gov/web/oge.nsf/All%20Legal%20Advisories/01F8E09232041FD185257E96 005FBBE8/$FILE/64ed9ad9bd294b45a88ac8729a97968a3.pdf?open.

147 *presided over a dinner of European business leaders*: "President Trump Dinner with European Business Leaders," C-SPAN, January 25, 2018, www.c-span.org /video/?440299-1/president-trump-makes-remarks-dinner-european-business -leaders&start=134.

148 *running the country like his business*: "Donald Trump Says He'll Run America Like His Business," Associated Press, October 27, 2016, http://fortune.com/2016/10 /27/donald-trump-hillary-clinton-business-management/.

148 *"the first presidential candidate to run and make money on it"*: Philip Bump, "Trump Once Figured He'd Be the First Person to Make Money Running for President. He Didn't," *Washington Post*, June 21, 2017, www.washingtonpost.com/news/politics /wp/2017/06/21/trump-once-figured-hed-be-the-first-person-to-make-money -running-for-president-he-didnt.

148 *Cohen, testified that Trump*: "Prepared Statement of Michael D. Cohen, Committee on Oversight and Reform, U.S. House of Representatives," February 27,

2019, available at https://assets.documentcloud.org/documents/5753202/Cohen-Prepared-Testimony.pdf.

148 The New York Times *published a mammoth article*: David Barstow, Susanne Craig, and Russ Buettner, "Trump Engaged in Suspect Tax Schemes as He Reaped Riches from His Father," *New York Times*, October 2, 2018, www.nytimes.com/interactive/2018/10/02/us/politics/donald-trump-tax-schemes-fred-trump.html.

150 *Washington turns out to have engaged in secret land purchases*: Seth Barrett Tillman, "Business Transactions and President Trump's 'Emoluments' Problem," *Harvard Journal of Law and Public Policy* 40 (2017): 761, https://papers.ssrn.com/sol3/papers.cfm?abstract_id=2937186. For the debate over the significance of this, see Eugene Kontorovich, "Did George Washington Take 'Emoluments'?" *Wall Street Journal*, April 13, 2017, www.wsj.com/articles/did-george-washington-take-emoluments-1492123033; Eugene Kontorovich, "George Washington Was the First President to Stay in the Real Estate Business," *Washington Post*, April 14, 2017, www.washingtonpost.com/news/volokh-conspiracy/wp/2017/04/14/george-washington-was-the-first-president-to-stay-in-the-real-estate-business; Jed Shugerman, "George Washington's Secret Land Deal Actually Strengthens CREW's Emoluments Claim," *Take Care Blog*, June 2, 2017, https://takecareblog.com/blog/george-washington-s-secret-land-deal-actually-strengthens-crew-s-emoluments-claim.

150 *Lyndon Johnson was the first to establish a supposedly blind trust*: Len Costa, "A Wink and a Nod: A New Scandal Exposes the Problem with Blind Trusts," *Legal Affairs*, January/February 2006, www.legalaffairs.org/issues/January-February-2006/toa_costa_janfeb06.msp.

150 *claims that this blind trust was a mockery*: Robert A. Caro, "The Years of Lyndon Johnson," *Atlantic Monthly*, October 1981, 43.

150 *Reagan executed a true blind trust*: Ronald Reagan, "Announcement of the Formation of a Blind Trust to Manage the President's Personal Assets," January 30, 1981, www.reaganlibrary.gov/research/speeches/13081a.

150 *kept the bulk of his assets outside of the trust*: Edward T. Pound, "Reagan's Worth Put at $4 Million," *New York Times*, February 23, 1981, www.nytimes.com/1981/02/23/us/reagan-s-worth-put-at-4-million.html.

150 *George H. W. Bush, even as vice president*: Jeff Gerth, "Bush's Blind Trust: Guarding Against Conflicts of Interest," *New York Times*, September 28, 1984, www.nytimes.com/1984/09/28/us/bush-s-blind-trust-guarding-against-conflicts-of-interest.html.

150 *the Clintons put their assets into a blind trust in 1993*: David Lauter, "Clintons Putting Financial Assets into Blind Trust," *Los Angeles Times*, May 20, 1993, http://articles.latimes.com/1993-05-20/news/mn-37415_1_blind-trust.

150 *during Hillary Clinton's first presidential run*: Patrick Healy, "To Avoid Conflicts, Clintons Liquidate Holdings," *New York Times*, June 15, 2007, www.nytimes.com/2007/06/15/us/politics/15clintons.html.

151 *presiding over chants of "lock her up"*: See, for example, "Presidential Candidate Donald Trump Rally in Pueblo, Colorado," C-SPAN, October 3, 2016, at timestamp 42:26, available at www.c-span.org/video/?416273-1/donald-trump -campaigns-pueblo-colorado.

151 *experts warned that only full divestment would resolve*: Kurt Eichenwald, "How the Trump Organization's Foreign Business Ties Could Upend U.S. National Security," *Newsweek*, September 14, 2016, www.newsweek.com/2016/09/23/donald -trump-foreign-business-deals-national-security-498081.html.

151 *handing control of his business to his children*: Eric Levitz, "If Clinton Needs to Close Her Foundation, Trump Needs to Dissolve His Company," *New York* magazine, September 14, 2016, http://nymag.com/intelligencer/2016/09/president -trumps-conflicts-of-interest.html; Nick Gass, "Trump Jr. Grilled on 'Blind Trust' Arrangement," *Politico*, September 16, 2016, www.politico.com/story /2016/09/donald-trump-jr-blind-trust-businesses-228269.

151 *"great business in total"*: Trump tweeted, consolidating the tweets, "I will be holding a major news conference in New York City with my children on December 15 to discuss the fact that I will be leaving my . . . great business in total in order to fully focus on running the country in order to MAKE AMERICA GREAT AGAIN! While I am not mandated to . . ." Donald J. Trump, Twitter, November 30, 2016, https://twitter.com/realDonaldTrump/status/803926488579973120; https://twitter.com/realDonaldTrump/status/803927774784344064.

151 *official Twitter account responded*: Office of Government Ethics, Twitter, November 30, 2016, https://twitter.com/OfficeGovEthics/status/804020925171646464.

151 *released an official statement*: Alina Seylyukh, "Not a Hack: U.S. Office of Government Ethics Tweets at Trump," NPR, November 30, 2016, www.npr.org/sections /thetwo-way/2016/11/30/503879587/not-a-hack-u-s-office-of-government -ethics-tweets-at-trump.

152 *Mr. Trump would take steps to avoid such conflicts*: "Trump Lawyer Offers SOLUTIONS for Trump's Conflicts of Interest-FNN," FOX 10 Phoenix, January 11, 2017, www.youtube.com/watch?v=9F85sZM9DBA. See also Josh Dawsey and Darren Samuelsohn, "Trump Drops 'No New Deals' Pledge," *Politico*, January 11, 2017, www.politico.com/story/2017/01/trump-business-ties-conflicts-233468.

152 *"no new deals"*: Trump tweeted, consolidating the tweets, "Even though I am not mandated by law to do so, I will be leaving my businesses before January 20th so that I can focus full time on the . . . Presidency. Two of my children, Don and Eric, plus executives, will manage them. No new deals will be done during my term(s) in office." Donald J. Trump, Twitter, December 12, 2016, https://twitter.com /realDonaldTrump/status/808528428123254785; https://twitter.com/real DonaldTrump/status/808529888630239232.

152 *Reporters were not permitted to inspect the contents*: CNN Politics, Twitter, January 11, 2017, https://twitter.com/CNNPolitics/status/819298681643995136.

152 *publicly critiqued the plan*: "Remarks of Walter M. Shaub, Jr., Director, U.S. Office of Government Ethics, as prepared for delivery at 4:00 p.m. on January 11, 2017,

at the Brookings Institution," available at www.brookings.edu/wp-content
/uploads/2017/01/20170111_oge_shaub_remarks.pdf.

153 *Shaub resigned*: Nicholas Fandos, "Government Ethics Chief Resigns, Casting Uncertainty Over Agency," *New York Times*, July 6, 2017, www.nytimes.com/2017/07
/06/us/politics/walter-shaub-office-of-government-ethics-resign.html.

153 *Trump administration's White House ethics lawyer*: Bess Levin, "White House
Ethics Lawyer Finally Reaches His Breaking Point," *Vanity Fair*, July 26, 2018,
www.vanityfair.com/news/2018/07/white-house-ethics-lawyer-finally-reaches
-his-breaking-point.

153 *Passantino later conceded*: R. Robin McDonald, "Trump's Former Ethics Czar
Reflects on White House's Legal Challenges," Law.com, December 3, 2018,
www.law.com/dailyreportonline/2018/12/03/trumps-former-ethics-czar
-reflects-on-white-houses-legal-challenges/.

154 *a bid to develop the space into a hotel*: "GSA Selects the Trump Organization as
Preferred Developer for DC's Old Post Office," General Services Administration, February 7, 2012, www.gsa.gov/about-us/newsroom/news-releases/gsa
-selects-the-trump-organization-as-preferred-developer-for-dcs-old-post
-office; Zach Everson, "Inside the World's Most Controversial Hotel," *Condé
Nast Traveler*, May 2, 2018, www.cntraveler.com/story/trump-hotel-dc-inside
-the-worlds-most-controversial-hotel.

154 *The hotel opened thirteen days before Donald Trump was elected*: Rick Massimo,
"Trump Attends Grand Opening of His DC Hotel," WTOP, October 26, 2016,
https://wtop.com/dc/2016/10/trump-speak-grand-opening-dc-hotel/slide/1/.

154 *originally planned to charge a little over $400*: Alexandra Berzon, "Trump Hotel in
Washington Saw Strong Profit in First Four Months of 2017," *Wall Street Journal*,
August 11, 2017, www.wsj.com/articles/trump-hotel-in-washington-saw-strong
-profit-in-first-four-months-of-2017-1502424589.

154 *the hotel has charged more than its competitors*: Cristina Alesci and Curt Devine,
"Exclusive: Data Show Trump's DC Hotel Was Pricier and Emptier Than Peers
in 2017," CNN, January 27, 2018, www.cnn.com/2018/01/27/politics/trump
-hotel-occupancy-rates-data/index.html.

154 *King Louis XVI gave Franklin*: Zephyr Teachout, *Corruption in America: From
Benjamin Franklin's Snuff Box to Citizens United* (Cambridge, MA: Harvard
University Press, 2014), 1–4, 26–28.

154 *The office produced a thirteen-page memorandum*: "Applicability of the Emoluments Clause and the Foreign Gifts and Decorations Act to the President's Re-
ceipt of the Nobel Peace Prize," Office of Legal Counsel, U.S. Department of
Justice, December 7, 2009, available at www.justice.gov/sites/default/files/olc
/opinions/2009/12/31/emoluments-nobel-peace_0.pdf.

154 *Obama did so and distributed the money to ten charities*: "The President Do-
nates Nobel Prize Money to Charity," White House, March 11, 2010, https://
obamawhitehouse.archives.gov/the-press-office/president-donates-nobel-prize
-money-charity.

155 *Roosevelt donated his prize money*: "Theodore Roosevelt Nobel Lecture," May 5, 1910, available at www.nobelprize.org/prizes/peace/1906/roosevelt/lecture/.

155 *Wilson may have just pocketed the cash*: PolitiFact was unable to ascertain "what Wilson did with his money" but noted that "one biography said Wilson was worried about his finances and suggested that he simply kept the money." See Angie Drobnic Holan, "Does Obama Need Congress' Permission to Get Nobel?" PolitiFact, October 29, 2009, www.politifact.com/truth-o-meter/statements /2009/oct/29/ginny-brown-waite/does-president-need-permission-congress -accept-nob/.

155 *though he has reportedly exerted great effort*: Gwladys Fouche, "No Need for Shinzo Abe: Trump Already Nominated for Nobel Peace Prize," Reuters, February 18, 2019, www.reuters.com/article/us-nobel-prize-peace/no-need-for-shinzo -abe-trump-already-nominated-for-nobel-peace-prize-idUSKCN1Q71IS.

155 *Trump's attorneys argued*: Morgan, Lewis & Bockius LLP, "White Paper: Conflicts of Interest and the President," January 11, 2017, available at https://assets .documentcloud.org/documents/3280261/MLB-White-Paper-1-10-Pm.pdf.

155 *Critics fear that Trump is inappropriately profiting*: See, for example, "Profiting from the Presidency," Citizens for Responsibility and Ethics in Washington, available at www.citizensforethics.org/profitingfromthepresidency/.

155 *Trump's luxury hotels in New York and Chicago are both suffering*: David A. Fahrenthold, Jonathan O'Connell, and Morgan Krakow, "At Trump's Big-City Hotels, Business Dropped as His Political Star Rose, Internal Documents Show," *Washington Post*, October 4, 2018, www.washingtonpost.com/politics/at-trumps-big -city-hotels-business-dropped-as-his-political-star-rose-internal-documents -show/2018/10/03/bd26b1d6-b6d4-11e8-a7b5-adaaa5b2a57f_story.html.

155 *But the D.C. hotel has thrived*: For Saudi use of the hotel, see David A. Fahrenthold and Jonathan O'Connell, "Saudi-Funded Lobbyist Paid for 500 Rooms at Trump's Hotel After 2016 Election," *Washington Post*, December 5, 2018, www.washingtonpost.com/politics/saudi-funded-lobbyist-paid-for-500-rooms -at-trumps-hotel-after-2016-election/2018/12/05/29603a64-f417-11e8-bc79 -68604ed88993_story.html. For Kuwait's use of the hotel, see David Corn, "Once Again, the Kuwaiti Government Puts Money Right into Trump's Pocket," *Mother Jones*, January 30, 2019, www.motherjones.com/politics/2019/01/donald-trump -hotel-kuwait-government-emoluments/. For use of the hotel by the Philippines, Turkey, and other countries, see Bernard Condon and Stephen Braun, "Philippines Latest Foreign Country to Book the Trump International Hotel," NBC Washington, April 28, 2018, www.nbcwashington.com/news/local/Philippines -Latest-Foreign-Country-to-Book-Rooms-at-the-Trump-International-Hotel -481144831.html.

156 *The State of Maine*: Scott Thistle and Kevin Miller, "Maine Paid for 40 Rooms at Trump Hotel for LePage, Staff," *Portland Press Herald*, February 17, 2019, www .pressherald.com/2019/02/17/maine-paid-for-40-rooms-at-trump-hotel-for -lepage-staff/.

156   *members of Congress have standing to raise the issue*: Memorandum Opinion, Richard Blumenthal, et al. v. Donald J. Trump, No. 17-1154 (D.D.C., September 28, 2018), available at www.courtlistener.com/recap/gov.uscourts.dcd .187220/gov.uscourts.dcd.187220.59.0_1.pdf.

156   *the governments of Maryland and the District of Columbia have standing*: District of Columbia and State of Maryland v. Donald J. Trump, No. 17-1596 (D.D.C., March 28, 2018), available at http://oag.dc.gov/sites/default/files/2018-03 /Emoluments_Standing_Opinion.pdf. For the Fourth Circuit Court of Appeals decision reversing, see In re Donald Trump, No. 18-2486 (Fourth Circuit, July 10, 2019), available at www.ca4.uscourts.gov/opinions/182486.P.pdf.

157   *When Reagan was elected*: "Constitution Is Cited as Bar to Pension for Reagan," Associated Press, August 29, 1987, www.nytimes.com/1987/08/29/us/constitution -is-cited-as-bar-to-pension-for-reagan.html.

157   *it did not qualify as an emolument*: "President Reagan's Ability to Receive Retirement Benefits from the State of California," Office of Legal Counsel, U.S. Department of Justice, June 23, 1981, available at www.justice.gov/file/22681 /download.

157   *In the Old Post Office Building lease*: "Evaluation of GSA's Management and Administration of the Old Post Office Building Lease," Office of Inspector General, U.S. General Services Administration, January 16, 2019, available at www.gsaig .gov/sites/default/files/ipa-reports/JE19-002%20OIG%20EVALUATION% 20REPORT-GSA%27s%20Management%20%26%20Administration% 20of%20OPO%20Building%20Lease_January%2016%202019_Redacted.pdf.

158   *Bill Clinton rightly got in trouble*: See, for example, "Lincoln Bedroom Guests Gave $5.4 Million," CNN, February 26, 1997, www.cnn.com/ALLPOLITICS /1997/02/26/clinton.lincoln/.

158   *including $700,000 for event space at a rate of $175,000 per day*: Ilya Marritz and Justin Elliott, "Trump's Inauguration Paid Trump's Company—With Ivanka in the Middle," *ProPublica*, December 14, 2018, www.propublica.org/article /trump-inc-podcast-trumps-inauguration-paid-trumps-company-with-ivanka -in-the-middle. See also Justin Elliott and Ilya Marritz, "New Evidence Emerges of Possible Wrongdoing by Trump Inaugural Committee," *ProPublica*, February 8, 2019, www.propublica.org/article/trump-inc-new-evidence-emerges-of -possible-wrongdoing-by-trump-inaugural-committee.

158   *appointments clause*: U.S. Constitution, Article II, Section 2.

158   *Hamilton believed that the senatorial role in appointments*: Alexander Hamilton, *Federalist* 76.

159   *Harry Truman's legacy was marred*: Felzenberg, *The Leaders We Deserved*, 111.

159   *James Barber writes*: Barber, *The Presidential Character*, 290.

159   *the director of OGE sent a letter*: Senator Charles Schumer released the letter in "Schumer Statement on Office of Government Ethics Letter Detailing 'Great Concern' with Cabinet Nominees Disclosures," January 7, 2017, available at www.democrats.senate.gov/newsroom/press-releases/schumer-statement

-on-office-of-government-ethics-letter-detailing-great-concern-with-cabinet
-nominees-disclosures.

160 *Tom Price, Scott Pruitt, Ryan Zinke, or Wilbur Ross*: Dan Mangan, "Trump's
Cabinet Has Been Rocked by a Number of Ethics Scandals—Here's a Complete Guide," CNBC, February 16, 2018, www.cnbc.com/2018/02/15/trump
-cabinet-officials-in-ethics-scandals.html.

160 *signed into law in 1967 by Lyndon Johnson*: 5 U.S. Code § 3110.

160 *named his wife*: Thomas L. Friedman, "Hillary Clinton to Head Panel on Health
Care," *New York Times*, January 26, 1993, www.nytimes.com/1993/01/26/us
/hillary-clinton-to-head-panel-on-health-care.html.

160 *the D.C. Circuit Court of Appeals noted*: Association of American Physicians and
Surgeons, et al. v. Hillary Rodham Clinton, et al., 997 F.2d 898 (D.C. Circuit,
1993).

161 *He initially claimed*: Rebecca Ballhaus, "Donald Trump's Children Won't Have
White House Roles," *Wall Street Journal*, November 17, 2016, www.wsj.com
/articles/donald-trumps-children-wont-have-white-house-roles-1479415773.

161 *Kellyanne Conway went on MSNBC's* Morning Joe: Jim Zarroli, "Trump Relatives' Potential White House Roles Could Test Anti-Nepotism Law," NPR, January 5, 2017, www.npr.org/2017/01/05/508382236/trump-relatives-potential
-white-house-roles-could-test-anti-nepotism-law.

161 *Office of Legal Counsel issued an opinion*: "Application of the Anti-Nepotism Statute to a Presidential Appointment in the White House Office," Office of Legal
Counsel, U.S. Department of Justice, January 20, 2017, www.justice.gov/sites
/default/files/opinions/attachments/2018/08/06/2017-01-20-anti-nepo-stat
-who.pdf.

161 *promoting their businesses in office*: Aliyah Frumlin, "Ivanka Trump's Company
Scrambles Over '60 Minutes' Bracelet Criticism," NBC News, November 15,
2016, www.nbcnews.com/news/us-news/ivanka-trump-s-company-scrambles
-over-60-minutes-bracelet-criticism-n684171.

161 *incomplete financial disclosures and untruthful security clearance forms*: Jonathan
O'Connell, Matea Gold, Drew Harwell, and Steven Rich, "In Revised Filing, Kushner Reveals Dozens of Previously Undisclosed Assets," *Washington Post*, July 21,
2017, www.washingtonpost.com/politics/kushner-failed-to-disclose-dozens
-of-financial-holdings-new-document-shows/2017/07/21/1a11a566-6e35-11e7
-96ab-5f38140b38cc_story.html; Kara Scannell, "Background Check Chief Has
'Never Seen' Mistakes and Omissions at Level of Jared Kushner Forms," CNN, February 13, 2018, www.cnn.com/2017/10/12/politics/jared-kushner-background
-check-form/index.html.

162 *granted his son-in-law a top secret security clearance*: Haberman, Schmidt, Gold-
man, and Karni, "Trump Ordered Officials to Give Jared Kushner a Security
Clearance." See also Josh Dawsey, Seung Min Kim, and Shane Harris, "Trump
Demanded Top-Secret Security Clearance for Jared Kushner Last Year Despite

Concerns of John Kelly and Intelligence Officials," *Washington Post*, February 28, 2019, available at www.washingtonpost.com/politics/trump-sought-top
-secret-security-clearance-for-jared-kushner-last-year-despite-concerns-of
-john-kelly-and-intelligence-officials/2019/02/28/2eacc72e-3bae-11e9-aaae
-69364b2ed137_story.html.

7. "The power to protect the guilty": Corrupting Justice

165 *announcing Sessions as his pick to be attorney general*: David Nakamura and Elise Viebeck, "Trump Chooses Sen. Jeff Sessions for Attorney General, Rep. Mike Pompeo for CIA Director," *Washington Post*, November 18, 2016, www.washingtonpost
.com/politics/trump-chooses-sen-jeff-sessions-for-attorney-general-rep-mike
-pompeo-for-cia-director-transition-sources-say/2016/11/18/.

166 *recusing himself from oversight of the Russia investigation*: Sessions announced his recusal "in the matters that deal with the Trump campaign" during a March 2, 2017, press conference, video of which is available at www.c-span.org/video/?424859-1
/attorney-general-jeff-sessions-recuses-russia-trump-campaign-investigations. At the time, the Department of Justice had not confirmed the existence of the Russia investigation. Sessions stated as much: "This announcement should not be interpreted as confirmation of the existence of any investigation or suggestive of the scope of any such investigation because we in the Department of Justice resist confirming or denying the very existence of investigations." See also "Attorney General Sessions Statement on Recusal," Department of Justice, March 2, 2017, www
.justice.gov/opa/pr/attorney-general-sessions-statement-recusal.

166 *Sessions's recusal was in line with the counsel of career government attorneys*: Sessions said at the press conference, "My staff recommended recusal. They said that since I had involvement with the campaign, I should not be involved in any campaign investigation. I have studied the rules and considered their comments and evaluation. I believe those recommendations are right and just. Therefore, I have recused myself in the matters that deal with the Trump campaign."

166 *Trump launched an aggressive campaign*: Trump's conduct in the matter is detailed in the Mueller report, Vol. II, 49.

166 *McGahn's calls were not the only ones*: Mueller report, Vol. II, 49.

166 *"I don't have a lawyer"*: Mueller report, Vol. II, 50.

166 *rendered himself useless for purposes of watching Trump's back*: In a December 28, 2017, interview with the *New York Times* reporter Mike Schmidt, Trump compared Sessions to Eric Holder, the first attorney general under Barack Obama, saying, "It's too bad Jeff recused himself. I like Jeff, but it's too bad he recused himself . . . Holder protected President Obama. Totally protected him." See "Excerpts from Trump's Interview with The Times," *New York Times*, December 28, 2017, www.nytimes.com/2017/12/28/us/politics/trump-interview-excerpts.html.

167 *McGahn backed off*: Mueller report, Vol. II, 50.

167 *the president pulled Sessions aside*: Mueller report, Vol. II, 51.

167 *calling Sessions at home to press it*: Mueller report, Vol. II, 107.

167 *"I can't do anything"*: Mueller report, Vol. II, 63.

167 *again directed his fury at Sessions*: Mueller report, Vol. II, 78–79.

167 *Sessions handed over a resignation letter*: Mueller report, Vol. II, 79–80.

167 *send a message through his former campaign manager*: Mueller report, Vol. II, 90–91.

167 *who never delivered the message*: Mueller report, Vol. II, 92–93.

167 *"would have picked somebody else"*: Trump made these comments during an Oval Office conversation with *Times* reporters Peter Baker, Maggie Haberman, and Michael S. Schmidt on July 19, 2017. See "Excerpts from The Times's Interview with Trump," *New York Times*, July 19, 2017, www.nytimes.com/2017/07/19/us/politics/trump-interview-transcript.html.

167 *"our beleaguered A.G."*: Trump tweeted, "So why aren't the Committees and investigators, and of course our beleaguered A.G., looking into Crooked Hillarys [*sic*] crimes & Russia relations?" Donald J. Trump, Twitter, July 24, 2017, https://twitter.com/realdonaldtrump/status/889467610332528641.

167 *he was again demanding that Sessions resign*: Mueller report, Vol. II, 95.

167 *"holy hell to pay"*: Graham made the statement to a group of reporters in the Senate halls. "Graham: Holy Hell to Pay If Sessions Is Fired," CNN, July 27, 2017, available at www.youtube.com/watch?v=wCafpKcnBJA.

168 *"Why aren't Dem crimes under investigation?"*: Donald J. Trump, Twitter, February 21, 2018, https://twitter.com/realDonaldTrump/status/966321700588711936.

168 *"DISGRACEFUL!"*: Trump tweeted, "Why is A.G. Jeff Sessions asking the Inspector General to investigate potentially massive FISA abuse. Will take forever, has no prosecutorial power and already late with reports on Comey etc. Isn't the I.G. an Obama guy? Why not use Justice Department lawyers? DISGRACEFUL!" Donald J. Trump, Twitter, February 28, 2018, https://twitter.com/realDonaldTrump/status/968856971075051521.

168 *tweeted invective*: Jennifer Hansler, "Trump's Twitter Attacks on Sessions: An Annotated Timeline," CNN, August 25, 2018, www.cnn.com/2018/08/25/politics/trump-sessions-twitter-timeline/index.html.

168 *Rumors of Sessions's imminent dismissal swirled*: See, for example, Carol D. Leonnig, Josh Dawsey, and Gabriel Pogrund, "Trump Privately Revived the Idea of Firing Sessions This Month, According to People Familiar with the Discussions," *Washington Post*, August 28, 2018, www.washingtonpost.com/politics/trump-privately-revived-the-idea-of-firing-sessions-this-month-according-to-people-familiar-with-the-discussions/2018/08/28/13e84a6c-aa40-11e8-a8d7-0f63ab8b1370_story.html. The story reports, "At least twice this month, Trump vented to White House advisers and his lawyers about the 'endless investigation' of his campaign and said he needs to fire Sessions for saddling his presidency with the controversy."

168 *The president's aides scrambled to control the fallout*: Leonnig, Dawsey, and Pogrund, "Trump Privately Revived the Idea of Firing Sessions This Month."

168 *Graham himself offered the compromise*: Lauren Fox and Jeremy Herb, "Lindsey

Graham Says Trump Could Replace Jeff Sessions After Midterms," CNN, August 23, 2018, www.cnn.com/2018/08/23/politics/lindsey-graham-jeff-sessions-replace/index.html.

168 *bypassing Rosenstein to name Sessions's chief of staff*: Peter Baker, Katie Benner, and Michael D. Shear, "Jeff Sessions Is Forced Out as Attorney General as Trump Installs Loyalist," *New York Times*, November 7, 2018, www.nytimes.com/2018/11/07/us/politics/sessions-resigns.html.

169 *Congress had sought to thread a needle*: For an account of the congressional purpose in creating the FBI director's term limit, see Andrew Kent, Susan Hennessey, and Matthew Kahn, "Why Did Congress Set a Ten-Year Term for the FBI Director?" *Lawfare*, May 17, 2017, www.lawfareblog.com/why-did-congress-set-ten-year-term-fbi-director.

170 *"tyrant-proofing"*: See Conor Friedersdorf, "Tyrant-Proof the White House—Before It's Too Late," *Atlantic*, March 8, 2016, www.theatlantic.com/politics/archive/2016/03/quick-limit-the-power-that-trump-or-clinton-would-inherit/472743/.

171 *the table-pounding of civil libertarians aside*: For examples of concerns raised regarding the National Security Agency, see, for example, Andy Greenberg, "Imagine If Donald Trump Controlled the NSA," *Wired*, October 19, 2016, www.wired.com/2016/10/imagine-donald-trump-controlled-nsa/.

172 *In a famous speech*: Robert H. Jackson, "The Federal Prosecutor," Address at Conference of United States Attorneys, Washington, D.C., April 1, 1940, available at www.roberthjackson.org/speech-and-writing/the-federal-prosecutor/.

173 *describes it as the essential element to Orbán's undermining of democracy*: David Frum, "How to Build an Autocracy," *Atlantic*, March 2017, www.theatlantic.com/magazine/archive/2017/03/how-to-build-an-autocracy/513872/.

173 *Reince Priebus and Steve Bannon became alarmed to learn*: Mueller report, Vol. II, 79–80.

174 *the standards for doing so*: Opening a preliminary investigation requires "information or an allegation indicating" that "activity constituting a federal crime or a threat to the national security has or may have occurred, is or may be occurring, or will or may occur and the investigation may obtain information relating to the activity or the involvement or role of an individual, group, or organization in such activity"; or that an action "may obtain foreign intelligence that is responsive to a foreign intelligence requirement." A full investigation "may be initiated if there is an articulable factual basis for the investigation that reasonably indicates" such circumstances. See "Attorney General's Guidelines for Domestic FBI Operations," U.S. Department of Justice, 20–22, available at www.justice.gov/archive/opa/docs/guidelines.pdf.

174 *is so vast*: The total number of criminal offenses under U.S. law is unknown. Ronald Gainer, a retired Justice Department official who oversaw an attempt to collate all U.S. crimes, told *The Wall Street Journal* in 2011, "You will have died and resurrected three times" and still not know how many crimes there are. See Gary

Fields and John R. Emshwiller, "Many Failed Efforts to Count Nation's Federal Criminal Laws," *Wall Street Journal*, July 23, 2011, www.wsj.com/articles/SB10 001424052702304319804576389601079728920.

174 *Levi Guidelines*: The guidelines were originally promulgated by Attorney General Edward Levi in 1976. The most recent version is formally titled "The Attorney General's Guidelines for Domestic FBI Operations."

174 *normative rules about contacts*: See, for example, Donald F. McGahn, "Communications Restrictions with Personnel at the Department of Justice," White House, January 27, 2017, available at www.politico.com/f/?id=0000015a-dde8-d23c -a7ff-dfef4d530000.

176 *"Lock her up!"*: For the origin and history of the "Lock her up" chant, see Peter W. Stevenson, "A Brief History of the 'Lock Her Up!' Chant by Trump Supporters Against Clinton," *Washington Post*, November 22, 2016, www.washingtonpost .com/news/the-fix/wp/2016/11/22/a-brief-history-of-the-lock-her-up-chant -as-it-looks-like-trump-might-not-even-try.

176 *supposed crimes by his political opponents*: See, for example, Trump's tweet that "Attorney General Jeff Sessions has taken a VERY weak position on Hillary Clinton crimes (where are E-mails & DNC server) & Intel leakers!" Donald J. Trump, Twitter, July 25, 2017, https://twitter.com/realDonaldTrump/status /889790429398528000.

176 *asking Sessions, on multiple occasions*: Mueller report, Vol. II, 107, 109.

176 *In one December 2017 meeting, Trump told Sessions*: Mueller report, Vol. II, 109.

176 *accuses enemies of crimes*: For an example of Trump accusing people of crimes, see Nicholas Fandos and Maggie Haberman, "Top Democrats Warn Trump over Comments on Michael Cohen," *New York Times*, January 13, 2019, www .nytimes.com/2019/01/13/us/politics/trump-cohen-testimony.html. See also Donald J. Trump, Twitter, July 27, 2019, https://twitter.com/realDonaldTrump /status/1155324390793515008.

176 *objects to prosecution of his allies*: For an example of him objecting to criminal prosecutions of his allies, see "Donald Trump: 'Manafort's a Good Man,'" BBC, August 21, 2018, video available at www.bbc.com/news/av/world-us-canada -45266609/donald-trump-manafort-s-a-good-man.

176 *based on no information other than what he has apparently seen*: For an example of Trump tweeting on a pending matter based on material he has seen on Fox News, see Maxwell Tani, "Trump Tweets About Fox News 'FBI Bombshell' During Scheduled Intel Briefing," *Daily Beast*, February 7, 2018, www.thedailybeast .com/trump-tweets-about-fox-news-fbi-bombshell-during-scheduled-intel -briefing. More generally, media analyst Matt Gertz has chronicled this behavior, which Gertz calls the "Trump-Fox Feedback Loop," and in which Trump has commented on matters ranging from the resignation of FBI general counsel Jim Baker to the possible investigation of the Uranium One deal, in a Twitter thread, available at https://twitter.com/MattGertz/status/948180198289178624, and

in an essay in *Politico Magazine*. See Matt Gertz, "I've Studied the Trump-Fox Feedback Loop for Months. It's Crazier Than You Think," *Politico Magazine*, January 5, 2018, www.politico.com/magazine/story/2018/01/05/trump-media -feedback-loop-216248.

176 *career officials and those*: For an example of Trump's attacks on career officials, see "How the hell is Bruce Ohr still employed at the Justice Department? Disgraceful! Witch Hunt!" Donald J. Trump, Twitter, August 29, 2019, https://twitter .com/realDonaldTrump/status/1034821067423014913. For an example of Trump attacking people he has appointed, see his tweets on Rod Rosenstein— for example, Donald J. Trump, Twitter, June 16, 2017, https://twitter.com /realDonaldTrump/status/875701471999864833. Trump tweeted, "I am being investigated for firing the FBI Director by the man who told me to fire the FBI Director! Witch Hunt."

176 *persistently reserves the right to pardon*: In an interview with the *New York Post*, Trump said in late November 2018 that he was still open to a pardon for former campaign chairman Paul Manafort, whom a jury had convicted and who had pled to an array of charges. See Marisa Schultz and Nikki Schwab, "Trump Says Pardon for Paul Manafort Still a Possibility," *New York Post*, November 28, 2018, nypost .com/2018/11/28/trump-says-pardon-for-paul-manafort-still-a-possibility/.

176 *dangles the possibility of firing or interfering*: Trump on many occasions discussed, publicly and privately, firing Jeff Sessions, Rod Rosenstein, and Robert Mueller. See, for example, Pamela Brown, Gloria Borger, Evan Perez, Jeff Zeleny, Dana Bash, and Dan Merica, "Trump Considering Firing Rosenstein to Check Mueller," CNN, April 10, 2018, www.cnn.com/2018/04/10/politics/trump -rod-rosenstein-robert-mueller/index.html. Trump also inquired about putting Geoffrey Berman, the Trump-appointed U.S. attorney for the Southern District of New York, in charge of the investigation into Michael Cohen after Berman had already recused himself. See Mark Mazzetti, Maggie Haberman, Nicholas Fandos, and Michael S. Schmidt, "Intimidation, Pressure and Humiliation: Inside Trump's Two-Year War on the Investigations Encircling Him," *New York Times*, February 19, 2019, www.nytimes.com/2019/02/19/us/politics/trump -investigations.html.

176 *publicly entertains the possibility of revoking the security clearances*: After the high-profile revocation of former CIA director John Brennan's security clearance, Trump threatened to revoke the clearance of the career Justice Department official Bruce Ohr. See Karen DeYoung and Josh Dawsey, "White House Drafts More Clearance Cancellations Demanded by Trump," *Washington Post*, August 17, 2018, www.washingtonpost.com/politics/former-intelligence-officials -rebuke-trump-for-pulling-brennans-security-clearance/2018/08/17/ea8382f2 -a20d-11e8-8e87-c869fe70a721_story.html.

177 *"I have absolute right to do what I want to do with the Justice Department"*: See Michael S. Schmidt and Michael D. Shear, "Trump Says Russia Inquiry Makes U.S.

'Look Very Bad,'" *New York Times*, December 28, 2017, www.nytimes.com /2017/12/28/us/politics/trump-interview-mueller-russia-china-north-korea .html.

177 *attorney general is a job created by Congress*: The position was created in the Judiciary Act of 1789 and is now codified at 28 U.S. Code § 503.

179 *wrote to Alexander Hamilton*: Letter from George Washington to Alexander Hamilton, October 1, 1792, available at www.loc.gov/resource/mgw2.032/?sp =330&st=text.

179 *"Whereas it appears to me"*: Letter from George Washington to William Rawle, March 13, 1793, available at www.loc.gov/resource/mgw2.023/?sp=353&st =text.

179 *He wrote in 1800 to Charles Lee*: Letter from John Adams to Charles Lee, May 16, 1800, available at https://founders.archives.gov/documents/Adams/99-02-02 -4344.

179 *In a letter to Edward Livingston*: Letter from Thomas Jefferson to Edward Livingston, November 1, 1801, available at https://founders.archives.gov/documents /Jefferson/01-35-02-0451.

180 *In a string of letters in 1807*: Jefferson's correspondence with George Hay, the United States District Attorney for Virginia throughout the Burr trial, is available at www.loc.gov/resource/mtj1.038_0446_0446/?st=text. His requests for trial testimony can be found in his letter to Hay of May 26, 1807.

180 *"to have it denied to be law"*: Letter from Thomas Jefferson to George Hay, June 2, 1807.

180 *He personally interviewed a witness*: Letter from Thomas Jefferson to George Hay, May 20, 1807.

180 *Bruce A. Green and Rebecca Roiphe note*: Bruce A. Green and Rebecca Roiphe, "Can the President Control the Department of Justice?" *Alabama Law Review* 70 (2018): 13, https://papers.ssrn.com/sol3/papers.cfm?abstract_id=3126856.

180 *Attorney General William Wirt actually wrote a legal opinion*: William Wirt, "Power of President to Discontinue a Suit," 2 Op. Att'y Gen. 53, July 27, 1827.

181 *followed up on Wirt's opinion*: Roger Taney, "Jewels of the Princess of Orange," 2 Op. Att'y Gen. 482, December 28, 1831.

182 *transferred them there to face trial by military commission*: "President Discusses Creation of Military Commissions to Try Suspected Terrorists," Bush White House Archive, September 6, 2006, available at https://georgewbush-whitehouse .archives.gov/news/releases/2006/09/20060906-3.html.

182 *"It's your call. You're the attorney general"*: Daniel Klaidman, *Kill or Capture: The War on Terror and the Soul of the Obama Presidency* (New York: Houghton Mifflin Harcourt, 2012), 149.

182 *Obama acquiesced*: For an account of the collapse of the plan to close the detention facility, see Peter Finn and Anne E. Kornblut, "Guantanamo Bay: Why Obama Hasn't Fulfilled His Promise to Close the Facility," *Washington Post,*

April 23, 2011, www.washingtonpost.com/world/guantanamo-bay-how-the
-white-house-lost-the-fight-to-close-it/2011/04/14/AFtxR5XE_print.html.

183 *President Franklin Delano Roosevelt personally ordered*: Goldsmith, *The Terror
Presidency*, 49–52.

183 *the administration negotiated a spy swap with Moscow*: White House Chief of Staff
Rahm Emanuel told PBS *NewsHour* that the president was fully briefed on and
endorsed the swap. See Basil Katz, "U.S. and Russia to Swap Spies After 10 Plead
Guilty," Reuters, July 7, 2010, www.reuters.com/article/us-russia-usa-spy/u-s-and
-russia-to-swap-spies-after-10-plead-guilty-idUSTRE66618Y20100708.

183 *While the Paul Manafort jury was deliberating*: Katelyn Polantz, Dan Berman,
Marshall Cohen, Liz Stark, and Kara Scannell, "Manafort Jury to Resume Delib-
erations Monday; Trump Calls Trial 'Very Sad,'" CNN, August 18, 2018, www
.cnn.com/2018/08/17/politics/paul-manafort-trial-friday/index.html; see also
Mueller report, Vol. II, 122–28.

184 *famously commented on the guilt of Charles Manson*: Robert B. Semple, Jr., "Nixon
Calls Manson Guilty, Later Withdraws Remark," *New York Times*, August 4,
1970, www.nytimes.com/1970/08/04/archives/nixon-calls-manson-guilty-later
-withdraws-remark-refers-to-coast.html.

184 *public remarks that seemingly exonerated*: Matt Apuzzo and Michael S. Schmidt,
"Obama's Comments About Clinton's Emails Rankle Some in the F.B.I.," *New
York Times*, October 16, 2015, www.nytimes.com/2015/10/17/us/politics/obamas
-comments-on-clinton-emails-collide-with-fbi-inquiry.html.

184 *public comments about Khalid Sheikh Mohammed's execution*: Josh Gerstein,
"Obama on Terror Trials: KSM Will Die," *Politico*, November 18, 2009, www
.politico.com/story/2009/11/obama-on-terror-trials-ksm-will-die-029661.

184 *prompted litigation over whether*: Joint Defense Motion to Dismiss for Unlawful
Influence, U.S. v. Khalid Sheikh Mohammed et al., AE 31, May 11, 2012, avail-
able at https://assets.documentcloud.org/documents/5782188/2012-05-11
-AE031-MAH-AAA-RBS-Joint-Defense.pdf.

184 *CIA pressure the FBI*: For a contemporary press account of the so-called smoking gun tape, see John M. Crewdson, "Nixon Ordered That the F.B.I. Be Told:
'Don't Go Any Further into This Case,'" *New York Times*, August 6, 1974, ny
times.com/1974/08/06/archives/nixon-ordered-that-the-fbi-be-told-dont-go
-any-further-into-this.html.

184 *demanded IRS investigations of people he perceived*: See, for example, Jack Nel-
son, "Nixon Targeted the Times, Tapes Show," *Los Angeles Times*, March 22,
1997, www.latimes.com/archives/la-xpm-1997-03-22-mn-40969-story.html. More
generally, see "Intelligence Activities and the Rights of Americans" (Church
Committee Report), Final Report of the Senate Select Committee to Study Governmental Operations with Respect to Intelligence Activities, Book II, April 26,
1976, pp. 94–95, www.intelligence.senate.gov/sites/default/files/94755_II
.pdf.

184 *political spying on domestic foes*: For a history of domestic spying by U.S. intelligence agencies under successive presidential administrations, see the Church Committee Report. See also Barton J. Bernstein, "The Road to Watergate and Beyond: The Growth and Abuse of Executive Authority Since 1940," *Law and Contemporary Problems* 40 (Spring 1976): 58–86.

184 *Charles A. Lindbergh and the New York office of the America First Committee*: See Justus D. Doenecke, "FDR's Sorry Domestic Spying Record," *Daily Beast*, April 14, 2017, www.thedailybeast.com/fdrs-sorry-domestic-spying-record. For spying against supporters of Lindbergh and the America First Committee, see Church Committee Report, 9, 33.

184 *Martin Luther King, Jr.*: See Bernstein, "The Road to Watergate and Beyond," 71–72; Church Committee Report, 11–12, 219–24.

184 *Mississippi Freedom Democratic Party*: See Bernstein, "The Road to Watergate and Beyond," 74; Church Committee Report, 234. See also Dallek, *Flawed Giant*, 162.

184 *members of Barry Goldwater's staff*: See Bernstein, "The Road to Watergate and Beyond," 74; Church Committee Report, 10, 227–28.

185 *"general intelligence information"*: See Church Committee Report, 25. See also J. Edgar Hoover, Confidential Memoranda, August 24, 1936, and August 25, 1936, both available at www.personal.psu.edu/dmc166/FDR%20Aug%201936%20 memos.pdf.

185 *Get Hoffa Squad*: For a history of the relationship between Attorney General Kennedy and Hoffa, including the activities of the "Get Hoffa Squad," see James Neff, *Vendetta: Bobby Kennedy Versus Jimmy Hoffa* (New York: Little, Brown, 2015).

186 *Most law enforcement took place at the hands*: Sara Sun Beale, "Federalizing Crime: Assessing the Impact on the Federal Courts," *Annals of the American Academy of Political and Social Science* 543 (January 1996): 40.

186 *private actions brought by*: For a history of private prosecutions in the early republic, see Robert M. Ireland, "Privately Funded Prosecution of Crime in the Nineteenth-Century United States," *American Journal of Legal History* 39, no. 1 (January 1995): 43–58. See also Allen Steinberg, "'The Spirit of Litigation': Private Prosecution and Criminal Justice in Nineteenth Century Philadelphia," *Journal of Social History* 20 (Winter 1986): 231–39.

186 *related to revenue crimes and slave catching*: Daniel Richman, "Partisan Politics and Federal Law Enforcement: The Promise and Corruption of Reconstruction," *Lawfare*, July 22, 2019, www.lawfareblog.com/partisan-politics-and-federal -law-enforcement-promise-and-corruption-reconstruction.

186 *no federal law enforcement agency*: See Daniel Richman, "The Past, Present, and Future of Violent Crime Federalism," *Crime and Justice* 34, no. 1 (2006): 384.

186 *created in the immediate aftermath*: Norman Ansley, "The United States Secret

Service—an Administrative History," *Journal of Criminal Law and Criminology* 47 (1956): 94, https://scholarlycommons.law.northwestern.edu/cgi/viewcontent.cgi ?article=4472&context=jclc.

186 *Only during Reconstruction*: Green and Roiphe, "Can the President Control the Department of Justice?" 49.

187 *The idea, write Green and Roiphe, was that*: Green and Roiphe, "Can the President Control the Department of Justice?" 51–52.

188 *Trump told a radio talk show*: "President Donald Trump to Larry O'Connor: I'm Very Unhappy the Justice Department Isn't Going After Hillary Clinton," WMAL, November 3, 2017, www.wmal.com/2017/11/03/listen-president-donald -trump-to-larry-oconnor-im-very-unhappy-the-justice-department-isnt-going-after -hillary-clinton/.

189 *Trump declared that it would be "appropriate" for him to ask*: Eliana Johnson, Darren Samuelsohn, Andrew Restuccia, and Daniel Lippman, "Trump: Discussing a Biden Probe with Barr Would Be 'Appropriate,'" *Politico*, May 11, 2019, www .politico.com/story/2019/05/10/trump-biden-ukraine-barr 1317601.

189 *for their private dinner at the White House and sought a pledge of his loyalty*: Comey, *A Higher Loyalty*, 233–44. See also Mueller report, Vol. II, 33–36.

189 *describes a series of private interactions*: For Trump lobbying Comey to drop the Flynn investigation, see Mueller report, Vol. II, 39–41. For Trump lobbying Comey to announce that he was not under investigation, see Mueller report, Vol. II, 57–59. For Comey's perception that Trump was trying to establish a patronage relationship with him, see Mueller report, Vol. II, 34. The Mueller report's description of the credibility of Comey's account of the loyalty oath dinner, and the president's denial of that account, appears in Vol. II, 35–36.

189 *public fury when Sessions recused himself*: Michael S. Schmidt and Julie Hirschfeld Davis, "Trump Asked Sessions to Retain Control of Russia Inquiry After His Recusal," *New York Times*, May 29, 2018, www.nytimes.com/2018/05/29/us /politics/trump-sessions-obstruction.html.

189 *only a shadow of his private rage*: An account of the extent of Trump's private expression of anger regarding the recusal is included in the Mueller report, Vol. II, 51, 78, 95.

189 *Trump pressured both Rosenstein*: See, for example, Mazzetti, Haberman, Fandos, and Schmidt, "Intimidation, Pressure and Humiliation: Inside Trump's Two-Year War on the Investigations Encircling Him." The story reports that Trump "repeatedly leaned on administration officials on behalf of the lawmakers— urging Mr. Rosenstein and other law enforcement leaders to flout procedure and share sensitive materials about the open case with Congress."

189 *Andrew McCabe*: Carol E. Lee, "Trump's Gripes Against McCabe Included Wife's Politics, Comey's Plane Ride Home," NBC News, January 29, 2018, www.nbcnews.com/politics/donald-trump/trump-s-gripes-against-mccabe -included-wife-s-politics-comey-n842161.

189 *he directed McGahn to order the firing of Special Counsel Robert Mueller*: Michael S. Schmidt and Maggie Haberman, "Trump Ordered Mueller Fired, but Backed Off When White House Counsel Threatened to Quit," *New York Times*, January 25, 2018, nytimes.com/2018/01/25/us/politics/trump-mueller-special-counsel -russia.html. See also Mueller report, Vol. II, 85.

190 *asked Whitaker to exercise control over the Southern District*: Mazzetti, Haberman, Fandos, and Schmidt, "Intimidation, Pressure and Humiliation: Inside Trump's Two-Year War on the Investigations Encircling Him."

190 *congressional Republicans who deployed their committees*: See, for example, Karoun Demirjian, "Devin Nunes, Targeting Mueller and the FBI, Alarms Democrats and Some Republicans with His Tactics," *Washington Post*, December 31, 2017, www.washingtonpost.com/powerpost/devin-nunes-targeting-mueller-and -the-fbi-alarms-democrats-and-some-republicans-with-his-tactics/2017/12/30 /b8181ebc-eb02-11e7-9f92-10a2203f6c8d_story.html.

190 *threaten to impeach Rosenstein over their demands for documents*: Kyle Cheney and Rachel Bade, "House Conservatives Threaten Rosenstein Impeachment Vote," *Politico*, September 25, 2018, www.politico.com/story/2018/09/25/congress -rosenstein-impeach-840110.

190 *Trump himself encouraged those demands*: See, for example, Trump's tweet, "If the FBI or DOJ was infiltrating a campaign for the benefit of another campaign, that is a really big deal. Only the release or review of documents that the House Intel-ligence Committee (also, Senate Judiciary) is asking for can give the conclusive answers. Drain the Swamp!" Donald J. Trump, Twitter, May 19, 2018, https:// twitter.com/realDonaldTrump/status/997951982467014656.

191 *Trump said that Holder had protected Obama*: Mueller report, Vol. II, 51.

191 *telling The New York Times*: "Excerpts from Trump's Interview with The Times."

192 *Bannon turned out to be right*: For Bannon's comment that Trump can't fire the FBI, see Mueller report, Vol. II, 64.

192 *mostly failed*: For one example, see Mueller report, Vol. II, 107–11: "From sum-mer 2017 through 2018, the President attempted to have Attorney General Ses-sions reverse his recusal, take control of the Special Counsel's investigation, and order an investigation of Hillary Clinton."

192 *the Justice Department has released unprecedented quantities*: See, for example, Charlie Savage, "Carter Page FISA Documents Are Released by Justice De-partment," *New York Times*, July 21, 2018, www.nytimes.com/2018/07/21/us /politics/carter-page-fisa.html.

192 *Political considerations have certainly influenced the FBI's handling*: See, for exam-ple, Matt Zapotosky, "FBI Agent Peter Strzok Fired Over Anti-Trump Texts," *Washington Post*, August 13, 2018, www.washingtonpost.com/world/national -security/fbi-agent-peter-strzok-fired-over-anti-trump-texts/2018/08/13 /be98f84c-8e8b-11e8-b769-e3fff17f0689_story.html.

8. "A TOTAL POLITICAL WITCH HUNT!": Investigating the President

196 *Barr had said that the Mueller*: Letter from Attorney General William Barr to House and Senate judiciary committee leaders, March 24, 2019, available at www.documentcloud.org/documents/5779688-AG-March-24-2019-Letter-to -House-and-Senate.html.

196 *At the press conference, Barr went further*: See "Attorney General William P. Barr Delivers Remarks on the Release of the Report on the Investigation into Russian Interference in the 2016 Presidential Election," Department of Justice, April 18, 2019, www.justice.gov/opa/speech/attorney-general-william-p-barr-delivers -remarks-release-report-investigation-russian.

197 *special counsel had not rendered a judgment*: Mueller report, Vol. II, 1–2.

198 *published the document that became*: Ken Bensinger, Miriam Elder, and Mark Schoofs, "These Reports Allege Trump Has Deep Ties to Russia," *BuzzFeed News*, January 10, 2017, www.buzzfeednews.com/article/kenbensinger/these -reports-allege-trump-has-deep-ties-to-russia.

198 *earlier CNN reporting*: Evan Perez, Jim Sciutto, Jake Tapper, and Carl Bernstein, "Intel Chiefs Presented Trump with Claims of Russian Efforts to Compromise Him," CNN, January 10, 2017 (updated January 12, 2017), www.cnn.com/2017 /01/10/politics/donald trump-intelligence-report-russia/index.html.

198 *"FAKE NEWS—A TOTAL POLITICAL WITCH HUNT!"*: Donald J. Trump, Twitter, January 10, 2017, https://twitter.com/realDonaldTrump/status/81899 0655418617856.

198 *In the wake of the briefing*: Comey, *A Higher Loyalty*, 224–25.

198 *did in a Moscow hotel in 2013*: The allegation can be found on page 2 of the so-called Steele dossier, published by *BuzzFeed* and available at https://assets .documentcloud.org/documents/3259984/Trump-Intelligence-Allegations .pdf#page=2.

198 *Comey later wrote*: Comey, *A Higher Loyalty*, 223–24.

199 *the FBI already had begun electronic surveillance*: Savage, "Carter Page FISA Documents Are Released by Justice Department."

199 *there was an active investigation*: Sadie Gurman, Eric Tucker, and Jeff Horwitz, "Special Counsel's Russia Investigation Includes Former Trump Campaign Chair," Associated Press, June 2, 2017, www.pbs.org/newshour/politics/ap-report-special -counsels-russia-investigation-includes-former-trump-campaign-chair.

199 *the bureau would interview another*: See Statement of the Offense, U.S. v. George Papadopoulos, No. 17-cr-182 (D.D.C., 2017), available at www.justice.gov/file /1007346/download.

199 *he would later plead guilty*: Flynn would later be charged with making false statements to investigators during the January 24, 2017, interview with FBI agents. See Information, U.S. v. Michael T. Flynn, No. 17-232 (D.D.C., 2017), available at www.justice.gov/file/1015026/download.

199 *acknowledged publicly to Congress*: "Full transcript: FBI Director James Comey Testifies on Russian Interference in 2016 Election."

199 *a fact that Trump repeatedly pressured Comey to make public*: Comey, *A Higher Loyalty*, 257–61. See also Mueller report, Vol. II, 57–61.

199 *the FBI had opened both a criminal investigation of possible presidential obstruction of justice*: Devlin Barrett, Adam Entous, Ellen Nakashima, and Sari Horwitz, "Special Counsel Is Investigating Trump for Possible Obstruction of Justice, Officials Say," *Washington Post*, June 14, 2017, www.washingtonpost.com /world/national-security/special-counsel-is-investigating-trump-for-possible -obstruction-of-justice/2017/06/14/9ce02506-5131-11e7-b064-828ba60fbb98 _story.html.

199 *a counterintelligence investigation of Trump*: Adam Goldman, Michael S. Schmidt, and Nicholas Fandos, "F.B.I. Opened Inquiry into Whether Trump Was Secretly Working on Behalf of Russia," *New York Times*, January 11, 2019, www.nytimes .com/2019/01/11/us/politics/fbi-trump-russia-inquiry.html.

200 *Mueller was appointed as special counsel*: See Order No. 3915-2017, "Appointment of Special Counsel to Investigate Russian Interference with the 2016 Presidential Election and Related Matters," Department of Justice, May 17, 2017, www .justice.gov/opa/press-release/file/967231/download. For additional information forming the predicate of the obstruction investigation subsequent to Mueller's appointment, see Mueller report, Vol. II, 12.

200 *"This is the single greatest witch hunt of a politician"*: Donald J. Trump, Twitter, May 18, 2017, https://twitter.com/realDonaldTrump/status/865173176854204416.

201 *as Nixon did before Trump*: Deanna Paul, "Nixon, Like Trump, Decried Investigations in His State of the Union Address. Months Later, He Resigned," *Washington Post*, February 7, 2019, www.washingtonpost.com/history/2019/02/07 /nixon-like-trump-decried-investigations-his-state-union-address-months -later-he-resigned/.

202 *the long-standing position of the executive branch is that a sitting president*: See "Amenability of the President, Vice President and Other Civil Officers to Federal Criminal Prosecution While in Office," Office of Legal Counsel, September 24, 1973. See also "A Sitting President's Amenability to Indictment and Criminal Prosecution," Office of Legal Counsel, October 16, 2000.

203 *culminated in Israel's attorney general recommending his criminal indictment*: David M. Halbfinger and Isabel Kershner, "Netanyahu Indictment Closer as Israeli Prosecutor Seeks Charges," *New York Times*, February 28, 2019, www.nytimes .com/2019/02/28/world/middleeast/benjamin-netanyahu-indicted.html.

205 *Federal criminal law was scant*: Beale, "Federalizing Crime: Assessing the Impact on the Federal Courts," 40.

205 *An intercepted letter*: Chernow, *Washington: A Life*, 732–34.

206 *"Exercising oversight authority"*: Matthew Waxman, "Remembering St. Clair's Defeat," *Lawfare*, November 4, 2018, www.lawfareblog.com/remembering-st -clairs-defeat.

206 *Congress believed that Adams was lying*: McCullough, *John Adams*, 493–98.

206 *Secretary of War George W. Crawford*: See Gerald S. Greenberg, "Ohioans vs. Georgians: The Galphin Claim, Zachary Taylor's Death, and the Congressional Adjournment Vote of 1850," *Georgia Historical Quarterly* 74, no. 4 (1990): 587–98, available at www.jstor.org/stable/40582231.

207 *the Whiskey Ring*: Chernow, *Grant*, 796–99.

207 *Grant pledged his cooperation*: Chernow, *Grant*, 799.

207 *"Let no guilty man escape"*: Ronald C. White, *American Ulysses: A Life of Ulysses S. Grant* (New York: Random House, 2016), 562.

208 *netting 350 indictments*: White, *American Ulysses*, 562.

208 *Grant even grudgingly allowed*: Chernow, *Grant*, 803–806.

208 *and moved to indict Babcock*: Chernow, *Grant*, 802–804.

208 *eventually acquitted with help from Grant's own testimony*: White, *American Ulysses*, 564.

208 *Grant demanded that those reports be publicly rebutted*: Chernow, *Grant*, 804.

209 *advise U.S. attorneys in the Midwest*: Chernow, *Grant*, 804–805.

209 *"withdrawal of your confidence & official support"*: Chernow, *Grant*, 808.

209 *involved a kickback scheme*: Dean, *Warren G. Harding*, 155–58.

209 *he sought specific legislation*: For a detailed account of the Teapot Dome special counsels, see Leslie E. Bennett, "One Lesson from History: Appointment of Special Counsel and the Investigation of the Teapot Dome Scandal," 1999, Brookings Institution, available at http://academic.brooklyn.cuny.edu/history/johnson/teapotdome.htm.

210 *Fall was convicted for receiving the bribes*: Dean, *Warren G. Harding*, 160.

210 *Harry Daugherty, was never charged with*: Dean, *Warren G. Harding*, 159–60.

210 *senior White House staff*: "Watergate Special Prosecution Force: Final Report," June 1977, 4–5.

210 *was forced to step down*: James M. Naughton, "Agnew Quits Vice Presidency and Admits Tax Evasion in '67; Nixon Consults on Successor," *New York Times*, October 10, 1973, http://movies2.nytimes.com/learning/general/onthisday/big/1010.html. For an account of the investigation into Agnew, see the 2018 MSNBC podcast *Bagman*, available at www.msnbc.com/bagman.

211 *very large iceberg of spying scandals*: See, for example, the Church Committee Report.

211 *refused to carry out the order to fire Cox*: "Watergate Special Prosecution Force: Final Report," 49.

211 *get the FBI to back off*: A transcript of the White House recording of this conversation is archived at the Nixon Presidential Library, with the relevant line at 16. Available at www.nixonlibrary.gov/sites/default/files/forresearchers/find/tapes/watergate/trial/exhibit_01.pdf#page=9.

211 *Nixon also sought to obstruct the separate investigation*: Rachel Maddow, "Turn It Off," *Bagman*, episode 4, MSNBC, November 12, 2018, www.nbcnews.com/msnbc/maddow-bag-man-podcast/transcript-episode-4-turn-it-n935286.

211 *Leon Jaworski*: "Watergate Special Prosecution Force: Final Report," 49.

211 *law professor Philip Heymann, who worked with Cox*: Philip B. Heymann, "The Art of the Cover Up," *Lawfare Research Paper Series*, November 13, 2017, 8, https://assets.documentcloud.org/documents/4196900/Heymann-Final.pdf.

213 *The court explained that*: United States v. Nixon, 418 U.S. 683 (1974).

215 *"the imperial presidency"*: See generally Schlesinger, *The Imperial Presidency*.

215 *"independent counsel" law*: See 28 U.S. Code §§ 591–99.

215 *created an automatic trigger*: 28 U.S. Code § 591.

215 *power to name the prosecutor*: 28 U.S. Code § 593.

215 *"full power and independent authority"*: 28 U.S. Code § 594.

215 *limited the circumstances*: 28 U.S. Code § 596(a).

215 *pardoned a group of Iran-Contra figures*: See Lawrence E. Walsh, "Final Report of the Independent Counsel for Iran/Contra Matters," Part 2, 48. Available at https://archive.org/details/WalshReport/page/n73.

216 *Reagan administration sought to have*: Morrison v. Olson, 487 U.S. 654 (1988).

216 *it concurrently appointed him as a special prosecutor under the old regulatory system*: Walsh report, Part 2, 32. Available at https://archive.org/details/WalshReport/page/n57.

216 *signed reauthorizations in 1983 and 1987, and in 1994*: Benjamin J. Priester, Paul G. Rozelle, and Mirah A. Horowitz, "The Independent Counsel Statute: A Legal History," *Law and Contemporary Problems* 62, no. 1 (Winter 1999): 11, available at https://scholarship.law.duke.edu/cgi/viewcontent.cgi?article=1117&context=lcp.

216 *In a* Washington Post *op-ed written in 1998*: Benjamin Wittes, "If Starr's So Bad, Fire Him," *Washington Post*, June 16, 1998, www.washingtonpost.com/archive/opinions/1998/06/16/if-starrs-so-bad-fire-him/.

217 *granting limited immunity*: See Walsh report, Part 2, 32–34. Available at https://archive.org/details/WalshReport/page/n57.

217 *to throw out convictions*: U.S. v. Oliver L. North, 910 F.2d 843 (D.C. Circuit, 1990); U.S. v. John M. Poindexter, 951 F.2d 369 (D.C. Circuit, 1992).

218 *The Lewinsky scandal broke in January 1998*: For an excellent history of this episode, see Michael Isikoff, *Uncovering Clinton: A Reporter's Story* (New York: Crown, 1999).

218 *until the Starr Report arrived in September 1998*: "Communication from Kenneth W. Starr, Independent Counsel Transmitting a Referral to the United States House of Representatives Filed in Conformity with the Requirements of Title 28, United States Code, Section 595(c)" ("The Starr Report"), Government Publishing Office, September 11, 1998, www.govinfo.gov/content/pkg/GPO-CDOC-106sdoc3/pdf/GPO-CDOC-106sdoc3-2.pdf.

219 *the current special counsel regulations*: 28 C.F.R. § 600 et seq.

220 *it would be improper*: Mueller report, Vol. II, 2.

221 *Charles Black, Jr., proved this point in three pithy sentences*: Charles L. Black, Jr., *Impeachment: A Handbook* (New Haven, CT: Yale University Press, 1998), 33.

223 *pressured his replacement Whitaker to get control over the investigation*: Mazzetti,

Haberman, Fandos, and Schmidt, "Intimidation, Pressure and Humiliation: Inside Trump's Two-Year War on the Investigations Encircling Him."

223 *Mueller report documents Trump's overtures*: Mueller report, Vol. II, 120–56.

223 *Manafort breached his plea agreement*: Mueller report, Vol. II, 127; Joint Status Report, U.S. v. Paul Manafort (D.D.C., November 26, 2018), available at https://assets.documentcloud.org/documents/5280674/D-D-C-1-17-Cr-00201-ABJ-455-0.pdf.

224 *openly admitting that both*: Trump told Lester Holt two days after dismissing James Comey that "regardless of recommendation I was going to fire Comey, knowing there was no good time to do it. And in fact when I decided to just do it, I said to myself, I said you know, this Russia thing with Trump and Russia is a made-up story." Partial transcript available at https://assets.documentcloud.org/documents/3718523/NBC-News-Exclusive-Interview-With-Donald-Trump.pdf.

9. "Without deliberation . . . or appreciation of facts": The Conduct of Foreign Affairs

228 *Recep Tayyip Erdoğan had reached Trump by phone*: Karen DeYoung, Missy Ryan, Josh Dawsey, and Greg Jaffe, "A Tumultuous Week Began with a Phone Call Between Trump and the Turkish President," *Washington Post*, December 21, 2018, www.washingtonpost.com/world/national-security/a-tumultuous-week-began-with-a-phone-call-between-trump-and-the-turkish-president/2018/12/21/8f49b562-0542-11e9-9122-82e98f91ee6f_story.html.

228 *"defeated ISIS in Syria, my only reason for being there"*: Donald J. Trump, Twitter, December 19, 2018, https://twitter.com/realDonaldTrump/status/1075397797929775105.

228 *"time to bring our great young people home"*: Donald J. Trump, Twitter, December 19, 2018, https://twitter.com/realDonaldTrump/status/1075528854402256896.

228 *said France's European affairs minister Nathalie Loiseau*: "Trump's Syria Withdrawal Announcement Criticized by Allies, Praised by Putin," Radio Free Europe/Radio Liberty, December 20, 2018, www.rferl.org/a/trump-syria-troop-pullout-islamic-state-russia-turkey-iran/29666375.html.

228 *British defense official shared*: The member of Parliament and British defense ministry official Tobias Ellwood tweeted, "I strongly disagree. It has morphed into other forms of extremism and the threat is very much alive." Tobias Ellwood, Twitter, December 19, 2018, https://twitter.com/Tobias_Ellwood/status/1075422159244324865.

228 *Kurdish forces, whom Turkey*: Zeina Karam and Sarah El Deeb, "Trump Move to Pull US Troops from Syria Opens Way to Turmoil," Associated Press, December 20, 2018, www.apnews.com/96768dcc51fd47f8997e0dd00371048b.

229 *Lindsey Graham fretted*: Steven T. Dennis, "Trump's Syria Decision 'Rattled the World,' Graham Says," *Bloomberg*, December 20, 2018, www.bloomberg

.com/news/articles/2018-12-20/trump-s-syria-decision-rattled-the-world-gop
-s-graham-says.

229 *Senator Marco Rubio put it*: David Brown, Gregory Hellman, and Burgess Everett,
"Republicans Rip Trump's Surprise Syria Withdrawal in Meeting with Pence,"
Politico, December 19, 2018, www.politico.com/story/2018/12/19/trump-us
-troops-in-syria-1068734.

229 *Republican-controlled Senate even passed a measure*: See roll call vote on Senate
Amendment 65 to S.1, 116th Congress, 1st Session, February 4, 2019, available at
https://assets.documentcloud.org/documents/5783832/U-S-Senate-U-S-Senate
-Roll-Call-Votes-116th.pdf.

229 *only prominent Republican who spoke up in favor*: Devan Cole, "Rand Paul: 'I'm
Very Proud of the President' for Syria Withdrawal Decision," CNN, December
23, 2018, www.cnn.com/2018/12/23/politics/rand-paul-syria-withdraw-cnntv
/index.html.

229 *were Russian president Putin and Turkish strongman Erdoğan*: See "Putin Warns of
Risk of Nuclear War, Talks Up Russian Economy in Annual Press Conference,"
Radio Free Europe/Radio Liberty, December 20, 2018, www.rferl.org/a/putin
-annual-news-conference-questions-journalists/29666377.html. Erdoğan, for
his part, wrote an op-ed endorsing Trump's position. See Recep Tayyip Erdoğan,
"Trump Is Right on Syria; Turkey Can Get the Job Done," *New York Times*, January 7, 2019, www.nytimes.com/2019/01/07/opinion/erdogan-turkey-syria
.html.

229 *a terse letter of resignation*: Letter from James Mattis to Donald Trump, December 20, 2018, available at https://assets.documentcloud.org/documents
/5656059/Mattis.pdf.

229 *announced that he was hastening his planned departure*: Rukmini Callimachi and
Eric Schmitt, "Splitting with Trump over Syria, American Leading ISIS Fight
Steps Down," *New York Times*, December 22, 2018, www.nytimes.com/2018/12
/22/world/brett-mcgurk-isis-resign.html.

229 *later criticizing the president's "snap decision"*: Brett McGurk, "Trump Said He
Beat ISIS. Instead, He's Giving It New Life," *Washington Post*, January 18, 2019,
www.washingtonpost.com/outlook/trump-said-hed-stay-in-syria-to-beat
-isis-instead-hes-giving-it-new-life/2019/01/17/a25a00cc-19cd-11e9-8813
-cb9dec761e73_story.html.

229 *personal attacks against Mattis and McGurk*: On Mattis, Trump tweeted, "When
President Obama ingloriously fired Jim Mattis, I gave him a second chance. Some
thought I shouldn't, I thought I should. Interesting relationship—but I also gave
all of the resources that he never really had. Allies are very important—but not
when they take advantage of U.S." Donald J. Trump, Twitter, December 22,
2018, https://twitter.com/realDonaldTrump/status/1076663817831153664.
On McGurk, Trump tweeted, "Brett McGurk, who I do not know, was appointed
by President Obama in 2015. Was supposed to leave in February but he just

resigned prior to leaving. Grandstander? The Fake News is making such a big deal about this nothing event!" Donald J. Trump, Twitter, December 22, 2018, https://twitter.com/realDonaldTrump/status/1076655729820471296.

230 *he tweeted indignantly*: Donald J. Trump, Twitter, December 20, 2018, https://twitter.com/realDonaldTrump/status/1075718191253504001.

230 *would "utterly destroy ISIS"*: See, for example, Jenna Johnson and Jose A. DelReal, "Trump Vows to 'Utterly Destroy ISIS'—but He Won't Say How," *Washington Post*, September 24, 2016, www.washingtonpost.com/politics/trump-vows-to-utterly-destroy-isis--but-he-wont-say-how/2016/09/24/911c6a74-7ffc-11e6-8d0c-fb6c00c90481_story.html.

230 *avoid overseas deployments*: Steve Holland, "Trump Lays Out Non-Interventionist U.S. Military Policy," Reuters, December 6, 2016, www.reuters.com/article/us-usa-trump-military/trump-lays-out-non-interventionist-u-s-military-policy-idUSKBN13W06L.

230 *commitments in Afghanistan and Syria and Iraq*: For an example of Trump's promise to get out of Afghanistan, see Daniella Díaz, "A History of Trump's Thoughts on Afghanistan," CNN, August 21, 2017, www.cnn.com/2017/08/21/politics/history-president-trump-remarks-afghanistan-tweets/index.html. For an example of his skepticism of deep engagement in Syria and Iraq, see Ben Jacobs, "The Donald Trump Doctrine: 'Assad Is Bad' but US Must Stop 'Nation-Building,'" *Guardian*, October 13, 2015, www.theguardian.com/us-news/2015/oct/13/donald-trump-foreign-policy-doctrine-nation-building. For Trump's underlying attitudes on the Iraq conflict, see "Transcript: Donald Trump Expounds on His Foreign Policy Views," *New York Times*, March 26, 2016, www.nytimes.com/2016/03/27/us/politics/donald-trump-transcript.html.

230 *sending precisely the opposite signals*: His own national security adviser at the time, John Bolton, had two months earlier declared that U.S. forces would stay in place as long as Iranian forces and their proxies remained in Syria. See Paul Sonne and Missy Ryan, "Bolton: U.S. Forces Will Stay in Syria Until Iran and Its Proxies Depart," *Washington Post*, September 24, 2018, www.washingtonpost.com/world/national-security/bolton-us-forces-will-stay-in-syria-until-iran-and-its-proxies-depart/2018/09/24/be389eb8-c020-11e8-92f2-ac26fda68341_story.html. And McGurk had doubled down days before the announcement, saying, "Americans will remain on the ground after the physical defeat of the caliphate, until we have the pieces in place to ensure that that defeat is enduring." See Press Briefing, Department of State, December 11, 2018, www.state.gov/briefings/department-press-briefing-december-11-2018/.

231 *At the Helsinki summit*: Julie Hirschfeld Davis, "Trump, at Putin's Side, Questions U.S. Intelligence on 2016 Election," *New York Times*, July 16, 2018, www.nytimes.com/2018/07/16/world/europe/trump-putin-election-intelligence.html.

232 *"fire and fury"*: Peter Baker and Choe Sang-Hun, "Trump Threatens 'Fire and

Fury' Against North Korea If It Endangers U.S.," *New York Times*, August 8, 2017, www.nytimes.com/2017/08/08/world/asia/north-korea-un-sanctions-nuclear -missile-united-nations.html.

232 *chummy summits with Kim Jong Un in Singapore*: See, for example, Mark Landler, "The Trump-Kim Summit Was Unprecedented, but the Statement Was Vague," *New York Times*, June 12, 2018, www.nytimes.com/2018/06/12/world/asia /north-korea-summit.html.

232 *"love letters"*: Philip Rucker and Josh Dawsey, "'We Fell in Love': Trump and Kim Shower Praise, Stroke Egos on Path to Nuclear Negotiations," *Washington Post*, February 25, 2019, www.washingtonpost.com/politics/we-fell-in-love-trump -and-kim-shower-praise-stroke-egos-on-path-to-nuclear-negotiations/2019/02 /24/46875188-3777-11e9-854a-7a14d7fec96a_story.html.

232 *abandon the NATO alliance*: Carol Morello and Adam Taylor, "Trump Says U.S. Won't Rush to Defend NATO Countries If They Don't Spend More on Military," *Washington Post*, July 21, 2016, www.washingtonpost.com/world /national-security/trump-says-us-wont-rush-to-defend-nato-countries-if -they-dont-spend-more-on-military/2016/07/21/76c48430-4f51-11e6-a7d8 -13d06b37f256_story.html.

232 *allies in Asia*: Mark Landler, "Trump Orders Pentagon to Consider Reduc- ing U.S. Forces in South Korea," *New York Times*, May 3, 2018, www.nytimes .com/2018/05/03/world/asia/trump-troops-south-korea.html.

232 *a law strengthening sanctions against Russia*: Peter Baker and Sophia Kishkovsky, "Trump Signs Russian Sanctions into Law, with Caveats," *New York Times*, August 2, 2017, www.nytimes.com/2017/08/02/world/europe/trump-russia -sanctions.html. See Public Law 115-44, available at www.govinfo.gov/content /pkg/PLAW-115publ44/pdf/PLAW-115publ44.pdf.

232 *gutting the foreign assistance budget*: See Marian L. Lawson, "Foreign Aid in the 115th Congress: A Legislative Wrap-Up in Brief," *Congressional Research Ser- vice*, January 11, 2019, https://fas.org/sgp/crs/row/R45458.pdf.

233 *makes her commander in chief*: U.S. Constitution, Article II, Section 2.

233 *to make treaties*: U.S. Constitution, Article II, Section 2.

233 *appoint ambassadors to other countries*: U.S. Constitution, Article II, Section 2.

233 *"receive Ambassadors and other public Ministers"*: U.S. Constitution, Article II, Section 2.

233 *a clause that is understood by some scholars*: Robert J. Delahunty and John C. Yoo, "The President's Constitutional Authority to Conduct Military Opera- tions Against Terrorist Organizations and the Nations That Harbor or Support Them," *Harvard Journal of Law & Public Policy* 25 (2002): 493. Write Delahunty and Yoo, "The centralization of authority in the President alone is particularly crucial in matters of national defense, war, and foreign policy, where a unitary executive can evaluate threats, consider policy choices, and mobilize military and diplomatic resources with a speed and energy that is far superior to any other

branch." See also Julian Mortenson, "Article II Vests Executive Power, Not the Royal Prerogative," *Columbia Law Review* 119 (2019).

234 *so-called executive agreements*: For an analysis of the modern use of executive agreements, see Curtis Bradley, Jack Goldsmith, and Oona A. Hathaway, "Executive Agreements: International Lawmaking Without Accountability?" *Lawfare*, January 9, 2019, www.lawfareblog.com/executive-agreements-international -lawmaking-without-accountability.

234 *move the embassy in Israel from Tel Aviv to Jerusalem*: Mark Landler, "Trump Recognizes Jerusalem as Israel's Capital and Orders U.S. Embassy to Move," *New York Times*, December 6, 2017, www.nytimes.com/2017/12/06/world /middleeast/trump-jerusalem-israel-capital.html.

234 *withdraw recognition of Venezuelan president*: "Statement from President Donald J. Trump Recognizing Venezuelan National Assembly President Juan Guaido as the Interim President of Venezuela," January 23, 2019, available at www .whitehouse.gov/briefings-statements/statement-president-donald-j-trump -recognizing-venezuelan-national-assembly-president-juan-guaido interim -president-venezuela/.

234 *wide authority over who can come into the United States*: See, for example, Immigration and Nationality Act, 8 U.S. Code, § 1182(f).

234 *designate foreign non-state groups as terrorist organizations*: 8 U.S. Code § 1189.

234 *impose criminal penalties on those who give "material support"*: 18 U.S. Code § 2339B.

234 *impose economic sanctions on countries and individuals*: See, for example, the International Emergency Economic Powers Act, 50 U.S. Code, Chapter 35.

234 *They give her the power to impose tariffs*: 19 U.S. Code § 1862.

234 *the power to declare national emergencies*: See the National Emergencies Act, 50 U.S. Code, Chapter 34. For an example of authority to take action pursuant to such a declaration, see 10 U.S. Code § 2808 concerning "construction authority in the event of a declaration of war or national emergency."

234 *"all necessary and appropriate force"*: Public Law 107-40, "Joint Resolution: To authorize the use of United States Armed Forces against those responsible for the recent attacks launched against the United States," September 18, 2001, 107th Cong., 1st Sess., available at www.govinfo.gov/content/pkg/PLAW -107publ40/pdf/PLAW-107publ40.pdf.

235 *Hamilton called "energy"*: Alexander Hamilton, *Federalist* 70.

235 *Arthur Schlesinger's famed work*: Schlesinger, *The Imperial Presidency*, 282–83.

235 *The Supreme Court famously declared*: U.S. v. Curtiss-Wright Export Corp., 299 U.S. 304 (1936).

237 *language of countless statutes*: For example, the major financial sanctions law gives the president broad powers, subject to regulations he promulgates, to "investigate, regulate, or prohibit" economic activity "to deal with any unusual and extraordinary threat" from outside the United States *"if the President declares a*

national emergency with respect to such threat" (emphasis added). See 50 U.S. Code §§ 1701–702. The law under which Trump imposed tariffs on steel and aluminum authorizes the president to impose such trade restrictions when the president "concurs" with the secretary of commerce that foreign imports threaten national security and requires that "if the President concurs, [he can] determine the nature and duration of the action that, in the judgment of the President, must be taken." See 19 U.S. Code § 1862.

237 *Dean Acheson gave a speech*: Dean Acheson, "Speech on the Far East," January 12, 1950, available at www.cia.gov/library/readingroom/docs/1950-01-12.pdf.

237 *This line excluded*: James I. Matray, "Dean Acheson's Press Club Speech Reexamined," *Journal of Conflict Studies* 22 (Spring 2002), available at https://journals .lib.unb.ca/index.php/jcs/article/view/366/578.

238 *if the president gets on the phone with his Mexican counterpart*: Philip Rucker, Joshua Partlow, and Nick Miroff, "After Testy Call with Trump over Border Wall, Mexican President Shelves Plan to Visit White House," *Washington Post*, February 24, 2018, www.washingtonpost.com/politics/after-testy-call-with -trump-over-border-wall-mexicos-president-shelves-plan-to-visit-white-house /2018/02/24/c7ffe9e8-199e-11e8-8b08-027a6ccb38eb_story.html.

238 *Neutrality Proclamation*: George Washington, "Neutrality of the United States in the War Involving Austria, Prussia, Sardinia, Great Britain, and the United Netherlands Against France," April 22, 1793, available at www.presidency .ucsb.edu/documents/proclamation-4-neutrality-the-united-states-the-war -involving-austria-prussia-sardinia.

239 *1823 State of the Union message to Congress*: James Monroe, "Seventh Annual Message," December 2, 1823, available at www.presidency.ucsb.edu/documents /seventh-annual-message-1.

239 *when the president sent a delegation to negotiate a treaty*: Both the Quasi-War with France in the 1790s and the War of 1812 ended not when presidents agreed to end them, but when negotiating delegations sent by those presidents reported back that they had struck deals. On the War of 1812, see Michael Beschloss, *Presidents of War* (New York: Crown, 2018), 89–91. On the Quasi-War, see McCullough, *John Adams*, 552.

240 *committed to shrinking the young navy*: Beschloss, *Presidents of War*, 9.

240 *Jefferson developed a loony scheme*: For Jefferson's ambitions to diminish U.S. naval capabilities, see Beschloss, *Presidents of War*, 8–9, 25–26.

240 *Even as tensions with Britain heated up*: For an account of the protracted negotiations and failures of military preparedness in the run-up to the War of 1812, see Beschloss, *Presidents of War*, chaps. 1 and 2, 7–63.

240 *The Mexican-American War was deliberately engineered by President James Polk*: For Polk's campaign promise to annex Texas and his engineering of war with Mexico, see Beschloss, *Presidents of War*, 103, 111–20.

241 *more than two months of intensive investigation and negotiation*: Beschloss, *Presidents of War*, chap. 8, "Maine Blown Up," 240–63.

241 *famous "madman theory"*: H. R. Haldeman recounted that Nixon said to him, "I call it the Madman Theory, Bob. I want the North Vietnamese to believe I've reached the point where I might do *anything* to stop the war. We'll just slip the word to them that, 'for God's sake, you know Nixon is obsessed about Communism. We can't restrain him when he's angry—and he has his hand on the nuclear button'—and Ho Chi Minh himself will be in Paris in two days begging for peace." H. R. Haldeman, *The Ends of Power* (New York: Times Books, 1978), 83. See also Garrett M. Graff, "The Madman and the Bomb," *Politico Magazine*, August 11, 2017, www.politico.com/magazine/story/2017/08/11/donald-trump-nuclear-weapons-richard-nixon-215478.

241 *summaries of the foreign policy actions*: A list of the Miller Center's resource pages for each president is available at https://millercenter.org/president. Each president has a dedicated web page for foreign affairs.

241 *"For most of American history"*: Michael Beschloss email to Benjamin Wittes, January 19, 2019.

242 *"We must as a nation be more unpredictable"*: "Transcript: Donald Trump's Foreign Policy Speech," *New York Times*, April 27, 2016, www.nytimes.com/2016/04/28/us/politics/transcript-trump-foreign-policy.html.

242 *tariffs on imported steel and aluminum*: Ana Swanson, "White House to Impose Metal Tariffs on E.U., Canada, and Mexico," *New York Times*, May 31, 2018, www.nytimes.com/2018/05/31/us/politics/trump-aluminum-steel-tariffs.html.

242 *threats to blow up NAFTA*: Katie Lobosco, "Trump's Threat to Override New NAFTA with Tariff on Mexican Cars Could Undermine Ratification," CNN, April 5, 2019, www.cnn.com/2019/04/05/politics/mexico-auto-tariffs-trump/index.html.

242 *serial offense to European allies*: See, for example, Susan B. Glasser, "How Trump Made War on Angela Merkel and Europe," *New Yorker*, December 17, 2018, www.newyorker.com/magazine/2018/12/24/how-trump-made-war-on-angela-merkel-and-europe.

243 *"partly to spare him"*: Lou Cannon, *President Reagan: The Role of a Lifetime* (New York: PublicAffairs, 2008), 539.

243 *Robert McFarlane*: Robert McFarlane, *Special Trust* (New York: Cadell & Davies, 1994), 21.

243 *Cannon concludes that*: Cannon, *President Reagan*, 540.

243 *"the president would do just about anything"*: George P. Shultz, *Turmoil and Triumph: My Years as Secretary of State* (New York: Charles Scribner's Sons, 1993), 816.

246 *The vote in favor of the declaration of war*: Pietro S. Nivola, "The 'Party War' of 1812," in *What So Proudly We Hailed*, ed. Pietro S. Nivola and Peter J. Kastor (Washington, D.C.: Brookings Institution Press, 2012), 12.

246 *it even provoked serious talk*: For an account of northern talk of secession during the War of 1812, see Benjamin Wittes and Ritika Singh, "James Madison, Presidential Power, and Civil Liberties," in *What So Proudly We Hailed*, 102–103.

246 *Gulf of Tonkin Resolution, which authorized it, passed nearly unanimously*: Public

Law 88-408, "Joint Resolution to promote the maintenance of international peace and security in southeast Asia," August 10, 1964, available at www.gov info.gov/content/pkg/STATUTE-78/pdf/STATUTE-78-Pg384.pdf.

246 *political pressure Johnson faced*: Beschloss, *Presidents of War*, 49, 516–38. And Richard Nixon in 1968 promised a secret plan to end the war—by winning it. See Beschloss, *Presidents of War*, 562–79.

247 *Nixon wanted an opening with China*: In 1967, before he was president, Nixon wrote an article in *Foreign Affairs* titled "Asia After Viet Nam," arguing that the United States had an extraordinary set of opportunities in Asia, including the opportunity to reorient China. See Richard M. Nixon, "Asia After Viet Nam," *Foreign Affairs*, October 1967, www.foreignaffairs.com/articles/asia/1967–10–01/asia-after-viet-nam. Later, as president, he declared that he would like to visit China before he died. Still later, he secretly sent Kissinger to meet with Chinese leader Mao Tse-tung. It wasn't until July 1971 that he revealed publicly his invitation to visit China, and he then worked to persuade both his party and the public at large that it was the right course. In other words, Nixon defied an established orthodoxy, but before doing so, he spent literally five years working to change that orthodoxy, to break it down, and to convince people that an alternative course was better. We are indebted to Michael Beschloss for this point. For an account of Nixon's engagement with China, see Margaret MacMillan, *Nixon and Mao: The Week That Changed the World* (New York: Random House, 2008).

247 *Trump was actually executing*: Scott R. Anderson and Yishai Schwartz, "On Waiving the Jerusalem Embassy Act (Or Not)," *Lawfare*, November 30, 2017, www.lawfareblog.com/waiving-jerusalem-embassy-act-or-not.

247 *twenty-two conservative members of the House*: The House clerk's roll call for the vote on H.R. 676 is available at http://clerk.house.gov/evs/2019/roll044.xml. The text of the resolution is available at https://www.congress.gov/bill/116th-congress/house-bill/676/text.

248 *adopt a credulous posture toward Saudi lies*: The White House's posture contradicted the assessment of the Central Intelligence Agency as briefed to members of Congress by CIA director Gina Haspel. See Josh Dawsey, "Trump Brushes Aside CIA Assertion That Crown Prince Ordered Killing, Defends Him and Saudi Arabia," *Washington Post*, November 20, 2018, www.washingtonpost.com/politics/trump-brushes-aside-cia-assertion-that-crown-prince-ordered-killing-defends-him-and-saudi-arabia/2018/11/22/d3bdf23c-ee70-11e8-96d4-0d23f2aaad09_story.html.

248 *lavished praise on figures such as Erdoğan of Turkey*: See, for example, David Morgan, "Trump Fist-Bumped Turkish Leader Erdogan, Said He 'Does Things the Right Way,'" CBS News, July 26, 2018, www.cbsnews.com/news/trump-fist-bumped-turkish-leader-erdogan-said-he-does-things-the-right-way/.

248 *Hungary's Viktor Orbán*: "Trump Praises 'Respected' Hungary PM Orbán," BBC, May 13, 2019, www.bbc.com/news/world-us-canada-48260165.

248 *the Philippines' leader Rodrigo Duterte*: David E. Sanger and Maggie Haberman,

"Trump Praises Duterte for Philippine Drug Crackdown in Call Transcript," *New York Times*, May 23, 2017, https://www.nytimes.com/2017/05/23/us /politics/trump-duterte-phone-transcript-philippine-drug-crackdown.html.

249 *once quipping that he wished "my people" would "sit up at attention"*: Candice Norwood, "Trump: I Want 'My People' to 'Sit Up at Attention' Like in North Korea," *Politico*, June 15, 2018, www.politico.com/story/2018/06/15/trump-north-korea -sit-up-attention-648969.

249 *even where it inflames the belief*: Trump's performance at the Helsinki summit is an illustrative case. Davis, "Trump, at Putin's Side, Questions U.S. Intelligence on 2016 Election."

249 *Trump had repeatedly asked what the point of having nuclear weapons*: "Trump Reportedly Asks Why US Can't Use Nukes: MSNBC," CNBC, August 3, 2016, www.cnbc.com/video/2016/08/03/trump-reportedly-asks-why-us-cant-use -nukes-msnbc.html.

249 *Barry Goldwater suggested that*: "Goldwater Poses New Asian Tactic; Says A-Arms Could Be Used to Expose Supply Lines of Reds in Vietnam," *New York Times*, May 24, 1964, www.nytimes.com/1964/05/25/archives/goldwater-poses-new -asian-tactic-says-aarms-could-be-used-to-expose.html.

250 *"In your guts, you know he's nuts"*: Kent Germany, "Lyndon B. Johnson: Campaigns and Elections," Miller Center, available at https://millercenter.org/president /lbjohnson/campaigns-and-elections.

250 *famous "daisy ad"*: Video of the ad is available at www.youtube.com/watch?v =2cwqHB6QeUw.

250 *Schlesinger writes that*: Schlesinger, *The Imperial Presidency*, 283.

10. "It squints towards monarchy": The Kingly Powers

253 *The president answered*: "Remarks by President Trump Before Marine One Departure," January 10, 2019, available at www.whitehouse.gov/briefings-statements /remarks-president-trump-marine-one-departure-30/.

254 *took to Twitter to declare he had "the absolute right"*: Trump tweeted, "As President I wanted to share with Russia (at an openly scheduled W.H. meeting) which I have the absolute right to do, facts pertaining . . ." Donald J. Trump, Twitter, May 16, 2017, https://twitter.com/realDonaldTrump/status/864436162567471104.

254 *the president told reporters from* The New York Times: See Michael S. Schmidt and Michael D. Shear, "Trump Says Russia Inquiry Makes U.S. 'Look Very Bad,'" *New York Times*, December 28, 2017, www.nytimes.com/2017/12/28/us /politics/trump-interview-mueller-russia-china-north-korea.html.

254 *tweeting in a fit of pique*: Donald J. Trump, Twitter, June 4, 2018, https://twitter .com/realDonaldTrump/status/1003616210922147841. The tweet appears to have responded to controversy following the publication by the *New York Times* of a letter from John Dowd to Robert Mueller from January 29, 2018. See "The Trump Lawyers' Confidential Memo to Mueller, Explained," June 2, 2018, www.nytimes .com/interactive/2018/06/02/us/politics/trump-legal-documents.html.

254 *In April 2019, Trump tweeted*: Trump tweeted, "Just out: The USA has the absolute legal right to have apprehended illegal immigrants transferred to Sanctuary
Cities. We hereby demand that they be taken care of at the highest level, especially by the State of California, which is well known or [*sic*] its poor management
& high taxes!" Donald J. Trump, Twitter, April 13, 2019, https://twitter.com
/realDonaldTrump/status/1117242926654947328.

254 *debated whether a president can pardon herself*: See, for example, Brian Kalt,
"Pardon Me: The Constitutional Case Against Presidential Self-Pardons," *Yale
Law Journal* 106 (1996–1997): 779; Ken Gormley, "Impeachment and the Independent Counsel: A Dysfunctional Union," *Stanford Law Review* 51 (1999): 323;
and Richard A. Posner, *An Affair of State: The Investigation, Impeachment, and
Trial of President Clinton* (Cambridge, MA: Harvard University Press, 1999),
107–108.

254 *statutory authority that falls*: For an explanation of the president's legal authorities with respect to Trump's national emergency declaration, see Jack Goldsmith, "What Is and Isn't a Big Deal in Trump's Executive Actions Related to the
Border," *Lawfare*, February 16, 2019, www.lawfareblog.com/what-and-isnt-big
-deal-trumps-executive-actions-related-border.

255 *the president had suddenly announced his pardon of Joe Arpaio*: "President Trump
Pardons Sheriff Joe Arpaio," White House statement, August 25, 2017, www
.whitehouse.gov/briefings-statements/president-trump-pardons-sheriff-joe
-arpaio/.

255 *The president's critics swiftly accused him of using the hurricane*: See, for example,
Chuck Schumer, who tweeted, "As millions of people in TX and LA are prep-
ping for the hurricane, the President is using the cover of the storm to pardon a
man who violated a court's order to stop discriminating against Latinos." Chuck
Schumer, Twitter, August 25, 2017, https://twitter.com/SenSchumer/status
/901251604384493569, and Chuck Schumer, Twitter, August 25, 2017, https://
twitter.com/SenSchumer/status/901251872056643584.

255 *As he told reporters*: Glenn Thrush and Julie Hirschfeld Davis, "Trump Eyed 'Far
Higher' Ratings in Pardoning Joe Arpaio as Hurricane Hit," *New York Times*,
August 28, 2017, www.nytimes.com/2017/08/28/us/politics/trump-finland
-harvey-arpaio-russia.html.

255 *He told Fox News in an interview*: Gregg Jarrett, "Trump 'Seriously Considering'
a Pardon for Ex-Sheriff Joe Arpaio," Fox News, August 14, 2017, www.foxnews
.com/politics/trump-seriously-considering-a-pardon-for-ex-sheriff-joe-arpaio.

255 *a federal court had enjoined Arpaio*: Order, Melendres v. Arpaio, No. 07-2513
(Dist. Ariz., December 23, 2011), available at www.acluaz.org/sites/default/files
/field_documents/12.23.2011-order-re-plaintiffs-summary-judgment-and
-class-certification-doc.-494.pdf. The court ruled that Arpaio's office "and all of
its officers are hereby enjoined from detaining any person based only on knowledge or reasonable belief, without more, that the person is unlawfully present
within the United States, because as a matter of law such knowledge does not

amount to reasonable belief that the person either violated or conspired to violate the Arizona human smuggling statute, or any other state or federal criminal law."

256 *the Constitution prevents officers*: See Terry v. Ohio, 392 U.S. 1 (1968).

256 *He violated the order again and again*: See Order re: Criminal Contempt, Melendres v. Arpaio, No. 07-2513 (Dist. Ariz., August 19, 2016), available at https://assets.documentcloud.org/documents/3032001/Arpaio-Criminal-Contempt-Order.pdf.

256 *finding Arpaio to be in criminal contempt*: See Findings of Fact and Conclusions of Law, U.S. v. Arpaio, No. 16-1012 (Dist. Ariz., July 31, 2017), available at https://assets.documentcloud.org/documents/6002555/Arpaio-Finding-of-Criminal-Contempt.pdf.

256 *endorsed Trump's presidential campaign and later even provided event security for his rallies*: See Diamond Naga Siu and Ted Hesson, "Trump: I'm 'Seriously Considering' Pardoning Joe Arpaio," *Politico*, August 14, 2017, www.politico.com/story/2017/08/14/trump-pardon-joe-arpaio-241621.

256 *Trump made clear that he liked the guy*: Trump said of Arpaio on Fox News shortly before pardoning him, "He's a great American patriot." See Jarrett, "Trump 'Seriously Considering' a Pardon for Ex-Sheriff Joe Arpaio."

256 *before Arpaio's conviction*: See Maggie Haberman, "Trump Asked Top Aides Months Ago If Arpaio Case Could Be Dropped, Officials Say," *New York Times*, August 26, 2017, www.nytimes.com/2017/08/26/us/politics/political-reaction-trump-pardon-arpaio.html.

256 *Senator Jeff Flake said*: Flake tweeted, "Regarding the Arpaio pardon, I would have preferred that the President honor the judicial process and let it take its course." Jeff Flake, Twitter, August 25, 2017, https://twitter.com/JeffFlake/status/901249192257101825.

256 *John McCain, said that pardoning*: McCain's statement reads in full, "No one is above the law and the individuals entrusted with the privilege of being sworn law officers should always seek to be beyond reproach in their commitment to fairly enforcing the laws they swore to uphold. Mr. Arpaio was found guilty of criminal contempt for continuing to illegally profile Latinos living in Arizona based on their perceived immigration status in violation of a judge's orders. The President has the authority to make this pardon, but doing so at this time undermines his claim for the respect of rule of law as Mr. Arpaio has shown no remorse for his actions." See "Statement by Senator John McCain on President Trump's Pardon of Joe Arpaio," August 25–26, 2017, available at https://web.archive.org/web/20180609084907/https://www.mccain.senate.gov/public/index.cfm/2017/8/statement-by-senator-john-mccain-on-president-trump-s-pardon-of-joe-arpaio.

256 *Legal scholars could*: For one example of this strain of criticism, see Bob Bauer, "The Arpaio Pardon," *Lawfare*, August 26, 2017, www.lawfareblog.com/arpaio-pardon.

257 *Commentators could rail*: See, for example, Margaret Talbot, "Why Does Donald Trump Like Joe Arpaio?" *New Yorker*, August 25, 2017, www.newyorker.com /news/daily-comment/why-does-donald-trump-like-sheriff-joe.

257 *solicited ideas for new names from his supporters*: See, for example, Rick Maese, "Trump Asked NFL Players for Pardon Suggestions. On Thursday, They Responded," *Washington Post*, June 21, 2018, www.washingtonpost.com/news /sports/wp/2018/06/21/trump-asked-nfl-players-for-pardon-suggestions-on -thursday-they-responded/.

257 *suggested that he might*: For Trump contemplating a commutation for Rod Blagojevich and a pardon for Martha Stewart, see Cristiano Lima, "Trump Floats Commutation for Blagojevich, Pardon for Martha Stewart," *Politico*, May 31, 2018, www .politico.com/story/2018/05/31/trump-floats-commutation-for-blagojevich -pardon-for-martha-stewart-615358.

257 *right-wing pundit Dinesh D'Souza*: See Peter Baker, "Trump Wields Pardon Pen to Confront Justice System," *New York Times*, May 31, 2018, www.nytimes.com /2018/05/31/us/politics/dsouza-pardon.html.

257 *former vice presidential aide Lewis "Scooter" Libby*: Chad Day and Catherine Lucey, "Trump Pardons Scooter Libby, Says He Was 'Treated Unfairly,'" Associated Press, April 13, 2018, https://apnews.com/46e832e8e7874372b3a92f2f9b 0b9cfd.

258 *he pardoned a former navy sailor*: Matt Zapotosky, "Trump Pardons Former Navy Sailor Convicted of Retaining Submarine Pictures in Case That Drew Comparisons to Clinton," *Washington Post*, March 9, 2018, www.washingtonpost .com/world/national-security/trump-pardons-former-navy-sailor-convicted -of-retaining-submarine-pictures-in-case-that-drew-comparisons-to-clinton /2018/03/09/401eae26-23e2-11e8-86f6-54bfff693d2b_story.html.

258 *Trump had once tweeted about the case*: Trump tweeted, "Crooked Hillary Clinton's top aid, Huma Abedin, has been accused of disregarding basic security protocols. She put Classified Passwords into the hands of foreign agents. Remember sailors pictures on submarine? Jail! Deep State Justice Dept must finally act? Also on Comey & others." Donald J. Trump, Twitter, January 2, 2018, https:// twitter.com/realDonaldTrump/status/948174033882927104.

258 *commuted the life sentence of a drug offender named Alice Marie Johnson*: Peter Baker, "Alice Marie Johnson Is Granted Clemency by Trump After Push by Kim Kardashian West," *New York Times*, June 6, 2018, www.nytimes.com/2018/06 /06/us/politics/trump-alice-johnson-sentence-commuted-kim-kardashian -west.html.

258 *commuted the sentences of Oregon ranchers*: Eileen Sullivan and Julie Turkewitz, "Trump Pardons Oregon Ranchers Whose Case Inspired Wildlife Refuge Takeover," *New York Times*, July 10, 2018, www.nytimes.com/2018/07/10/us /politics/trump-pardon-hammond-oregon.html.

258 *Iowa kosher meatpacking executive*: Mitch Smith, "President Commutes Sentence

of Iowa Meatpacking Executive," *New York Times*, December 20, 2017, www
.nytimes.com/2017/12/20/us/president-trump-iowa-commutation.html.

258 *boxing champion Jack Johnson*: John Eligon and Michael D. Shear, "Trump Pardons
Jack Johnson, Heavyweight Boxing Champion," *Washington Post*, May 24, 2018,
www.nytimes.com/2018/05/24/sports/jack-johnson-pardon-trump.html.

258 *pardoned a soldier*: Mihir Zaveri, "Trump Pardons Ex-Army Soldier Convicted
of Killing Iraqi Man," *New York Times*, May 6, 2019, www.nytimes.com/2019/05
/06/us/trump-pardon-michael-behenna.html.

258 *pardoned the convicted fraudster Conrad Black*: "Statement from the Press Secretary Regarding Executive Clemency for Lord Conrad M. Black of Crosshar-
bour," White House, May 15, 2019, www.whitehouse.gov/briefings-statements
/statement-press-secretary-regarding-executive-clemency-lord-conrad-m-black
-crossharbour/. See Conrad Black, *Donald Trump: A President Like No Other*
(Washington, D.C.: Regnery, 2018).

258 *pardoned Patrick Nolan*: "Statement from the Press Secretary Regarding Executive Clemency for Patrick Nolan," White House, May 15, 2019, www.whitehouse
.gov/briefings-statements/statement-press-secretary-regarding-executive
-clemency-patrick-nolan/. See also Bill Keller, "Prison Revolt: A Former Law-
and-Order Conservative Takes a Lead on Criminal-Justice Reform," *New Yorker*,
June 22, 2015, www.newyorker.com/magazine/2015/06/29/prison-revolt.

258 *dangling clemency before those individuals implicated*: See, for example, Schultz
and Schwab, "Trump Says Pardon for Paul Manafort Still a Possibility"; and
Mueller report, Vol. II, 127.

258 *his lawyers hinted privately to Paul Manafort and Michael Cohen*: For Trump
counsel's interactions with Manafort, see Mueller report, Vol. II, 123–24. For
his counsel's interactions with Cohen, see Mueller report, Vol. II, 147.

258 *told Michael Flynn to stay strong*: On April 25, 2017, Flynn reportedly told associates, "I just got a message from the president to stay strong." See Michael Isikoff,
"As Investigators Circled Flynn, He Got a Message from Trump: Stay Strong,"
Yahoo News, May 18, 2017, www.yahoo.com/news/investigators-circled-flynn
-got-message-trump-stay-strong-145442727.html.

258 *had messages passed to Flynn*: Mueller report, Vol. II, 43.

259 *the very antithesis of the constitutional command*: Quinta Jurecic and Benjamin
Wittes, "Take More Care: Did the President Tell Subordinates to Violate the Law?"
Lawfare, April 13, 2019, www.lawfareblog.com/take-more-care-did-president-tell
-subordinates-violate-law.

259 *besotted with the pardon power*: At the time, Quinta Jurecic argued this very point.
See Quinta Jurecic, "Donald Trump's Pardon Power and the State of Exception,"
Lawfare, June 11, 2018, www.lawfareblog.com/donald-trumps-pardon-power
-and-state-exception.

260 *Senator Rand Paul had suggested to Trump that he revoke*: Paul tweeted, "Today I
will meet with the President and I will ask him to revoke John Brennan's security

clearance!" Rand Paul, Twitter, July 23, 2018, https://twitter.com/RandPaul
/status/1021359932795482112.

260 *when then press secretary Sarah Huckabee Sanders was asked*: Press briefing by
Press Secretary Sarah Sanders, July 23, 2018, available at www.whitehouse.gov
/briefings-statements/press-briefing-press-secretary-sarah-sanders-072318/.

260 *he had, in fact, revoked Brennan's clearance*: Statement from the President, July
26, 2018, available at https://content.govdelivery.com/attachments/USWHPO
/2018/08/15/file_attachments/1055816/Statement%2Bfrom%2Bthe%2BPresi
dent.pdf.

260 *The statement was actually dated just a few days after*: Julie Hirschfeld Davis and
Michael D. Shear, "Trump Revokes Ex-C.I.A. Director John Brennan's Security
Clearance," *New York Times*, August 15, 2018, www.nytimes.com/2018/08/15
/us/politics/john-brennan-security-clearance.html.

261 *penned an opinion article in* The Washington Post: William H. McRaven, "Revoke
My Security Clearance, Too, Mr. President," *Washington Post*, August 16, 2018,
www.washingtonpost.com/opinions/revoke-my-security-clearance-too-mr
-president/2018/08/16/8b149b02-a178-11e8-93e3-24d1703d2a7a_story.html.

261 *Franklin Delano Roosevelt issued the first executive order*: Executive Order 8381,
"Defining Certain Vital Military and Naval Installations and Equipment," 5 FR
1147, March 22, 1940. FDR did cite statutory authority and not inherent constitutional power at the time.

261 *Prior to that, classification decisions were treated*: See Jennifer K. Elsea, "The Protection of Classified Information: The Legal Framework," Congressional Research
Service, May 18, 2017, available at https://fas.org/sgp/crs/secrecy/RS21900.pdf,
citing Harold Relyea, "The Presidency and the People's Right to Know," in Harold
Relyea and Larry Berman, *The Presidency and Information Policy*, Vol. 1, 16–18
(1981).

261 *The Supreme Court articulated the principle clearly in 1988*: Department of the
Navy v. Egan, 484 U.S. 518 (1988).

262 The New York Times *reported that*: Haberman, Schmidt, Goldman, and Karni,
"Trump Ordered Officials to Give Jared Kushner a Security Clearance."

262 *thumbed his nose at anti-nepotism*: John Wagner and Ashley Parker, "Trump's
Son-in-Law, Jared Kushner, to Join White House as Senior Adviser; No Formal
Role for Ivanka Trump," *Washington Post*, January 9, 2017, www.washingtonpost
.com/news/post-politics/wp/2017/01/09/tumps-son-in-law-jared-kushner
-expected-to-join-white-house-as-a-senior-adviser. The Justice Department's
Office of Legal Counsel cleared the appointment on January 20, 2017. See Memorandum Opinion of the Counsel to the President, "Application of the Anti-
Nepotism Statute to a Presidential Appointment in the White House Office,"
January 20, 2017, www.justice.gov/sites/default/files/olc/opinions/attachments
/2017/01/20/2017-01-20-anti-nepo-stat-who_0.pdf. The Justice Department later
released documents revealing that the OLC had previously advised presidents that

such appointments were unlawful and that the January 20 memo overruled those opinions. See Josh Gerstein, "DOJ Releases Overruled Memos Finding It Illegal for Presidents to Appoint Relatives," *Politico*, October 3, 2017, www.politico.com /story/2017/10/03/justice-department-legal-memos-presidents-appoint-relatives -243395.

262 *Kushner's business owed more than a billion dollars*: Caleb Melby and David Kocieniewski, "Kushners' Troubled Tower: Debt, Empty Offices and Rising Fees," *Bloomberg*, March 22, 2017, www.bloomberg.com/news/articles/2017-03-22 /kushners-troubled-tower-debt-empty-offices-and-rising-fees.

262 *meeting with Chinese nationals with whom he was negotiating*: Susanne Craig, Jo Becker, and Jesse Drucker, "Jared Kushner, a Trump In-Law and Adviser, Chases a Chinese Deal," *New York Times*, January 7, 2017, www.nytimes.com/2017/01 /07/us/politics/jared-kushner-trump-business.html.

262 *attempted to establish a back channel with the Kremlin*: Ellen Nakashima, Adam Entous, and Greg Miller, "Russian Ambassador Told Moscow That Kushner Wanted Secret Communications Channel with Kremlin," *Washington Post*, May 26, 2017, www.washingtonpost.com/world/national-security/russian-ambassador-told -moscow-that-kushner-wanted-secret-communications-channel-with-kremlin /2017/05/26/520a14b4-422d-11e7-9869-bac8b446820a_story.html.

262 *he'd failed to disclose*: Jo Becker and Matthew Rosenberg, "Kushner Omitted Meeting with Russians on Security Clearance Forms," *New York Times*, April 6, 2017, www.nytimes.com/2017/04/06/us/politics/jared-kushner-russians-security -clearance.html.

262 *At the White House, he'd taken on*: Wagner and Parker, "Trump's Son-in-Law, Jared Kushner, to Join White House as Senior Adviser."

262 *his close personal relationship with Saudi Crown Prince*: Carol D. Leonnig, Shane Harris, Josh Dawsey, and Greg Jaffe, "How Jared Kushner Forged a Bond with the Saudi Crown Prince," *Washington Post*, March 19, 2018, www.washingtonpost .com/politics/how-jared-kushner-forged-a-bond-with-the-saudi-crown-prince /2018/03/19/2f2ce398-2181-11e8-badd-7c9f29a55815_story.htm.

262 *Reports came out that*: Shane Harris, Carol D. Leonnig, Greg Jaffe, and Josh Dawsey, "Kushner's Overseas Contacts Raise Concerns as Foreign Officials Seek Leverage," *Washington Post*, February 27, 2018, www.washingtonpost.com /world/national-security/kushners-overseas-contacts-raise-concerns-as-foreign -officials-seek-leverage/2018/02/27/16bbc052-18c3-11e8-942d-16a950029788 _story.html.

263 *Eventually even his interim clearance was downgraded*: Kaitlan Collins, Kevin Liptak, and Pamela Brown, "Kushner Security Clearance Is Downgraded," CNN, February 28, 2018, www.cnn.com/2018/02/27/politics/jared-kushner-security -clearance/index.html.

263 *Everything was aboveboard*: Philip Rucker, Carol D. Leonnig, Matt Zapotosky, and Devlin Barrett, "Jared Kushner Receives Permanent Security Clearance, an

Indication He May No Longer Be a Focus of the Special Counsel," *Washington Post*, May 23, 2018, www.washingtonpost.com/politics/jared-kushner-receives -permanent-security-clearance-ending-uncertainty-over-his-status/2018/05 /23/b4a57fae-5eb6-11e8-9ee3-49d6d4814c4c_story.html.

263 *Trump had personally intervened*: Haberman, Schmidt, Goldman, and Karni, "Trump Ordered Officials to Give Jared Kushner a Security Clearance."

263 *lying to the public about it ever since*: See, for example, Peter Baker and Maggie Haberman, "Trump, in Interview, Calls Wall Talks 'Waste of Time' and Dismisses Investigations," *New York Times*, January 31, 2019, www.nytimes.com/2019/01/31 /us/politics/trump-wall-investigations-interview.html. The story reported that "Mr. Trump said he played no role in directing White House officials to arrange for Jared Kushner, his son-in-law and senior adviser, to receive a top-secret clearance."

263 *Kellyanne Conway went on Fox News*: Rebecca Morin, "Kellyanne Conway Says Trump Has 'Absolute Right' to Order Security Clearances," *Politico*, March 1, 2019, www.politico.com/story/2019/03/01/kellyanne-conway-trump-security -clearance-1197534.

264 *earlier advocated for lifetime tenure*: Klarman, *The Framers' Coup*, 228–29.

265 *warned of the perils*: "Speech of Patrick Henry," June 7, 1788, available at www .let.rug.nl/usa/documents/1786-1800/the-anti-federalist-papers/speech-of -patrick-henry-(june-7-1788).php.

266 *Sanders noted that*: Press briefing by Press Secretary Sarah Sanders, March 3, 2018, available at www.whitehouse.gov/briefings-statements/press-briefing-press -secretary-sarah-sanders-050318/.

266 *dismissed a secretary of state*: The secretary of state "learned he had been fired on Tuesday morning when a top aide showed him a tweet from Mr. Trump announcing the change, according to a senior State Department official." See Peter Baker, Gardiner Harris, and Mark Landler, "Trump Fires Rex Tillerson and Will Replace Him with C.I.A. Chief Pompeo," *New York Times*, March 13, 2018, www .nytimes.com/2018/03/13/us/politics/trump-tillerson-pompeo.html.

266 *an attorney general*: Baker, Benner, and Shear, "Jeff Sessions Is Forced Out as Attorney General as Trump Installs Loyalist."

266 *a White House counsel*: Julie Hirschfeld Davis, Michael S. Schmidt, and Maggie Haberman, "Don McGahn to Leave White House Counsel Job This Fall, Trump Says," *New York Times*, August 29, 2018, www.nytimes.com/2018/08/29/us /politics/don-mcgahn-white-house-counsel-trump.html.

266 *a White House chief of staff*: Peter Baker and Maggie Haberman, "Reince Priebus Is Ousted Amid Stormy Days for White House," *New York Times*, July 28, 2017, www.nytimes.com/2017/07/28/us/politics/reince-priebus-white-house -trump.html.

266 *he bullied a national security adviser*: Trump announced former national security adviser H. R. McMaster's resignation and replacement by tweet: "I am pleased to announce that, effective 4/9/18, @AmbJohnBolton will be my new National

Security Advisor. I am very thankful for the service of General H. R. McMaster who has done an outstanding job & will always remain my friend. There will be an official contact handover on 4/9." Donald J. Trump, Twitter, March 22, 2018, https://twitter.com/realDonaldTrump/status/976948306927607810.

266 *another chief of staff*: See Annie Karni and Maggie Haberman, "John Kelly to Step Down as Trump, Facing New Perils, Shakes Up Staff," *New York Times*, December 8, 2018, www.nytimes.com/2018/12/08/us/politics/john-kelly-chief -staff-trump.html.

266 *and a homeland security secretary*: Zolan Kanno-Youngs, Maggie Haberman, Michael D. Shear, and Eric Schmitt, "Kirstjen Nielsen Resigns as Trump's Homeland Security Secretary," *New York Times*, April 7, 2019, www.nytimes.com /2019/04/07/us/politics/kirstjen-nielsen-dhs-resigns.html.

266 *he could order information released to the public*: See Mazzetti, Haberman, Fandos, and Schmidt, "Intimidation, Pressure and Humiliation: Inside Trump's Two-Year War on the Investigations Encircling Him." The paper reported that Trump "repeatedly leaned on administration officials on behalf of the lawmakers— urging Mr. Rosenstein and other law enforcement leaders to flout procedure and share sensitive materials about the open case with Congress."

267 *Pat Cipollone wrote in a letter*: Letter from Pat Cipollone to Elijah Cummings, March 4, 2019, available at https://oversight.house.gov/sites/democrats.oversight .house.gov/files/documents/2019-03-04_2%20Cipollone%20to%20EEC %20re%20Security%20Clearances.pdf.

267 *broad statutory language*: 50 U.S. Code § 1621.

268 *declaring a specious national emergency*: Peter Baker, "Trump Declares a National Emergency, and Provokes a Constitutional Clash," *New York Times*, February 15, 2019, www.nytimes.com/2019/02/15/us/politics/national-emergency -trump.html.

268 *a resolution of disapproval*: H.J. Res. 46, "Joint resolution relating to a national emergency declared by the President on February 15, 2019," 116th Congress, 1st Session, available at www.congress.gov/bill/116th-congress/house-joint -resolution/46/text. 50 U.S. Code § 1622 authorizes Congress to pass a joint resolution of disapproval to terminate the declaration.

268 *Trump vetoed that resolution*: Michael Tackett, "Trump Issues First Veto After Congress Rejects Border Emergency," *New York Times*, March 15, 2019, www .nytimes.com/2019/03/15/us/politics/trump-veto-national-emergency.html.

268 *Congress couldn't muster the votes needed*: Emily Cochrane, "House Fails to Override Trump's Veto, Preserving National Emergency Order," *New York Times*, March 26, 2019, www.nytimes.com/2019/03/26/us/politics/national-emergency-vote.html.

268 *"power to persuade"*: See chap. 3, "The Power to Persuade," in Neustadt, *Presidential Power and the Modern Presidents*.

269 *concept of pardons long predates the establishment of European monarchies*: Examples of pardons are found in the Code of Hammurabi, in ancient Greece, and

in the New Testament, where the Roman procurator Pontius Pilate hesitatingly pardons the robber Barabbas instead of Jesus.

269 *"analogous in theory and practice to divine grace"*: Kathleen Dean Moore, "Pardon for Good and Sufficient Reasons," *University of Richmond Law Review* 27 (1993): 282, https://scholarship.richmond.edu/cgi/viewcontent.cgi?article=2033&context =lawreview.

269 *The British Crown*: William F. Duker, "The President's Power to Pardon: A Constitutional History," *William & Mary Law Review* 18 (1977): 497–500, https:// scholarship.law.wm.edu/cgi/viewcontent.cgi?article=2444&context=wmlr.

269 *Despite trends among the early states*: See Duker, "The President's Power to Pardon," 500–501.

269 *the Supreme Court has interpreted the presidential pardoning power*: See Ex Parte Wells, 59 U.S. 307 (1855): "At the time of our separation from Great Britain, that power had been exercised by the king, as the chief executive. Prior to the revolution, the colonies, being in effect under the laws of England, were accustomed to the exercise of it in the various forms, as they may be found in the English law books . . . At the time of the adoption of the Constitution, American statesmen were conversant with the laws of England, and familiar with the prerogatives exercised by the crown."

269 *Chief Justice John Marshall wrote*: United States v. Wilson, 32 U.S. 150 (1833).

269 *James Iredell took the view*: Jonathan Elliot, ed., *The Debates in the Several State Conventions on the Adoption of the Federal Constitution as Recommended by the General Convention at Philadelphia in 1787*, Vol. IV (Philadelphia: J. B. Lippincott, 1941), 111.

270 *"too sanguinary and cruel"*: Alexander Hamilton, *Federalist* 74.

270 *pardon participants in the Whiskey Rebellion*: George Washington, "Proclamation— Granting Pardon to Certain Persons Formerly Engaged in Violence and Obstruction of Justice in Protest of Liquor Laws in Pennsylvania," July 10, 1795, available at www.presidency.ucsb.edu/documents/proclamation-granting-pardon-certain -persons-formerly-engaged-violence-and-obstruction.

270 *had urged Washington to deal aggressively with the rebels*: See Carrie Hagen, "The First Presidential Pardon Pitted Alexander Hamilton Against George Washington," *Smithsonian*, August 29, 2017, www.smithsonianmag.com/history/first -presidential-pardon-pitted-hamilton-against-george-washington-180964659/.

270 *State of the Union address*: George Washington, Seventh Annual Message, December 8, 1795, available at www.presidency.ucsb.edu/documents/seventh-annual -address-congress.

270 *pardoned participants in a rebellion in Pennsylvania*: John Adams, "Proclamation— Granting Pardon to Certain Persons Engaged in Insurrection Against the United States in the Counties of Northampton, Montgomery, and Bucks, in the State of Pennsylvania," May 21, 1800, available at www.presidency.ucsb.edu/documents /proclamation-granting-pardon-certain-persons-engaged-insurrection-against -the-united.

270 *James Madison agreed to pardon an unsavory group of pirates*: Jeffrey Crouch, *The Presidential Pardon Power* (Lawrence: University Press of Kansas, 2009), 56.

270 *Abraham Lincoln employed mass amnesty of Confederates*: Duker, "The President's Power to Pardon," 510–11.

270 *Jimmy Carter issued a mass pardon of draft resisters*: Proclamation 4483, "Granting Pardon for Violations of the Selective Service Act," August 1964 to March 28, 1973, White House, January 21, 1977, www.justice.gov/pardon/proclamation-4483-granting-pardon-violations-selective-service-act.

270 *Truman, Carter, Clinton, and Obama*: For Truman's and Carter's commutations of the sentence of Oscar Collazo, see Associated Press, "Oscar Collazo, 80, Truman Attacker in '50," published in *New York Times*, February 23, 1994, www.nytimes.com/1994/02/23/obituaries/oscar-collazo-80-truman-attacker-in-50.html. For Clinton's clemency actions, see John M. Broder, "12 Imprisoned Puerto Ricans Accept Clemency Conditions," *New York Times*, September 8, 1999, www.nytimes.com/1999/09/08/us/12-imprisoned-puerto-ricans-accept-clemency-conditions.html. For Obama's commutation of Oscar López Rivera's sentence, see Christopher Mele, "Obama Commutes Sentence of F.A.L.N. Member Oscar Lopez Rivera," January 17, 2017, *New York Times*, www.nytimes.com/2017/01/17/us/obama-commutes-sentence-of-faln-member-oscar-lopez-rivera.html.

271 *Ronald Reagan commuted the life sentence of a foreign spy*: Bernard Gwertzman, "U.S. Releases 4 and East Bloc 25 in Spy Exchange on Berlin Bridge," *New York Times*, June 12, 1985, www.nytimes.com/1985/06/12/world/us-releases-4-and-east-bloc-25-in-spy-exchange-on-berlin-bridge.html.

271 *Warren Harding grew concerned*: Dean, *Warren G. Harding*, 126–29.

272 *Trump tweeted of D'Souza*: The full tweet reads "Will be giving a Full Pardon to Dinesh D'Souza today. He was treated very unfairly by our government!" Donald J. Trump, Twitter, May 31, 2018, https://twitter.com/realDonaldTrump/status/1002177521599860736.

272 *whom the White House claimed*: "Statement from the Press Secretary Regarding the Pardon of Dinesh D'Souza," May 31, 2018, www.whitehouse.gov/briefings-statements/statement-press-secretary-regarding-pardon-dinesh-dsouza/.

272 *About Libby, the president said*: "Statement from the Press Secretary Regarding the Pardon of I. 'Scooter' Lewis Libby," April 13, 2018, www.whitehouse.gov/briefings-statements/statement-press-secretary-regarding-pardon-scooter-lewis-libby/.

272 *"has been treated unfairly"*: Philip Rucker, "Trump Says He Feels 'Very Badly' for Flynn Because Lies to FBI Have 'Ruined His Life,'" *Washington Post*, December 4, 2017, www.washingtonpost.com/news/post-politics/wp/2017/12/04/trump-says-he-feels-very-badly-for-flynn-because-lies-to-fbi-have-ruined-his-life.

272 *as has his former campaign manager*: Schultz and Schwab, "Trump Says Pardon for Paul Manafort Still a Possibility."

272   *As Mueller wrote*: Mueller report, Vol. II, 132–33.

273   *Hamilton argued that the gravity of the responsibility*: Alexander Hamilton, *Federalist 74*.

273   *Edmund Randolph warned*: James Madison, *Notes of Debates in the Federal Convention of 1787 Reported by James Madison* (Athens: Ohio University Press, 1987), 646.

273   *he proposed an amendment that would prevent pardons for treason*: Duker, "The President's Power to Pardon," 502.

273   *George Mason put a finer point on the peril*: George Mason, "Objections to the Constitution of Government Formed by the Convention," in Max Ferrand, *The Record of the Federal Convention of 1787*, Vol. 1 (New Haven, CT: Yale University Press: 1966), 639.

274   *mentions of pardons*: Duker, "The President's Power to Pardon," 478.

274   *the convention delegates were persuaded*: Duker, "The President's Power to Pardon," 501–506.

274   *debated making the presidential veto absolute*: Madison, *Notes of Debates in the Federal Convention of 1787*, 63.

274   *it debated allowing the executive an unfettered hand*: Madison, *Notes of Debates in the Federal Convention of 1787*, 517.

274   *using clemency energetically*: See, for example, Sari Horwitz, "Obama Grants Final 330 Commutations to Nonviolent Drug Offenders," *Washington Post*, January 19, 2017, www.washingtonpost.com/world/national-security/obama-grants -final-330-commutations-to-nonviolent-drug-offenders/2017/01/19/41506468 -de5d-11e6-918c-99ede3c8cafa_story.html.

275   *that they don't use it enough*: See, for example, Richard W. Stevenson, "Washington Talk; A Presidential Power This President Uses Rarely," *New York Times*, December 25, 2002, www.nytimes.com/2002/12/25/us/washington-talk-a -presidential-power-this-president-uses-rarely.html.

275   *President Bill Clinton disregarded the Justice Department*: Broder, "12 Imprisoned Puerto Ricans Accept Clemency Conditions."

275   *Clinton relied on the advice of his White House counsel*: See, for example, Debra Burlingame, "The Clintons' Terror Pardons," *Wall Street Journal*, February 12, 2008, www.wsj.com/articles/SB120277819085260827.

276   *he directed the pardon attorney*: Ken Belson and Eric Lichtblau, "A Father, a Son, and a Short-Lived Presidential Pardon," *New York Times*, December 25, 2008, www.nytimes.com/2008/12/26/us/26pardon.html.

276   *Bush directed the Office of the Pardon Attorney*: Statement by the press secretary, December 24, 2008, https://georgewbush-whitehouse.archives.gov/news /releases/2008/12/20081224-5.html.

277   *Jeanine Pirro or Rudy Giuliani*: For Pirro, see Eliana Johnson and Andrew Restuccia, "Trump Dangled Administration Job to Judge Jeanine," *Politico*, June 7, 2018, www.politico.com/story/2018/06/07/jeanine-pirro-trump-white-house

-630378. For Giuliani, see Mike Allen, "Trump Ponders Rudy Giuliani for At-torney General," *Axios*, July 24, 2017, www.axios.com/exclusive-trump-ponders-rudy-giuliani-for-attorney-general-1513304393-156c083d-c170-41a5-ada5-0123d8711a35.html.

277 *Justice Oliver Wendell Holmes, who wrote*: Biddle v. Perovich, 274 U.S. 480 (1927).

278 *Bill Clinton's last-minute pardon*: John Solomon, "In Final Act, Clinton Issues Pardons," Associated Press, January 20, 2001, www.washingtonpost.com/wp-srv/aponline/20010120/aponline162547_000.htm.

278 *George H. W. Bush's pardon of six people*: David Johnston, "Bush Pardons 6 in Iran Affair, Aborting a Weinberger Trial; Prosecutor Assails 'Cover-Up,'" *New York Times*, December 25, 1992, https://archive.nytimes.com/www.nytimes.com/books/97/06/29/reviews/iran-pardon.html.

278 *the act was deeply unpopular*: See, for example, Paul L. Montgomery, "Some Mixed Reactions in Foley Square," *New York Times*, September 9, 1974, www.nytimes.com/1974/09/09/archives/some-mixed-reactions-in-foley-square-some-opinions-in-foley-square.html.

Conclusion:
"A man unprincipled in private life desperate in his fortune, bold in his temper"

281 *Lindsey Graham's prediction*: Lindsey Graham, Twitter, May 3, 2016, https://twitter.com/LindseyGrahamSC/status/727604522156228608.

282 *At 10:39 p.m., the networks projected*: For a detailed account of the timeline of the election night, including the times at which individual states were called, see Ciara McCarthy and Claire Phipps, "Election Results Timeline: How the Night Unfolded," *Guardian*, November 9, 2016, www.theguardian.com/us-news/2016/nov/08/presidential-election-updates-trump-clinton-news.

282 *FiveThirtyEight took heat*: See, for example, Josh Katz, "Why Are the Different Presidential Forecasts So Far Apart?" *New York Times*, September 29, 2016, www.nytimes.com/2016/09/30/upshot/why-are-the-different-presidential-forecasts-so-far-apart.html.

282 *put Clinton's odds of victory at 70 percent*: "2016 Election Forecast," FiveThirty Eight, https://projects.fivethirtyeight.com/2016-election-forecast/.

283 *analyst like Jack Goldsmith*: Goldsmith, "Will Donald Trump Destroy the Presidency?"

284 *"senatorial courtesy"*: Joseph P. Harris, "The Advice and Consent of the Senate" (Berkeley: University of California Press, 1953), 40–41.

284 *Carter from consciously dismantling the norm with respect to circuit judges*: "First, Carter set out to dismantle the traditional method of selecting lower court judges—senatorial courtesy—which had perpetuated the old white boys' network. Second, Carter directed the appellate merit selection committees to make 'special efforts' to identify minorities and women for appellate vacancies." Nancy Scherer, "Diversifying the Federal Bench: Is Universal Legitimacy for the U.S. System Possi-

ble?" *Northwestern University Law Review* 105, no. 2 (2015): 587–633, at 595, https://scholarlycommons.law.northwestern.edu/cgi/viewcontent.cgi?referer =https://www.google.com/&httpsredir=1&article=1169&context=nulr.

284 *Reagan, capitalized on the demolished norm*: Commenting on the phenomenon in 1982, W. Gary Fowler observed that "while Carter's promise attracted only mild attention, the 1980 Republican Party platform, ultimately embraced by President Reagan, stirred controversy. Although all presidents (including Carter) have chosen judges on the basis of philosophy, the Republican platform specifically called for the appointment of judges who had 'the highest regard for protecting the rights of law-abiding citizens' and who hold views 'consistent with the belief in the decentralization of the federal government and efforts to return decision-making power to state and local elected officials.'" In order to implement his partisan and political vision, Reagan did not have to change the selection process at all. Carter had already done the work for him. The breach of a norm simply became the accepted mode of operation. W. Gary Fowler, "A Comparison of Initial Recommendation Procedures: Judicial Selection Under Reagan and Carter," *Yale Law & Policy Review* 1, no. 2 (1982): 307, available at https://digitalcommons.law.yale.edu/cgi /viewcontent.cgi?referer=&httpsredir=1&article=1012&context=ylpr.

284 *David Priess notes*: David Priess, *How to Get Rid of a President: History's Guide to Removing Unpopular, Unable, or Unfit Chief Executives* (New York: PublicAffairs, 2018), 6.

285 *James Madison famously warned*: James Madison, *Federalist* 10.

285 *Hamilton presciently warned of a Trump-like figure*: Alexander Hamilton, "Objections and Answers Respecting the Administration of the Government," August 18, 1792, available at https://founders.archives.gov/documents/Hamilton /01-12-02-0184-0002.

286 *having recognized the risks, the founders placed a remarkable faith*: While Hamilton entertained the theoretical possibility of a bad president, he also argued that the process of elections "affords a moral certainty, that the office of President will never fall to the lot of any man who is not in an eminent degree endowed with the requisite qualifications." He acknowledged that perhaps "talents for low intrigue, and the little arts of popularity" would suffice to win a single state, but a candidate would need "a different kind of merit, to establish him in the esteem and confidence of the whole Union, or of so considerable a portion of it as would be necessary" to win the presidency. "It will not be too strong to say that there will be a constant probability of seeing the station filled by characters preeminent for ability and virtue." Alexander Hamilton, *Federalist* 68.

287 *"faithless electors"*: Lilly O'Donnell, "Meet the 'Hamilton Electors' Hoping for an Electoral College Revolt," *Atlantic*, November 21, 2016, www.theatlantic.com /politics/archive/2016/11/meet-the-hamilton-electors-hoping-for-an-electoral -college-revolt/508433/.

287 *only seven electors broke with their obligations*: Ed O'Keefe, "With Electoral College Vote, Trump's Win Is Official," *Washington Post*, December 19, 2016,

www.washingtonpost.com/politics/the-electoral-college-is-poised-to-pick
-trump-despite-push-to-dump-him/2016/12/19/75265c16-c58f-11e6-85b5
-76616a33048d_story.html.

292 *swear an oath of office*: The oath required of government employees is codified at 5
     U.S. Code § 3331. The oath of enlistment for uniformed military personnel is codi-
     fied at 10 U.S. Code § 502(a). The naturalization oath of renunciation and allegiance
     is codified at 8 U.S. Code § 1448(a).

ACKNOWLEDGMENTS

WRITING A BOOK ABOUT FAST-DEVELOPING, ONGOING EVENTS WAS an undertaking unlike anything either of us has done before. Doing so while simultaneously editing a daily publication focused on issues at the center of a protracted political maelstrom was, to put it mildly, a challenge. We could not have hoped to face this challenge and complete this project without the assistance of a number of people to whom the following thanks do not do justice.

We had superlative research assistance throughout our work on this project. Sarah Grant, Sabrina McCubbin, Helen Klein Murillo, and Cody Poplin each did extensive historical and legal research that informed major sections of the book. Mikhaila Fogel, Matthew Kahn, and Jacob Schulz ran down hundreds of citations and helped us annotate the manuscript, correcting any number of errors along the way.

The book benefited enormously from the thoughtful and challenging comments given by Bob Bauer, Michael Beschloss, Daniel Drezner, William Galston, Jack Goldsmith, Quinta Jurecic, Christopher Klein, David Kris, Jonathan Rauch, Daniel Richman, Jeffrey Tulis, and Matthew Waxman. The manuscript was vastly improved by the detailed attention of our editor, Alex Star, who also helped us conceptualize the book's integration of history and contemporary analysis. Our agents, Anna Sproul-Latimer and Gail Ross, helped us turn a project that started its life as a series of posts on *Lawfare* during the 2016 presidential campaign into the cohesive treatment this book represents. Our copy editor, Maxine Bartow, saved us from myriad errors.

Life does not stop when you're working on a book in the middle of a national crisis. Our spouses, Tamara Cofman Wittes and Brendan Hennessey, and Susan's mom, Mary Grad, covered for us in a thousand different ways and created space for us to write. Our children cut us slack and kept us grounded. We love you guys.

Nor did the business of *Lawfare* go on hiatus when the site's two senior editors decided to immerse themselves in a major project. Quite apart from their direct contributions to the book, the staff of *Lawfare* have in so many ways kept the trains running. We are privileged and grateful to work beside this team. More generally, the site's contributors and staff have provided a remarkable community of experts devoted to serious discussion of the presidency and of Trump's challenges to it—a community that has cumulatively offered the furnace out of which many of the ideas discussed in these pages were forged.

Finally, this book describes and analyzes the institutions that comprise the executive branch and the American presidency. But those institutions are really just people. To the federal civil servants who stand guard and seek to do what is right in trying times, thank you.

INDEX

A NOTE ABOUT THE AUTHORS

Susan Hennessey and Benjamin Wittes are the executive editor and editor in chief, respectively, of *Lawfare*. Hennessey is a senior fellow at the Brookings Institution and a CNN contributor; she was previously an attorney at the National Security Agency. Wittes is a senior fellow at the Brookings Institution and the author of *Law and the Long War* and *The Future of Violence*, among other books.